# THE AVRO
# LANCASTER

## A COMPREHENSIVE GUIDE FOR THE MODELLER

## Manchester and Lincoln

Richard A. Franks

**SAM Publications**

**Front cover:**
The cover artwork depicts a Manchester of No. 57 Squadron, a Lancaster of No. 57 Squadron and a Lincoln B.2 and was created exclusively for this publication by Michele Marsan.

## Modellers Datafile No.4
## The Avro Lancaster
## Manchester & Lincoln
by Richard A. Franks

First published in 2000 by SAM Publications
4 Princeton Court, Pilgrim Centre
Brickhill Drive, Bedford.
MK41 7PZ, United Kingdom

ISBN 0 9533465 3 6

Typeset by DMZee Marketing Ltd, 4 Princeton Court, Pilgrim Centre, Bedford MK41 7PZ United Kingdom
Series Editor Richard A. Franks
Designed by Simon Sugarhood
Printed and bound in the United Kingdom by Printhaüs

### The Modellers Datafile Series.
• No.1 – De Havilland Mosquito - Out of Print
• No.2 – Hawker Hurricane *
• No.3 – Supermarine Spitfire (Part 1 Merlin Powered)*
• No.4 – Avro Lancaster (Inc Manchester & Lincoln) *
• *No.5 – Supermarine Spitfire (Part 2 Griffon Powered) [Due Winter 2000]*
* Available

### Acknowledgments
A word of thanks must go to the following people and organisations, without whose help and encouragement this title would never have happened: The Department of Records & Information Services, Royal Air Force Museum, Hendon, The Aircraft & Exhibits Department, Royal Air Force Museum, Hendon, The Photographic Department, Royal Air Force Museum, Hendon, Rolls-Royce Heritage Trust, Derby, The Battle of Britain Memorial Flight, RAF Coningsby. Lincolnshire Aviation Heritage Centre, East Kirkby. Mike Belcher, Pablo Calcatera, Andy Cline, Bill Coffman, David Frowan, Jim Grant, Jim Lyzun, David Lennox, and Derek Pennington.

Also a large vote of thanks to the following organisations and firms that readily supplied products for inclusion in this title.

Aeroclub, 5, Silverwood Avenue, Ravenshead, Nottingham. NG15 9BJ Tel: 44 (0)115 967 0044 Fax: 44 (0)115 967 1633

AeroMaster Products, 2615 NW, 20th Avenue, Miami, Florida FL 33142, USA Tel 305 635 3134 Fax: 305 638 4197

Airfix, Humbrol Ltd, Marfleet, Hull, North Humberside. HU9 5NE Tel: 44 (0)1482 701191 Fax: 44 (0)1482 712908

(Minicraft) Toyway, P.O. Box 55, Unit 20, Jubilee Trade Centre, Jubilee Road, Letchworth, Herts. SG6 1SG Tel: 44 (0)1462 672509 Fax: 44 (0)1462 672132

Neil Burkill, Paragon Designs, 39, Cantley Lane, Norwich, Norfolk. NR4 6TA Tel: 44 (0)1603 507152 Fax: 44 (0)1603 506057

# Contents

# Contents

# Preface

'City of Lincoln', PA474
operated by the BBMF,
RAF Coningsby

In this, the fourth title in our Modeller's Datafile series, we will cover a classic type in the form of the Lancaster. To fully understand this machine though it is also necessary to consider its predecessor, the Manchester, and its successor, the Lincoln. Although conceived from the outset with the static scale models in mind, this series of books has already proved extremely popular with radio controlled model makers and aviation enthusiasts and historians. What follows will be a concise history of these three types, along with all those details that modellers crave.

This title is again on a subject that is a personal favourite. I think one of my happiest, and most vivid, memories as a child involves the BBMF's Lancaster. After spending a lovely summer's day on a picnic with my parents and elder sister,

we were just a few miles from home driving up to the crest of a hill outside where I lived when, out of the sky to our left came the BBMF flight, low and slow with the Spitfire and Hurricane on either wing tip of the Lanc. Pure nostagia! For me the sound of four Merlins 'turning and burning' cannot be beaten, although a Moto Guzzi V8 at full song comes close, but that's another story, and another passion.

I hope you enjoy what follows to the same extent as I have enjoyed writing it.

*Richard A. Franks*

Bedford
July 2000

## Photographs

A great number of the photographs used in this title have come from the Royal Air Force Museum's (RAFM) extensive collection. Each picture can be obtained from the RAFM, using the 'P' prefixed number shown in brackets at the end of each caption.

For more details and an up-to-date price list contact the Photographic Department of the RAFM on +44 (0) 20 8205 2266.

Royal Air Force Museum
**HEND☉N**
Britain's National Museum of Aviation

# Glossary

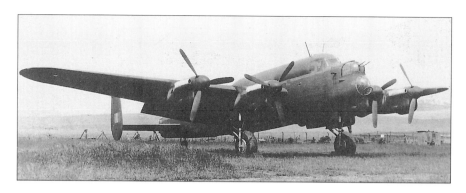

AA . . . . . . . . Anti-Aircraft
A&AEE . . . . . Aeroplane & Armament Experimental
          Establishment
Air Cdre . . . . Air Commodore (RAF)
ACM . . . . . . . Air-Chief Marshal (RAF)
AFC . . . . . . . . Air Force Cross (RAF)
AFDU . . . . . . Air Fighting Development Unit
AFEE . . . . . . . Airborne Forces Experimental
          Establishment
AGLT . . . . . . Automatic Gun-laying (Turrets)
AI . . . . . . . . . Airborne Interception (radar)
Air Mshl . . . . Air Marshal (RAF)
AMWD . . . . . Air Ministry Works Department
AOC . . . . . . . . Air Officer Commandiing
AP . . . . . . . . . Armour Piercing
ASC . . . . . . . . Air Support Control
ASR . . . . . . . . Air Sea Rescue
ASV . . . . . . . . Air to Surface Vessel (Radar)
ASWDU . . . . Anti-submarine Warfare Development
          Unit
ATA . . . . . . . . Air Transport Auxiliary
ATC . . . . . . . . Air Training Corps
AVM . . . . . . . Air Vice Marshal (RAF)
A.V. Roe. . . . . (Sir) Alliott Verdon-Roe
AWA . . . . . . . . Armstrong-Whitworth Aircraft
B (Mk). . . . . . Bomber Aircraft
BAFO. . . . . . . British Air Forces of Occupation
BBU . . . . . . . . Blind Bombing Unit
BCAMS . . . . . Bomber Command Aircraft Maintenance
          Squadron
BCIS . . . . . . . Bomber Command Instructor's School
BDU. . . . . . . . Bomber Development Unit
BEF . . . . . . . . British Expeditionary Force
BEAC . . . . . . . British European Airways Corporation
BOAC. . . . . . . British Overseas Airways Corporation
BS . . . . . . . . . British Standard
BSAAC. . . . . . British South American Airways
          Corporation
BSDU. . . . . . . Bomber Support Development Unit
C (Mk). . . . . . Freighter or Passenger Aircraft
Capt . . . . . . . . Captain
CGS . . . . . . . . Central Gunnery School
CMF. . . . . . . . Central Mediterranean Force
CO . . . . . . . . . Commanding Officer
CSE . . . . . . . . Central Signal Establishment
Do . . . . . . . . . Dornier
DFC . . . . . . . . Distinguished Flying Cross
DFM . . . . . . . Distinguished Flying Medal
D.H. . . . . . . . . de Havilland
DSO . . . . . . . . Distinguished Service Order
DTD. . . . . . . . Directorate of Technical Development
EAAS . . . . . . . Empire Air Armament School
EANS. . . . . . . Empire Air Navigational School
ECFS . . . . . . . Empire Central Flying School
EFS . . . . . . . . Empire Flying School
ETPS . . . . . . . Empire Test Pilots School
FAA . . . . . . . . Fleet Air Arm
F.E. . . . . . . . . . Far East (standard)
FEAF . . . . . . . Far East Air Force
Fg Off . . . . . . Flying Officer (RAF)
FIDO . . . . . . . Fog Investigation and Dispersal
          Operation
Flt Ltn . . . . . . Flight Lieutenant
Flt Sgt . . . . . . Flight Sergeant

F.N. . . . . . . . . Frazer Nash
FRU . . . . . . . . Fleet Requirements Unit
FS. . . . . . . . . . Federal Standard
FTS . . . . . . . . Flying Training School
Gal . . . . . . . . . Gallons
GCB . . . . . . . . Knight Grand Cross of the Bath
Gee. . . . . . . . . Navigational Device
G-H . . . . . . . . Radar Blind Bombing System
GLO . . . . . . . . Ground Liaison Officer
Grp Capt . . . . Group Captain (RAF)
GR . . . . . . . . . General Reconnaissance
H2S . . . . . . . . Airborne Radar Navigational and
          Target Location Device
HAL. . . . . . . . Hawker Aircraft Ltd.
HC Flt . . . . . . Heavy Conversion Flight
HCU. . . . . . . . Heavy Conversion Unit
HMS . . . . . . . His/Her Majesty's Ship
H.P. . . . . . . . . Handley Page
HQ . . . . . . . . . Headquarters
IFF. . . . . . . . . Identification Friend or Foe
JASS. . . . . . . . Joint Anti-submarine School
JG. . . . . . . . . . Jädgschader
KBE . . . . . . . . Knight Commander of the Order of the
          British Empire
KCB . . . . . . . . Knight Commander of the Bath
kg. . . . . . . . . . Kilogram
KG . . . . . . . . . Kampfgeschwader (Luftwaffe)
LAC . . . . . . . . Leading Aircraftsman
lb . . . . . . . . . . Pound
LFS . . . . . . . . Lancaster Finishing School
L.G. . . . . . . . . Landing Ground
LORAN . . . . . Long Range Navigational Aid
lt. . . . . . . . . . . Litre
Lt Cdr . . . . . . Lieutenant Commander (Royal Navy)
Lt Col. . . . . . . Lieutenant Colonel
MAC . . . . . . . Mediterranean Air Command
Maj . . . . . . . . Major
MAP . . . . . . . Ministry of Air Production
MC. . . . . . . . . Medium Capacity (bomb)
Me. . . . . . . . . . Messerschmitt (also Bf)
MEAF . . . . . . Middle East Air Force
Mk . . . . . . . . . Mark
ML. . . . . . . . . ML Aviation Ltd.
Monica . . . . . Airborne Radar Warning Device
MOS . . . . . . . Ministry of Supply
MOTU . . . . . Marine Operational Training Unit
MR. . . . . . . . . Maritime Reconnaissance
MU . . . . . . . . Maintenance Unit (RAF)
NCO. . . . . . . . Non-commissioned Officer
NEAF. . . . . . . Near East Air Force
No. . . . . . . . . . Number
NTU. . . . . . . . Night Training Unit (Pathfinder Force)
OBE . . . . . . . . Order of the British Empire
Oboe . . . . . . . Ground-controlled Blind-bombing
          Radar System

OTU. . . . . . . . Operational Training Unit
PEE . . . . . . . . Proof and Experimental Establishment
PFF . . . . . . . . Pathfinder Force
Plt Off . . . . . . Pilot Officer (RAF)
POW . . . . . . . Prisoner of War
PR . . . . . . . . . Photographic Reconnaissance
PRU . . . . . . . . Photographic Reconnaissance Unit
RAAF . . . . . . Royal Australian Air Force
RAE. . . . . . . . Royal Aircraft Establishment
RAF . . . . . . . . Royal Air Force
Radar. . . . . . . Radio Detection and Ranging
RATO. . . . . . . Rocket Assisted Take-Off
RCAF. . . . . . . Royal Canadian Air Force
REAF. . . . . . . Royal Egyptian Air Force
Rebecca. . . . . Radar Navigational Aid
RHU . . . . . . . Reserve Holding Unit (RAF
          Waddington)
RNAS. . . . . . . Royal Naval Air Station
RNZAF . . . . . Royal New Zealand Air Force
RR . . . . . . . . . Rolls-Royce
RSAF . . . . . . . Royal Swedish Air Force
RWE . . . . . . . Radio Warfare Establishment
SAAF. . . . . . . South African Air Force
Sgt . . . . . . . . . Sergeant
SMR. . . . . . . . School of Maritime Reconnaissance
SOC . . . . . . . . Struck Off Charge
SofTT . . . . . . School of Technical Training
(Spec) . . . . . . Special
Sqn . . . . . . . . Squadron
Sqn Ldr . . . . . Squadron Leader (RAF)
T . . . . . . . . . . Trainer
TI. . . . . . . . . . Target Indicator
TDU. . . . . . . . Torpedo Development Unit
TFU . . . . . . . . Telecommunications Flying Unit
TT . . . . . . . . . Target Tug
UK . . . . . . . . . United Kingdom
USAAC . . . . . United States Army Air Corps
USAAF . . . . . United States Army Air Force
USS . . . . . . . . United States Ship
VC . . . . . . . . . Victoria Cross
VE-Day . . . . . Victory in Europe Day
VHF. . . . . . . . Very High Frequency
VIP . . . . . . . . Very Important Person
VJ-Day. . . . . . Victory in Japan Day
WAAF . . . . . . Woman's Auxiliary Air Force
Wg Cdr . . . . . Wing Commander (RAF)
WO . . . . . . . . Warrant Officer
Window . . . . Strips of aluminium foil dropped to
          disrupt enemy radar defences
W/T. . . . . . . . Wireless Telegraphy
WU . . . . . . . . Western Union
/G. . . . . . . . . . Suffix letter added to aircraft serial
          number denoting that it carried special
          equipment and was to be guarded at all
          times.

# The Manchester

## Chapter 1

Manchester B Mk I, L7284,
EM•D of No. 207 Squadron
in flight
*(©RAFM P0016514)*

By the mid-1930s the RAF's frontline bomber squadrons were still equipped with outdated types. Eight squadrons had the H.P. Heyford, three still had the Vickers Virginia and only one (No. 38 Sqn) had a 'modern' type in the form of the Fairey Hendon. Even this machine, although at least a monoplane, was still of metal and fabric construction. In America the USAAC test flew the Boeing 299 (later XB-17) in July 1935, and in Germany the newly acknowledged Luftwaffe was flying types as 'airliners' that would soon prove themselves as bombers in WWII (Heinkel He 111, Dornier Do 17 and Junkers Ju 88).

The first truly modern monocoque construction bomber, the A.W. Whitley, flew on the 17th March 1936 and the Wellington (which although of alloy geodetic construction, still had fabric covering) followed later in the year.

On 8th September 1936 the Air Ministry issued Specification No. P13/36 which called for a twin-engined medium bomber of 20 tons that was capable of cruising at 275mph on two-thirds power at 15,000ft with a 3,000lb bomb load for 2,000 miles. Service ceiling was to be 28,000ft and in the event of the loss of one engine, the type was to be able to maintain a height of 10,000ft. The type was also to have armoured protection and power-operated turrets and the maximum bomb load was to be 8,000lb. Limitations were applied to the size of the main components, so they could be handled by the ground equipment then in service with the RAF, and the design was also to be capable of dive bombing (at an angle of 60° to conceal the type and also to offer better accuracy of ordnance delivery), torpedo dropping (this led to the very long bomb bay as the torpedoes of the time were 18ft 3in long), troop carrying and supply dropping! It should be realised that at this time the Air Staff was formulating 'Expansion Programme F' and this called for a substantial force of heavy bombers but, due to financial restrictions imposed on the nation in the 1930s, all new designs were to

incorporate as great an offensive capability as possible (value for money!). The long range and heavy bomb load of the type was to be achieved by the use of catapult take-off. Now, although at a later stage the various other roles envisaged for the type were dropped, it was not until a 37,000lb Manchester was hurled down the runway at Farnborough on a trolley, that the catapult idea was finally dispensed with. Many may question the sanity of such a requirement in a machine of this size, but due to the length of runways at RAF bases of the time, the design would have to take off in 500 yards with a 1,000lb bomb load or 700 yards with a 3,000lb bomb load and 2,000 miles worth of fuel!

Six firms (A.V. Roe, Boulton Paul, Bristol, Handley Page, Short Brothers and Vickers) were approached to tender designs for this new specification in August 1936, and in November 1936 the specification was also sent to Fairey and Hawker. Only three companies submitted designs in regard to this specification: Avro (Type 679), Handley Page (HP 56) and Hawker. Only the Avro design was built to meet the P.13/36 requirement, although it should be noted that the HP 56 was later to lead to the Halifax when the Vulture engines required for the P.13/36 specification were not

Manchester B Mk I, L7380,
EM•W of
No. 207 Squadron
*(©RAFM P004023)*

**Manchester
B Mk I, L7277**
*(©RAFM P004022)*

**Manchester prototype (L7247)
showing the ventral gun turret
in the extended position**
*(via R. Sturtivant)*

**Winston Churchill inspecting
the crew of Manchester
L7322 of No. 207 Squadron,
RAF West Raynham, 6th June
1941** *(©RAFM P009996)*

available in large enough numbers. Handley Page cancelled the HP 56 and started work on a revised layout using four Rolls-Royce Merlin engines (a path the Manchester was to follow as well, although for totally different reasons). The Design Tender submitted to the Air Ministry by Avro in late February 1937 bore little resemblance to the Manchester that emerged. The design used many new techniques, with a monocoque alloy fuselage built on hoops and stringers and secured with flush rivets. The design had to offer the best capacity with the least overall size and initially the Type 679 design had a span of just 72ft. The specification had called for a maximum bomb load of 8,000lb, but by having a bomb bay nearly two-thirds the overall fuselage length, and by being a mid-wing design with all the fuel carried in the wings, Avro were able to improve on this to a maximum envisaged load of 12,000lb. Just four crew members were intended for this initial design and mock-ups of the cockpit area were built at the Newton Heath works to ensure that this layout was correct. The long range operations envisaged for the type led Avro to design a sound-proofed sleeping/rest area in the mid-section that would accommodate two relief crewmen for this type of operation.

As can be seen much rested on the potential 1,700hp Rolls-Royce Vulture engines. In the end this was to be the Achilles Heel of the design, as this engine's layout meant that everything depended on adequate lubrication of the bearings of its single crankshaft. The oil in use within the RAF at this time was not of sufficient quality to withstand the demands being made on it by this new engine, and as a result the Manchester (as the Avro Type 679 had been called) was plagued with engine problems from day one. Rolls-Royce also experienced problems in producing the engine, as distortion of the crankcases was being experienced during casting. The

initial trials with the Vulture were undertaken with an engine fitted into the Hawker Henley prototype (K5115); this was later joined by another similarly modified Henley (L3302), as the engine soon proved to be unreliable. Testing continued through 1939 and 1940 and the engine type was also used in the new Hawker Tornado. Throughout all of these tests the engine showed signs of overheating, and coolant circulation problems were a major headache. Poor oil circulation also led to a drop in pressure with any increase in altitude and severe aeration of the oil. Modifications to these engines included a larger header tank and revised coolant flow, but they never fully cured the problems. The modifications did unfortunately raise the overall weight of the Vulture engine by more than a ton per pair. The Manchester had been designed from the outset to maximize all available potential and as a result there was insufficient capacity for the type to suffer a weight gain without any increase in the power offered from its engines. This combined to spell the end of the Manchester, as it was dangerously underpowered.

By early 1938 Rolls-Royce had serious doubts about the development potential of the Vulture engine and so alternative engines for the Manchester were sought; the Bristol Hercules was considered, but at 1,350hp they would not have been powerful enough to even get the type off the ground! There were also concerns that Rolls-Royce could not actually make the Vulture in sufficient numbers and it was at

this point that Handley Page were instructed by the Air Ministry to redesign their HP 56 tender to accept four Merlin engines (something that at the time Sir Frederick Handley Page complained most strongly about). During the 1937/8 period the Avro design underwent many changes, as did the specification to which it was designed, and many meetings were held between the Air Ministry, RAF and major sub-contractors for the project. Considering the obvious amount of uncertainty about the design, it is interesting to note that an order for 200 was placed on the 1st July 1937, 'straight off the drawing board'. On the 26th August 1937 the torpedo carrying capability was dropped, followed by the catapult launch requirement on the 4th July 1938 and the dive bombing requirement on the 11th August 1938 (the latter item was dropped as the 60° angle required for the dive was considered unobtainable). All of these requirements were shelved because there was a pressing need to get a modern bomber into production. What must be considered though is that although the catapult system requirement was dropped, the first twenty airframes produced were too advanced to take advantage of the weight saving this offered, and so they were built still able to withstand the stresses of a catapult launch. In fact the first prototype did undertake accelerated take-off (not catapult) and dive bombing trials as a result. The number of changes to the requirement for the design made by the Air Staff and RAF lead to huge delays in the building of the first two prototypes. Many time-wasting requests were made by the Air Ministry, including the ability to take alternative engines, interchangeable fuel tanks, redesigned bomb bay and even alternative materials instead of alloy for the overall constructions (these included steel and even laminated paper!). The major external changes made at this time included the replacement of the inset fins with elliptical fins and rudders on the ends of the tailplanes and the increase in span from 72ft to 80ft 2in.

Expansion Programme L had, by the end of 1938, called for the procurement of 3,500 medium and heavy bombers and 1,500 of these were to be Manchesters. To meet this huge requirement the Manchester Production Group consisting of Avro, Armstrong Whitworth, Fairey and Metropolitan-Vickers was established. A further 200 Manchesters were ordered from Avro with another 100 from Metropolitan-Vickers in 1939. Armstrong Whitworth and Fairey were to join production with 300 each of the type in late 1939 and early 1940, but in the end many of these machines were actually built as Lancasters.

Work on the Type 679 had continued though and on the 25th July 1939 the prototype took off from Ringway with Capt H.A. 'Sam' Brown at the controls, assisted by Bill Thorn and two engineers. The first flight lasted just 17 minutes, and although Brown signalled to the assembled crowd that all was well, there were some serious problems to overcome. The initial tests proved the type's performance was poor and a substantial increase in wing area would be required. The type

was also unstable in the longitudinal axis. All of this was to lead to the increase in span from 80ft 2in by 9ft 11in to 90ft 1in. The aircraft was soon to be transferred to A&AEE Boscombe Down, but during the delivery flight the port engine stopped and the pilot (Bill Thorn) had to make a wheels-down landing in a field at Charnes Hall, Staffordshire. This emergency was caused by the fuel cock being tuned to 'reserve' instead of 'main'! After various hazards had been removed from the take off run, the Manchester took off again on the 1st December and returned to Ringway for checks. Sam Brown eventually took the aircraft to Boscombe Down on the 10th December A third fin on the dorsal spine

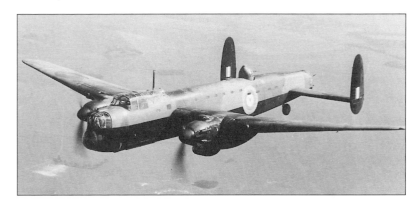

between the tailplanes was added, and its initial 'shark fin' profile was replaced after a few days with a more rounded version. The first prototype's flying was cut short after just two days, when on the 12th December the engines failed at just 300ft after take off and it crash landed in a cabbage field. The aircraft was only lightly damaged and so it was sent to Newton Heath for repair. Test flying soon resumed, but on the 23rd December engine failure occurred again and even at 3,000ft, height could not be retained and it crashed just short of the boundary at Boscombe. Damage to the airframe and engines was such that development flying stopped, as the problems with the Vultures were far from over, and the dismantled airframe was sent back to Woodford.

The design's weight had escalated and the Deputy Director of Technical Development advised Avro that the Manchester had to have its all-up weight drastically reduced. In the end, with the help of thinner gauge metal skinning, the weight was reduced by 1,500lb, but it was too late for the first 200 production machines which were in an advanced state of construction. Repairs to L7246 were completed rapidly by May 1940 and the aircraft was soon joined in the testing programme by the second prototype (L7247). This machine had a smaller dorsal fin fitted from the outset and it also had the front and rear turrets installed (although without any guns). It flew for the first time on the 26th May 1940. Initially this machine had auxiliary 'bench seat' elevators fitted under the main elevators, but this interim solution to the type's longitudinal stability was soon to be replaced with a more permanent correction. This took the form of new tailplanes of an increased span (33ft) and was incorporated with an improved elevator that had its hinge set back by 24%. The first prototype returned to A&AEE in May 1940 and tests showed that the increased span and tailplanes were essential, as the type was still woefully unstable. By July the aircraft had the 90ft 1in span and the revised elevators (although the short [28ft] tailplanes were still fitted) and it was joined in the test prgramme by the second prototype (L7247).

Manchester B Mk Ia, L7320, which was operated by the A&AEE between March and December 1941 on various trials *(via R. Sturtivant)*

Manchester B Mk I, L7319, EM•X of No.207 Squadron *(©RAFM P006299)*

Manchester prototype L7246, August 1939 *(©RAFM P005200)*

Repairs being carried out on Manchester B Mk IA, L7477, QR•N of No. 61 Squadron after its involvement on the raids on Scharnhorst and Gneisenau on the 12th February 1942 *(©RAFM P0019789)*

Manchester B Mk I, L7282, EM•J of No. 207 Squadron
*©RAFM P0022535)*

Repairs being carried out on Manchester B Mk IA, L7477, QR•N of No. 61 Squadron after its involvement on the raids on Scharnhorst and Gneisenau on the 12th February 1942 *(©RAFM P0019790)*

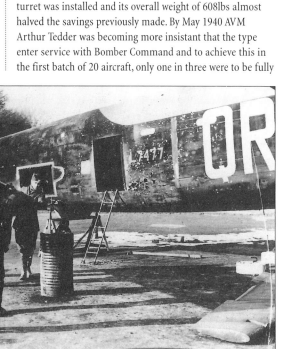

Turret installations trials were conducted using L7247, but initial trials with the round F.N.20 rear turret were not successful and the type was dropped, similarly the D-section F.N.4 resulted in uncontrollable pitch changes when trained to the port or starboard. The stresses imposed on the airframe by the movement of the turret was such that it actually twisted the rear fuselage. The cause was high pressure in front of the elevators, which forced them down. To overcome this the fuselage was lengthened and the turret located six inches further aft. Wedges were cut out of the inner faces of the elevators, the turret was faired into the fuselage and all screw fixings were replaced with rivets. Test flights with this new installation proved that all the previous problems had been overcome. All weight saving on the design came to nought, as by this time the F.N.21A ventral gun turret was installed and its overall weight of 608lbs almost halved the savings previously made. By May 1940 AVM Arthur Tedder was becoming more insistant that the type enter service with Bomber Command and to achieve this in the first batch of 20 aircraft, only one in three were to be fully

equipped. These machines were to become gunnery and bombing trainers to help crews become accustomed to them. The Air Ministry now dictated that the F.N.21A turret was not to be installed, and two hand-held Browning or Vickers gas-operated machine guns were to be fitted instead. Although instructions were issued, somewhere between nine and eleven of the first production batch had these turrets installed. In service this turret was usually removed and most of the subsequent machines never had any provision for the turret incorporated. A mid-upper F.N.7A turret was also to be installed, as this type had been designed for the Botha, which had been cancelled, and as a result there were examples now available for installation. The Manchester, Stirling and Halifax all used this turret and the Manchester with it fitted was redesignated Mk IA.

By September 1940 L7247 was at A&AEE with the revised elevator appendages. These were not the metal skinned versions fitted to L7246, but metal framed and fabric covered, they also included nose balance and inset geared balance tabs. The type also had the 33ft span tailplanes and the revised (production) profile to the central vertical fin.

## Production

As time was soon to tell, the Manchester had unfortunately been ordered in quantity (200) right off the drawing board. Production of these machines started in July 1939, and as has already been recounted, at this stage the problems associated with the type's Vulture engines were still in the initial stages of investigation. The first production machine (L7276) was delivered to A&AEE on the 5th August 1940 and it was fitted with the 90ft 1in span mainplanes and two of the modified

Vulture II engines (now rated at 1,850hp). This machine retained the old 28ft tailplanes, and it was only with the 21st production machine that the new 33ft unit would be incorporated. Initial trials with L7246 proved that performance and take off were much improved and apart from a few minor problems there was only one major concern; the F.N.21A ventral turret. This 'low drag' turret induced a speed loss of 16mph, one gun would often jam during firing, the viewing lens was often obscured by oil leaking from the bomb door jacks and it could not be retracted when the aircraft was at cruising speed. All of these factors proved the turret to be more trouble than it was worth and on the 1st July 1940 the order was given to delete the turret from all production Manchesters.

The future of the Manchester was still in doubt as the engines were still troublesome and when AVM Charles Portal advised the Air Staff on the 28th August 1940 that all Bomber Command heavy bombers were to have four engines, it seemed as if the Manchester would fail before it even reached service. Chadwick and the rest of his design team knew that the only way forward was with the Manchester III and its four Merlin engines. Even though by October 1940 Rolls-Royce assured Avro that the new Vulture II engine was fully developed, problems still persisted and with pressure from the Minister for Aircraft Production (Lord Beaverbrook) and Sir Frederick Handley Page to see the Manchester cancelled in favour of the Halifax, it was a very dark time indeed. Eventually it was thought best to plan production of both the Halifax and Manchester III (Lancaster), so development and production of the Manchester continued. Rolls-Royce had now discovered the cause of the coolant problems with the Vulture, which arose from contamination of the coolant in the coolant passages. This was caused by oil left in these passages during the production process. A 100% ethylene glycol coolant would dissolve this oil, but the 30% glycol/pressurised water system of the Vulture did not. The Vulture was not without fault though, and as the build-up to service entry commenced in late September 1940 the engine still suffered with excessive temperature and local 'hot spots'.

## Service

No. 207 Squadron was to be the first to receive the Manchester, and it had been reformed at Waddington on the 1st November as part of No. 5 Group for the task. Some of their flight and ground crews had been detached to Boscombe Down to undertake familiarisation work with the Manchester, but unserviceable aircraft had left little for the flight crews to do, but lots for the ground crews! The squadron's first aircraft (L7279) was collected from No. 6 MU

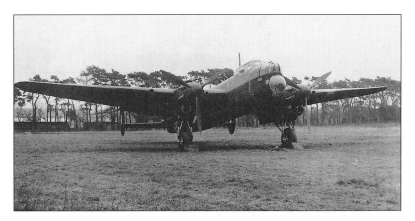

(RAF Brize Norton) on the 6th November 1940 and taken to Boscombe down. Two days later this machine was flown to Waddington and it was joined by their second machine (L7278) on the 10th. On the 21st November orders were given to make L7278 and L7279 undertake 500 hours of flying with Rolls-Royce engineers on board to assure the modifications carried out by them in the first part of the month were successful. The 'hot spots' in the coolant system were traced to air locks in the two coolant pumps. This lead to either

pump stopping, followed by seizure of the engine and it was overcome with a balance pipe between the pumps. By the end of November 1940 the two existing airframes had been joined by L7283 and L7284. Problems experienced in these machines included the lack of any heating, frequent failure of the Ermeto hydraulic couplings and the lack of an engine-driven air compressor (for the brakes). In December the squadron gained L7280 and L7286. By the end of 1940 some twenty-five production Manchesters had been completed and, after a visit by Their Majesties, King George VI and Queen Elizabeth in January 1941, the squadron was declared operational. By the end of January 1941 the squadron had fourteen machines (L7278-80, L7282-4, L7286, L7288, L7290-2, L7294 and L7298-9). In early February these

**Manchester B Mk IA, L7320**
(©RAFM P006300)

**Hawker Henley K5115 was used as a test-bed for the Vulture engine**
(©Rolls-Royce Ltd)

**The Manchester prototype (L7246) ground running at Ringway in July 1940**
(©BAe)

were supplemented with the arrival of seven more machines. The decision was made to make another squadron (No. 57) from B Flight of No 207 Squadron. They were to use the older machines, while No. 207 Squadron got the newer examples and this did mean that No. 57 squadron was initially only seen in a non-operational role. The first operational mission by No. 207 Squadron was on the 24th February 1941, when six machines (L7279, L7284, L7286, L7288, L7294 & L7300) set out for Brest. All machines returned, although L7300 diverted to Boscombe Down, and L7286 landed at Middle Wallop. L7284 crashed on landing due to a hydraulics failure that led to the bomb doors being open for the entire return trip and the undercarriage refusing to go down. Even with the emergency pneumatic system the starboard leg would not come down. Roy Chadwick was a guest at Waddington on this day and he talked to the pilot about how he could get the leg down, but with all these options exhausted, the pilot (Fg Off P.R Burton-Gyles) executed a perfect emergency landing on the port main and tail wheels, leaving the aircraft's starboard wing up as long as possible. L7284 therefore became the first Manchester damaged during operational service.

On the 25th February 1941 No. 97 Squadron was formally created at Waddington and it was hoped to transfer eight aircraft to it. This took place on the 27th when L7283, L7290,

L7291, L7292, L7294, L7298 and L7299 were transferred. The squadron moved to Coningsby in March, with its aircraft following later that month. The second raid by No. 207 Squadron took place on the 26th February 1941 and was with five aircraft (L7286, L7288, L7292, L7294 and L7300) against Cologne. L7286 had oil pressure problems and had to return to base, and L7294 suffered a number of hydraulic leaks. The squadron's third operation, due to continuing serviceability problems, saw just two machines (L7302 and L7312) go on the raid to Brest on the 3rd March. Raids by 207 Squadron followed on the 12th/13th March (Hamburg), 20th March (Lorient), 27th March (Dusseldorf), 30th March (Brest), 4th April (Brest) and 6th April (Brest). No 97 Squadron made its debut with a raid on Kiel on the 8th April 1941. By the 13th April 1941 some fifteen raids had been completed but a general grounding order was issued, so that checks and modifications could be made to the engines. This was followed by a similar order on the 30th June. The end of the Vulture came as result of all these problems combined with the fatal crash of L7295 which was operated by Rolls-Royce on the 26th May 1941.

The first use of the 4,000lb 'Cookie' in a Manchester was undertaken by 207 Squadron Manchesters (L7317, L7377 and L7379) on the 2nd May 1941, when they attacked Hamburg. L7379 was lost in this raid, although all the crew got out. No. 61 Squadron was soon to become operational with the Manchester and it undertook its first operation with Nos. 207 and 97 squadrons on the 21st June 1941 against Boulogne. Mk IAs were starting to be delivered to the squadrons in late 1941 and the Manchester equipped squadrons were boosted by No. 83 Squadron when it joined Nos. 207 and 61

squadrons machines on a raid on Boulogne on the 28th/29th
January 1942.

The Manchester was to take part in the 1,000 bomber raid
on Cologne on the 30th/31st March 1942, as well as the
similar sized raid on Essen on the 1st/2nd June 1942. The
final operation of the Manchester before it was withdrawn
from frontline service was another 1,000 bomber raid on
Bremen on the 25th/26th June 1942.

## The End

In all some 200 Mk I and Mk IA airframes were built. The type
undertook 1,269 sorties and dropped 1,826 tons of bombs and
mines in just five months in 1941. Losses were high though,
with 63 machines lost on operations and a further 59 lost due
to mechanical failures and training accidents.

Further development of the Manchester design was
instigated, mainly to deal with the unsuitable nature of the
Vulture engines. Napier Ltd were sent an airframe to test-fit
Sabre engines to, but in the end it was never completed and
the aircraft ended its days without outer wing panels as a
ground test stand. The airframe was also considered for two
Bristol Centaurus engines, and although these engines were
actually installed onto a Manchester, it was never test flown

L7246 was used for
frictionless take-off trials at
Farnborough and is seen here
rigged in a flying position on
the test rails
(©Crown Copyright)

because development of the next version of the Manchester
had already commenced. Both the Sabre and Centaurus
powered versions were to have been Mk IIs (Mk IIA and
Mk IIB), but they were all superseded by the Mk III which
had four Merlin engines and was later renamed Lancaster.

Manchester prototype L7247
with the central
'shark' fin

# From Manchester to Lancaster

## Chapter 2

On the 18th April 1940 Roy Chadwick wrote to the Air Ministry making proposals for the various Manchester variants. The list ended with the Mk III with its four Merlin engines and a note stating that 'this type will probably be given another name later'.

With the obvious problems associated with the Manchester's Vulture engines, an incomplete airframe was taken from the production line in mid-1940 (the precise date is unknown) and modified to take four Rolls-Royce Merlin engines. Accommodating these engines on the existing Manchester wing was not possible, but as development on the extension of the Manchester wing had already been undertaken, wing spar extensions were already available. These extensions increased the span by 12ft (to 92ft 1in) and the Merlin 'power eggs' that had been developed for the Beaufighter Mk II were installed. This revised airframe was allocated the Avro type No. 683 and the first prototype (BT308) flew for the first time on the 9th January 1941. At this time the airframe still had the triple fin assembly of the Manchester and it underwent a large number of tests with the A&AEE at Boscombe Down from 28th February. By September BT308 had lost the Manchester three-fin assembly and had also gained the 33ft tailplane assembly. In May the first prototype had been joined by the second (DG595). This airframe was fitted with four Merlin XX engines and had a revised and strengthened undercarriage to deal with the increased weight.

With the obvious problems the Manchester was experiencing and the success of the Type 683 (now named Lancaster) all Manchester production ceased with L7526

Lancaster B Mk II of No. 61 Squadron
(©RAFM P0019786)

and the remainder of that contract were completed as Lancaster B Mk Is. The first Lancaster (L7527) was flown at Woodford on the 31st October 1941 and was soon passed to A&AEE Boscombe Down. Later it moved to the TFU at Hurn for the installation of its radio equipment.

## Into Service

The first Squadron to receive the Lancaster had been identified at an early stage as No. 44 (Rhodesia) Squadron and it received its first three machines (L7537, L7538 & L7541) on the 24th December 1941. These had been supplemented with a further twenty-one airframes by the 25th March 1942. Although the new machines brought about an urgent need to train flight and ground crews, the similarities with the Manchester meant that the squadron

Lancaster B Mk II of No. 115 Squadron
(©RAFM P015482)

Bombing up a Lancaster B Mk I with incendiary clusters

was able to undertake its first operation to lay mines in the Heligoland Bight on the 3rd March with four machines. On the 10th March two aircraft went on a bombing raid to Essen and at the same time eight of the squadron's machines were detached to RAF Lossiemouth in preparation for an attack on the Tirpitz at Trondheim.

The second squadron to equip with the Lancaster was No. 97 (Straits Settlements) Squadron at RAF Coningsby. The unit had already flown the Manchester (having been formed from B Flight of No. 207 Squadron at Waddington) and it received its first Lancaster in January 1942. So quick

was the transition from Manchester to Lancaster that the squadron undertook its first mission with the type (mine laying off the Fresian Islands) on the 20th March. However, on the 26th March 1942 all of No. 97 Squadron's Lancasters were grounded after one was lost due to a structural failure of the wing. No. 5 Group instructed all squadrons to ground the Lancaster and make inspections of the wings and in all, eight machines were found to be in need of rectification. On the 4th April 1942 twelve Lancasters (six from each squadron) took off for a daylight raid on the submarine diesel engine site of the Maschinenfabrik Augsburg Nürnburg AG. Unfortunately the group was bounced by Messerschmitt Bf 109s of JG.2 and as a result only two of the No. 44 Squadron machines reached the target (Sqn Ldr D.J. Nettleton and Fg Off Garwell). Although the target was heavily damaged in the raid just five of the twelve machines limped home. It would be another six months before, on the

17th October 1942, the Lancaster was used in a daylight operation and this time the target was the Schneider works at Le Creusot. The method of operation coupled with practice and good security ensured that the force met little resistance, but because of a lack of daylight bombing practice the factory suffered little damage (even with 100 tons of explosives being dropped on it!). The Lancaster spent the next eighteen months operating by night.

Bombing at night was always a problem, as pinpoint accuracy to the target was difficult with no electronic navigational aids. This all changed in early 1942 when 'Gee' was introduced. Developed by the TRE since 1940 this system used pulsed signals from three transmitters and was not effected by compass or speed errors or by variable winds (all factors that effected 'dead-reckoning' navigation). Depending on the curvature of the Earth and the height of the aircraft the system had a 350-400 mile range and the TRE envisaged that the system would be effective for about six months before the Germans jammed it. As a result operational use was not to start until 200 machines had been installed with the system. The first raid to use Gee was against Essen and of

Lancaster B Mk II, DS689, CW•S of No. 26 Squadron
(via R. Sturtivant)

Lancaster B Mk Is of No. 50 Squadron
(©RAFM P0019719)

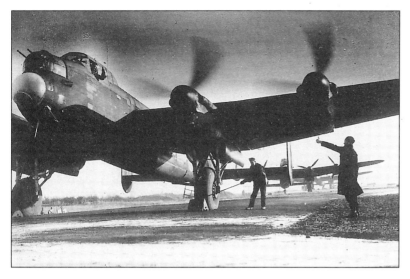

Lancaster B Mk I of No. 467 Squadron, RAF Waddington, March 1944 (©RAFM P0020922)

Lancaster B Mk Xs under construction at Victory Aircraft factory, Canada, 28th January 1944

struggled to overcome, and in August 1942 the Pathfinder Force (PFF) was formed. The PFF used experienced crews to find and mark targets and utilised Nos. 7 (Stirling), 35 (Halifax), 83 (Lancaster) and 156 (Wellington) to undertake the work. The task of developing radio counter-measures and radar aids was undertaken by No. 109 Squadron. The force was commanded by Gp Capt D. Bennett and on the 8th January 1943 it became No. 8 (PFF) Group.

The first operation of the PFF was on the 18th August 1942, but unfortunately at this time the Germans had successfully jammed Gee and so their raid against the Flensburg submarine yard was not a success.

## Attacks on Germany

By March 1943 the bombing of Germany had commenced, and on the 5th March 442 bombers attacked the Krupp factory in the heart of Essen. The raid saw the first use of

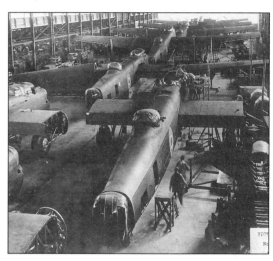

the 211 aircraft that took part, just eighty-two machines had Gee. The results were poor though as, at maximum range Gee was accurate only within four to five miles, and so pinpointing the target was still up to the bomb aimer. To help matters a hooded flare was developed, and this later became known as the Target Indicator (TI) bomb.

### Operation Millennium

By May 1942 the average number of bombers available for a raid was just 350, so the idea of launching a 1,000 bomber raid would seem impossible. However, the Prime Minister and Bomber Command planned such an offensive, called Operation Millennium, as both a morale booster and test. The date for the raid was the 30th May 1942 and the target was Cologne. Of the 1,037 aircraft used, 367 came from Operational Training Units, but 75 Lancasters took part. 2,100 tons of bombs were dropped and Cologne was extensively damaged for the loss of 44 aircraft.

### PFF

The problems associated with accurate identification and marking of a target was one that Bomber Command had

the new Oboe bombing and navigation aid, and Oboe-equipped Mosquitos and PFF Lancasters lead the raid. Between March and July Essen was visited five more times and the last raid was on the 25th July when 700 aircraft took part. The next city to suffer in a similar

Lancaster B Mk Is of No. 467 Squadron, being loaded with bombs
(©RAFM P0020923)

manner was Duisburg, which had over 5,000 tons of bombs dropped on it in five raids. The raid on Wuppertal-Barmen on the 29th/30th May saw the loss of 33 of the 534 bombers involved and most of these were lost to radar-equipped night fighters, something that was to remain a constant threat to the bombers throughout WWII. Hamburg was attacked by 791 bombers on the 25th July and this raid saw the first use of 'window' aluminium strips cut to the same length as the frequency of the German radar systems, which effectively blinded them by filling them with possible 'targets'. The PFF was now equipped with the plan position indicator H2S radar and the bombers were using a high proportion of incendiaries. The city was attacked three more times in as many days, with over 2,000 tons of ordnance being dropped each time.

## Peenemünde

This name is now well known to us all as the source of the Vengeance Weapons (V1 and V2), but it was not until April 1943 that the British Government took seriously the information it had been receiving from Oslo and the USA about these weapons. Initial PR missions over Peenemünde highlighted torpedo-shaped objects, about 40ft long, and so a raid was instigated. The date was set for the 17th/18th August 1943, and because of the distance involved, a feint

attack would need to be arranged to try and draw off the German night fighters. In the end twenty Mosquitos dropped masses of flares on Berlin and successfully fooled the Germans into sending nearly 200 nightfighters up to intercept them (where they were promptly shot at by their own AA defenses!). Nearly 600 bombers headed to Peenemünde, lead by the master bomber flown by Gp Capt J.H. Searby of No. 82 Squadron. Over 2000 tons of bombs were dropped on the dispersed site, but the cost was high. Forty aircraft (including seventeen Lancasters) failed to return and because of the dispersed nature of the buildings at Peenemünde, hundreds of slave workers were also killed.

## Berlin

It had been the wish of both 'Bomber' Harris and Winston Churchill to take the bombing offensive to Berlin, but the other industrial sites had taken priority. Now with these targets attacked, thoughts turned to the German capital, and it received the attention of Bomber Command on the 23rd and 31st August and 3rd September. Losses were very high amongst the Halifax and Stirling groups, so the third raid was done just by Lancasters (losing 20 aircraft in the

Lancaster B Mk III, QR•M of No. 61 Squadron after a wheels-up landing at Blida in July 1943
*(©RAFM P007279)*

Lancaster B Mk I, W4315, VN•G of No. 50 Squadron, and her crew
*(©RAFM P004440)*

Crew members relax on the nose of Lancaster B Mk II, WS•Z of No. 9 Squadron
*(©RAFM P007187)*

Lancaster B Mk I, KM•H of No. 44 Squadron, RAF Dunholm Lodge, 20th June 1943
(©RAFM P016432)

A Lancaster B Mk I of No. 83 Squadron in flight

Lancaster B Mk I, R5689, VN•N of No. 50 Squadron in flight
(©RAFM P003465)

process). Many raids took place on Berlin, with sixteen being undertaken between October 1943 and March 1944. During these Bomber Command lost 492 aircraft but they destroyed over four square miles of the capital and a large number of factories and amenities.

## 1943-4

This period was to see a large number of strategic raids and these include the 'Big Weeks' raids combining USAAF and RAF machines. Frankfurt was attacked on the 22nd/23rd March 1944 by 800 bombers, and in the raid on Nürnburg on the 31st March, 94 of the 800 bombers sent were lost, the highest loss rate of any night of the war. Munich was raided on the night of the 24th/25th April 1944, and this was when Wg Cdr Cheshire flew his Mosquito B Mk VI to just 700ft over the target to drop a new marker flare. Despite heavy flak and damage to his aircraft he continued to circle the target to correct the bombs being dropped by No. 617 Squadron above him! For this and many other courageous acts Cheshire was awarded the VC.

## D-Day

This operation marked the end of the Pinpoint raids that had been carried out until this point by Bomber Command, and saw the Lancaster being used in a very different manner. With the invasion planned Bomber Command turned its attention to railways, coastal defenses, harbours

and airfields; all items that would be closely associated with any offensive landing by the Allies. The 'Transportation Plan' was approved on the 15th April 1944 and this identified the railway system as a prime target during the build up to D-Day. By the 3rd June 1944 over 42,000 tons of bombs had been dropped on railway and marshalling yards in over 8,800 sorties. The Région Nord system was extensively damaged resulting in many diversions, and by the time of the invasion the French railway system was unable to be used to bring German reinforcements to the beachhead. Strategic targets in Germany were still attacked, when the opportunity arose, but military installations and ammunition dumps were the main targets. The 21st Panzer Division HQ at Mailly le Camp was attacked by 362 bombers on the 3rd May 1944. Heavy raids on the coastal batteries resulted in just one still being in action by the time of the landings. On the 6th June Lancasters attacked the marshalling yard at Caen and No. 617 Squadron's Lancasters took part in Operation Taxable, an operation where they and No. 218 squadron flew in a manner intended to simulate two large fleets of ships. The ruse worked, and blinded by 'Window', the German batteries opened fire on the imaginary fleet!

Villers Bocage was attacked on the 30th June 1944 by 258

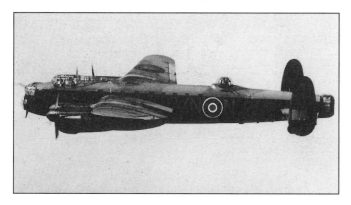

Lancaster B Mk I, VN•N of No. 50 Squadron in flight

Lancaster B Mk I, ND991, VN•P of No. 50 Squadron, RAF Skellingthorpe, 1945
*(via R. Sturtivant)*

A line-up of Lancaster B Mk IIIs of No. 50 Squadron
*(©RAFM P0019721)*

Lancaster B Mk I, W4419, VN•Q of No. 50 Squadron in flight
*(©RAFM P013901)*

Lancaster B Mk II, LM321, PH•H² of No. 12 Squadron, RAF Wickenby, 1943
*(©RAFM P008576)*

Lancaster B Mk III, ED888, PM•M² of No. 105 Squadron
*(©RAFM P0016830)*

Lancaster B Mk I, PO•E of No. 467 Squadron
*(©RAFM P010296)*

Lancaster B Mk I, W4366, PH•R of No. 12 Squadron, RAF Wickenby 1943
*(©RAFM P013781)*

Lancaster B Mk I, R5868 RO•S of No. 467 Squadron with the crew assembled prior to a mission *(©RAFM P000249)*

**Lancaster B Mk III, LM419, PG•S of No. 619 Squadron in flight**

**Lancaster B Mk I of Nos. 463 and 467 Squadrons in flight, during a raid on Bremen in 1945** *(©RAFM P007008)*

aircraft and Caen was attacked on the 7th/8th July with over 10,000 tons of bombs being dropped. Raids in support of the ground troops continued with attacks in support of the British Second Army south of Caumont on the 30th July. Attacks on the dykes in Holland were undertaken to flood the low-lying areas during October 1944. Attacks on oil and transportation systems continued, as well as attacks on pockets of resistance at the French ports in support of ground troops. Le Havre was first, and this port was finally captured on the 12th September 1944. Next was Boulogne, which fell on the 26th September, and Calais which fell early in October. Operations in support of the Russian advance was also undertaken, and it was in such an operation that the historic city of Dresden was attacked twice in February

1945. Unfortunately intelligence that informed Bomber Command that this city was a communications centre was later found to be false and the city in fact housed thousands of refugees. The loss of life can never be accurately known, but the attacks on Dresden have since been held up as an example of the unnecessarily aggressive strategies of men like 'Bomber' Harris, at a time when Germany was 'obviously' beaten. No matter what you believe, these strategies brought the war to a decisive end, by crippling the German forces and facilities, and the Avro Lancaster was one of the main weapons that took the war to the very heart of Germany.

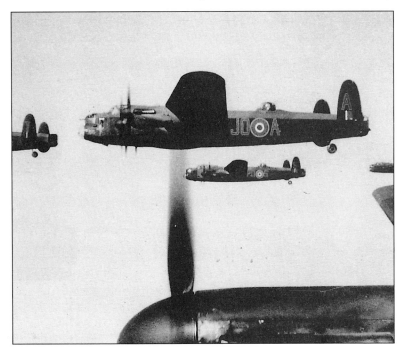

# Special Operations

## Chapter 3

Group shot of members of No. 617 Squadron celebrating in London after the raid. Guy Gibson can be see in the middle (third from right), while Dr Barnes Wallis is on the extreme left
*(©RAFM P004443)*

## The Dams Raid

Probably the most well known raid of the war, the attack by No. 617 Squadron on the hydro-electric generating dams in the Ruhr valley was also one of the most effective in relation to the number of aircraft lost.

The go-ahead for the raid (code-name Operation Chastise) was issued on the 26th February 1943, and in the three months that followed the special mines and the modified aircraft to carry them were created, and No. 617 squadron was specially formed and trained for the task. Tests with the new mines, codename Upkeep, had taken place using a Vickers Wellington, and the first Lancaster modified to carry the weapon (ED765/G) was delivered to RAE Farnborough on the 8th April 1943. This aircraft was soon joined by ED817/G on the 20th April and test drops of the weapon proceeded on the Ashley Walk Bombing Range and at Reculver in Kent. Initial drops lead to the disintegration of the weapon and it was not until the 29th April that a successful drop was made.

No. 617 Squadron had been formed specially to undertake this raid, although they had no idea of their target. The squadron was commanded by Wg Cdr Guy Gibson, who was a veteran pilot with 157 operations to his credit. The squadron initially undertook practice during daylight, but this soon changed to night. Low-level flying at night in the Lake District did little to endear them with the locals, and the squadron was still unaware of their intended target. The first production modified B Mk III, ED824/G, arrived at No. 617's base (RAF Scampton) on the 18th April 1943 and the final (twentieth) was delivered on the 13th May. These machines had the bomb doors removed, V-struts added either side to hold the mine, no mid-upper turret and spot lights built into the new fairings within the bomb bay. Initial trials with a Ford V8 engine to spin the Upkeep mine proved this to be too heavy, so with the removal of the bomb doors the spare capacity of the VSG hydraulic motor was used instead. The standard CSBS (Course Setting Bomb Sight) was found to be useless, but because two of the targets had gun towers 600ft apart, a simple bit of geometry

Lancaster B Mk III (Special), ED825/G
*(©RAFM P011881)*

**Lancaster B Mk III (Special), ED825/G**
*(©RAFM P011882)*

**A close-up of the 'Upkeep' mine under Lancaster B Mk III (Special), AJ•G of No. 617 Squadron**
*(©RAFM P011917)*

**Another close-up of the 'Upkeep' mine under Lancaster B Mk III (Special), AJ•G of No. 617 Squadron**
*(©RAFM P011916)*

allowed a Y-shaped metal frame with two nails on each tip to be created to make the simplest bomb sight. In the short time No. 617 Squadron had existed it undertook over 2000 hours of flying and dropped 2,500 practice bombs.

The raid itself was planned to take place on the night of the 16th/17th May, as this was when the water level in the dams was within 1 metre of their maximum. One aircraft was damaged prior to the raid, when Sqn Ldr Maudsley dropped a mine from too low and the water spray ripped off the aircraft's flaps. With only nineteen of the intended twenty machines now ready for the raid, ED825/G was flown in from Boscombe Down to act as a spare. In the end this machine was flown on the raid by Flt Lt J McArthur when his machine (ED923/G) went unserviceable whilst it was taxying out. It was not until the 15th May that the crews learned of their targets: the Moehne, Eder and Sorpe dams. The Sorpe dams along with the Ennepe, Uster and Schwelme were identified as low priority and alternative targets if the Moehne and Eder could not be seen. These latter dams were all earth banked, while the Moehne and Eder were made of reinforced concrete. The attack had to consist of a dive from 2000ft to precisely 60ft at 232mph and the mine was dropped half a mile from the target so it could skip over the anti-torpedo nets and then settle against the dam wall.

The raid consisted of two flights; one of nine aircraft in three waves taking off at ten minute intervals, and the other consisting of five aircraft in a loose formation. The five reserve aircraft would follow two hours behind. The second group took off first, as their northern route to the target was longer. This group was to have been lead by McArthur, but his unserviceable aircraft let him down and he went as a reserve. Gibson led the first formation, which

actually took off second at 2130 hours. The flight in was at only 40ft and surprisingly this group only lost one aircraft during this stage. The first mine was dropped by Gibson against the Moehne Dam at 00:30 on the 17th May and at 00:50 the codeword was transmitted to advise their base that the dam had been breached. Those that had dropped their mines headed for home, but Gibson got the remainder of the group together and headed for the Eder. This target was much more challenging, as the valley was covered with fog and 1000ft high summits had to be cleared during the approach. The first mine dropped was by Sqn Ldr Maudsley, but he did it too late and as a result it hit the top of the dam and exploded. The next attempt was by Flt Lt D. Shannon and the final mine dropped was by Plt Off Knight. Initially these weapons seemed to have had no effect, but slowly cracks appeared in the dam and eventually it ruptured. Because of the design of the Sorpe, the two mines dropped on it did little and the one mine dropped on the Ennerpe also had no effect.

The raid cost the lives of eight Lancaster crews (only two survived and were captured), but 330 million tons of water flooded the Ruhr valley causing widespread damage to both industrial and domestic property. Guy Gibson received a VC for his part in the raid, and 32 other decorations were presented to other members of No. 617 Squadron.

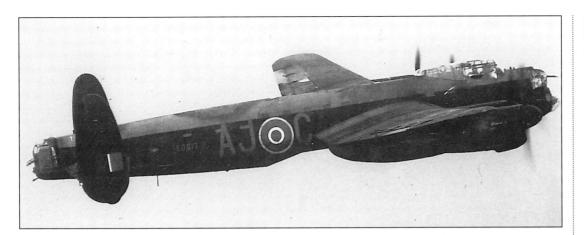

## Tallboy

This 12,000lb Deep Penetration bomb was designed by Dr Barnes Wallis (who also designed the Upkeep mine) and was used for the first time on the 9th June 1944 to block the railway tunnel at Saumar. This effectively stopped the German Panzer divisions from getting to the D-Day beachhead from Bordeaux. This weapon was dropped from 40,000ft and spun gently as it fell, reaching supersonic speeds before hitting the ground and penetrating 100ft. Lancasters carried this weapon inside the bomb bay, as it fitted in quite neatly with only the addition of special 'bulged' bomb bay doors being needed. Once again it was No. 617 Squadron, now based at Woodhall Spa, that was equipped with such Lancasters. The raid on the Saumar tunnel was marked by Wg Cdr Cheshire of the PFF in a Mosquito, and the Tallboys were dropped from just 10,000ft. The weapons did not explode until they were 100ft down and it was not until the next day that the PR photos showed that one bomb had hit the tunnel, penetrated 100ft and exploded, filling the tunnel. Other bombs had produced craters 100ft wide and 70ft deep!

The next target for Tallboy was Le Havre, on the 14th June 1944. Fifteen bombs were dropped by No. 617

Squadron on the E-boat pens there. Three bombs penetrated the concrete roof of the pens and destroyed them, and the 400 other bombers following up the Tallboy raid ensured none of the E-boats escaped. On the 15th June Boulogne was attacked with ten Tallboys, resulting in the destruction of 133 boats.

The Tallboy was to be used on the Tirpitz (see elsewhere), but probably one of the oddest uses was the proposed low-level drop of one against the flood gates of the Kembs Dam at the Belfort Gap. No. 617 Squadron was once again to

Wg Cdr Guy Gibson and a group of No. 106 Squadron crews with Manchesters in the background
(©RAFM P0018415)

Lancaster B Mk I (Special), of No. 617 Squadron during an attack on Arnesberg Bridge on the 19th March 1945
(©RAFM P0022483)

Wg Cdr Guy Gibson and King George VI at RAF Scampton in 1943
(©RAFM P0018732)

undertake the raid and it was split into two groups; one would bomb at 8000ft, while the rest went in at low-level. The date was set for the 7th October 1944, and during the raid the AA fire was concentrating on the group at high level and allowed one Tallboy to be dropped at low-level, lodging itself into one of the flood gates. Unfortunately the AA reacted quickly and the next two Lancasters were shot down before they could drop their bombs. The delay fuse on the first bomb went up 30 minutes later and the huge torrent of water that flooded out even left boats in nearby Switzerland high and dry!

The Tallboy was used in early 1945 during daylight

operations, as little German fighter resistance remained, and one of its last uses was against the Bielefeld Viaduct near Bremen. The viaduct was surrounded by marshland and the Tallboy had no noticeable effect; obviously a bigger weapon was needed. The Heligoland was the next target for the Tallboy, and after this No. 617 undertook its last operation of the war when it set off on the 25th April 1945 for the Eagle's Nest at Berchtesgaden. The target was obscured with snow however, so they dropped their bombs on the nearby SS barracks.

## V-1

The raids on Peenemünde had had no real affect on the development of the V-1, although it seriously slowed work on the V-2. These weapons were launched off concrete ramps and of the 140 constructed by early 1944, Bomber Command, USAAF and the 2nd TAF had destroyed all bar ten of them by D-Day. A pre-fabricated version of the ramp was developed and seen for the first time on the 27th April, and a week after D-Day V-1s were being launched from these difficult-to-detect sites. Massive underground sites for V-1 storage and production were suspected at Watten, Wizernes, Nucourt and Mimoyecques and so it was up to No. 617 Squadron to destroy them. The first target was Watten, and on the 19th June 1944 fifteen Tallboy equipped Lancasters attacked and destroyed it. The target was once again marked by Cheshire, although this time he was assisted by Dave Shannon, and this was to be the first daylight use of the Tallboy. Wizernes was the next target, although the first two sorties were aborted due to cloud cover. The third sortie on the 24th June went ahead and after five hits the massive chalk quarry, in which the store was situated, collapsed.

## The Battleships

Throughout the war the German battleships Bismark and Tirpitz, battle cruisers Scharnhorst and Gneisenau and pocket battleships Admiral von Sheer, Graf Spee and Deutschland (later renamed Lützow) had been a thorn in the sides of the Allies. After various Bomber Command and Royal Navy attacks just two ships were left: Admiral von Scheer and Tirpitz (along with the Admiral Hipper). These ships were moored at Trondheimfjord and the first raids against them were undertaken by Halifaxes in late March and early April 1942. Through 1943 and 1944 the RAF and Royal Navy launched a number of attacks against the Tirpitz in the various fjords in which she was moored. By the 2nd August 1944 it was decided that the ineffective nature of the previous attacks dictated that a special attack with Tallboy Lancasters of No. 617 Squadron should be undertaken. The range of this attack, 3000 miles, was prohibitive for these machines, so it was decided to fly the aircraft out to Russia, then attack on the return leg. On the 10th September the Lancasters of Nos. 9 and 617 Squadrons took off for the 11-12 hour trip. Bad weather and incompatible radio

beacons led to the loss of a number of the Lancasters, although most of these were subsequently ferried on to the correct location and only six airframes were lost due to landing in marsh land. Bad weather delayed the operation until the 15th September, when twenty-eight Lancasters headed for Altenfjord. The smoke screen was intense and many of the Lancasters returned to Yagodnik airfield with their Tallboys still on board. Even though the raid had seemed to be ineffective, the Tirpitz had been damaged, but she also moved from Altenfjord. It took a while to locate her again, being repaired at Tromsö, but now she was 200 miles nearer Scotland. To attack the Tirpitz from Scotland would require 300 gallons more fuel, and to do this Wellington and Mosquito long range fuel tanks were collected and squeezed inside the Lancasters fuselages. Now the aircraft were two tons over their limit, so the more powerful Merlin 24 engines needed to be installed. Sufficient numbers of these engines were found and both Nos. 617 and 9 Squadron's Lancasters were modified. The raid had to take place before the long winter nights set in at Tromsö at the end of November, so the Lancasters set off to Lossiemouth from

Lancaster B Mk I (Special) of No. 15 Squadron in flight, 1945 (©RAFM P009937)

Woodhall Spa on the 28th October. They left Lossiemouth at 0100 on the 29th and headed towards Tromsö at low level. In the end the wind veered and mist covered the fjord, so that the bombs were dropped blind and the results were disappointing. Only one aircraft, which crash landed in Sweden, was lost though. After an aborted re-run on the 4th November the squadron took off once more from Lossiemouth on the 12th November. The drop zone was clear when the squadrons approached, and No. 617 started, followed by No. 9. The fighters moved close to Tromsö were

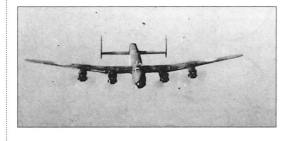

Lancaster B Mk I (Special) of No. 15 Squadron in flight, 1945 (©RAFM P009938)

too late, as the bombs hit the battleship's foredeck, starboard side and funnel. The great ship slowly turned turtle and it was only later that it was discovered that the first attack had damaged her beyond repair and the move to Tromsö was only to make her an 'unsinkable fortress'.

Attention now turned to the last pocket battleship, Lützow, which was at Swinemünde. Two attempts failed due to low cloud, but on the 16th April 1945 No. 617 Squadron attacked it and, although one aircraft was lost, a near-miss tore the entire bottom off the ship and it settled in shallow water.

## Grand Slam

The first two Grand Slams were delivered to Woodhall Spa on the 13th March 1945, and these 22,000lb bombs were loaded onto suitably modified Lancaster B Mk Is the next

day. To carry this weapon the Lancaster had to have more powerful Merlin engines fitted as well as a strengthened undercarriage and bomb bay. In the event only one of the two Lancasters was serviceable, and it therefore left with the other Tallboy Lancasters of the squadron to attack the Bielefeld Viaduct. The weapon landed just 30 yards from the viaduct and in the ensuing explosion a large section of it simply fell into the resulting crater. Five Grand Slams were dropped on the Arnsberg viaduct on the 19th March, with the Arbergen and Nienburg bridges being hit on the 21st and 22nd March. The final railway bridge of the Ruhr was hit by two Grand Slams and two Tallboys on the 23rd and this marked the end of this type of target for these weapons.

## Electronic Warfare

By 1944 a large number of radio and radar systems had been installed in the Lancaster. These included the Gee and $H_2S$ systems already mentioned, but also G-H, IFF, 'Village Inn', Monica and Mandril. One of the most secret squadron was No. 101 Squadron which was based at Ludford Magna. Their Lancasters carried ABC, which involved an eighth crew member who spoke German and transmitted false messages to the Luftwaffe *Wilde Sau* nightfighters. ABC equipped Lancasters can be identified by 36in mast antenna; one under the nose and two on the dorsal spine. Mandril was a very simple electronic-countermeasure, as it used a microphone in one engine nacelle to transmit amplified engine noise to block the German radio transmissions. Village Inn was the AGLT gun laying system installed below the rear turret of late-war Lancasters.

Lancaster B Mk I (Special), PB995 in flight (©RAFM P014426)

# Test-Beds

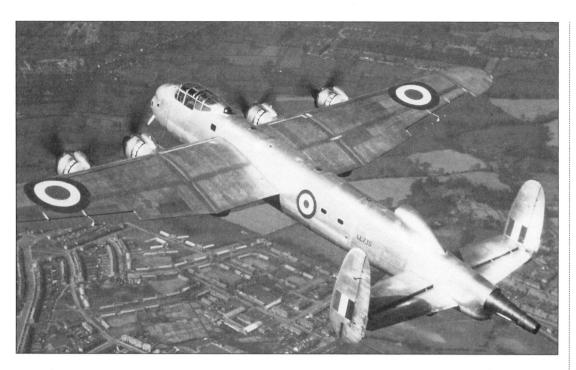

## Chapter 4

Lancaster B Mk II, Beryl
test-bed in flight (©C.E.Brown)

I t is not surprising to find that the Lancaster and Lincoln
were extensively used for engine testing, and all of these
machines are listed in a little more detail below. With the war
situation, its short service life, and its own problems with
powerplants, it can be no surprise to read that the Manchester
was never involved in any trials work, other than the odd
catapult trial at A&AEE.

## Lancaster - Merlin

Many airframes were utilised by Rolls-Royce during the
development of the Manchester, Lancaster and Lincoln.
Lancaster R5849 can be considered the first test-bed though, as
it undertook development work that was involved with a new
version, instead of research and modification work undertaken
by the airframes previously used by Rolls-Royce. This machine
initially undertook trials with the Merlin XX engines, which
were tailored to suit their location (e.g port inner, starboard
outer etc). After it completed these trials it was fitted with
Merlin 28s and in so doing it became the prototype B Mk III.
This aircraft was soon involved in the development of the
Universal Power Plant (UPP), which was basically a system that
would introduce a common cowling of circular cross-section.
This new cowling would allow all ancillary equipment on the
engines to be fitted to, or behind, the bulkhead. With the existing
cowlings, each was different, and therefore not interchangeable,
but it was hoped that the new UPP would allow quick and easy
engine changes as well as allowing space for progressively larger
engines to be fitted without the need for modification. R5849
was initially fitted with two Merlin 28s inboard and two UPP
Merlin 68s outboard, and flew for the first time in this
configuration on the 6th May 1943. On the 11th June however it
suffered a fire on landing approach and was subsequently totally
destroyed. DV170 was converted to the same configuration as
R5849 to continue the development work, and flew in August
1943. The inboard engines were soon changed to Merlin 38s and
the outboard to Merlin 85s. The Merlin 85 was basically a 68
with an auxiliary gearbox and it was intended for the new
Lancaster Mk IV, which became the Lincoln. DV170 was first
flown in this configuration on the 3rd November 1943 and on
the 7th December 1943 DV199 flew with four Merlin UPPs (68s
inboard and 85s outboard), thus becoming the prototype
Lancaster Mk VI. Only seven other airframes (JB713, JB675,
ND418, ND479, ND558, ND673 and ND784) were converted to
Mk VI standard by Rolls-Royce at Hucknall, and five were to see
service with the RAF. JB675 and ND558 were retained by
Rolls-Royce for UPP development trials with DV199 and ND784
later becaming the Armstrong-Siddeley Mamba test-bed.

## Lancaster - Dart

This turboprop engine was installed in the nose of Lancaster
NG465, which had arrived at Rolls-Royce in August 1945, and it
flew for the first time on the 10th October 1947. Later, to assist

Lincoln B Mk II, RE418
Proteus test-bed, Luqa 1948
(©RAFM P013713)

in determining the effects of icing on the type, a water spray frame was added to the nose of the Lancaster. Once enough ice had formed on the engine the de-icing equipment was switched on. The effectiveness of this equipment could then be judged, and as chunks of the melting ice were ingested by the engine, their effects could be determined as well. The flying career of NG465 ended after 800 flying hours on the 22nd January 1954, when it crashed on Holiwell golf course whilst attempting a forced landing.

## Lancaster - Metropolitan-Vickers F2

Metropolitan-Vickers had started development work on an axial compressor gas turbine engine and by 1940 the F1, as it was known, was producing 2,600lb of thrust. Further development led to the F2 and by 1943 a flight-ready engine (F2 No.3) was prepared. This engine was installed by Armstrong Whitworth in the rear fuselage of the prototype Lancaster (BT308); it was rated at 1,800lb of thrust and was test flown on the 29th June 1943 in BT308. A year later the sole Lancaster B Mk II (LL735) used for test purposes was converted in a similar manner. This machine was later fitted with the ultimate development of the F2, in the form of the F2/4 Beryl.

## Lancaster - ASX

Armstrong Siddeley were contracted to produce an axial jet engine in 1942 and in 1943 they produced the ASX which offered 2,600lb of thrust. Lancaster Mk VI ND784 was converted by Air Service Training to carry this new engine in the bomb bay. It made its first flight in this configuration in June 1945, and development flights totalling 48 hours were undertaken before it was decided to develop the turboprop version (the ASP) instead.

## Lancaster - ASP (Python)

When Armstrong Siddeley decided to develop the turboprop version of their ASX engine, Lancaster TW911 was converted to carry two of these engines in the outboard positions. Called the Python, the ASP was twice the weight of a Merlin and in its initial form had a long nacelle that positioned the air intake just aft of the spinner. Flight testing began on the 3rd January 1949, and a short time after this the cowlings were shortened by 4ft 9in to bring the intakes nearer the wing leading edge.

## Lancaster - Mamba

The ASX test-bed, ND784, was passed to Air Service Training after the termination of that project to be converted to accept another engine. The Mamba 2 was installed in the nose of this machine and it flew for the first time on the 14th October 1947. The test programme was joined by a second converted Lancaster (SW342) and this machine featured an icing test rig in front of the Mamba. Because this rig was much smaller, the propeller blades on the Mamba had to be truncated and widened. This machine flew like this for the first time in June 1949 and in 1951 it had an Adder jet engine installed in the tail. The Adder was a 1,050lb thrust pure jet version of the Mamba, but was only intended as a short-life unit for radio-controlled

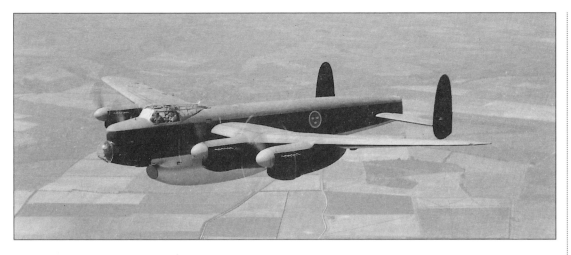

Lancaster Tp.80 was used to test the STAL Dovern and RM6, and is seen here on a test flight before delivery

targets. A long-life version of the Adder, the Viper, was installed in its place in the tail of SW342 in November 1952. Initially trials were conducted with the 1,640lb thrust Viper 3, but later in the programme a Viper 7R was installed for reheat trials.

## Lancaster - Sapphire

The Sapphire can trace its roots back to the Metropolitan-Vickers F2/4 Beryl, as the F9 development of this engine by Metropolitan-Vickers was taken over by Armstrong Siddeley and named the Sapphire. This engine was first test flown in the outboard positions of Lancaster VM733 on the 19th January 1950.

## Lancaster - Dovern

STAL (Svenska Turbinfabriks AB Ljungström) and Svenska Flygmotor AG started work in 1949 on an axial jet engine. The former worked on an axial compressor engine, while Svenska Flygmotor worked on a radial compressor design. The former proved successful, and was rated at 7,275lb thrust. This was soon christened the Dovern and it was to be flight tested in a Lancaster. The machine chosen for this job was one of the surplus machines (RA805) from the Argentine contract and it was delivered to Air Service Training for conversion work on the 22nd June 1950. Once completed, and registered as G-11-29, the type was test flown on the 24th April 1954. The conversions made to this machine included the shackles for the engine in the bomb bay, plus stainless steel sheeting on the underside of the fuselage to protect it from the jet exhaust. The escape hatch was modified to create an air dam to ensure that the crew would not

be sucked into the engine in the event of an emergency exit, and a retractable tailwheel unit with twin wheels was installed. It was passed to Sweden in May 1951, where a Type 3 Dovern engine was installed and it was given the RSAF (Royal Swedish Air Force) serial 80001 and designated the Tp.80. The type was operated by Kungl Flgfor Nalningon at Malmslätt and flew for the first time in this configuration on the 27th June 1951. By

Lincoln B Mk II, RE418 Proteus test-bed, Luqa 1948
(©RAFM P013712)

June 1952 the Dovern Type 6A was installed. The Dovern project was shelved in November 1952, when Rolls-Royce agreed to supply an Avon engine and the RSAF decided that this engine would be a better option for the Saab-32 Lansen project that was in the initial planning stages. With the loss of the Dovern project, the Tp.80 was not grounded, instead it started flight trials with the RM2, which was a licence-built D.H. Ghost 50 intended for the new Saab J-29 Tunnan. The need for an afterburner version of the RM2 (to power the J-29D) had been identified as early as 1950, but it was not until July 1953 that an

Lancaster B Mk VI prototype (JB675) shown here with Rolls-Royce and fitted with the new Universal Power Plants. Note the mix of three and four-blade propellers
(© RR Heritage Trust)

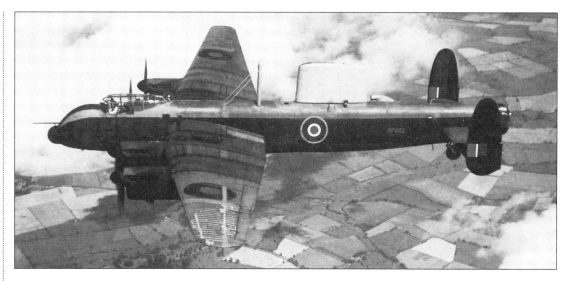

**Lancaster de-icing aircraft in flight** (©C.E.Brown)

**Lancaster B Mk III Nene test-bed in flight** (©C.E. Brown)

**Close-up of the icing rig fitted to the nose of the Dart engine test-bed** (©RR Heritage Trust)

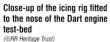

airworthy example was sent to Malmslätt for installation under the Tp.80. Tests with this engine continued throughout the 1953-1955 period, and in early 1956 80001 was refurbished. Flight testing of the RM6, which was an afterburner-equipped licence-built Avon, was to be undertaken in 80001 for the J-32 and J-35 fighters. Prior to this the Tp.80 had been repainted aluminium overall with silver dope flying surfaces and all serials and codes in black.

Throughout its service in Sweden the Tp.80 had given many hours service, but had suffered with cracking of the exhaust stacks on numerous occasions. On the 7th May 1956 it suffered a broken rocker arm in the No.1 engine that started a fire, and the decision was made to abandon the aircraft. Because it was at just

800ft the pilot decided to climb before ordering everyone out. The fuel lines had ruptured inside the No. 1 engine though and fuel was not flowing properly to the No. 2 engine, so it did not respond correctly. Without the correct power from the second engine, and trimmed for a feathered port engine, the assymetric power that resulted made the aircraft go out of control. Although two of the three test engineers managed to bale out, the third and the pilot were killed when 80001 crashed near the church in the village of Slaka.

## Lancaster - Orenda

The Orenda engine was a 6,000lb thrust gas turbine that followed on from the previously un-flown Chinook engine, and it was test flown in a Lancaster Mk X. This machine, FM209, was converted to carry two Orenda engines in the outboard positions and it flew for the first time on the 13th July 1950. This machine continued to test the Orenda until it was lost in a fire in 1956.

## Lancastrian - Nene

The Lancastrian was ideally suited to the role of test-bed, as not only did its passenger-carrying capacity give space for all the test crews, but the retention of the inboard piston engines ensured that the failure of the test engines should not result in the loss of the test aircraft. Being four-engined the type also allowed two engines to be tested simultaneously, and the bomber lineage of the Lancastrian meant it had lots of fuel tankage for the thirsty new jet engines. The first Lancastrian to arrive at Hucknall was PD167 (later renumbered VH737) in August 1945. This airframe was initially put in store at Church Broughton, and as a result was not the first Lancastrian to become a test-bed. That honour falls to VH742, which arrived at Hucknall in October 1945 and was converted with Nenes placed in the outboard engine nacelles. To achieve this, the flaps and elevators had to be modified to give clearance on the

extended nacelles of the new Nene powerplants. It flew for the first time after conversion on the 14th August 1946. The aircraft attended the SBAC show at Radlett on the 10th September 1946 and excited the aviation press by taking groups up for flights (this was the first time 'civilians' had ever flown in a jet powered aircraft).

The test programme was now joined by VH737, when in April 1946 it returned to Hucknall and conversion work commenced. By January 1947 the outboard engines had been replaced with Nenes and the first flight took place on the 17th. In April the

aircraft moved to RAE Farnborough for trials and returned to Hucknall in August to have an icing spray rig installed on the port outer Nene. The inboard Merlin 24s were replaced with Tudor powerplants (Merlin 621s) in November 1948, and it was test flown in this configuration in January 1949.

Both VH742 and VH737 continued development flights for the Nene. VH742 was the first to stop this work in August 1949, when it was passed to the workshops at Hucknall for Tay engine installation. This work continued very slowly until the Tay was cancelled in October 1949, and the airframe was dismantled and passed to the Gunnery Ranges at Shoeburyness on the 24th

Lancastrian VM704 fitted with Griffon 57s inboard [with contra-rotating propellers] and Merlin 623s outboard
(©Rolls-Royce Ltd)

Lancastrian VM728 fitted with Merlin 600s inboard and 641s outboard (©Rolls-Royce Ltd)

Lancaster TW911 with Pythons outboard in the original [long] nacelles
(©Rolls-Royce Ltd)

October 1950, for use as a gunnery target. VH737 was to continue development trials with the Nene until March 1952, when it was retired after 406 (flying) hours.

## Lancastrian - Merlin 600s

The 600 series Merlin was designed for use in the new Tudor airliner and Lancastrian VM728 was used to test the operational limitations of this new engine series. The aircraft had water-methanol injected Merlin 600s inboard and Merlin 641s outboard and undertook a 1,000 hour flight testing programme between September 1947 and June 1948.

## Lancastrian - Avon

The AJ65 Avon engine developed by Rolls-Royce was their first gas turbine with co-axial compressor. Lancastrian VM732 had previously been involved with noise reduction trials for the Tudor and DC-4M, but it was converted to carry Avon engines in the outboard positions and flew for the first time with these

engines on the 15th August 1948. During the August 1948 to September 1949 period this machine undertook 273 hours of development flying on the Avon, and then it was joined by another Lancastrian (VL970). This machine had its inboard Merlin T24s replaced with Merlin 623s and the port Avon had a water spray frame installed. This aircraft flew for the first time on the 16th June 1949, and it continued to undertake Avon development work for seven years. Unfortunately this extensively used aircraft was lost in a fatal crash on the 29th March 1955.

## Lancastrian - Clyde

The large 3,500shp Clyde turboprop developed by Rolls-Royce in the 1940s was to have been tested in Lancastrians VM704 and VM733. However, before any conversion work could commence the Clyde project was dropped due to the other commitments Rolls-Royce had at that time. VM733 was to be involved with Rotol and de Havilland propeller comparison trials before moving on to do work on the Sapphire, and VM704 was to become a hybrid with both Griffon and Merlin engines.

## Lancastrian - Hybrid (Griffon/Merlin)

Lancastrian VM704, having been diverted from the Clyde programme (see above) was fitted with Merlin 623 Tudor engines in the outboard positions and Griffon 57 Shackleton engines in the inboard positions. This combination gave a staggering 8,420hp and it flew for the first time on the 19th October 1948. Throughout the test programme this machine also tested Merlin 625 and 641s in the outboard positions and after 500 hours, it was retired in May 1952.

## Lancastrian - Ghosts

De Havilland started gas turbine development work in 1941 with work on the H1 (Goblin) and this was later developed into the 4,000lb thrust H2 Ghost. Initial trials were undertaken in a Vampire, but Lancastrian VM703 was later converted to take the engines in the outboard positions. This aircraft flew for the first time on the 24th July 1947 and the engines featured the central intake for the Comet airliner (Ghost 50). A second airframe, VM729, was also converted to carry Ghosts, although most of its work was around certification of the engine for use in the Comet.

## Lincoln - Derwent

Lincoln SX971 was converted by Air Service Training for the National Gas-Turbine Establishment at Pyestock to carry a Rolls-Royce Derwent in a special nacelle under the bomb bay. The aircraft was delivered to the NGTE (based at Bitteswell) in May 1951 and then moved with the NGTE to Farnborough in August 1952. When the aircraft ceased being used it was sent to No. 10 MU, RAF Hullavington in 1956, before being sold as scrap to International Alloys in August 1957.

## Lincoln - Phoebus

The Bristol Phoebus was first installed in the specially modified bomb bay of Lincoln RA643 by Napiers at Luton. Tests only continued for 23$^1/_2$ hours before the trials were abandoned and RA643 was returned to the RAF.

## Lincoln - Theseus

The first Lincoln converted to take the Theseus was RA716, which flew for the first time with these engines in the outboard positions on the 17th February 1947. Later RE339 and RE418 were also modified to carry the Theseus and were operated by the specially-formed Theseus Lincoln Flight, Transport Command, RAF Lyneham. Between May 1948 and May 1952

these machines logged 1,000hrs, and later both RE418 and RE339 (with Pythons fitted) served with the ARDU in Australia.

## Lincoln - Proteus

This massive turbo-prop engine weighed 2,900lbs and was fitted in the outer engine stations of Lincoln RF368. This was followed by SX972, which was loaned to Bristol in 1948 and flew for the first time with the Proteus installed on the 12th December 1950. This aircraft logged 958hrs with the engine installed before being returned to the RAF and scrapped at No. 49 MU, RAF Colerne in July 1953.

## Lincoln - Python

Initial tests of the Python were carried out in Lancaster TW911 (see entry elsewhere), then the programme was joined by Lincoln RE339 (originally used for Theseus trials). Finally RF403 joined the team with the A.S. Pythons installed in the outer engine stations. Later RF403 was passed to the ARDU at Woomera, Australia for ballistic trails and was eventually dumped at Tocumwal, NSW in 1958.

## Lincoln - Naiad

The Naiad gas-turbine was installed in the nose of Lincoln RF530 as early as 1948 by D. Napier & Son. With the cancellation of the Naiad's potential user, the Blackburn YB1, the project was abandoned and RF530 later passed to Rolls-Royce for use as a test-bed for their new Tyne engine. Later however Napiers installed a mock-up Naiad in the nose of Lincoln RF402 and used this in a number of experiments and research relating to de-icing.

## Lincoln - Nomad

Another Napier design, the Nomad, was a massive (two ton) compound diesel/gas turbine engine. It was tested in the nose of Lincoln SX973, but the type proved unsuccessful and the whole project was abandoned.

Lancaster TW911 with the Pythons in the shortened [by 4ft 9in] nacelles
*(©Rolls-Royce Ltd)*

Lancaster PA474 at the moment it took off from RAF Henlow for Waddington after being parked outside for two years

Lancastrian VM703 flying with the inboard Merlins shut down and the outboard Avons doing all the work

**Lancastrian VH742, fitted with Nene engines in the outboard positions**
(©Rolls-Royce Ltd)

### Lincoln - Avon

RA716 had originally been used for Bristol Theseus trials, but was passed to Air Service Training in May 1951 to be converted to test the new Rolls-Royce Avon jet engines. These motors were installed in the outer engine stations. Later RA716 served with the Bombing Trials Unit at West Freugh, before being sold to International Alloys in November 1957 as scrap.

### Lincoln - Tyne

Lincoln RF530 came to Hucknall in August 1954, when the massive Tyne turbo-prop was installed in the nose. This aircraft was re-registered G-37-1 and flew for the first time on the 28th June 1956. From January 1959 an icing rig was installed forward of the propeller, with camera to record the effects. This machine was retired from use in June 1962, although trials on the engine continued with an Ambassador, due to the need to have a larger diameter propeller fitted for the proposed installation of the type in the Transall and CL44.

**The ASX installed in the bomb bay of Lancaster Mk VI, ND784**
(©Rolls-Royce Ltd)

# Lincoln - Other Test Beds

*Although no other engines were tested in a Lincoln, the type was used by a number of government establishments for various trials.*

### Radar Trials

Lincolns RF561 and RF342 were used for radar trials at the TFU, RAF Defford. Later these machines were both operated by the Telecommunications Flying Unit, before RF561 moved to the RAE at Farnborough, and RF342 undertook de-icing trial work with Napiers. RE342 later moved to a museum at Southend, before being sold. Today I believe she lies derelict at North Weald airfield. RF561 ended its days as a gunnery target on the P&EE ranges at Shoeburyness.

### Brabazon

Lincoln B Mk I, RE284 was taken out of storage and loaned to the Bristol Aeroplane Company to undertake trials work with the undercarriage of the new Brabazon airliner. The Brabazon had an all-up weight of 129 tons so a complex and strong bogie undercarriage was designed for it. This, in a scaled-down form, was installed in RE284 and first air tested on the 7th March 1947. The aircraft was still in use in 1949, although it was probably scrapped later.

### Napier De-Icing

It has already been seen that a number of aircraft were used by Napier for de-icing research. After use in the Naiad trials, RF402 was used for heater development work on behalf of the Ministry of Supply. In 1956 the aircraft was fitted with a complex spraying rig, water tanks in the bomb bay and camera to record the effects. Aerofoil test sections were mounted vertically on the top of the fuselage, aft of this rig, and the aircraft flew with a number of test sections installed. The test programme was also undertaken by RF342, which in turn later became G-APRJ. In 1957 RF402 was re-registered as G-APRP and although it flew for a while longer, in the end it was used as a source of spares to keep G-APRJ flying.

### Laminar Flow Research

Probably the most famous test bed is the ex-Cranfield Lancaster PA474, simply because it is still flying with the BBMF, but this machine was actually replaced by a Lincoln (RF342) because the available airframe hours on PA474 were getting too low. Previously involved with de-icing trials at Napiers, RF342 (G-APRJ) was moved to Cranfield and undertook a number of flights with various laminar flow wing sections mounted on her back, before being finally retired and sold to a museum. Her last flight was on the 9th May 1967, when she flew from Cranfield to Rochford Airport, Southend.

# The Lincoln

## Chapter 5

**Lincoln B Mk II, 'D', ground running her engines**
(©RAFM P001332)

T he Lincoln, as has already been noted, was originally the Lancaster Mk IV. Although the prototype Lincoln (Mk IV) first flew on the 9th June 1944, it was not until the 9th November 1944 that the second prototype took to the air. This gives some indication of the changing pace of the war, and the low priority with which the Lancaster's replacement was viewed. By the end of 1944, Lancasters were fully meeting the requirements of Bomber Command, and there was little need to quickly bring into production a replacement. With the changing tide of war, even the manufacturers themselves were starting to consider post-war requirements, and so Avro was more concerned with new passenger carrying aircraft (like the York and Tudor) than the Lincoln.

It was hoped that Lancaster production could be scaled down from 284 a month in November 1944 to a total phasing out in November 1945, while Lincoln production could be started at 66 a month in March 1945, peaking at 200 a month from August 1945 to June 1946. In the end the capitulation of Japan in August 1945 and the removal of the need for any

Bomber Command involvement in the Far East (Tiger Force) meant that none of these figures were ever met. Lincoln production lines were set up at Chadderton and Yeadon (Avro), Trafford Park (Metropolitan-Vickers), Baginton and Bitteswell (Armstrong Whitworth). In the end Yeadon only built six Lincolns before being shut in the post-war depression. Deliveries of Lincolns started in February 1945, although the numbers were very small and most went to trials units and MUs. Some of the first arrived at the TFU at Defford (including RE229), but these early machines suffered

**The second production Lincoln B Mk I, RE228, January 1945**
(©Real Photos)

**Lincoln B Mk II, RF560 of the Telecommunications Flying Unit, RAF Defford**
(©RAFM P013025)

Lincoln B Mk II, RF561 of the
Telecommunications Flying
Unit, RAF Defford
(©RAFM P013027)

with many problems, most of which related to vibrations. The large wing of the Lincoln flexed (it could move eight feet without snapping) and the engines 'nodded' due to harmonics that were identical between engines and airframe. In the end this was overcome at TFU by fitting four-blade propellers to the engines, which instantly cured the problem. The first production Lincoln (RE227) went to A&AEE in April 1945, while the second (RE228) and fourth (RE230) were sent to Rolls-Royce for engine trials. The first RAF unit (as opposed to MUs or research establishments) to receive the Lincoln was the BDU at RAF Feltwell, which received RE240 on the 21st May 1945. It is worth noting that all of these early

Lincoln B Mk II of
No. 7 Squadron
(©RAFM P011918)

machines had a Martin mid-upper and F.N.121 rear turret fitted, as the Bristol and B.P turrets were not ready.

The prototype B Mk II (RE289) was delivered to Langar on the 6th July 1945, although production B Mk IIs were already coming off the production line at Armstrong Whitworth by June 1945. The Mk IIs were modified Mk Is and were fitted with Merlin 68 engines. Considering the intended use of Lincolns in Tiger Force, RF370 was sent to Khartoum in August 1945 for tropical trials. On the 26th November 1945 the order was given to modify all B Mk Is with the installation of Merlin 85 engines and issue them to training units, although records show that no B Mk I was ever issued, and they all remained in storage until they were scrapped.

## Into Service

The first units to receive the Lincoln were No. 57 Squadron at RAF East Kirkby and No. 75 Squadron at RAF Spilsby. The former received RF385 on the 22nd August, followed by RF386 and RF387 on the 27th, while No. 75 Squadron received RF383, RF388 and RF389 a few days later. In November 1945, the Lincoln Service Trials Flight, as the No. 57 Squadron contingency had been named, moved to RAF Scampton. Here flight testing and service trials continued with the Lincoln progressively moving towards the projected 82,000lb maximum take-off weight. Unfortunately these early machines suffered many problems, specifically relating to the Merlin 68 engines, and both squadrons got little flying time in as a result. By the end of 1945 No. 75 Squadron disbanded and so No. 44 (Rhodesia) Squadron took their place as a Lincoln Service Trials Flight. No. 44 Squadron received three new Mk IIs (RE406, RE406 & RE407) in February 1946, but these moved on to No. 57 Squadron by July 1946. Three new B Mk IIs (RE377, RE379 and RE380) were passed to No. 57 Squadron from Avro in March 1946 and on the 2nd April 1946, Bomber Command finally accepted the Lincoln for squadron service.

Further problems persisted, as although the type had been accepted for service use, many of the airframes held in store were found to have serious corrosion. A special works party was set up in December 1946 to deal with this, and at this stage the troublesome Merlin 68 was being superseded by the Merlin 68A. No. 1 Group (formerly Nos 1 & 5 Groups in WWII) was steadily re-equipped with the Lincoln and from late 1946 this group was responsible for Meteorological work for weather prediction. Squadrons involved included Nos. 50, 57, 61 and 101 and they continued in the role until the task was taken over by the Hastings of No. 202 Squadron. During 1947 No. 3 Group started to swap its Lancasters for Lincolns, and the initial trials squadron for this group (No. 44 Squadron) was the first to receive production Lincolns, followed by No. 15 Squadron in February, No. 90 Squadron in April and No. 138 Squadron in September.

Lincoln B.2, RF389, AA•A of
No 75 Squadron
(via R. Sturtivant)

February 1947 saw new designations for the Lincoln, as the terms B Mk II/IIIG and B Mk II/IVA (later to become B.2/3G and B.2/4A when the coding system changed to Arabic numerals) came into being. These related to the type of $H_2S$ radar carried and it was hoped that No. 1 Group could be equipped with Lincoln Mk II/IVAs, while No. 3 Group would get the Mk II/IIIGs. In the end it took two more years to achieve this, with No. 9 Squadron getting the first Mk II/IVAs. Throughout 1949 and 1950 more and more squadrons equipped with the Lincoln, and most of these airframes came out of store, being modified at MUs or Avro's before going for final acceptance with BCAMS at Binbrook. During August to October 1949 the last 3 Group squadrons, Nos. 35, 115, 149 and 207 Squadrons finally swapped their Lancasters for Lincolns. This was followed by Nos. 148 and 214 Squadrons at Upwood in January and February 1950. At this date the total number of Lincoln squadrons in Bomber Command was 22, with around 200 aircraft. Because of the limitations and problems encountered with the Lincoln, it was soon obvious that it could not be used in the nuclear deterrent role, so, after much controversy, the Boeing B-50 was ordered to fulfil the role. The first Lincoln unit to receive the Washington (as the B-50 was known in RAF service) was No. 115 Squadron at RAF Marham in June 1950. This were followed by No. 90 Squadron in October, No. 149 Squadron in November and No. 15 Squadron in January 1951. Later Nos. 35, 44, 57 & 207 Squadrons were also to operate the Washington, with most crews being ex-Lincoln.

The arrival of jet-bombers in the form of the E.E. Canberra in 1951 was to signal the end of the large piston bomber. The first Lincoln squadron to go over to the Canberra was No. 101 Squadron in May 1951, followed by No. 617 in January 1952, No. 12 in April 1952 and No. 9 in May 1952. January 1952 was to see the first deployment of the Lincoln abroad, when No. 148 Squadron went out to Egypt to deal with the Nasser/Neguib coup. The squadron was based at Shallufa, although it did not see much action and spent most of its time there as a 'show of strength'. In June 1952 No. 148 squadron was replaced by No. 100 Squadron and they remained in the area until August 1952, when they flew home. On the 4th August 1953 the whole of the Waddington Wing (comprising Nos. 100, 61 and 49 Squadrons) moved to Wittering. Throughout 1954 Nos. 148 and 7 Squadrons operated in Malaya, and No. 148 Squadron carried out the last Lincoln sortie in Malaya in April 1955. No. 148 Squadron came back to the UK to join No. 7 Squadron before they both disbanded on the 1st July 1955. No. 47 Squadron came back from Kenya a month later and also disbanded. V-Force training was being undertaken by Lincolns of Nos. 83 and 97 Squadrons, while No. 199 Squadron continued to undertake ECM work, but by the end

of 1955, most Lincolns were being replaced by jet-powered aircraft and they were all consigned to the scrap yard.

## Malaya

No history of the Lincoln can miss out the type's involvement in the troubles in Malaya. After the Lancasters of No. 7 Squadron's involvement in January 1947, the Lincolns of No. 97 squadron were sent out during April and May 1948. Unfortunately the communist terrorists were not put off by these 'show of strength' exercises and it was therefore decided that heavy bombers should join the other aircraft of the FEAF in the campaign.

This campaign, called Firedog, saw the first Lincoln unit (No. 57 Squadron at Waddington) mobilised in March 1950.

Strikes were carried out within two days of the squadron arriving at Tengah (on the Malayan Peninsular of Singapore). Bombing aids like H2S were useless over the jungle and no Gee chain existed in the area to help, so all bombing was done 'by eye'. Political 'channels' meant that authority had to be sought before a suspected terrorist target could be bombed, and as a result the terrorists often knew the bombers were coming and had simply moved on. In June 1950 the Lincolns of No. 57 Squadron handed over to No. 100 Squadron, and flew back home. No. 100 Squadron was joined by the No. 1 Squadron (RAAF) in July 1950 and they both carried out bombing raids until No. 100 Squadron was recalled in December. This time the

**Lincoln B.2, RE311, 48• of
No. 116 Squadron, 1953**
(via r. Sturtivant)

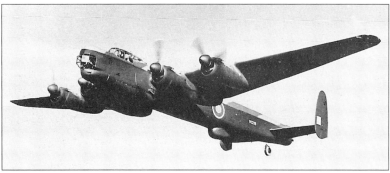

**Lincoln B Mk I, RE228 in flight**

**Lincoln B Mk II, DX•L of
No.57 Squadron**
(©RAFM P015405)

squadron was replaced by No. 61 Squadron, but instead of shipping each squadron's aircraft to and from the UK, No. 61 Squadron simply took over the aircraft of No. 100 Squadron. The squadron remained on active service in the area until it returned home in April 1951, and with the RAAF squadron still present, it seemed as if the RAF's involvement was over in Malaya.

This was not the case, as two years later, No. 83 Squadron left its Hemswell base for Tengah in August 1953. The squadron took two other aircraft crewed by Hemswell-resident No. 97 Squadron, as well as spares and ground crews. The first operation was undertaken in the area on the 5th September 1953 along with the RAAF Lincolns of No. 1 Squadron. Operations during this period were also undertaken from Kuala Lumpur and Butterworth airfield and on the 28th October 1953, Operation Bison was launched. This saw the Lincolns of No. 1 Squadron (RAAF) and No. 83 Squadron (RAF) dropping 15 million propaganda leaflets on 200 locations. Although the Lincolns also took supplies to the Cocos Islands in support of the England-New Zealand Air Race during September and October 1953, the two 97 Squadron machines came home in mid-November. Operations continued throughout 1953 and into 1954 and No. 83 Squadron's last operation in the area was on the 13th January 1953. By this stage the first four Lincolns had already set off for the UK and they were to be replaced by No. 7 Squadron. The final four No. 83 Squadron crews left Tengah on the 24th January 1954. By the end of the month No. 7 Squadron was fully operational and started operations along with the RAAF squadron. Apart from getting involved with the very protracted shipment of radio-active material from the American test on Bikini Atoll to the UK, the squadron continued on operations until it returned to the UK in April. Their place was taken by No.

148 Squadron, who also got involved with moving radio-active material. No. 148 Squadron was relieved by No. 7 Squadron in mid-July, with these swapping back over again in mid-October. The next changeover took place in April 1955, when No 148 Squadron was replaced by No. 101 Squadron, only this time, the replacement aircraft were Canberras, not Lincolns. The RAAF machines remained in the area until 1958, but the RAF's involvement there with its Lincolns had ceased.

## Kenya

During 1953 groups of Kikuyu tribesmen were making forceful claims on various areas of the country. These tribesmen were known as Mau Maus, and as their terrorism moved closer to Nairobi, the RAF's Lincolns were called in. All operations took place from Eastleigh airfield and the squadrons involved included Nos. 49 (Nov 1953 to Jan 1954), 100 (Jan 1954 to Mar 1954), 61 (Mar 1954 to June 1954), 214 (June 1954 to Dec 1954) and 49 (Dec 1954 to June 1955). No. 49 Squadron, the first in the area, arrived from Shallufa in November 1953. Initially just three aircraft were involved, and the idea was to undertake a number of limited bombing raids before returning to the rest of the squadron at Shallufa. The first raid was undertaken by SX979 on the 18th November, but quite unexpectedly the three machines were joined by the rest of the squadron at Eastleigh. Operations commenced, but usually only involved one to four aircraft at any one time. Most targets were in the Aberdare mountains, the slopes of Mount Kenya or the forests north of Nairobi. The Lincoln was ideal for the job, as Eastleigh airfield was 5,500ft above sea level and Mount Kenya was 17,000ft high, so its high operational ceiling made it ideal for bombing runs in this sort of country. No. 49 Squadron returned home in January 1954 and was replaced by No. 100 Squadron, who in turn were replaced by No. 61 Squadron in March 1954 (No. 100 Squadron having returned home to disband). Unfortunately No. 61 Squadron was to suffer the loss of an entire crew during a night raid on the 22nd March, when RE297 hit the Ruathia Ridge. The squadron came home in June 1954 and was replaced by No. 214 Squadron. During a raid on the 14th August 1954, three Lincolns were making low-level runs when the delayed bombs from the first ignited those dropped by the second and those being dropped by the third. The bombs just being dropped by the third aircraft actually detonated under it, and the shrapnel shattered the controls and seriously injured the Flight Engineer. With both starboard engines out (the pitch controls having been jammed at fine), the pilot got the aircraft back to Eastleigh, but the Flight Engineer died of his wounds. Being able to bomb at 20,000ft was achieved with the use of an AA No 3 Mk VII radar based on top of Mount Alsop, which allowed the Lincoln crews to use it as a beacon to pin-point their positions. In November the replacement crews from No. 49 squadron started to arrive, and by early December No. 214 Squadron went home. Unfortunately No. 49 Squadron was to suffer a fatal loss on the 19th February 1955, when SX984 hit a radio aerial and knocked its entire tail off, the aircraft climbing, stalling at 300ft and crashing, killing all on board. The Mau Mau's resolve was breaking through and they were being pushed further north, so it came as no surprise for No. 49 squadron to receive a communication in July to say they they would soon go home. The squadron's last operation was on the 16th July 1955 and it set off from Kenya to the UK on the 28th July. The Lincoln's involvement in Kenya was at an end.

**Lincoln B Mk II having bombs loaded aboard**
(©RAFM P015406)

## Aden

When No. 7 Squadron disbanded in January 1952, a number of it's crews were on detachment in Aden and they remained there to form No. 1426 Flight. This flight, which was officially formed at Khormaksar with six Lincolns, was meant to undertake a 'policing' role along the borders of the Aden Protectorate. Command of the squadron quickly passed from Bomber Command to HQ British Forces, Aden Protectorate, and as a result the Flight was very much 'on a limb' with no RAF support. By the end of January a Flight Commander was appointed, so the ex-7 Squadron crews stood down and went home. With few serviceable planes or current crews, little happened for the next few weeks. Eventually two Lincoln crews arrived along with more ground crew and so a CO was also appointed to the flight. In March two new Lincolns

**Lincoln B Mk II, SX983, KO·X of No. 115 Squadron**
(©RAFM P015552)

**Lincoln B Mk I in flight**

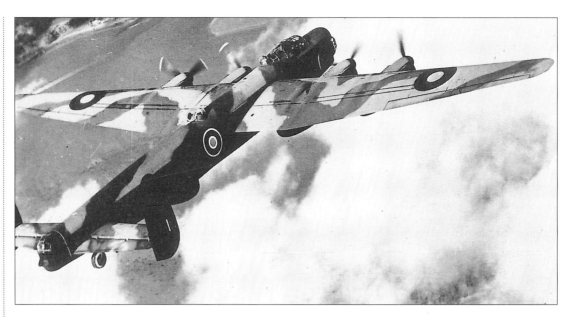

**Lincoln B Mk II, RF505 in flight from RAF Watton in 1962**
*(©D. Pennington)*

arrived and by mid-April all five crews were operational. Operations for the flight consisted of long patrols over the featureless terrain, along with reconnaissance, supply dropping and the occasional attack on tribesmen who were gun-running or illegally crossing the borders. Because of the very poor quality of the maps of this area, it soon fell to No. 1426 Flight to map the entire Aden area. Unfortunately the focal lengths of the F.24 camera carried in the Lincoln was wrong for the huge diversity of land contours in the area. After weeks of trying the squadron had to admit defeat and a detachment of PR Meteors was sent out from the UK to do the job (which they did in one day!). With the Suez Crisis, the whole flight (plus passengers) flew to Bahrain on the 6th November 1956. Standing patrols were undertaken by the flight, until the 22nd, when they all flew back to Aden.

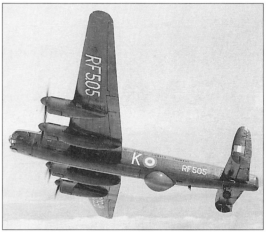

**Lincoln B Mk II, RF386 of No. 57 Squadron in flight**

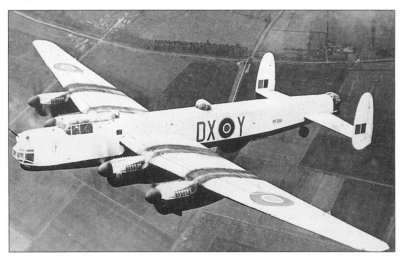

By January 1957 the first Shackleton MR.2s of No. 37 Squadron were starting to arrive. This was to mark the end of the Lincoln's involvement in the Aden area. The 'final' Lincoln sortie took place on the 16th January 1957 and in this sortie the Lincolns actually fired on the rebels, as well as being fired back at. By the 9th January just a few crews and machines remained in Aden and on the 21st the last two aircraft (RE322 and RF558) were ferried back to the UK. Unfortunately RE322 suffered a broken camshaft and had to return to Khormaksar for repairs. A week later RE322 and the crews all made their way back to the UK and the Lincoln's involvement in Aden came to an end.

With the end of this operation the Lincoln's use as a front line aircraft with the RAF also came to a close.

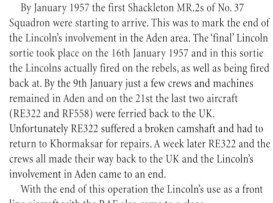

**Lincoln B.2, RF507, HW•G of No. 100 Squadron**
*(via R. Sturtivant)*

Lincoln, RA685, M• of No. 157
Squadron, RAF Kinloss, 1962
*(via R. Sturtivant)*

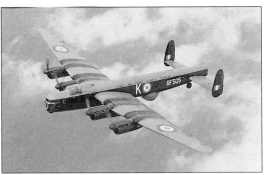

Lincoln B.2s, SX983, SX987,
RF295 & RE347 on a
bombing raid during
Operation Firedog
*(via R. Sturtivant)*

Three shots of Lincoln B Mk II,
RF505 in flight from RAF
Watton in 1962
*(©D. Pennington)*

Lincoln B.2s WD143, RA115,
RF351 and SX944 (camera
ship) of the Bomber
Command Bombing School
seen in formation over
Binbrook on the 5th
September 1958
*(via R. Sturtivant)*

# The Lancaster & Lincoln in Argentina

Chapter **6**

**by Raul Wright**

The technical innovations of the Second World War, with the developments in both weapons and aircraft, were not only viewed by those involved with the conflict those outside were also taking a great deal of notice. The Republic of Argentina was one of the first non-combatant nations to consider the use of wartime technical advancements. The Fuerza Aerea Argentina (FAA - Argentinian Air Force) was the first military element to be reformed, on the 5th January 1945, with a fleet of Curtiss Hawk 75s in the fighter role and Northrop A-8s and Martin 139WAAs as bombers. From the very beginning the high command knew that these machines were already obsolete, and so they started negotiations with the British Government to obtain war surplus materials, including aircraft.

In 1946 an agreement was reached for the purchase of 100 Gloster Meteor Mk IVs, fifteen Lancaster B Mk Is and thirty Lincoln B Mk IIs. The purchase of these aircraft was off-set against the debt that the British Government owed Argentina for the purchase of food from them in the Second World War.

## The Lincoln

The largest number of these machines were to be supplied directly from the Avro plant at Chadderton, with the entire order being delivered to the Fuerza Aerea Argentina within one year from the signing of the contract. To meet this timescale, Avro bought back twelve airframes from the Air Ministry in June 1946 and refurbished and modified them before sending them to Argentina. The remaining airframes (18) were all built at Chadderton specifically for the contract. In the first batch of ex-RAF machines, the $H_2S$ radar and all other RAF radar equipment was removed and two machines (B-004 and B-005) were fitted with dual controls for crew training. The first machine (B-001) was handed over to delegates of the FAA at a special ceremony at Chadderton during Aeronautic Week. This airframe was then flown across to Argentina under the command of two pilots from Avro and an FAA official (Lieutenant Rodolfo Otero). On arrival the aircraft was dismantled and shipped to Buenos Aires, where it was re-erected, but not without considerable difficulty due to the sheer size of the airframe. Other aircraft from the order started to make their way across to Argentina during December and each of these machines was crewed by staff from British South American Airways and Skyways Airlines. Training of the FAA crews took place at Langar from October 1947, where B-005 was used as a conversion trainer (having been fitted with dual controls). Deliveries of the aircraft to Langar started with the arrival of B-002, B-004, B-009, B-010, B-011 and B-012. These were followed in March 1948 with the arrival of B-005, B-007 and B-008, with the final batch of B-006 and B-003 arriving in October. The second batch of Lincolns were all new, being made by Armstrong-Whitworth Ltd at Bagington. These machines were all registered in the B-013 to B-030 series for service with the FAA.

The operational history of the Lincoln in Argentina began in 1948, where they were seen flying in formation for the first time during the nation's anniversary celebrations. Between December 1951 and February 1952 these machines were involved with operations in the Antarctic under 'Operation Penguino' and 'Operation Enlance'. These operations consisted of supply flights in support of the Antarctic Research Groups on the ground and were under the control of the Fuerza Aerea del Tareas Antarticas. The first loss of a Lincoln by the FAA was experienced in 1950, when B-019 was lost in bad weather near the city of Rio Gallegos. Everyone aboard this aircraft perished, and even a later (1983) search for this machine drew a complete blank.

During 1952 a number of exercises were undertaken and these involved the bomber elements of the FAA together with the IA-24 Calquin, Fiat G-55 and the Gloster Meteor. In September 1952 the Lincolns of the FAA made their first visit to a foreign country: Chile. These machines were in Chile during celebrations to mark the anniversary of their independence. Losses during the service of the type included B-018, B-001 and B-023, all of which exploded in the air whilst on bombing exercises. B-020 was lost after just two exercises and B-030 was lost during the Antarctic Campaign in 1952/1953. B-019 was lost in the 'Tierra del Fuego' with the loss of all on board and B-012 was transferred to the Specialist School of the FAA as an instructional airframe.

During the Freedom Revolution that overthrew General Juan D.Peron, the president of the Argentine Republic, the Lincolns were used for the first time in real bombing operations against hostile forces. 1955 saw the loss of both B-009 and the B-028, both of which crashed during bombing exercises. By 1957 there were just sixteen Lincolns left, with four in reserve. As some of these machines were fitted with $H_2S$ Mk III, it was decided to try and use them in the anti-shipping/submarine role. The remainder still had the older $H_2S$ Mk II fitted and so could not be used in this role. The first machine to receive a 'modern' ASV radar in a retractable 'dustbin', was B-024. With this radar, and in the company of B-020 and B-029, they tracked an unidentified submarine in the Golfo Nuevo off Santa Cruz. Although the submarine was also pursued by other means, it submerged and the contact was broken, although the operation had proved the suitability of the Lincoln in the role. Another task assigned to the Lincolns was that of fire fighting. The aircraft simply carried General Purpose (G.P.) bombs, and dropped them on the fire. The resulting blast was supposed to consume all the oxygen and put the fire out, although it obviously could not be used in built-up areas! In October 1964 B-029 was destroyed by fire in the Aeroparque at Buenos Aires. By the beginning of 1965 only six Lincolns remained, and so they were all removed from active service. In 1966 seven were scrapped, while B-004 (marked as 'B-010') was placed on exhibition in the National Museum of Aeronautics, and B-016 (marked as 'B-017') is a gate guardian at the V Air Brigadeat Villa Reynolds-Sans Luis.

## The Lancaster

The Lancasters operated in Argentina, unlike the Lincolns, were all ex-RAF machines, and were obtained as surplus once their RAF service had come to an end. The FAA were given fifteen airframes that were subsequently registered B-031 to B-045. The first ten airframes, plus B-045, were all Vickers-Armstrong built, while the remainder were all Metropolitan-Vickers machines. Initially these machines were given B Class British registrations from G-11-14 to G-11-28 and it was with these registrations that they undertook test flights in the UK. The first machine was delivered to Argentina on the 8th September 1948 and was immediately allocated to the First Regiment of Bombardiers under the command of Colonel Pringles. This machine was registered as O00-1 ('O' for observer) and carried out photographic and plotting missions from Reconquista attached to Group 1 (Observation & Connection). During December 1948 B-034, B-039, B-036, B-042 and B-044 arrived in Argentina, and formed the 2nd Regiment of Bombardiers. It has often been said that the small number of Lancasters available made their role as bombers difficult, but to be truthful, the Lincoln was used in this role more, leaving the Lancasters in reserve.

One of the curious things about the airframes was that Vickers demanded that they be shipped with the $H_2S$ radar installed. Only the first machine had no radar installed, although it is not known if these machines also retained their 'Monica' (IFF) system. Both the Lancaster and Lincoln were the first machines operated by the FAA with an airborne radar system, and they were both therefore used in airborne surveillance and bombing roles as a result. Because these machines were fitted with $H_2S$ and the 'magnetron' valve that powered it (generating 10000 watts at a 10cm frequency), the FAA was told that they had to be parked on grass at all times, and could not be left on asphalt or concrete runways or dispersals! On the 16th April 1951 all remaining Lancasters were taken off front-line service and placed in reserve at Reconquista-Entre Riosm. This did not mark the end of their use, as on the 22nd April 1952 they were all brought out of storage and reconditioned for active service once more. Both B-036 and B-042 were lost in crashes during 1954, and by 1960 there were just twelve Lancasters left. By 1962, further losses and conversions coupled with the need to retire B-031 left just eight machines in service. The conversion mentioned was B-038, which was sent to the Taller Region, Cuarto-Córdoba, where it was modified for the transport role and re-registered as T-038. By 1963 B-032, B-034, B-039 and B-044 also joined the ranks of retirees. One Lancaster that did see a massive amount of service was B-040. This machine undertook a photographic survey of the whole of Argentina, comprising over 6,600 km$^2$ under 'Operation Poses'. By this stage an acute lack of spares meant that T-038, B-033 and B-043 all had to be removed from service. B-040's end was not to be a happy one, as it was involved in a terrible accident in the city of Rio Gallegos-Santa Cruz.

The end of the Lancaster's operational life with the FAA came at the same time as the Lincoln in 1966. Under Resolution 446-66, Reserved Air Bulletin 1615, dated the 7th July all the remaining Lancasters and Lincolns were withdrawn from service and scrapped. Regrettably no Lancasters were preserved in an Argentinian museum.

## The Lancastrians

Before the FAA ever operated the Lancaster, the nation's Merchant Air Fleet received three Lancastrian C Mk IVs. The first machine was registered LV-ACS and was lost in bad weather over Brazil later in its career. The other two machines were LV-ACU and LV-ACV; LV-ACU was used as a personal transport by Eva Perón during her European tour and returned to Argentina on the 22nd August 1947. In 1948 LV-ACU was re-registered as T-66, while LV-ACV became T-65. LV-ACV was only to remain in service until June 1949, when corrosion was discovered in its wings and it was grounded.

In 1957 Lancaster B-045 was converted to Lancastrian configuration and it was subsequently re-registered T-62. This gave two Lancastrians in service, but T-66 was lost in an accident on the 16th October 1957, when it crashed at El Alto airport, Boliva with the loss of three crew members. T-62 was re-registered as T-102, but in 1959 it too was lost in a fatal accident when it crashed near San Andrés of Giles with the loss of all passengers and crew.

One machine not mentioned here, as it was supplied as a Lancaster, is B-003. This machine was modified to Lancastrian standard and registered as LV-ZEI. In this guise it was used in support of the Antarctic operations by the Fuerza Aerea del Tareas Antarticas. At one stage this machine was christened Cruz del Sur (Southern Cross) but was eventually lost in an accident during July 1961.

## Special Weapons

Inspired by the Dams Raid undertaken by No. 617 Squadron in World War Two, the FAA decided in 1953 to form a special bomber group to attack dams and dykes. During July 1953 the Brigadier Apicella was formed with six Lincolns under the control of Brigadier Neithardt. Practice flights were undertaken over the waters of the Dyke San Roque in Córdoba. By the end of this training, flights at less than 10 metres at 280km/h were being achieved. Even though the group was formed and all the practice was undertaken, no bombs were ever produced and the whole project was eventually dropped.

## PT 1

With the arrival in Argentina of ex-Henschel designers Werner Von Baumach and the Henrici brothers, plans were made to continue the development of the wartime Henschel Hs 293 air-to-surface missile. This radio-controlled missile was called PT-1 and its preparation and development was undertaken under the title 'Operation Soverina'. Initial aerodynamic tests were carried out under C-47 (S.No. T-51), while Gloster Meteor I-087 was used as the high-speed chase plane. In the Taller Regional, Rio Cuarto Lancaster B-036 was modified to act as a mothership for the PT-1. This missile was carried under the closed bomb bay of the Lancaster and the first test launches were satisfactory. All did not go to plan though, as the Lancaster was lost in an emergency landing on the Rio de la Plata river on the 20th July 1953, which resulted in the total destruction of the aircraft and deaths of both Von Baumbach and one of the Henrici brothers.

Work continued on the project though, and B-037 was soon modified to act as a replacement mothership. Another Lancaster (B-038) also joined the research and was used to film the trajectory of the missile in its initial stages after launch, with the Gloster Meteor following it through the rest of its flight. It was at this stage that the designation of the weapon was changed from PT-1 to PAT-1; a technical amendment due to the change in role from 'radio-guided missile' to 'guided air missile'. Test launches were undertaken on the ranges near Córdoba, but they were not a total success as a missile went out of control in its final phase of flight, and crashed on a railroad. During the Revolution of September

1965 it was decided to use the PAT-1 in combat, but B-037 was attacked on the ground before it could be used and so the weapon was never used in anger. Tests continued with B-043 as the mothership in and around Punta Indio, Buenos Aires as well as over the waters of the Rio de la Plata. The programme was to come to an abrupt end when the new President of the Argentine Republic, Doctor Arturo Frondizi, ordered its cancellation.

Today only one PAT-1 exists, and it is exhibited in the Museum of the Military School of the Nation in Buenos Aires.

What the Lancaster and Lincoln actually contributed to the FAA was considerable. They represented the first four-engine aircraft flown by the nation and were the first equipped with radar. As well as strengthening both the offensive and defensive ability of the FAA, their service and operations also lead to a great improvement in the logistical infrastructure needed to support them. With the loss of these two machines from the FAA inventory the idea of a strategic force was also lost, as the Douglas A-4 Skyhawk and BAC Canberra Mk 62 that replaced them did not have that capacity. For almost 20 years these two heavies served with the Fuerza Aerea Argentina, and it is a testament to the quality of the design that they were able to fill the role so successfully for so long.

# Post-War Service

## Chapter 7

Lancaster B Mk VIIs of
No. 617 Squadron in flight
(©RAFM P002769)

## • The Lancaster

### Royal Air Force

One of the first tasks to be undertaken by Bomber Command, was not as such in the 'post-war' period. As early as February 1945 a Lancaster (HK696) had been at Netheravon for supply dropping trials. In this configuration the Lancaster was fitted with five panniers in the bomb bay, capable of carrying seventy 25lb sacks in each.

With the worsening situation in the final days of the war, the people of Holland found themselves surrounded and cut off. Food was very scarce and so to get over the ground blockade Bomber Command was called in to air-drop food. This work was carried out under Operation Manna, and it commenced on the 28th April. Various squadrons undertook this mercy work, but No. 115 Squadron did the first sortie. In just a two-week period, Lancasters of Bomber Command flew over 3,000 sorties and dropped 6,685 tons of food and supplies in support of Operation Manna.

The next role to face the Lancasters was that of repatriation of Allied POWs under Operation Exodus and Dodge. The first operation was to return POWs from Europe. This required a number of Lancasters to be converted to carry 25 passengers (uncomfortably!) and the first sortie was undertaken on the 4th May from Brussels. During May over 3,000 sorties were undertaken and over 74,000 POWs were returned home. Operation Dodge was a similar task, but to return POWs from Italy and the Central Mediterranean.

### Tiger Force

Even with the end of the war in Europe, the war in the Pacific was still going on, so thoughts turned to sending Lancasters of Bomber Command into this theatre. Initially it was intended to use the long-range Lancaster IV (Lincoln) for the role, but with so many Lancasters available trails were undertaken to increase the fuel capacity of the type. Initially two machines had been tested with 1,200 gallon 'saddle tanks' although all that fuel over their heads was not popular with the crews. Advanced navigation equipment was developed by the CNS and tropical equipment like enlarged radiators were developed for the Lancaster. By the end of 1944 plans were in place to set up three groups, with ten squadrons each, to operate in the Pacific. The Lancasters for these groups were converted from those coming off the Vickers Armstrong and Armstrong Siddeley production lines, and this work was

Lancaster B Mk VII, NX678, WS•S of No. 9 Squadron at Salbani
(©RAFM P002768)

Lancaster, JE•C of No. 195 Squadron dropping food during 'Operation Manna' in 1945
(©RAFM P007095)

Lancaster B Mk VII (FE), NX776, GAD•F of the EAAS, RAF Manby (via r. Sturtivant)

Lancaster MR Mk III of No. 38 Squadron
(©RAFM P001720)

use in the theatre, and their machines were designated B Mk VII (Special), as they were also capable of carrying a Tallboy or Grand Slam bomb. Squadrons equipped with the F.E. machines prior to going out to the Far East also included Nos. 35, 70, 104, 115, 138 and 207, but in the end they were not needed, as the dropping of the atomic bombs on Hiroshima and Nagasaki during August 1945, brought the war to an end. The Tiger Force deployment was officially cancelled on the 2nd September. The first Tiger Force Lancaster squadrons had not been envisaged to deploy to Okinawa until November, so all the converted aircraft never even left the UK.

## Air Sea Rescue & Maritime Reconnaissance

Although the Lancaster was to be used in the maritime reconnaissance role, it was only initially intended as an interim machine until the maritime version of the Lincoln (later to become the Shackleton) arrived. The Mk II airborne lifeboat weighing 3,750lbs had already been carried by the Warwick, but a more powerful carrier aircraft was required. To meet this

requirement a number of B Mk III Lancasters were taken out of storage and sent to Cunliffe Owen at Eastleigh for conversion. These machines were fitted with Merlin 224s and various other special equipment so that the lifeboat would be fitted via the 4,000lb bomb shackle under the bomb bay doors. In this configuration the type was redesignated ASR Mk III (later ASR Mk 3). The Mk II lifeboat was 30ft long and 6ft 6in wide, powered by a 900cc Austin marine engine, and was capable of a range of 600 miles.

The first machine (ND589) was actually converted by Avro, but all operational versions were converted by Cunliffe Owen. The first unit to equip with the ASR Mk III was No. 279 Squadron in December 1945 and they undertook the first drop of a Mk II lifeboat on the 10th December. The next squadron to equip was No. 179 Squadron at RAF St. Eval in February 1946, although they only continued until September that year. No. 279 Squadron disbanded in March 1946 but by this time ASR Mk IIIs were serving alongside the GR Mk IIIs of Nos. 203 and 210 Squadron in the UK, plus No. 38 Squadron in the Middle East and No. 1348 ASR Flight in Pegu, Burma. In August 1950 the Mk IIA lifeboat was introduced, but it is unlikely that the ASR Mk III ever carried these, as the type was made obsolete in the same month. Some airframes did remain at RAF St. Mawgan for crew training, but the last (RF325) was sent to RAF Wroughton in December 1956 for scrapping.

The Lancaster was also converted to undertake the General Reconnaissance role, and as such was designated as the GR Mk III (or GR Mk 3). This aircraft could also carry a Mk II airborne lifeboat and although the $H_2S$ radome was retained, it actually contained ASV radar more suited to its maritime role. The mid-upper turret was removed, and windows were cut in the fuselage sides, forward of the tailplanes. The first squadron to operate the type was No. 210 Squadron at RAF St. Eval, when it reformed in June 1946. Nos 203 and 224 Squadrons

undertaken by Short Brothers. These machines (B Mk Is, IIIs & VIIs) were designated as F.E. (Far East) and the conversion consisted of the fitment of Merlin 24 engines, the removal of the mid-upper turret, installation of an F.N.82 (2x 20mm cannon) rear turret, fitment of an additional 400 gallon long range fuel tank in the bomb bay and the installation of American SCR-522 radio equipment (this was to be compatible with the existing equipment in the Far East). Two specialist squadrons (Nos. 9 and 617) were also envisaged for

were also soon equipped with the GR Mk III, and by August 1947 they were all involved in rotating detachments to Ein Shemer (Palestine) under Operation Bobcat. The GR Mk IIIs were retained in their role until 1953 when they were replaced with the Neptune MR.1 and Shackleton. As with the ASR Mk III, the GR Mk III was to see its final service with the School of Maritime Reconnaissance at RAF St. Mawgan.

## Post-war Service Abroad - Egypt

During the 1945 to 1947 period four Lancaster squadrons (Nos. 37, 40, 70 and 104) were used to patrol the canal zone from bases at Shallufa and Abu Sueir. These machines were also used to ship mail to UK and their last Lancaster left No. 49 Squadron's charge in 1950, when this unit re-equipped with the Lincoln.

## Africa

Aerial survey work in Africa was undertaken by the specially modified PR Mk I Lancasters of Nos 82 and 683 Squadrons. The last aircraft (PA427) was withdrawn from this area in December 1953.

## Other Trials & Special Aircraft

One trial that the Lancaster was connected with was that of in-flight refuelling. Four Lancasters were loaned to Flight Refuelling Ltd for trials with in-flight refuelling, two acting as tankers and the other two acting as receivers. The tankers were fitted with a hose drum of 250ft of refuelling pipe in the rear fuselage (aft of the bomb bay). In the bomb bay itself were fitted two 600 gallon fuel tanks. Four pilots and eight operators

were detached from the BDU to Flight Refuelling at Staverton to undertake some 36 sorties. The success of these trials was to lead Flight Refuelling to continue development work once the BDU detachment had ended, and once again the Lancaster was chosen for the task. Trials continued at Staverton and for many of these converted Lancaster tanker G-33-2 was used. This machine was involved with the trials of the 'probe and drogue' system using Meteor Mk III EE397 in 1949, and this is the system of in-flight refuelling that is still in use to this day. It was the combination of these two machines that set a 12 hour endurance record on the 7th August 1949, during which the Meteor was refuelled no less than ten times by the Lancaster.

# Lancaster - Foreign Service

*War surplus Lancasters were sold to a number of countries in the post-war period.*

## Argentina

The first foreign operator of the Lancaster in the post-war period was Argentina, who placed an order with Avro for fifteen machines in 1947. These machines were taken out of storage and refurbished under Avro Works Order Sales 106 and

Lancaster B Mk I, PA441,
KO•K of No. 115 Squadron,
Luqa, 1948
(©RAFM P013692)

supplied to the Argentine Air Force during 1948 and 1949. All of these machines were given codes in the B-031 to B-045 series. The aircraft were allocated construction numbers 1450 to 1464 by Avro, and were test flown in the UK with civil registrations G-11-14 to G-11-28.

All pilot training with the Argentine Air Force crews was undertaken by Avro at their Langar facility. Once the crews were fully trained on the Lancaster they were allowed to undertake the very long delivery flight back to Argentina under the supervision of BSAA and Skyways crews. Delivery of all fifteen machines took place between May 1948 and January 1949. In Argentina these machines were operated by II Grupo de Bombardeo, III Brigada Aerea and some later saw service with the Paratroop Training School at Cordoba. Unfortunately a shortage of spares as well as suitable bombs and ammunition soon precluded the type's use in the intended bomber role. During their service ten airframes were lost in crashes, whilst B-034, B-038 and B-040 were later converted to transports and

re-registered as T-034, T-038 and T-040 respectively. What remained of the Lancaster fleet was finally retired in 1966.

For more details of these, and the Lincoln's use in Argentina, see Chapter 6.

## Egypt

Egypt was the second foreign operator of the Lancaster in the post-war period. They placed an order for nine refurbished B Mk Is and these airframes came out of store at Langar to be refurbished at Bracebridge Heath. All the airframes were updated, and all RAF radar equipment removed and although all armament was also removed, the turrets remained. In this form the aircraft were test flown in the UK with registrations G-11-60 to G-11-68.

All of these aircraft were ferried to Egypt in late 1950 and allocated Arabic codes 1801 to 1809 for Royal Egyptian Air Force service. Based at Almaza these machines saw very limited use due to a lack of spares, although it would seem that some (possibly just 3) saw action during the 1956 Suez campaign.

The ultimate fate of these machines is unknown, so maybe one day they will reappear from the sands of the Egyptian desert!

## France

France was to be the final foreign operator of the Lancaster in the post-war period. In all fifty-four Lancasters were supplied to the Aéronavale. Their supply had been agreed in 1948 and was funded under the Western Union (later to become the Western European Union) agreement. Western Union was a forerunner of NATO and was eventually absorbed into NATO when the USA and Canada joined. The fifty-four machines comprised thirty-two B Mk Is and twenty-two B Mk VII and each was converted to B Mk I (modified) standard with the removal of the mid-upper turret, installation of overload fuel tanks in the bomb bay, fitment of rear observation windows in the rear fuselage, plus the installation of ASV radar, ASR equipment and a lifeboat pick-up point (the latter modification was not made to all airframes). In this configuration they closely resembled the RAF Maritime Reconnaissance (GR/MR) standard. All of these machines bore a WU (Western Union) serial from 01 to 54.

The first machine (WU01) was handed over to Escadrille de Reception et Convoyage 70 during a ceremony at Woodford in January 1952, after which it flew to France (Les Mureaux). This

Lancaster B Mk I, PA417 at
Luqa, 1948
(©RAFM P013702)

Lancaster GR Mk III, SW366,
H•Z of the School of
Maritime Reconnaissance,
St Mawgan, seen here at
Blackbushe in 1956
(via R. Sturtivant)

Lancaster B Mk I of No. 230
OCU after crash landing at
RAF Lindholme, 1st July 1948
(©RAFM P0019723)

Lancaster B Mk VII, NX739
seen awaiting disposal. The
bulged bomb doors of the
later versions are well
illustrated in this shot
(via R. Sturtivant)

first machine was allocated to No. 24 Flotille (10F and 9S) at Lahn-Bihoué, Brittany. Other squadrons to operate the remaining airframes included 10S at St Raphael, 2F at Port Lyautey (Morocco), 52S, 55S and 56S (also all in Morocco) and 11F and 5S of No. 25 Flotille at Lartique. No. 9S later moved to Noumea (and Tontouta), New Caledonia (South Pacific) where they used their machines in the maritime reconnaissance role. The machines used for this role were initially WU16, WU27 and WU41, but they were eventually replaced by WU13, WU15 and WU21. Most of the aircraft flying from bases in France and North Africa stayed in service until 1961, when they were gradually replaced by Lockheed Neptunes. Those based in the South Pacific remained in service until 1964, and WU13 eventually returned to the UK (as NX611), where it can still be

seen today at East Kirkby.

An additional five B Mk VIIs were converted with Lincoln undercarriage and rudders and used in the air-sea rescue role by the Aéronavale. These machines were allocated serials FCL-01 to FCL-05 and from early 1954 they operated in the Mediterranean from bases at Maison Blanche (Algeria) and Agadir (Morocco).

## Russia

Mention must also be made of Russian use of the Lancaster. Although no Lancaster airframes were ever officially supplied to Russia during or after the war, it is believed that they did manage to salvage a number of airframes that crashed in Russia, and built flying examples. It is not known how many machines were built, and if they were ever used operationally, however it is thought that at least one machine that flew was made up of a substantial amount of ME559. This machine was an ex-617 Squadron airframe and had crashed in Russia on the 18th September 1944 during the outward leg of the operation against Tirpitz.

## Canada

Canada was to use a large number of Lancasters in the post-war period, most of which were actually built there by Victory Aircraft and had been flown back to Canada by ex-RCAF wartime crews. Eight RCAF squadrons from No. 6 Group returned to Canada in the immediate post-war period and they formed No. 664 Wing at Greenwood, Nova Scotia as part of the perceived requirements of Tiger Force. The war in Japan ended before the Wing could get fully operational, and so it was never used operationally.

With the end of hostilities, Canada now looked towards peacetime requirements. Most of the airframes were initially put in storage, but as they were all ex-operational machines many had high flying hours and with no post-war bomber role for the Lancaster foreseen in the RCAF, many of them were subsequently scrapped. Those that remained were to be modified and served in a number of diverse roles within the RCAF in the next twenty years. In all some 230 airframes were modified, although all of these modifications were carried out on B Mk X (later B Mk 10) airframes. The modifications resulted in the following types:

- Mk 10AR Area Reconnaissance (often incorrectly referred to as 'Arctic Reconnaissance')
- Mk 10BR Bomber Reconnaissance
- Mk 10DC Drone Controller
- Mk 10MR Maritime Reconnaissance (later redesignated 10MP 'Maritime Patrol')
- Mk 10N Navigation Trainer

Lancaster B Mk X, FM213 (CX-213) of No.107 Rescue Unit, RCAF

Lancaster B Mk VII, NX739 was on loan to English Electric and is seen here with the prototype Folland Midge parked under its nose

Lancaster B Mk Is, G-AHJW and G-AHJT of Flight Refuelling Ltd

Lancaster B Mk II, G-33-2 of Flight Refuelling Ltd refuelling Meteor F.III EE397 in flight, 6th August 1947
*(© C.E. Brown)*

- Mk 10O Orenda jet engine test-bed
- Mk 10P Photographic Reconnaissance
- Mk 10S 'Standard' airframes
- Mk 10SAR Search and Rescue

**NOTE:** This list is not in the order in which these machines entered service with the RCAF.

Many sources list the 10U, being 'unmodified' examples in store, but no official Canadian documentation can be found referring to this designation, so for the purposes of this book it has been ignored.

The starting point for all 10-series airframes was the B Mk X (B Mk 10 after 1950), and to identify this 'starting' point, the designation Mk 10S was allocated to all airframes in store. All conversions undertaken in the post-war period on the B Mk X airframes was done by Avro (Canada) Ltd, as the

Four shots of Lancaster FM148 of the Winter Experimental Establishment in the 'RAF' scheme in the summer of 1947
*(© J.Lyzun/FlightDecs)*

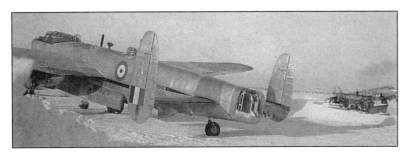

Victory Aircraft facility had closed with the cessation of hostilities. Once the Korean War started, Avro (Canada) were committed to CF-100 production and so all Lancaster conversion work was then sub-contracted to de Havilland (Canada) Ltd.

A couple of Mk 10S airframes did see service with the RCAF and two were used to evaluate the type's suitability with the Winter Experimental Establishment (WEE) at Namao, Alberta. The first was KB739, which joined the WEE in the Spring of 1945. This machine was soon found to be too war-weary and was therefore replaced with FM148 in early 1946. This machine undertook many years of climate evaluation work with the WEE before being passed to the Air Armament School at Trenton for use in bombing and gunnery training. The only other Mk 10Ss to see service was a single example that was used for fighter affiliation work with 103 RU (KB801), and FM118 which was acquired by the Army and subsequently used as a gunnery target.

The first actual post-war conversion was the 10P. Before the war survey work had started to map all of Canada. In 1944 No. 13 (Photo) Squadron was created to resume this task, but the areas left to cover by the end of the war were some of the most inhospitable and their mixed fleet of aircraft types was not up to the task. Lancasters KB884 and KB917 were allocated to the squadron for trials, and although these machines were very war-weary, their usefulness in the photographic survey role was soon apparent. Avro (Canada) were contracted to convert FM212 to Mk XP (later Mk 10P) configuration late in 1946. In 1947 this machine undertook a number of trials, and after further modifications it was issued to No. 413 Squadron (as No. 13 (Photo) Squadron had now been designated). An initial order for eight airframes was submitted and these were FM207, FM208, FM212 (the prototype), FM214, FM215, FM216, FM217 and FM218. All of these machines were in service by 1949 and FM212 and FM218 were used for further modification work, while FM215 was used for short-range navigational aid (SHORAN) trials and FM208 eventually became the prototype Mk XN. The initial batch was soon supplemented by three more machines (FM120, FM122 and FM199) in 1950. Fitted with the tri-metrogen three-camera installation in the rear fuselage and SHORAN navigational equipment No. 413 Squadron was soon joined in the survey work by No. 408 Squadron, while supply of equipment to these squadrons during their various detachments was undertaken by No. 414 Squadron. By November 1950 all photo-survey work had been taken over by No. 408 Squadron and the Mk 10P was to be the last Lancaster type to seen RCAF service, with FM212 making the last flight on the 11th March 1964.

The XN navigational trainer was to have been the second conversion to see service with the RCAF, but was delayed by the onset of the Korean War. The prototype Mk XN (FM208) was completed by Avro (Canada) for service with the Air Navigational School at Summerside, Price Edward Island. Initially FM208 and FM211 were to be the only Mk XNs, but sufficient pressure was applied to get three more (FM206, KB826 & KB986) converted. Of these, four were allocated

celestial names; FM208 *Polaris*, FM211 *Zenith*, FM206 *Northern Cross* and KB826 *Orion*. All of these machines saw continued service until they were declared obsolete in 1957.

The Mk XBR was initially designed to meet a high and low-level bombing and reconnaissance role as well as being able to undertake all-weather, long-range patrols, escort, general reconnaissance, anti-submarine and limited strike operations! The initial requirement was seen as fifteen machines, and these would consist of eight for the Bomber Reconnaissance squadron, while the remaining machines would be used in the SAR role. The first squadron to have the type was No. 405 (BR) Squadron at Greenwood, Novia Scotia and in all thirteen machines were built. The first was FM221, which acted as a prototype for the series, and there were three additional pre-production machines (FM222, FM228 and KB961) that acted as development airframes. Production machines included KB907, KB919, KB925, KB946, KB957, KB965, KB973, KB995 and KB996. By 1950 the whole idea of a combined bomber/reconnaissance machine had been dropped and each of the airframes delivered was initially in the bomber configuration, although it was easy to convert them to the reconnaissance role. With the loss of the bomber/reconnaissance task, the Mk XBRs were soon dispersed amongst the various maritime patrol and composite squadrons to undertake a new task.

The maritime reconnaissance Mk 10MR was produced in the greatest number (between 70 and 75) and was a modification based on the existing Mk 10BR. The first Mk 10MRs entered service with No. 2 OTU at Greenwood, Novia Scotia during the Winter of 1950. Nos 404 and 405 Squadrons were also equipped with the type, the former operating East Coast patrols (covering the North Atlantic under the terms of Canada's commitment to NATO), while the

latter operated on the West Coast. Various excercises showed that the type was adequate for the role, but that the radar equipment was not. To overcome this the type was updated with sonobuoy systems, APS-33 search radar in place of the $H_2S$ and more navigational aids. The type carried on in service until 1955/6, with the East Coast contingent retiring their machines for Neptunes in 1955, while the West Coast coverage continued until early 1956. It was during this last stage of the type's use that its role was changed to Maritime Patrol and the remaining airframes were redesignated Mk 10MP.

With the establishment of the International Civil Aviation Organisation (ICAO) at Montreal, the RCAF felt that it should make an effort to support any requirements set out by this organisation. One of its first requirements was the setting up of a long-range search network to cover the entire Atlantic region. The RCAF set up No. 10 Group covering the East Coast, No. 11 Group covering the central area and No. 12 Group covering the West Coast, and all of these groups were equipped with Lancasters. In this role the Mk 10S was only slightly modified, as the initial need for them was urgent. Initially these machines had no official mark, being referred to as Mk 10S&R, and once the Mk 10MR was delivered to the SAR squadrons,

**Lancaster Mk XP (FM216) of No. 413 (P) Squadron. One of the trimet camera ports is visible just below the roundel**
*(© J.Lyzun/FlightDecs)*

**FM148 in its original wartime camouflage with yellow tailplanes, spinners and wing tips**
*(© J.Lyzun/FlightDecs)*

**Lancaster Mk 10P, FM120 of No. 408 (R) Squadron, based at RCAF Rockcliffe, photographed in the air near Ottawa in June 1961**
*(©RCAF via J.Lyzun/FlightDecs)*

Line up of Lancaster Mk 10Ns at Churchill, Manitoba on a training flight c.1952. Similar to the Mk 10P version, the Mk 10N had no astrodome on the nose cupola. Spinners are black
(©W. Flinn via J.Lyzun/FlightDecs)

Although there was only one built, Avro Canada's engine test vehicle was given the official designation, Lancaster Mk 10O, and is seen here over southern Ontario
(©National Aviation Museum via J.Lyzun/FlightDecs)

Lancaster Mk 10AR, KB839 of No. 408 Squadron comes in to land. Note the mass of antenna and radomes on the undersides of this aircraft
(©J. Whorwood via J.Lyzun/FlightDecs)

the 'Mk 10S&R' disappeared. Once the Mk 10MRs were retired from these squadrons the Mk 10S&R reappeared on their strength once again, although these were actually just Mk 10BR and MK 10MR/MP machines with all armament removed for the SAR role. These aircraft continued in this role up until 1964, when they were retired.

The final version of the Mk 10 to see service with the RCAF was the Mk 10AR (Area Reconnaissance). Canada claimed sovereignty of the whole of the Arctic Archipelago, but had not really patrolled this vast area to ensure there were no infringements. With Soviet infringements into the area in the pre- and post-war period, the need to extend the existing ice reconnaissance flights into these areas was becoming apparent. An alternative was discussed in March 1952, although initially the Tactical Air Group asked for the existing machines of No. 408 Squadron to undertake this (an impossible task considering all the other work No. 408 Squadron was doing at this time!). By the Spring of 1952 work on the new Mk 10AR was under way, although it was basically just a Mk 10P fitted with powerful search radar, camera, electronic surveillance and ECM equipment. Three machines (KB839, KB882 & KB976) were produced, with a 40in extension to the nose, AN/APS-42 and UPD-501 radars plus no less than ten cameras. These machines undertook the role of air surveillance over the Arctic from 1952 right through to the type's eventual retirement in 1964.

Two additional machines that should be mentioned were not actually 'in service' with the RCAF, as one was an engine test-bed and the other was a launch/control platform. The former was the Mk 10O, which was used as a test bed for the Orenda engine intended for the CF-100. FM209 was converted to the role, with a TR.5 Orenda engine fitted in lieu of each outboard engine. Conversion was agreed in December 1949 and the airframe was ready by the Spring of

1950, undertaking its first flight with the Orendas on the 13th July. Test flying continued with this machine until the airframe was destroyed in a hanger fire on the 24th July 1956. The other machine was the Mk 10DC (Drone Controller), and two airframes (KB848 & KB851) were converted. The conversions were undertaken by Fairey Aviation, starting work in January 1957, and the type was similar to the Mk 10MR but with the addition of a drone control system, an operator and a movie camera. The type was fitted with a special pylon, on which was mounted a Type 51 shackle, under each outer wing pylon. On this was suspended a Ryan KDA-4 Firebee recoverable drone. The programme with these drones was to continue until 1961, when both airframes were declared obsolete and scrapped.

### Australia

During the war it had been decided that Lancaster B Mk III production would be set up in Australia, but plans for this slipped and by 1944 it had been decided that the B Mk VII version would be more suited to the long-patrol environment of the Pacific Theatre. In the end full-scale production of the Lancaster never happened in Australia, as by the time everything was in place to start, the war had ceased with Japan as well.

## • The Lincoln

As the Lincoln was developed too late for service in WWII, please refer to Chapter 5 for details of the type's use by the RAF in the post-war period.

## Foreign Service

### Argentina

For the Argentinian use of the Lincoln please refer to Chapter 6.

## Canada

It was intended to transfer Lancaster production at the Victory Aircraft (Malton, Ontario) plant over to Lincolns, but with the end of WWII, the need diminished, and was eventually removed altogether. In the end only one Lincoln B Mk XV (FM300) was completed. This aircraft flew for the first time on the 25th October 1945, but never entered service with either the RAF or RCAF. Eventually after a couple of flights the aircraft was put in store and subsequently scrapped in mid-1946.

## Australia

Probably the biggest post-war use of the Lincoln was by the RAAF. Actually just 85 Lincoln Mk 30 airframes were assembled at the Government Aircraft Factory at Fisherman's Bend, Melbourne. The first five of these (A73-1 to A73-5) were actually made from components shipped out from the UK, and A73-1 first flew on the 12th March 1946. This machine was handed over to the Lincoln Development Flight at RAAF Laverton on the 24th May. The first Lincoln actually manufactured in Australia, A73-6, was delivered to the Development Flight in November. All acceptance trials on Lincolns for the RAAF were carried out at No. 1 Aircraft Performance Unit, Point Cook.

Conversion of crews to the Lincoln started with the setting up of a Conversion Unit at RAAF East Sale in mid-1947. The first two crews to complete their conversion course took their machines to Amberley and started to re-equip No. 82 (Bomber) Wing with the type. The Liberators of Nos. 12, 21 and 23 Squadrons, which were also based at Amberley, were soon replaced with Lincolns too and in February 1948 these squadrons were renumbered as Nos. 1, 2 and 6 Squadrons. The first loss the RAAF suffered was on the 17th February 1948, when A73-11 overshot the runway and stalled, spinning in and killing all (16) on board. It was two years before the next fatal accident, when A73-44 dived into the ground near Amberley. During October 1949 to February 1950, five RAAF and five RAF Lincoln crews took part in Operation Cumulative. This operation saw the crews undertaking 11-13 hour flights to Darwin or Kalgoorlie, which was equivalent to flying one and a half times the distance from London to Moscow.

The original Merlin 85B engines fitted to the initial batch of

Lincolns soon proved very unreliable, and with Packard-built 68s impossible to get either, an alternative had to be found. At this time there were a large number of new Spitfire Mk VIIIs in store, so their Merlin 66 engines were removed and used to supplement the outboard Merlin 85Bs in the Lincoln fleet. After A73-51 the Australian-built Merlin 102s were installed, and as stocks grew, many of the older Lincolns were retro-fitted with the 102 as well. The Merlin 102 was initially tested at ARDU Laverton installed in Lincoln A73-41, and from August 1949 to March 1950 this aircraft undertook an extensive flight test programme, with tropical trials held at Darwin. The engines proved to be much more reliable than the previous ones, and the 10% performance increase also allowed the Lincolns to be stressed to a take-off weight of 82,000lbs (instead of the usual 75,000lbs).

During 1953 both Nos. 6 (at Woomera) and 2 (at Richmond) Squadrons were involved in the UK atomic trials. The first

One of the two Lancaster Mk 10DC models modified to carry a Firebee drone under each wing. Light colours on wing and fuselage indicate Dayglo areas
(©National Aviation Museum via J.Lyzun/FlightDecs)

The only Lincoln B Mk XV ever produced seen outside the Victory Aircraft plant. Note all the ex-RAF/RCAF B Mk X in storage in the background

device was detonated on the 15th October and the Lincolns of No. 6 Squadron tracked the resulting cloud. The cloud was continually tracked, initially by No. 6 Squadron, then by USAF B-29s and finally by Lincolns of No. 2 Squadron. A73-25 was used to sample the centre of the cloud, with an air filter under the starboard wing and a Geiger counter under the signaller's seat. With additional fuel on board, this machine stayed airborne for 12 hours, but on landing it was given a wide berth by everyone! No. 1 Squadron went to Malaya in July 1950 and this left Nos. 2 and 6 Squadrons as the main elements of No. 82

(Bomber) Wing. No. 2 Squadron also took on the mantle of training replacement crews for No. 1 Squadron during its time in Malaya, while No. 6 Squadron was often attached to the School of Land/Air Warfare undertaking trials for stores and supply dropping. The Lincoln also served with training and experimental units, such as the Central Flying School, School of Air Navigation, Air Armaments School and School of Photography, all of which were based at RAF East Sale, Victoria. Most of the Lincolns here were older machines with the unreliable Merlin 85Bs or later versions that were very

'weary' after many years squadron service. Of these machines A73-2 *Nyhuan* (Aboriginal for 'Scout' or Pathfinder), A73-15 *Brenool* ('Traveller') and A73-8 *Gundawarra* ('Weapons Thrower') were famous examples. The former two were operated by the School of Air Navigation and the latter used by the Air Armament School. A73-2 undertook an aerial survey of 45,000 square miles of Australia in December 1946, and this included the area that was soon to become the Woomera weapons test range. This aircraft undertook a number of extremely long flights during the late 1940s and early 1950s, and it remained in service until late 1953, when it was scrapped at East Sale.

The Lincoln Mk 30 was to leave service with No. 2 Squadron on the 18th November 1953, when the squadron converted to the Canberra, while No. 6 Squadron had to wait until July 1955. The last Lincolns of No. 6 Squadron were transferred to the Lincoln Development Flight at Amberley on the 11th July 1955, where this flight had been given full squadron status, and continued in the role of a training flight for No. 1 Squadron who were still based in Malaya.

## Special Duties

The Aircraft Research and Development Unit (ARDU) at RAAF Laverton was basically similar in role to the A&AEE in the UK. This unit undertook a mass of development work on the Lincoln and was involved in the adoption of the Merlin 102 and 66 (ex-Spitfire) engines into the Lincoln, as well as trials with an airborne lifeboat, rockets and even a pilot's reflector gunsight. Of these trials the use of A73-34 for cosmic ray measurements and A73-29 for rainmaking trials are probably the best known. The former was fitted with special equipment in 1957 by a team from the University of Tasmania as Australia's contribution to the International Geophysics Year. A73-29's use for rainmaking was undertaken by Detachment B of the ADRU on behalf of the Scientific and Industrial Research Organisation. The

A rare photo of a No. 407 Squadron Lancaster Mk 10MR fitted with guns. Although the front and rear turrets were armed on missions (the mid-upper turret was removed), the guns were quickly removed once the aircraft returned to base
(via J.Lyzun/FlightDecs)

Flight Refuelling Ltd's Lancaster G-AHJW fitted with a refuelling drum and hose in the bomb bay and used for 'hose and drogue' refuelling trials
(© FR Ltd)

Detachment used Dakotas to 'seed' the clouds with silver iodide in the hope that this would produce rain, while A73-29 did the same thing but used a half-million volt electrostatic charge. This was done with a four foot long drogue called *Betsy*, to which was attached a nylon cable through which the charge was passed. Most of these trials were carried out over the Southern Alps or Blue Mountains.

The RAAF Lincoln will always be linked with the rocket research facility at Woomera. Initially the air trails unit was provided by Lincolns of the ADRU, which were based at Salisbury and Edinburgh as Nos. 1 and 2 Air Trials Units. With no airstrip at Woomera, the nearby grass strip at Mallala was reopened. The bomb ballistics range adjacent to the rocket range at Woomera was the area in which the Lincolns operated. Fitted with a revised vertical camera in the aft fuselage, these machines started bomb ballistic trials in 1949. Because the 29,000ft ceiling of the Australian-built Lincolns was not good enough for the trials as they progressed, sixteen RAF Lincolns were obtained, as they could fly to 32,000ft. These included the two Python test-beds RE339 and RF403, which could operate at 43,000ft. Operations at this, and the lower 32,000ft, proved problematical, and oxygen supply for the crews was the main concern. Eventually the Lincoln's role at Woomera was taken by the Canberra, and only one (RE418) of the original sixteen RAF Lincolns returned The remainder, which comprised RA638, RA640, RA644, RE258, RE259, RE339, RE423 and RF403 were all scrapped at Woomera.

## Long Nose - The MR.31

No. 10 Squadron RAAF formed at Garbutt (now Townsville) on the 1st March 1949. Their first Lincolns (A73-12 and A73-22), were both Mk 30s and arrived at the base on the 12th September. A detachment was posted to Darwin, arriving there on the 30th June 1950, to cover the squadrons increased area of responsibility. The squadron and its detachment undertook search and rescue and general reconnaissance missions, but by

Armstrong-Whitworth built Lincoln B Mk II, WD148 seen here in the colours of the RAF Signals Command

Lancaster Mk 10MR, KB889 of No. 107 (RU) Squadron
(©L. Milberry via J.Lyzun/FlightDecs)

A common sight in the early 1950s was a former Mk 10P, MR/MP or BR returned to active service in the search and rescue role
(© via J.Lyzun/FlightDecs)

Lincoln B Mk II, RF535 of the ETPS (©RAFM P0021281)

1952 it had changed to anti-submarine warfare. In these initial stages the squadron had operated the 'short nose' MR.30, but operational experience showed this type to be unsuitable for the role and so a new version was developed.

The modification of the Mk 30 consisted externally of a 6ft 6in extension to the nose, and the first machine thus modified (A73-48) was undertaking trials at Nowra in early 1953, before being passed to No. 10 Squadron on the 10th March. All conversions were either undertaken by the Servicing

Lancaster Mk 10P, FM212, served with No. 408 Squadron and is seen here in the last paint scheme applied before the type was retired (©Collect-Aire via J.Lyzun/FlightDecs)

Department (conversion of ex-service Mk 30s) or the Main Assembly Workshops (those taken directly off the production line for conversion) of the Government Aircraft Factory at Fisherman's Bend. As well as the prototype (A73-48), eight more Mk 30s were converted by the Government Aircraft Factory, plus two more (A73-28 and A73-67) by the RAAF at Amberley. Nineteen brand-new airframes were constructed at Fisherman's Bend, and the first of these were known simply as 'Mk 31'. Later they were further modified for anti-submarine work and were titled 'MR.31'. All late-series production machines were finished

to this standard and were known as MR.31s. Initial machines also had the unreliable Merlin 85B, and, as with the Mk 30, these were soon replaced with the Merlin 102.

No. 10 Squadron had initially received the prototype in early 1953, and this was rapidly joined by three more. Although most equipment stayed the same between the Mk 30 and MR.31, the $H_2S$ radar was modified to accept an ASV Mk 7 unit, which was more suited to the role of the type. The type was stressed for an auw of 82,000lb and along with jettisonable fuel cells in the bomb bay it was also able to carry an airborne lifeboat. On the 20th May 1953 No. 10 Squadron's title was changed from General Reconnaissance (GR) to Maritime Reconnaissance (MR).

In twelve years of operation with the type, No. 10 Squadron only suffered one fatal crash, and this was when A73-64 hit Mount Superbus, killing all (including a nurse and very ill two-day old baby) on board. The Lincoln MR.31 had only ever been intended as an interim anti-submarine aircraft and in October 1959 the decision was taken to replace it with the Lockheed Neptune. By June 1961, when severe corrosion in the main spars of the Lincolns with No. 10 Squadron saw the entire fleet grounded, the type's days were numbered. The last operational sortie was undertaken in A73-65 on the 4th June 1961 and the last ever RAAF Lincoln flight took place on the 14th June, when the same machine flew to Darwin for use in fire-fighting training.

One of the two 'saddle tank' Lancasters

Lincoln MR.31, A73-61 of No. 10 Squadron, RAAF at Townsville (©RAFM P0021280)

# 'Civvy Street'

## The Civil Lancaster & the Lancastrian

## Chapter 8

**Lancaster B Mk X of Trans-Canada Air Lines**
*(©RAFM P0021278)*

### Civil Conversions

The first conversion of a Lancaster into a civil transport was undertaken when British-built B Mk III, R5727 was authorised to be modified in March 1943. The aircraft had the nose and tail turrets faired over, the mid-upper turret removed, three windows added to the back of the fuselage, and all camouflage paint removed by Victory Aircraft. This machine was handed over to Trans-Canada Air Lines becoming Fleet No. 100 and it undertook freight carrying trials between Moncton and Goose Bay. It came back to the UK on the 15th May and was modified further by A.V. Roe Ltd. The turret locations were properly faired over and the short nose was modified to house the navigator, with the upper portion glazed. Other modifications included the fitment of fuel tanks in the bomb bay to increase the range to 4,000 miles and the installation of ten passenger seats in the rear fuselage. This machine had the camouflage re-applied and was registered CF-CMS and inaugurated the Trans-Atlantic Air Service, which was run by TCA for the Canadian Government, on the 22nd July 1943. After a mail run from Dorval (Canada) to Prestwick (Scotland), the type was issued with a British CofA (Certificate of Airworthiness) to carry passengers. TCA supplemented CF-CMS with the conversion of two Mk Xs (KB702 and KB703), which became CF-CMT and CF-CMU. These became known as Mk X Transporters, and CF-CMT made the first Atlantic crossing on the 12th January 1944. Two more aircraft were developed for TCA requirements, becoming CF-CMV and CF-CMW. These machines differed from the previous conversions and were designated Lancaster XPPs (Mk X Passenger Plane). These machines had a longer nose than the previous examples (for mail carriage), a new tail, a mail compartment was added to the front of the bomb bay, two 400 Imp gallon long-range tanks were added to the bomb bay as well and five seats were fitted to either side of the rear fuselage with a window for each. These machines were delivered to TCA during July and September 1944. During August 1944 an additional four more Lancaster XPPs were acquired, becoming CF-CMX, CF-CMY, CF-CMZ and CF-CNA. These machines were finished to a better standard than the previous examples, although CF-CMT and CF-CMU were later brought up to the same standard. Later CF-CMY, CF-CMZ and CF-CFA were transferred to Flight Refuelling Ltd and used in the Berlin Airlift as G-AKDO, G-AKDP, G-AKDR and G-AKDS. With the end of the war, revenue-earning passengers were carried. The Montreal to Prestwick service was extended on the 15th September 1946 to London. These machines made their 1000th Atlantic crossing in December 1946 and on the 15th May 1947 the Lancaster was replaced by the Canadair 4 North Star.

By the end of 1943, A.V. Roe produced drawings for the new 'Lancaster Airmail'. This machine had a streamlined

**Lancastrian I, G-AGME at Luqa, 1948**
*(©RAFM P013720)*

Lancaster G-AGJI of BOAC in February 1944

Lancaster B Mk I, G-AHJJ of Flight Refuelling Ltd
(©RAFM P0020910)

nose and tail, the former allowing access to the 2000lb luggage storage area. Seats were shown for twelve passengers, although this did not actually happen until the Lancastrian C Mk 3. Instead it was usual for nine seats and three settees to be placed on the port fuselage side, with windows on the starboard side only. The first British-built Lancaster to be converted for civil use was DV379 (G-AGJI). The conversion started in November 1944 and included the replacement of the Merlin 22 engines with (civil) T 24s. The aircraft did not have the long nose and tail extensions associated with the Lancastrian instead it had small fairings that truncated these areas. It was handed over to the BOAC Development Flight at Hurn on the 20th January 1944, and was then moved to its new base at Croydon. In May 1944 it went to Rolls-Royce to have the Merlin T-102 fitted in annular (Tudor) engine nacelles. Post-war the type had all its camouflage removed and it continued in service until November 1946, before being finally scrapped at Colerne late in 1947.

## Lancastrian I

The 'Lancaster Airmail' mentioned above was further developed by Avro and in 1944 was put into production as the Type 691. This machine featured a 500 gallon fuel tank in the bomb bay and was later called the Lancastrian I. The first example, G-AGLF (ex-VB873) was delivered to the BOAC Development Flight at Hurn. It received its CofA on the 7th February 1945 and in April it made a record-breaking flight from Hurn to New Zealand in three and a half days.

Twenty-three Lancasters from the end of the production line were converted to Lancastrians. These were serial numbers PD140-146 and PD159-172 and had originally been intended for the RAF. They were all allocated new serial numbers and finished as nine-passenger aeroplanes for service with BOAC. These machines were registered from G-AGLS to G-AGMM, although G-ALGI was not allocated,

and they were operated on the 'Kangaroo Service' by both BOAC and Qantas crews (the Qantas crews took over at Karachi). This route was between the UK and Australia, and was established by G-AGLV flown by Capt E. Palmer on the 31st May 1945. Initially the UK terminal was at Hurn, but on the 28th May 1946 it was transferred to Heathrow. Although it lost some £1,400,000 per annum, it was seen as a 'prestige' line for BOAC. This route was soon being covered in Lockheed Constellations by Qantas, so BOAC used its Lancastrians to ship cargo. The Lancastrian remained on this service until replaced by the York in August 1950.

From the 11th April 1948 BOAC also operated the Lancastrian, in conjunction with South African Airways, to do a weekly mail service from London to Johannesburg.

Lancaster B Mk III, G–AHJU of
Flight Refuelling Ltd
(©RAFM P0020911)

This service continued until the 12th August 1949. Another route that the Lancastrian was used on, albeit for a very short time, was the London-Colombo-Singapore route. This passenger service only remained with the Lancastrian from February 1948 to November 1949, when the route was taken over by Canadair 4 Argonauts.

## Lancastrian C Mk 2

Because of its commitments in India, Australia and the Far East the RAF had a need for a long-range transport, so it placed an order for thirty-three Lancastrian C Mk 2s. These aircraft featured nine seats and T 24 engines and they were delivered from Woodford between October 1945 and March 1946. Initially they entered RAF service with the Lancastrian Training Flight at Full Sutton, although this Flight eventually became No. 231 Squadron. Two machines (VM728 and VM729) were used by the Handling School of the ECFS, while VL968 was used by the EANS, No. 232 Squadron in India had VM733 and VM735, VM701 was with No. 511 Squadron at Lyneham and the remainder were with No. 1359 (VIP) Flight also based at Lyneham.

By the end of 1948 three of these passed to BOAC, two (plus two for spares) went to BSAAC (becoming G-AKMW *Star Bright* and G-AKTB *Star Glory*) and four went to Skyways. Those that did remain with the RAF were on the strength of No. 24 Squadron, as this squadron had absorbed No. 1359 (VIP) Flight in June 1946.

## Lancastrian 3

This version of the Lancastrian was specifically created for use by BSAA (British South American Airways), but in the end they only actually operated six of the eighteen ordered. A reduction in operating weights, coupled with a reduction in the size of the crew and galley areas, allowed, thirteen seats to be installed (seven on the port side and six on the starboard). The six machines operated by BSAA were

registered G-AGWG (*Star Light*), G-AGWH (*Star Dust*), G-AGWI (*Star Land*), G-AGWJ (*Star Glow*), G-AGWK (*Star Trial*) and G-AGWL (*Star Guide*).

The first operational use of this Lancastrian variant was undertaken by G-AGWG *Star Bright* when it took off from Heathrow on the 1st January 1946 for proving flights to Lisbon, Bathurst, Natal, Montevideo and Rio de Janerio. Further flights were inaugurated as far as Carácas but during their operations BSAA lost four of its six Lancastrian 3s (G-AGWH being the one only recently discovered in the Andes).

Lancaster G-AHJV of BSAA
in flight
(©RAFM P100035)

The remaining twelve Lancastrian 3s ordered were registered G-AHBT to G-AHCE. Of these G-AHBT (City of New York), G-AHBV (City of Canberra) and G-AHBW (City of London) were operated by Silver City Airways. G-AHBT and G-AHBU were later passed on to Skyways and became Sky Ranger and Sky Path respectively, while G-AGBW went to Qantas as VH-EAV. Of the remaining aircraft, G-AHBZ (Sky Ambassador), G-AHCA and G-AHCC (Sky Chieftain) went to Skyways, while G-AHBX (I-AHBX Maestale),

Lancastrian I at Luqa, 1948
(©RAFM P013719)

**Lancaster G-AHJV of BSAA
in flight**
*(©RAFM P100034)*

G-AHBY (I-AHBY Libeccio), G-AHCB (I-AHCB Grocale), G-AHCD (I-AHCD Sirroco) and G-AHCE (I-DALR Borea) were operated by Alitalia (Alitalia registration and name shown in brackets).

## Lancastrian C Mk 4

The last Lancastrian contract was for eight C Mk 4s for the RAF. These were basically just military versions of the Lancastrian 3, and were allocated serial numbers TX283 to TX290. Of these it is known that seven were eventually passed to civil operators. These consisted of TX284 (G-AKFF Sky Ruler with Skyways), TX285 (G-AKLE) as

spares for Skyways, TX286 (G-AKFG) as Sky Minister with Skyways, and TX287 (LV-ACU), TX288 (LV-ACS) and TX289 (G-ACV) for Flota Aérea Mencante in Argentina. The last machine is G-AKJO Sky Envoy with Skyways which has never had its associated RAF serial number clarified. The last three machines (TX287-9) were later passed on to the Argentine Air Force.

In all just 82 Lancastrians were built, along with nine Canadian Lancaster Transports, but they played a key role in the development of world air travel as we know it today.

**Lancastrian I at Luqa, 1948**
*(©RAFM P013721)*

**Lancaster B Mk X of
Trans-Canada Air Lines**
*(©RAFM P0021277)*

# The Basics

As you would expect with such a famous type, there have been a large number of kits produced of the Lancaster. The same does not go for the Manchester and Lincoln however. Nearly all of these kits are in 1/72nd scale, but there were also a couple in 1/48th, 1/96th scale and a single example in 1/144th. To date there have been no attempts at any of these types in any scale larger than 1/48th, which is bit of a relief!

## (ex-Crown) 1/144th Scale Lancaster B Mk I

### B Mk I

This kit was originally released by Crown in the 1970s and has also been released under the Academy label in 1993. The model is currently (2000) available in the Minicraft range.

The decal options in the current example (#14403) we have are:
- 1. W4794, PH•V.

No squadron is quoted on the instructions, but this machine served with No. 12 Squadron.

This very simple kit comprises forty-five green parts plus five in clear plastic. Panel lines are all raised and the interior is devoid of any detail except a plain flat 'floor' in the cockpit area. The propellers don't seem to represent either standard or 'paddle' versions, although the kit does include just the spinners, so you can build the kit 'in flight'. The undercarriage legs are too long and the tyres are both too big in diameter and too narrow in cross-section. This results in the completed model looking very 'leggy'. The exhaust shrouds are completely the wrong shape and there are no trim tabs on the rudder. None of the fuselage windows are moulded other than as raised lines and the mid-upper turret surround is too shallow. The main canopy is too steep at the front and looks far too bulbous overall. The mid-upper turret glazing is too flat for an F.N.50, looking more like a Martin version. The tail turret is too narrow and there are no slots in the glazings for the guns (just holes in the clear section). The nose turret is too shallow and the wrong shape. The strengthening strip along the fuselage side looks far too big in this scale.

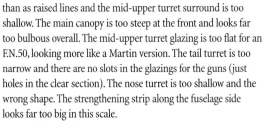

Accuracy wise, this kit has a span of 209mm and a length of 142mm. This equates in 'scale' terms to a span of 98ft 8in and a length of 67ft 2in, making the model 3ft 4in (7mm) short in span and 1ft 8in (3.5mm) short in length. These may seem small amounts, but in this small scale it makes the overall model well under-scale.

### Verdict
As is so often the case, this model is your only option in this scale: until someone else comes up with a better one.

## 1/96th scale Lancaster B Mk I

### B Mk I
This kit (#F359) was released in 1959 and is no longer available. It was also issued under the Novo label.

The decal options in the example we had are;
- 1. VN•N, R5689.

The instructions give no details of the squadron with which this aircraft operated, but it was No. 50 Squadron.

This is a real old kit, and it shows. The odd size is due to the fact that there were no real 'standard' sizes at the time it was released, and this scale had been in common use by Frog for many years for its bigger-sized kit subjects. The kit features recessed panel lines and no rivets. The propellers are far too narrow and the upper wing roundel locations are engraved into the wing panel (not uncommon for a kit of this vintage). There are no trim tabs on the rudders and there is no cockpit interior what-so-ever. The canopy does not feature any side bulges (due to the complex mould this would require) although strangely their existence is represented with engraved lines on the canopy itself. The mid-upper turret is the wrong shape, being flat like a Martin version. The nose turret does not feature slots for the guns, instead it has holes for each barrel. The nose blister is far too shallow for even an early version.

Dimensionally this model has a span of 324mm and a length of 221mm. This equates to a 102ft span and a length of 69ft 4in in 'scale' terms. This makes the model spot on in span and just 6in (less than 1.5mm) short in length, which is good enough in anyone's books. Not bad for a 41 year old kit!

### Verdict
An odd scale, and a basic model make this kit in its later 'non-collectable' form little more than a curio, and unless you want to add one in its original form to your Frog kit collection, I would leave this one for the kids to play with.

## 1/72nd scale Lancaster B Mk I (first mould)

### B Mk I
This kit (#5001) was originally issued in 1958 and was replaced in 1979 with the new mould for the B Mk I/III reviewed elsewhere. This original version is no longer available.

The decal options in the example we had were;
- 1. PR•G, W4783, 'G-George', No. 460 Squadron (RAAF), RAF Binbrook, May 1944.

This kit features the best bit of box art I can recall. I remember making this kit when I was eight, and at that time the model was well outside my pocket money budget. I got it as a present and spent ages just looking at the box - stunning! Inside you will find a typical 1950s kit, in that it is very basic. Cockpit interior consists of just a basic floor, a poor representation of the pilot's seat and some very basic crew figures. The propellers represent the narrow blade type, but still seem a bit too narrow. The mid-upper turret glazing is too big and is the wrong shape for an F.N.50 or a Martin 250. All of the fuselage windows are cut out, so check your references as some options will require some, or all, of these to be filled. The kit features the early style bomb aimer's glazing and the main canopy looks odd. The front section of the canopy seems to have too steep a windscreen and the side blisters are supplied as separate parts, therefore making for a very difficult couple of join lines to hide.

Dimensionally this model measures out at a span of 432mm and a length of 293mm. This is 102ft and 69ft in 'scale' terms, making the model accurate in span and just 6in (2mm) short in length.

### Verdict

For its day it was 'the' model to have and as one of the earliest Lancaster kits produced in injection moulded plastic is deserves a place in the history books. If you want to make a Lancaster you would be better off going for the later Airfix examples, and keeping this one as a collectors piece.

## 1/72nd scale Lancaster B Mk I/III (new mould)

### B Mk I/III

This kit was released in 1979 and replaced the original 1958 version. It is currently (2000) available

The current version (#08002) offers the following colour options;

- 1. PM•M2, ED888, No. 103 Squadron.
- 2. HW•A, ND458, 'Able Mabel', No. 100 Squadron.
- 3. WS•J, 'Johnny Walker' (originally a No. 9 Squadron machine) as applied to PA474, BBMF, RAF Coningsby, 1995.
- 4. PM•M2 (ex-ED888, No. 103 Squadron) as applied to PA474, BBMF, RAF Coningsby.

When this kit arrived back in 1979 it was hailed as the best kit of the Lancaster thus far produced. To date no-one else has produced another example, so it still holds the top honours. The kit is moulded in grey plastic with raised panel lines and rivets. The entire cockpit floor/bomb bay roof is included, although detail inside the cockpit area is very limited.

There are the pilot's seat and control column, as well as decals for the instrument panel and Flight Engineer's panel, but the whole interior could do with updating. The kit features the early-style shallow nose blister, as well as narrow propellers and this may explain why the box says 'B Mk I', while the instructions state 'B Mk III'. Once again, due to mould limitations, the side blisters on the main canopy are separate items, but there is the DF loop included inside the cockpit area. Twin downward identification lights are included in the port lower wing panel and a clear H2S radome is also included. In this standard bomber version you get a nice 4000lb 'Cookie', as well as a number of standard (albeit not very convincing) bombs and the Cookie even has all its stencils supplied as decals.

The model measures out (according to Airfix) at 432mm span and 293mm length. In 'scale' that equates to a span of 102ft and a length of 69ft, making this model once again accurate in span and 6in (2mm) short in length.

### Verdict

Really the only horse in town. To be truthful the raised panel lines and rivets are a pain, as the fit of the parts is not that good and when you sand away all the filler, you will also lose all the surface detail. It has been twenty-one years since this kit's release, so hopefully we will get a 'new' example from someone else before too much longer. In the meantime this is the basis for just about every commercial conversion set currently available in 1/72nd scale.

## 1/72nd scale Lancaster B Mk III (Special)

### B Mk III 'Dambuster'

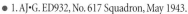

This kit was released in 1993, and is a modified version of the standard B Mk I/III kit. It is currently (2000) available.

The current version (#08004) offers the following colour options;

- 1. AJ•G. ED932, No. 617 Squadron, May 1943.
- 2. AJ•S, ED912, No. 617 Squadron, May 1943.

This kit is identical to the standard B Mk I/III reviewed previously and the only difference is the inclusion of an additional sprue in white plastic with all the necessary Upkeep components. The mould has been modified with an 'insert' to blank off the mid-upper turret location, the only problem being that the raised panel lines and rivets in this area don't match those on the surrounding fuselage! The Upkeep mine is shown with the wooden 'shuttering' fitted and the revised bomb bay area comes with separate struts and pulley and belt assemblies. The kit does not include the ventral gun fitted to these machines, nor does it make any mention of the two lights specially installed under the type for the Dams Raid in May 1943.

The model measures out (according to Airfix) at 432mm span and 291mm length. This is odd, as this is not the same as the standard kit, ever though the moulds are identical! In 'scale' that equates to a span of 102ft and a length of 68ft 4in, making this model once again accurate in span and 1ft 6in (6mm) short in length. I must admit when I measured the model I built, I agree with the previous 293mm, making the model just 6in (3mm) short, which is as accurate as you are going to get in this scale.

### Verdict

Based as it is on the 'best' 1/72nd scale Lancaster, this version is certainly better than the old Revell one, but still lacks the overall detail we would all like to see in a Lancaster kit in this scale.

## 1/72nd scale Lancaster B Mk I

### B Mk I

This kit was released in 1976, but is no longer available.

The decal options in the example we had were;

- 1. KC•B of No. 617 Squadron, 1945.
- 2. WS•Y of No. 9 Squadron, 1945.

The most important element of this kit is that it includes the bulged bomb doors and Tallboy bomb, unlike the Matchbox kit that includes the doors but no bomb. All panel lines are raised and the kit features only basic interior detail. The modeller will have to add the instrument panel and throttle box, plus the armour plate behind the pilot's seat and the Flight Engineer's folding seat.

Inaccuracies include the mid-upper turret, which does not show the distinctive 'bulbous' shape of the F.N.50 fitted in that position. The tailwheel needs modification to correctly depict the later 'Marstrand' anti-shimmy tyre fitted. The main wheels also need a bit of filler, as most examples seem to have large sink marks. The kit also features an odd anomaly, as the inner engine nacelles feature raised panel lines, while the outer ones are totally devoid of any panel lines at all!

### Verdict
Today one of these kits will set you back as much as £25, over fourteen times its original release price, as it is prized more as a collector's piece than a model. It is still worth considering though, as most kits plus conversion to make a Tallboy version would cost this much, so if you can find one, it is well worth having.

## 1/72nd scale Lancaster B Mk I

### B Mk I
This kit was first issued by Revell in the early 1960s and surprisingly, it is still (2000) available.

The current version (#04328) offers the following colour options;
- 1. PG•J, LM378, No. 619 Squadron, RAF Dunholme Lodge, April 1944.
- 2. CA•R, EE136, 'Spirit of Russia', No. 189 Squadron, RAF Fulbeck, December 1944.

Note: Both of these options are for B Mk IIIs!

This kit is currently (2000) moulded in a disgusting brown colour, and the age of the moulds is evident. The panel lines are surprisingly engraved (not bad for a kit of the 1960s), and all the rivets are raised. The kit features a wealth of 'moveable' parts, which was the vogue of the era, and these include the bomb doors, flaps, gun turrets and control surfaces, all of which compromise the accuracy. The bomb bay itself includes representations of the bomb load moulded very unconvincingly in half-relief. The crew figures included are very poor mouldings and the flight crew are depicted holding fighter-style control columns. The cockpit interior consists of just the floor and seat, neither of which is very convincing. The propeller blades are the narrow type, so once again references must be sought to see if these are correct for the colour options offered. All the fuselage windows are just moulded as recesses, and although this is fine for the rear ones (as many of these were painted out anyway), the ones by the radio operator's and bomb aimer's stations will need to be opened up. The canopy features no side blisters, and this omission is almost certainly due to the complexity of mould required to achieve it. The mid-upper turret is the wrong shape, being too 'tall' and cylindrical. The fairing around it is separate, which is good, and as this kit was later released in Dambuster form, it also features a blanking plate to cover the ventral gun turret position. The cross-section of each of the engines nacelles is too wide also, making each unit look too 'squat'.

Revell state that this model has a span of 440mm and a length of 242mm. That gives the model a 'scale' span of 104ft and a length of 57ft 4in. As you can see that makes the span 2ft (8mm) too long and the length some 12ft 2in (51mm) short! If their claimed dimensions are correct, this one is very inaccurate.

### Verdict
Very much a 'blast from the past', this one. Certainly surpassed by more recent kits, but still a popular kit as Revell® seem to keep on reissuing it. It has both good and bad parts, but to be truthful, the age of the mouldings means this one doesn't deserve the amount of input required to make it presentable.

## 1/72nd scale Lancaster 'Dambuster'

### 'Dambuster'
This kit was first issued by Revell in 1964, but at the time of writing (2000) it has not been seen for many years.

This kit (#H-202) offered the following colour option;
- 1. AJ•G, ED932/G, No. 617 Squadron, May 1943.

This kit is based on the Mk I mould, as reviewed previously and all the comments made for that kit apply here also. This version does feature a blanking plate for the mid-upper turret, as well as a revised bomb bay area and Upkeep mine. The Upkeep mine is moulded without the 'shuttered' exterior seen in the more recent Airfix example, but it does feature the pulleys without a moulded belt, so this can be added with fine wire thereby being far more 'in-scale'. The kit also makes use of the ventral gun location, with a fully rotating gun plate and two barrels.

As far as the scale accuracy of this kit goes, it is the same as the previous B Mk I version reviewed, so not very good!

### Verdict
Once again this kit is now just a curio, and one that deserves a place in any kit collection, but has been surpassed by the recent Airfix example if you want to build one.

## 1/72nd scale Lancaster B Mk I/III

### B Mk I/III
This kit (#PK-602) was released in 1980, but at the time of writing (2000) it is not currently available.

The decal options in the example we had were;
- 1. WS•J, NG266, 'Jane' of No. 9 Squadron, Bardney, 1944
- 2. ZN•A, RS677, 'Admiral Chattanoga' of No. 106 Squadron, RAF Coningsby, September 1942.
- 3. A66-1 based at RAAF Tocoumwal, NSW, 1945.

This kit has not been around for many years now, and at the time of writing this book (2000) it is still a 'collectors kit'. The annoying thing about the kit is that although the Tallboy markings and bulged bomb bay doors are included, the bomb itself is not! Panel lines are engraved, although in true Matchbox style they are a little overdone. The cockpit interior features just a section of the floor and the pilot's seat is the wrong shape. Like the Airfix kit, the mid-upper turret glazing is split vertically and the resulting join is very hard to hide. The good thing about the mid-upper gun position is that the fairing around it is a separate part, which is very helpful when using this kit as the basis of a conversion. The odd thing is that the nose is separate. Whether Matchbox were looking at producing some other variants (Lancastrian?) or they just ran out of mould space, we will never know. The join is a bit of a bind

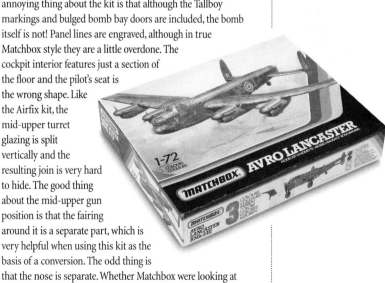

though and difficult to cover. The ventral radome is a separate part, which is good, but is not moulded in clear plastic, which is bad. Only paddle blade propellers are included, so check your references if building any other colour options using this kit. The control linkage on the control surfaces are moulded as simple wedges and could be refined. The kit also features inserts at the leading edge of the wing for each engine nacelle. Once again this results in a complex joint, but were Matchbox thinking of doing a radial powered Mk II? The final point with this kit is that the bulged side blisters on the canopy are supplied separately, and these will result in some unsightly joins, but they are unavoidable without complex multi-part moulds.

The decal sheet is up to the usual standards of the day, but it does include a full set of stencils.

### Verdict

One of my favourites to be truthful. I recall making this kit about five times as a kid, and I never even noticed that the Tallboy was missing (who would when they were eight!). The kit is currently (2000) unavailable, and is likely to remain so as the current holders of the licence to use the Matchbox tools (Revell®) will lose it at the end of 2000.

## 1/48th scale Lancaster B Mk I/III

### B Mk I/III

This kit was originally released by Tamiya in 1976. It has been available on and off over the years, but as of early 2000 when this title was written, it was not readily available.

The decal options in the example we had were;
- 1. B Mk I, PO•S, R5868, No. 467 Squadron
- 2. B Mk III, XH•L, ME545, 'Lovely Lou', C Flight, No. 218 Squadron.
- 3. B Mk I, ZN•Y, W4118, 'Admiral Prune', No. 106 Squadron, RAF Syerston.

Still the only 1/48th scale Lancaster kit ever produced this kit features raised panel lines and rivets. The interior, although well detailed with flight deck and even the 1154/1155 radio combination at the radio operator's station, is still a bit basic considering the size of the model. The gun turrets are well detailed and even the mid-upper one, which often perplexes mould makers, is split horizontally and thereby has the resulting joint hidden. The bomb bay features a Cookie as well as a mixed bag of bombs and the kit even includes two Merlin engines. These are pretty basic in this scale and need a lot of work done to them. All the control horns are moulded separately and the H2S radome is in clear plastic. Both plain and bulged side panels for the main canopy are included, which is a neat touch. Separate tip lights are also included, but the big drawback with this kit is that the early (shallow) style nose glazing is the only part included. For B Mk Is this is fine, but most B Mk IIIs (and it was retro-fitted into B Mk Is) had the later, deeper, style. The propeller blades are the later paddle type and the main wheels feature a checked tread.

### Verdict

'The' kit to have for this scale. With the excellent accessory sets from Flightpath this kit can be made into a highly detailed model.

Being the only one in its scale, it is also the basis of all Lancaster conversions, including those to Manchester and Lincoln. If you see one (or more) on the shelf, buy it, you will not regret it.

## 1/48th scale Lancaster B Mk I/III (Special)

### B Mk I/III 'Special'

This kit was originally released by Tamiya in 1976, and is a modified version of the standard B Mk I/III. Once again, at the time of writing (2000), this kit is not readily available.

The decal options in the example we had were;
- 1. B Mk I (Special), YZ•P, PD133, No. 617 Squadron, RAF Woodhall Spa.
- 2. B Mk I (Special), YZ•S, PD112, No. 617 Squadron, RAF Woodhall Spa.
- 3. B Mk III (Special), AJ•G, ED932/G, flown by Wg Cdr G. Gibson, No. 617 Squadron, May 1943.
- 4. B Mk III (Special), AJ•P, ED909/G, flown by Flt Lt H.B. Martin, No. 617 Squadron, May 1943.
- 5. B Mk III (Special), AJ•T, ED923/G, flown by Flt Lt J.C. McCarthy, No. 617 Squadron, May 1943.
- 6. B Mk III (Special), AJ•Y, ED924/G, flown by Flt Sgt L.T. Anderson, No. 617 Squadron, May 1943.
- 7. B Mk III (Special), AJ•L, ED929/G, flown by Flt Lt D.J. Shannon, No. 617 Squadron, May 1943.

This version was also released in 1976 and is basically a slightly revised version of the B Mk I/III reviewed previously. The kit is very similar to the standard bomber version, so all the comments made about that kit apply here also. The only modifications include the revised bomb bay with Upkeep mine for the Dambusters version and a Grand Slam bomb. Blanking covers for the mid-upper and nose turrets are included, the latter for the Dambuster and both for the Grand Slam options. Finally a ventral turret is included for the Dambuster options.

Dimensionally the kit has a span of 648mm which equates exactly to 102ft and a length of 441mm which is 69ft 4in in 'scale' terms. The former dimension is spot on, while the latter is about two scale inches (less than 2mm) short.

The above tells you what is (or isn't) currently available in 1/144th, 1/96th, 1/72nd and scales. Please note that we have deliberately omitted vac-formed kits from this list, as although they may be available at the time of writing, most accessories and conversions covered elsewhere in this title, will be designed for the above-listed injection moulded kits.

Now that we have a starting point it is time to get a better understanding of the actual aircraft, so read on...

---

### Thanks

Our thanks to Humbrol Ltd (Airfix) and Toyway (Minicraft) for supplying samples for use in this section.

# Colour Side-views • 1

Avro Manchester I, L7288/EM•H of Nº 207 Squadron, RAF
Waddington, September 1941. Standard finish of Dark Earth/Dark
Green/Night. Medium Grey codes and Dull Red serial, the latter
partly overpainted by 'M' of code

Avro Manchester I, L7453/EA•T of Nº 49 Squadron, RAF
Scampton, mid-1942. Note wavy dividing line between upper
colours and underside Night, and revised markings in the form of
C1 roundels on fuselage and narrow white portion on fin flash, a
rare combination for a Manchester

Avro Manchester I, L7427/OL•Q of Nº 83 Squadron, RAF
Scampton, March 1942. Medium Grey codes and Dull Red serial.
Note mission tally of ten red bombs on nose. Lost on its 15th
sortie on April 8/9, 1942

Avro Manchester I, L7417/ZN•V of Nº 106 Squadron, RAF
Coningsby, May 1942. Medium Grey codes, Dull Red serial and
late style straight (high) demarcation line between upper colours
and Night. Lost on May 19, 1942 on a cross-country flight

**Scale 1:120**  Colour Art © Richard J. Caruana

Avro Manchester IA, L7319/EM•S of Nº 207 Squadron, RAF
Waddington, March 1942. Medium Grey codes, Dull Red serial

Avro Manchester IA, R5833/OL•N of Nº 83 Squadron (B Flight),
RAF Scampton, April 1942. Mediium Grey codes, Dull Red serial;
note nose art consisting of a yellow moon and white stars.
Scripts reads "AR HYD Y NOS", Welsh for "All through the night"

Avro Manchester IA, L7463/OF•P 'Jill' of Nº 97 Squadron, RAF
Coningsby, November 1941. Mediium Grey codes and Dull Red
serial. Name under cockpit is 'SRI.GAJAH' (Elephant – all aircraft
in this unit had names related to animals and birds). Tally shows
four missions as at November 8, 1941

Avro Lancaster B.I, R5556/KM•C of Nº 44 (Rhodesia) Squadron,
RAF Coningsby, 1942. Early style markings including A1 roundels
and equal-bar fin flashes, together with Medium Grey codes;
serial is Dull Red. Note ventral turret. Later went on to 1661HCU
where it was damaged beyond repair on 13.03.43

**Scale 1:120**   Colour Art © Richard J. Caruana

Avro Lancaster B.III, LM624/DX•A of Nº 57 Squadron, RAF East
Kirby, early 1945. 'A' of code is repeated on nose, just aft of side
window. Fin markings usually covered both outer and inner faces

Avro Lancaster B.I, HK795/TK•B of Nº 149 Squadron (C Flight),
RAF Methwold, March 1945. Yellow H-G bars around fins and 'B'
of code repeated under nose turret. Note bulged bomb bay and
ventral turret

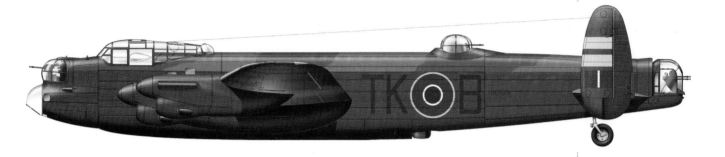

Avro Lancaster B.I, PB817/G, IQ•Q of Nº 150 Squadron, RAF
Hemswell, later 1944. The 'G' suffix to serial denotes that aircraft
was fitted with secret equipment and had to be guarded. Aircraft
survived the war and was stuck off charge on 02.06.47

Avro Lancaster B.I, PD441/PG•B of Nº 619 Squadron, RAF
Strubby, 1945. Aircraft later served with Nº 463 Squadron and
was struck off charge on 02.06.47

**Scale 1:120**   Colour Art © Richard J. Caruana

Avro Lancaster B.I, ME701/JO•F of N° 463 Squadron (RAAF), RAF Skellingthorpe, Summer 1944. 'Whoa Bessie' under cockpit; unusual are the roundel proportions, typical of all aircraft of this unit, and the use of 'milk bottles' for bomb mission tally. This aircraft was badly damaged by flak over Beauvoir on 29.06.44 and deemed beyond repair

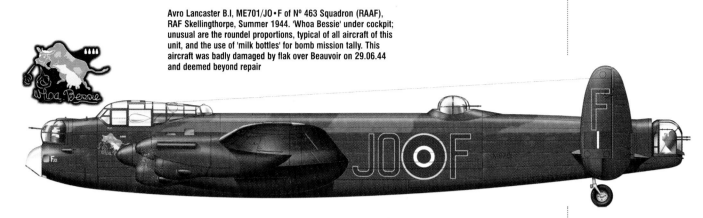

Avro Lancaster B.I, ME499/AS•D of N° 166 Squadron, RAF Kirmington, Spring 1945. High-visibility 'Daylight' markings consisting of yellow wingtips, fins and rudders on this particular Lancaster, though these varied from aircraft to aircraft

Avro Lancaster B.X, KB772/VR•R of N° 419 (Moose) Squadron (RCAF), RAF Middleton St. George, mid-1944. 'Ropey' is shown at the time it had 66 missions marked under its cockpit. Note 'sharkmouth' decoration on all four engines. It was transferred to Canada with a number of others of 419 Squadron's Lancs in June 1945

Avro Lancaster B.III, EE176/QR•M of N° 61 Squadron, RAF Skellingthorpe, Summer 1944. 'Mickey the Moocher' is shown with 83 mission marks on the nose, although it eventually went on to perform a total of 128 operations, after which it became a ground instructional airframe (5260M) in May 1945

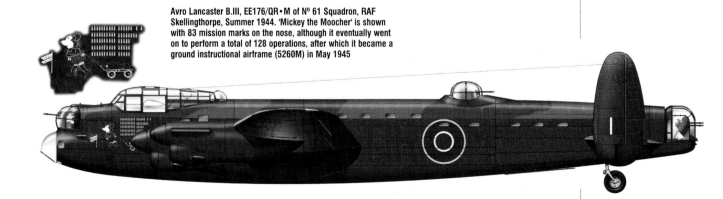

Scale 1:120   Colour Art © Richard J. Caruana

Avro Lancaster B.III, ED623/UM • M² 'Ali Oop', Nº 626 Squadron,
RAF Wickenby, April 1944. Note early shallow bomb aimer's
nose blister. This aircraft later moved to Nº 101 Squadron and
then various conversion units until struck off charge on 04.10.46

Avro Lancaster B.I (F.E.), TW657/TL • C of Nº 35 Squadron, based
at Graveley, as painted for a US Tour in 1946

Avro Lancaster B.III, ED539/PO • V of Nº 467 Squadron, RAF
Bottesford, Summer 1943. Note the Kookaburra within the 'V' on
the nose has Hitler's head dangling from its beak. Missing over
Berlin on 28.01.44

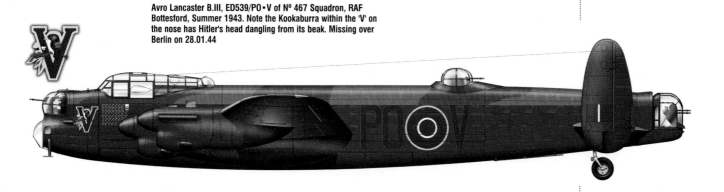

Avro Lancaster B.III, ED905/BQ • F 'Press on Regardless', of Nº
550 Squadron, RAF Waltham, late 1944. It is shown as it
appeared on its 100th mission of November 4, 1944. Note unusual
proportion of white area in both fuselage roundel and fin flash

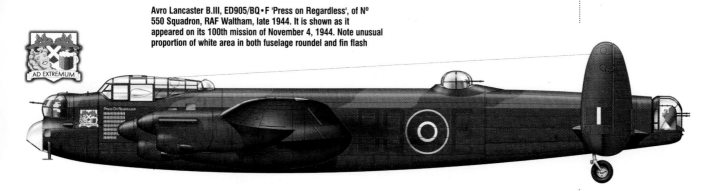

Scale 1:120   Colour Art © Richard J. Caruana

Avro Lancaster B.II, LL670/J9•P of 1668 Heavy Conversion Unit, Bottesford, early 1945. Aircraft shows signs of previous ownership by Nº 115 and 514 Squadrons, mainly in faint G-H marks on fin and sortie tally under the cockpit. Note deepened bomb-bay and overpainted rear fuselage windows. Struck off Charge on 08.02.45

Avro Lancaster B.II, DS626/KO•J of Nº 115 Squadron. East Wretham, March 1943. Note shallow-type bomb-aimer's perspex fairing and personal marking (designed by the mid-upper turret gunner, Flt Sgt W.B. Baker) ahead of cockpit. Struck off charge on 20.03.45 after having served also with Nos. 426, 408 squadrons and 1668 HCU

Avro Lancaster B.II, DS604/QR•W of Nº 61 Squadron, RAF Syerston, January 1943. It appears to wear a non-standard upper Dark Earth and Dark Green pattern in parts, probably due to local retouching. Note no spinners, and shallow bomb-aimer's perspex nose fairing

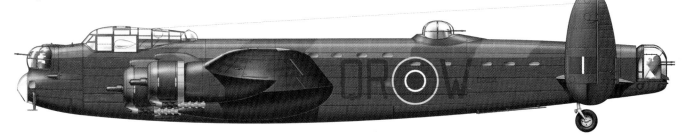

Avro Lancaster B.I, 1803, of the Royal Egyptian Air Force, 1952. Medium Sea Grey upper surfaces, Night undersides. Note Avro's logo under the fin flash

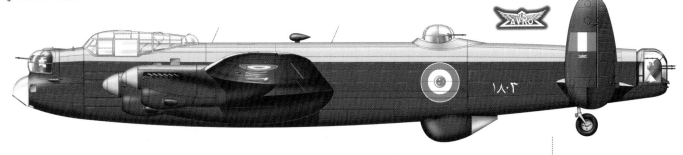

**Scale 1:120** Colour Art © Richard J. Caruana

# Colour Side-views • 7

Avro Lancaster 10MR, FM104/CX•104, of Nº 107 Rescue Unit, Royal Canadian Air Force, Torbay (Newfoundland). This is the early Rescue scheme for Canadian Lancasters: natural metal upper fuselage, fin and rudder and front section of engine cowlings; rest of airframe is Gloss Light Grey. Wingtips (upper and lower) are red except for ailerons; also red are upper and lower fixed surfaces of horizontal tailplane while the movable section is Gloss Light Grey

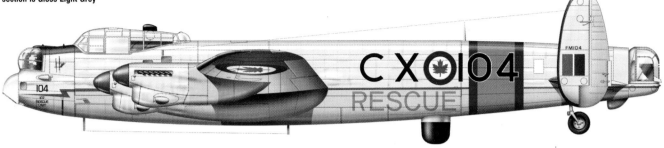

Avro Lancaster MR.1, WU27, of Flottilla 9S 'Noumea' French Aéronavale, New Caledonia, 1963. Unit badge is carried on both sides of fuselage front. This is ex-B.I (Armstrong-Whitworth-built) TW651, one of the few of this mark to be converted for MR duties in October 1952

Avro Lancaster MR.7, 105/Q of the French Secrétariat Géneral a l'Aviation Civile et Commerciale, North Africa, 1959. This aircraft was originally a B.VII (RT679) built by Austin Motors and delivered to France as FCL-05. Note extended lower rudder

Avro Lancaster MR.3, RF325/H•D of the School of Maritime Reconnaissance, RAF St Mawgan, 1956. Gloss Dark Sea Grey overall finish which was eventually adopted for the Shackleton. Note code on starboard side reads H-D; unit badge on both sides

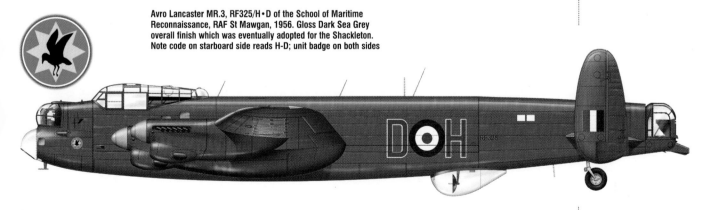

Scale 1:120  Colour Art © Richard J. Caruana

Avro Lancaster B.III, JA845/F•CXT, of the Empire Central Flying School, Autumn 1945. Faintly visible is the bomb log of its previous service with Nº 106 Squadron; aircraft was struck off charge on 21.10.47. Badge on both sides of the nose; code on starboard side reads: CXT-F

Avro Lancaster B.VI (converted from B.III), ND673/F2•V of Nº 635 Squadron, RAF Downham Market, late 1944. Note lack of spinners, quite often removed from Lancasters fitted with Merlin 28s in cylindrical cowlins such as this; also faired over (and painted) nose turret position, while although mid-upper turret has been removed and faired over, the patch appears to be unpainted

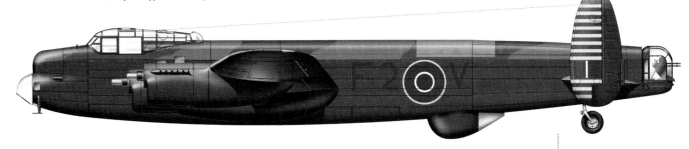

Avro Lancaster B.III (Special), ED912/AJ•S of Nº 617 Squadron, RAF Coningsby, December 1943. One of the B.IIIs converted to carry the Dam Buster's bomb, it flew on the memorable raid of May 16, 1943 with the individual letter 'N', piloted by Flt Lt L.G. Knight. It is shown here after its identity was changed to 'S' in November 1943. The Barnes Wallis bomb mechanism was still in place at that time

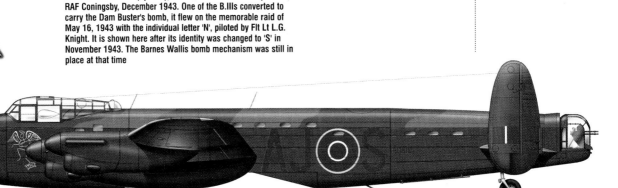

Avro Lancaster B.I (Special), PD121/YZ•Z of Nº 617 Squadron, RAF Woodhall Spa, March 1945 carrying the 22,000lb Grand Slam bomb. Finish is Light Earth/Light Green/Ocean Grey with yellow codes outlined in red, red serial and yellow 'Z' on nose. The code is repeated above and below fixed section of the horizontal tail surfaces (see plan views page). Bomb is light grey green with black front section

**Scale 1:120**  Colour Art © Richard J. Caruana

Avro Lancaster B.I (Special), PD131/LS•V of Nº 15 Squadron, during Operation Front Line, 1946. Serial is repeated in white under the wings, reading from leading edge under port, and from trailing edge under starboard

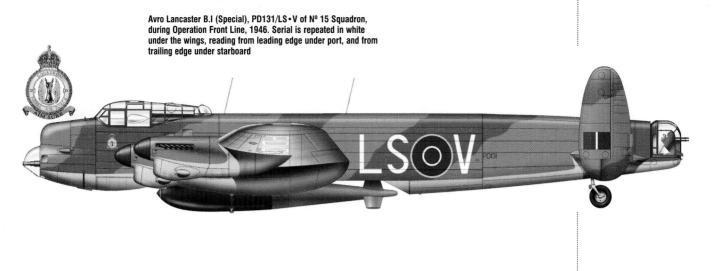

Avro Lincoln B.II, RF507/KC•O, of Nº 617 Squadron, during a tour of the USA in 1947. 'B' roundels above wings

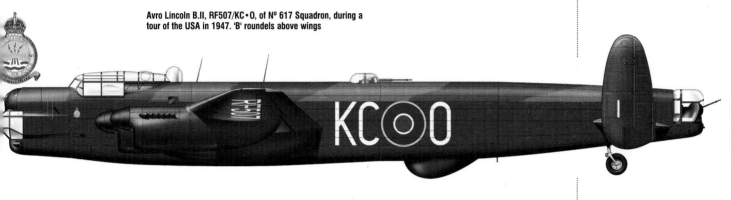

Avro Lincoln B.II, RE386/DX•Y of Nº 57 Squadron. Upper wing roundels are type 'C'

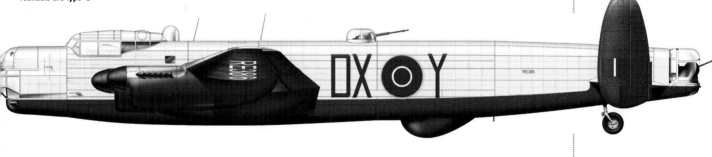

Avro Lincoln B.II, RF424/SR•F of Nº 101 Squadron, RAF Binbrook, 1950. Stripes on fin indicate Binbrook formation leader for King's Birthday mass flypast. 'C' roundels above wings

**Scale 1:120**  Colour Art © Richard J. Caruana

Avro Lincoln B.II, RF562/SN•N of Nº 230 OCU, July 1950. Badge on nose surmounted by 'N' in white

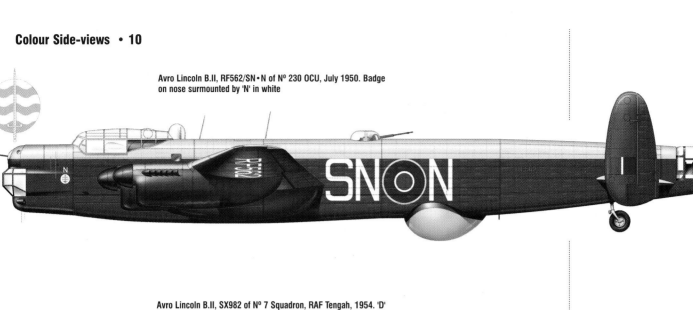

Avro Lincoln B.II, SX982 of Nº 7 Squadron, RAF Tengah, 1954. 'D' type roundels on fuselage sides and above wings. Note command pennant under cockpit; blue spinners identified Nº 7 Squadron

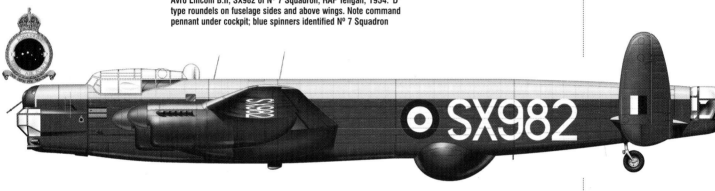

Avro Lincoln B.30, A73-36 of Nº 1 Squadron, Royal Australian Air Force, July 1958. Aircraft carries an impressive tally of 157 strikes under the cockpit, aft of the unit's badge. Note '36' repeated on nose under glazed bomb aimer's position. 'Kangaroo' roundels are carried on the fuselage sides only, wing roundels (upper and lower) being standard post-war 'D' Type

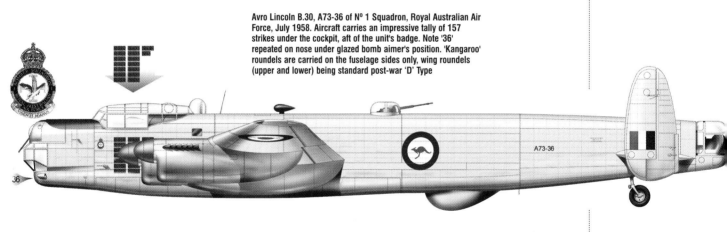

Avro Lincoln (B.II standard less radar), B-022 of the Fuerza Aerea Argentina. This was one of 18 Lincolns specially built for Argentina by Armstrong Witworth. Standard Medium Grey/Black scheme. Code repeated in white under port wing and above starboard wing; roundels carried under starboard wing and above port wing only. Unlike RAF practice, fin flashes were carried on the outside face only

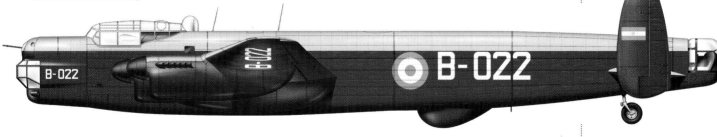

**Scale 1:120**  Colour Art © Richard J. Caruana

# Cockpit Interior Artwork • 1

**Key to illustration**

- 1 ASI Correction Card Holder
- 2 Blind Approach Visual Indicator
- 3 Blind Flying Panel
- 4 Watch Holder
- 5 Fire Extinguisher Push Buttons
- 6 Clock
- 7 Main Magneto Switches
- 8 Undercarriage Position Indicator Switch

- 9 Steering Indicator
- 10 Flap Position Indicator
- 11 Boost Gauge (2)
- 12 RPM Indicator (2)
- 13 Engine Starter Push-button (2)
- 14 Suction Gauge
- 15 Vacuum Pump Change-over Control Cock
- 16 Air Temperature Gauge
- 17 Propeller Feathering Controls
- 18 Bomb Jettison Control
- 19 Container Jettison Push-button
- 20 Bomb Release Master Switch
- 21 Undercarriage Position Indicator
- 22 Hydraulic Brake Pressure Gauge
- 23 Signalling Switch Box (Identification Lamps)
- 24 Two-speed Supercharger Control Lever
- 25 Fuel Cock Control Lever (2)
- 26 Mixture Control
- 27 Throttle Lever (2)
- 28 Propeller Speed Control Lever (2)
- 29 Landing Lamp Dimmer Lever
- 30 Fuel Jettison Lever
- 31 Landing Lamp Switch
- 32 Signalling Switch Box (Formation-keeping Lamps)
- 33 Oxygen Regulator
- 34 P.4 Compass Deviation Card Holder

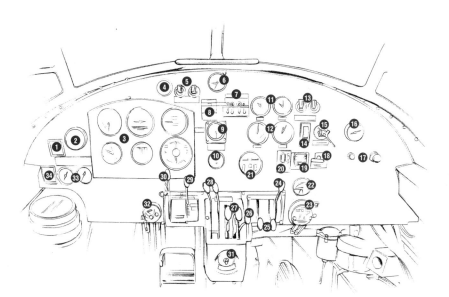

Colour Art © Michele Marsan

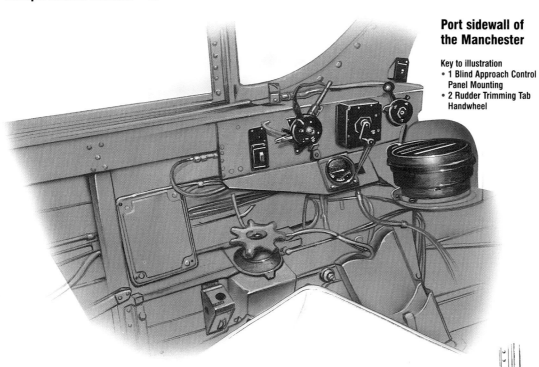

## Port sidewall of the Manchester

Key to illustration
- 1 Blind Approach Control Panel Mounting
- 2 Rudder Trimming Tab Handwheel

- 3 Automatic Pilot Control Main Switch
- 4 Oxygen Socket
- 5 TR.9F Frequency Change Switch
- 6 Automatic Pilot Clutch Lever
- 7 Automatic Pilot Altitude Control
- 8 P.4 Magnetic Compass
- 9 Automatic Pilot Triple Brake Pressure
- 10 Map Case & Course & Height Indicator Stowage
- 11 Automatic Pilot Control Cock
- 12 Blind Approach Plug Stowage
- 13 Bomb Doors Control Lever

## Starboard sidewall of the Manchester

Key to illustration
- 1 Heating Air Diffuser
- 2 Aldis Signalling Lamp Stowage

- 3 Camera Exposure Indicator Wedge Plate
- 4 Panel for R.3003 Visual Indicator and Switch
- 5 Front Gunner's Parachute Stowage

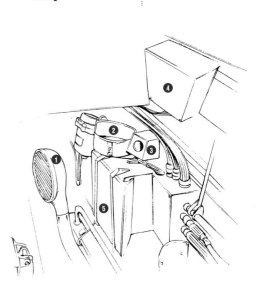

Colour Art © Michele Marsan

## Lancaster Instrument panel

### Key to illustration

- 1 Blind Flying Instrument Panel
- 2 DF Indicator
- 3 Landing Lamp Switches
- 4 Undercarriage Indicator Switch

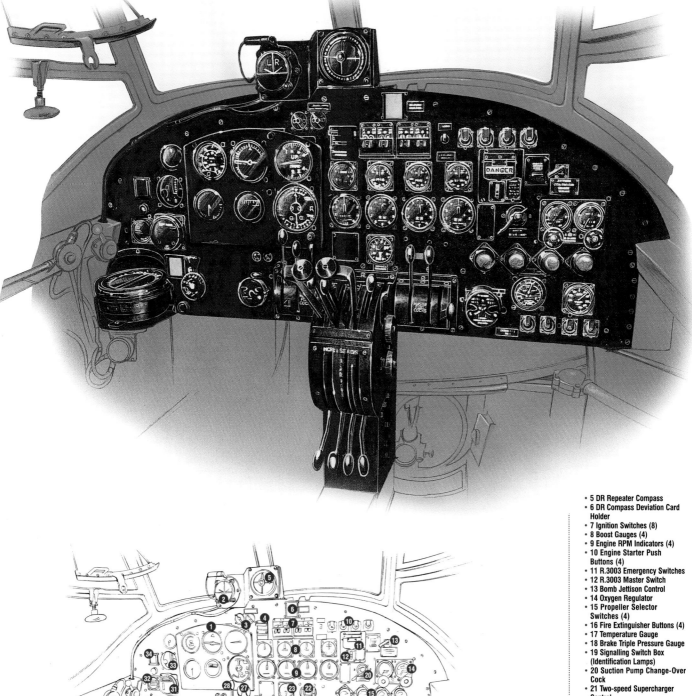

- 5 DR Repeater Compass
- 6 DR Compass Deviation Card Holder
- 7 Ignition Switches (8)
- 8 Boost Gauges (4)
- 9 Engine RPM Indicators (4)
- 10 Engine Starter Push Buttons (4)
- 11 R.3003 Emergency Switches
- 12 R.3003 Master Switch
- 13 Bomb Jettison Control
- 14 Oxygen Regulator
- 15 Propeller Selector Switches (4)
- 16 Fire Extinguisher Buttons (4)
- 17 Temperature Gauge
- 18 Brake Triple Pressure Gauge
- 19 Signalling Switch Box (Identification Lamps)
- 20 Suction Pump Change-Over Cock
- 21 Two-speed Supercharger Control
- 22 Starboard Master Engine Cocks (2)
- 23 Clock
- 24 Throttle Levers (4)
- 25 Friction Adjusters
- 26 Propeller Speed Controls (4)
- 27 Port Master Engine Cocks (2)
- 28 Boost Control Cut-Out (Inoperative)
- 29 Signalling Switch Box (Recognition Lamps)
- 30 Compass
- 31 Undercarriage Position Indicator
- 32 Flap Indicator
- 33 Beam Approach Visual Indicator
- 34 ASI Correction Card Holder

Colour Art © Michele Marsan

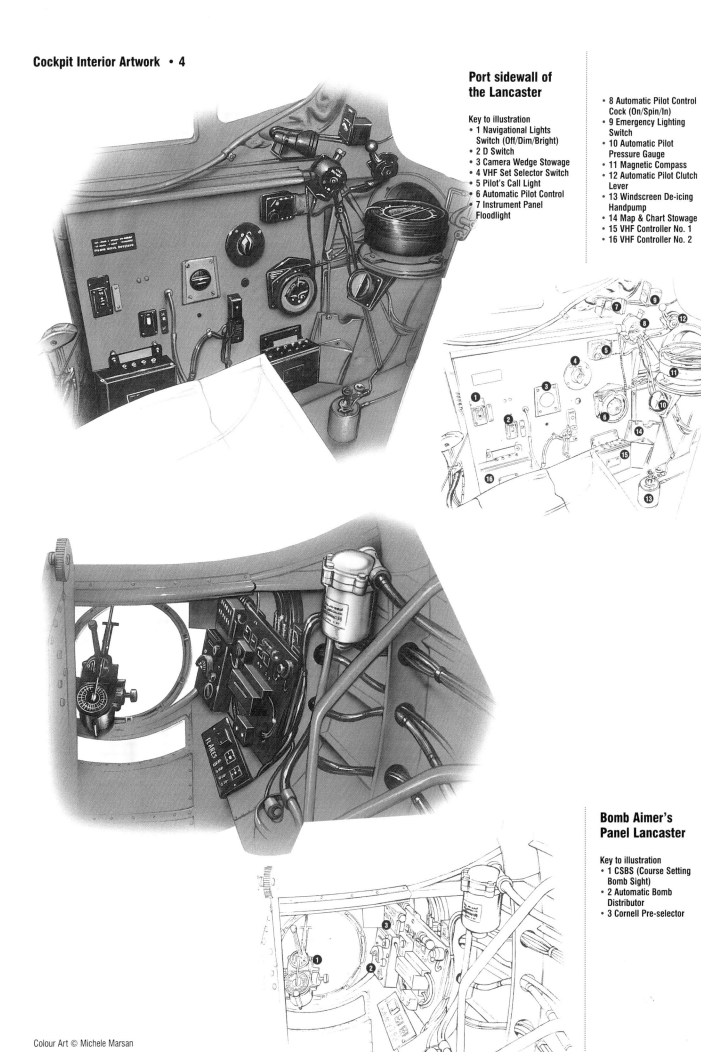

## Port sidewall of the Lancaster

Key to illustration
- 1 Navigational Lights Switch (Off/Dim/Bright)
- 2 D Switch
- 3 Camera Wedge Stowage
- 4 VHF Set Selector Switch
- 5 Pilot's Call Light
- 6 Automatic Pilot Control
- 7 Instrument Panel Floodlight

- 8 Automatic Pilot Control Cock (On/Spin/In)
- 9 Emergency Lighting Switch
- 10 Automatic Pilot Pressure Gauge
- 11 Magnetic Compass
- 12 Automatic Pilot Clutch Lever
- 13 Windscreen De-icing Handpump
- 14 Map & Chart Stowage
- 15 VHF Controller No. 1
- 16 VHF Controller No. 2

## Bomb Aimer's Panel Lancaster

Key to illustration
- 1 CSBS (Course Setting Bomb Sight)
- 2 Automatic Bomb Distributor
- 3 Cornell Pre-selector

Colour Art © Michele Marsan

# Lincoln
## Instrument panel

### Key to illustration

- 1 ASI Correction Card Holder
- 2 Beam Approach Visual Indicator
- 3 Blind Flying Panel
- 4 P.4 Compass Lamp Switch
- 5 Downward Identification Lamp Colour Selector Switch
- 6 External Lamps Warning Lamp
- 7 External Lamps Master Switch
- 8 Cockpit Lamps Switch
- 9 Navigation Lamps Switch

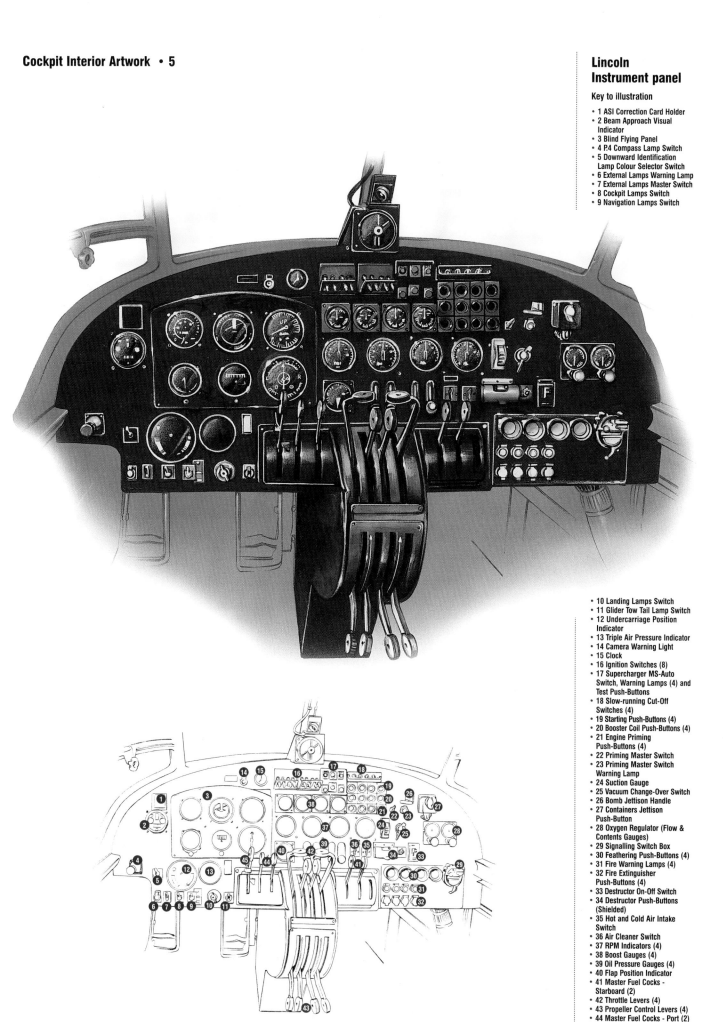

- 10 Landing Lamps Switch
- 11 Glider Tow Tail Lamp Switch
- 12 Undercarriage Position Indicator
- 13 Triple Air Pressure Indicator
- 14 Camera Warning Light
- 15 Clock
- 16 Ignition Switches (8)
- 17 Supercharger MS-Auto Switch, Warning Lamps (4) and Test Push-Buttons
- 18 Slow-running Cut-Off Switches (4)
- 19 Starting Push-Buttons (4)
- 20 Booster Coil Push-Buttons (4)
- 21 Engine Priming Push-Buttons (4)
- 22 Priming Master Switch
- 23 Priming Master Switch Warning Lamp
- 24 Suction Gauge
- 25 Vacuum Change-Over Switch
- 26 Bomb Jettison Handle
- 27 Containers Jettison Push-Button
- 28 Oxygen Regulator (Flow & Contents Gauges)
- 29 Signalling Switch Box
- 30 Feathering Push-Buttons (4)
- 31 Fire Warning Lamps (4)
- 32 Fire Extinguisher Push-Buttons (4)
- 33 Destructor On-Off Switch
- 34 Destructor Push-Buttons (Shielded)
- 35 Hot and Cold Air Intake Switch
- 36 Air Cleaner Switch
- 37 RPM Indicators (4)
- 38 Boost Gauges (4)
- 39 Oil Pressure Gauges (4)
- 40 Flap Position Indicator
- 41 Master Fuel Cocks - Starboard (2)
- 42 Throttle Levers (4)
- 43 Propeller Control Levers (4)
- 44 Master Fuel Cocks - Port (2)
- 45 Boost Cut-Out Control (Merlin 68 Engines Only)

Colour Art © Michele Marsan

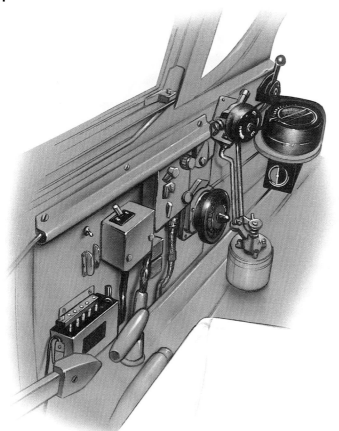

## Port sidewall of the Lincoln

Key to illustration
- 1 Transmitter/Receiver Control
- 2 Bomb Door Lever
- 3 Fuel Jettison Handle
- 4 Mixer Box
- 5 Windscreen De-icing Pump
- 6 Beam Approach Control Unit
- 7 Call Lamp & Push-Button
- 8 Pitch Control
- 9 Automatic Pilot Control Cock
- 10 Automatic Pilot Clutch Lever
- 11 Automatic Pilot Air Pressure and Trim Gauge

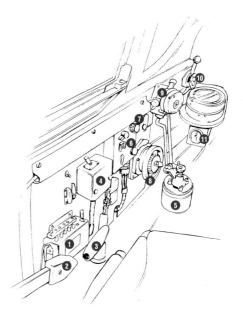

## Starboard sidewall of the Lincoln

Key to illustration
- 1 Radiator Shutter Control Over-Ride Switches (4)
- 2 Elevator Trimming Tab Control Wheel
- 3 Rudder Trimming Tab Control Wheel
- 4 Flaps Control Handle
- 5 Aileron Trimming Tab Control Wheel

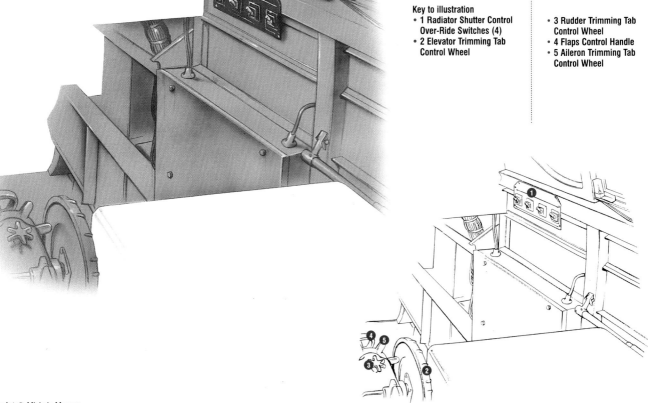

Colour Art © Michele Marsan

# Understanding the Subject

## Chapter 10

I n this chapter we will take a look at each version of the
Manchester, Lancaster and Lincoln, highlighting differences
between each version, as well as giving details of how to
model them in 1/72nd and 1/48th scale.

The following review has been based on a detailed study of
thousands of photographs and close reference to all the official
publications for each type. This has been backed up with the
information carried in a number of the titles listed in Appendix X
of this book, along with many a pleasant hour in and around
preserved examples here in the UK.

We appreciate that there are many areas of these types that

we may highlight in a different manner to that which has been
accepted so far, and we also know that we will still miss things,
so if anyone reading this has points they would like to raise and
has evidence to back them up, we would love to hear from you.
Any reprinted examples of this title in the future can therefore
incorporate any new information that may be brought to light.

NOTE: All items shown are to 1/72nd scale, 1/48th scale is in
brackets ( ). No details of 1/32nd or 1/24th scale models have
been included as, to date, there is no commercially available kit
on which to base a static model in these two scales.

# Manchester

### Prototype
### (1st, L7246)
**Kits: 1/72nd: Airfix Lancaster B Mk I/III & Paragon Conversion (#72050)**
**1/48th: Tamiya Lancaster B Mk I/III & Paragon Conversion (#48127)**

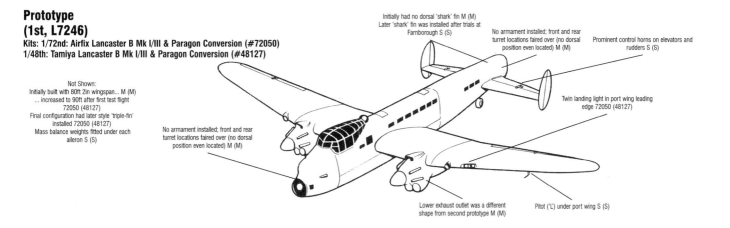

Not Shown:
Initially built with 80ft 2in wingspan... M (M)
... increased to 90ft after first test flight
72050 (48127)
Final configuration had later style 'triple-fin'
installed 72050 (48127)
Mass balance weights fitted under each
aileron S (S)

No armament installed; front and rear
turret locations faired over (no dorsal
position even located) M (M)

Lower exhaust outlet was a different
shape from second prototype M (M)

Initially had no dorsal 'shark' fin M (M)
Later 'shark' fin was installed after trials at
Farnborough S (S)

No armament installed; front and rear
turret locations faired over (no dorsal
position even located) M (M)

Prominent control horns on elevators and
rudders S (S)

Twin landing light in port wing leading
edge 72050 (48127)

Pitot ('L') under port wing S (S)

### (2nd, L7247)
**Kits: 1/72nd: Airfix Lancaster B Mk I/III & Paragon Conversion (#72050)**
**1/48th: Tamiya Lancaster B Mk I/III & Paragon Conversion (#48127)**

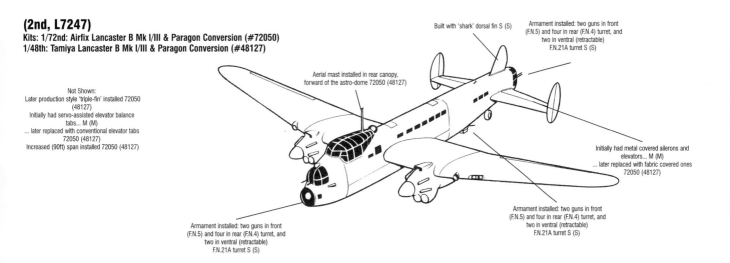

Not Shown:
Later production style 'triple-fin' installed 72050
(48127)
Initially had servo-assisted elevator balance
tabs... M (M)
... later replaced with conventional elevator tabs
72050 (48127)
Increased (90ft) span installed 72050 (48127)

Armament installed: two guns in front
(F.N.5) and four in rear (F.N.4) turret, and
two in ventral (retractable)
F.N.21A turret S (S)

Aerial mast installed in rear canopy,
forward of the astro-dome 72050 (48127)

Built with 'shark' dorsal fin S (S)

Armament installed: two guns in front
(F.N.5) and four in rear (F.N.4) turret, and
two in ventral (retractable)
F.N.21A turret S (S)

Initially had metal covered ailerons and
elevators... M (M)
... later replaced with fabric covered ones
72050 (48127)

Armament installed: two guns in front
(F.N.5) and four in rear (F.N.4) turret, and
two in ventral (retractable)
F.N.21A turret S (S)

## Mk I (Initial Production Qty 20)
Kits: 1/72nd: Airfix Lancaster B Mk I/III & Paragon Conversion (#72050)
1/48th: Tamiya Lancaster B Mk I/III & Paragon Conversion (#48127)

Not Shown:
Initial machines had ventral F.N.21A turret...
S (S)
First ten airframes had 'flat' bomb doors,
as per the prototypes M (M)

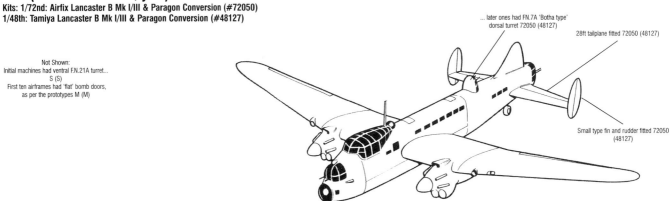

... later ones had FN.7A 'Botha type'
dorsal turret 72050 (48127)

28ft tailplane fitted 72050 (48127)

Small type fin and rudder fitted 72050
(48127)

## Mk Ia (21st & subsequent)
Kits: 1/72nd: Airfix Lancaster B Mk I/III & Paragon Conversion (#72050)
1/48th: Tamiya Lancaster B Mk I/III & Paragon Conversion (#48127)

Not Shown:
For all Mk I/Ia = Initial bomb load was
8x250lb bombs, later modified to carry
4,000lb of bombs

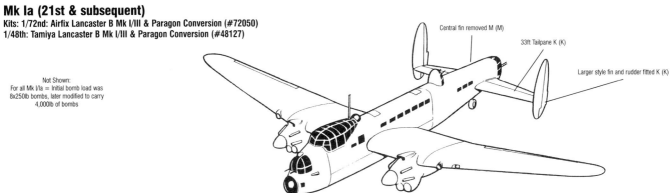

Central fin removed M (M)

33ft Tailpane K (K)

Larger style fin and rudder fitted K (K)

# Lancaster

## Prototype
## (1st BT308)
Kits: 1/72nd: Airfix Lancaster B Mk I/III & Paragon Conversion (#72065)
1/48th: Tamiya Lancaster B Mk I/III & Paragon Conversions (#48140)

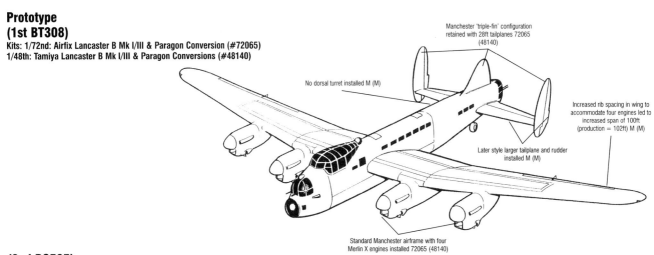

Manchester 'triple-fin' configuration
retained with 28ft tailplanes 72065
(48140)

No dorsal turret installed M (M)

Increased rib spacing in wing to
accommodate four engines led to
increased span of 100ft
(production = 102ft) M (M)

Later style larger tailplane and rudder
installed M (M)

Standard Manchester airframe with four
Merlin X engines installed 72065 (48140)

## (2nd DG595)
Kits: 1/72nd: Airfix Lancaster B Mk I/III
1/48th: Tamiya Lancaster B Mk I/III

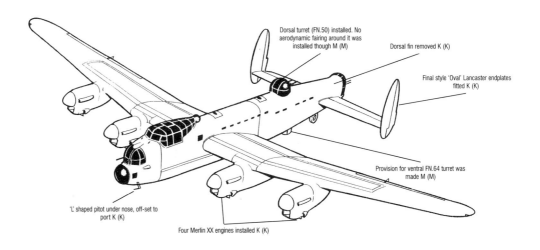

Dorsal turret (FN.50) installed. No
aerodynamic fairing around it was
installed though M (M)

Dorsal fin removed K (K)

Final style 'Oval' Lancaster endplates
fitted K (K)

Provision for ventral FN.64 turret was
made M (M)

'L' shaped pitot under nose, off-set to
port K (K)

Four Merlin XX engines installed K (K)

## Mk I ('B Mk I' from 1942)
**Kits: 1/72nd: Airfix Lancaster B Mk I/III**
**1/48th: Tamiya Lancaster B Mk I/III**

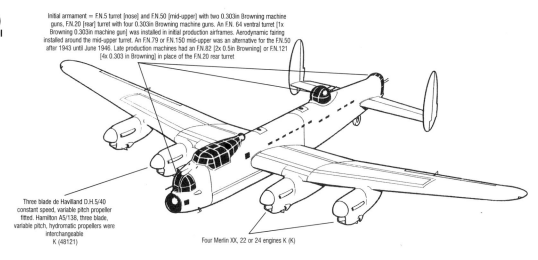

Initial armament = F.N.5 turret [nose] and F.N.50 [mid-upper] with two 0.303in Browning machine guns, F.N.20 [rear] turret with four 0.303in Browning machine guns. An F.N. 64 ventral turret [1x Browning 0.303in machine gun] was installed in initial production airframes. Aerodynamic fairing installed around the mid-upper turret. An F.N.79 or F.N.150 mid-upper was an alternative for the F.N.50 after 1943 until June 1946. Late production machines had an F.N.82 [2x 0.5in Browning] or F.N.121 [4x 0.303 in Browning] in place of the F.N.20 rear turret

Three blade de Havilland D.H.5/40 constant speed, variable pitch propeller fitted. Hamilton A5/138, three blade, variable pitch, hydromatic propellers were interchangeable K (48121)

Four Merlin XX, 22 or 24 engines K (K)

## B Mk I 'Special' (Mod No. 1693 a/c serials; PB592, PB995-998, PD112-139)
**Kits: 1/72nd: Airfix Lancaster B Mk I/III & Paragon**
**conversion 72009 (48123)**
**1/48th: Tamiya Lancaster B Mk I Special**

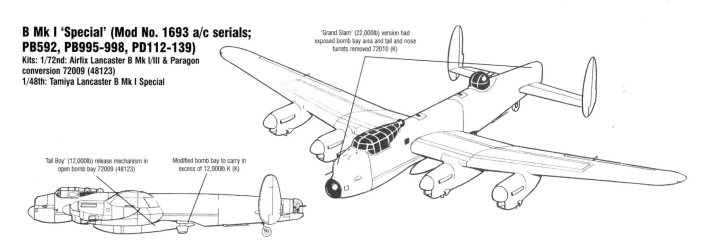

'Grand Slam' (22,000lb) version had exposed bomb bay area and tail and nose turrets removed 72010 (K)

Tall Boy' (12,000lb) release mechanism in open bomb bay 72009 (48123)

Modified bomb bay to carry in excess of 12,000lb K (K)

## 'Saddle Tank'
**Kits:1/72nd: Airfix Lancaster B Mk I/III**
**1/48th: Tamiya Lancaster B Mk I/III**

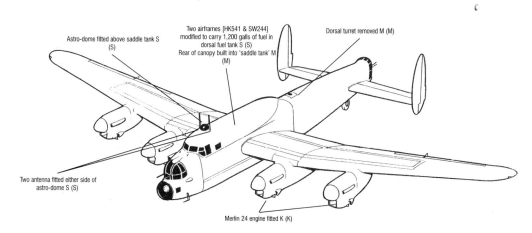

Astro-dome fitted above saddle tank S (S)

Two airframes [HK541 & SW244] modified to carry 1,200 galls of fuel in dorsal fuel tank S (S)
Rear of canopy built into 'saddle tank' M (M)

Dorsal turret removed M (M)

Two antenna fitted either side of astro-dome S (S)

Merlin 24 engine fitted K (K)

## B Mk I (FE): Tropicalised machines for 'Tiger Force'
**Kits: 1/72nd: Airfix Lancaster B Mk I/III**
**1/48th: Tamiya Lancaster B Mk I/III**

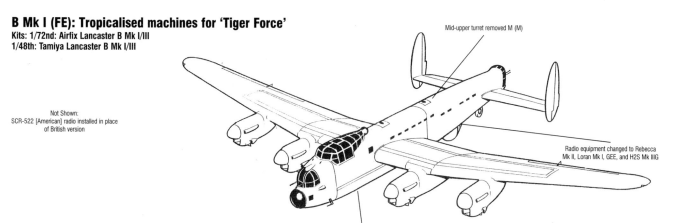

Mid-upper turret removed M (M)

Not Shown:
SCR-522 [American] radio installed in place of British version

Radio equipment changed to Rebecca Mk II, Loran Mk I, GEE, and H2S Mk IIIG

400 gallon tank installed in bomb bay

## B Mk II – Prototype (1st DT810)
**Kits: 1/72nd: Airfix Lancaster B Mk I/III & Paragon Conversion (#72048)**
**1/48th: Tamiya Lancaster B Mk I/III & Paragon Conversion (#48120)**

FN.64 ventral turret [1x 0.303 machine gun] installed 72011/72049 (48125/48126)

Not Shown:
H2S never became standard in the Mk II, so no ventral radome installed M (M)

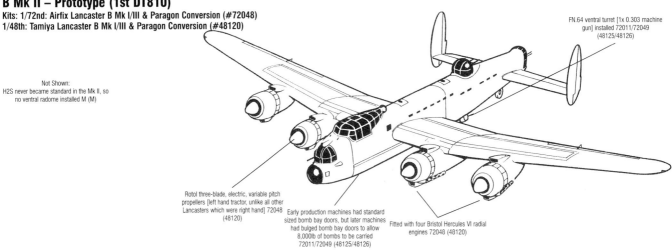

Rotol three-blade, electric, variable pitch propellers [left hand tractor, unlike all other Lancasters which were right hand] 72048 (48120)

Early production machines had standard sized bomb bay doors, but later machines had bulged bomb bay doors to allow 8,000lb of bombs to be carried 72011/72049 (48125/48126)

Fitted with four Bristol Hercules VI radial engines 72048 (48120)

## Production
**Kits: 1/72nd: Airfix Lancaster B Mk I/III & Paragon Conversion (#72048)**
**1/48th: Tamiya Lancaster B Mk I/III & Paragon Conversion (#48120)**
**Note: Same as prototype except:**

Aerial leads from top of each fin to either side of cockpit canopy. Port lead has secondary section going into the astro-dome S (S)

FN.64 ventral turret installed. This led to a pronounced 'step' in the bulged bomb bay door edge because it stopped right behind the ventral turret 72011/72049 (48125/48126)

FN.64 ventral turret installed. This led to a pronounced 'step' in the bulged bomb bay door edge because it stopped right behind the ventral turret 72011/72049 (48125/48126)

Hercules VI or XVI radial engines fitted 72048 (48120)

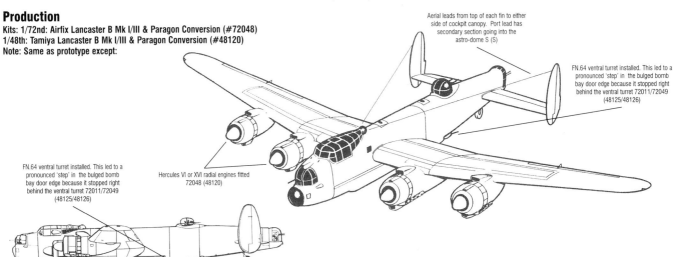

## B Mk III – Prototype – (1st 'Packard-powered' R5849)
**Kits: 1/72nd: Airfix Lancaster B Mk I/III**
**1/48th: Tamiya Lancaster B Mk I/III**

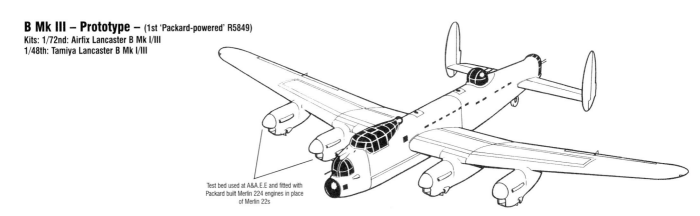

Test bed used at A&A.E.E and fitted with Packard built Merlin 224 engines in place of Merlin 22s

## (1st 'official' W4114)
**Kits: 1/72nd: Airfix Lancaster B Mk I/III**
**1/48th: Tamiya Lancaster B Mk I/III**

Same armament as B Mk I

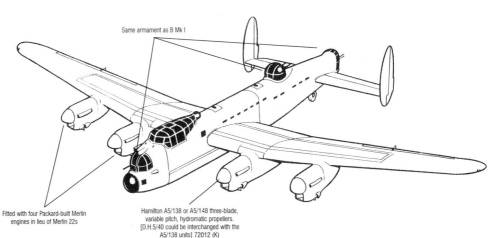

Fitted with four Packard-built Merlin engines in lieu of Merlin 22s

Hamilton A5/138 or A5/148 three-blade, variable pitch, hydromatic propellers. [D.H.5/40 could be interchanged with the A5/138 units] 72012 (K)

## Production

Kits: 1/72nd: Airfix Lancaster B Mk I/III
1/48th: Tamiya Lancaster B Mk I/III
Note: Same as W4114 except;

Not Shown:
Early production machines had ventral
FN.64 turret fitted, but these were all
removed from January 1944 72011/72049
(48125/48126)

FN.82 (2x 0.5in) or FN.121 (4x 0.303in)
turrets with A.G.L.T installed post-war S
(S)

Larger bomb aimer's glazing fitted [this
could be retro-fitted to B Mk Is as well] S
(S)

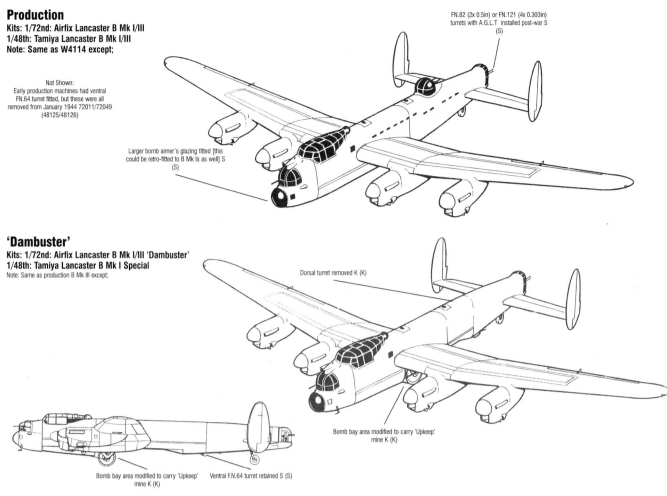

## 'Dambuster'

Kits: 1/72nd: Airfix Lancaster B Mk I/III 'Dambuster'
1/48th: Tamiya Lancaster B Mk I Special
Note: Same as production B Mk III except;

Dorsal turret removed K (K)

Bomb bay area modified to carry 'Upkeep'
mine K (K)

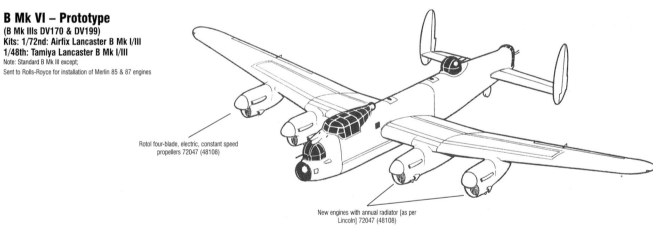

Bomb bay area modified to carry 'Upkeep'
mine K (K)

Ventral F.N.64 turret retained S (S)

## B Mk VI – Prototype

(B Mk IIIs DV170 & DV199)
Kits: 1/72nd: Airfix Lancaster B Mk I/III
1/48th: Tamiya Lancaster B Mk I/III
Note: Standard B Mk III except;
Sent to Rolls-Royce for installation of Merlin 85 & 87 engines

Rotol four-blade, electric, constant speed
propellers 72047 (48108)

New engines with annual radiator [as per
Lincoln] 72047 (48108)

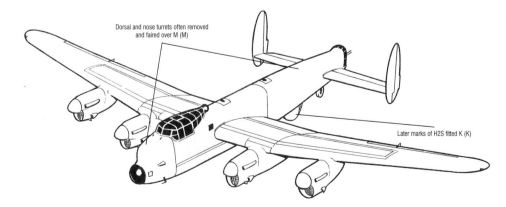

## Production (all converted B Mk IIIs)

Kits: 1/72nd: Airfix Lancaster B Mk I/III
1/48th: Tamiya Lancaster B Mk I/III
As prototype except;

Note
JB675 flew with Merlin 68, 102, 150, 620,
621, 630 and 641 engines as a test bed
until July 1948

Not Shown:
Large amount of radar jamming equipment
carried

Dorsal and nose turrets often removed
and faired over M (M)

Later marks of H2S fitted K (K)

## B Mk VIII (Interim)

Designation [not adopted] for Austin Motors-built B Mk Is with Martin mid-upper turret installed. Never built
with this turret installed and all [NX548-589 and NX603-610] were delivered as standard B Mk Is

## B Mk VII (F.E.)
[Basically B Mk Is with early B Mk III modifications]

## Prototype – (NN801)
Kits: 1/72nd: Airfix Lancaster B Mk I/III
1/48th: Tamiya Lancaster B Mk I/III

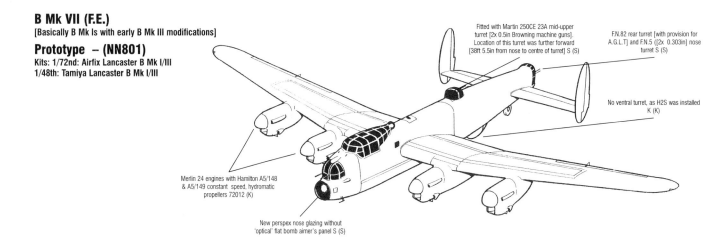

Fitted with Martin 250CE 23A mid-upper turret [2x 0.5in Browning machine guns]. Location of this turret was further forward [38ft 5.5in from nose to centre of turret] S (S)

F.N.82 rear turret [with provision for A.G.L.T] and F.N.5 ([2x 0.303in] nose turret S (S)

No ventral turret, as H2S was installed K (K)

Merlin 24 engines with Hamilton A5/148 & A5/149 constant speed, hydromatic propellers 72012 (K)

New perspex nose glazing without 'optical' flat bomb aimer's panel S (S)

# Lincoln

## Prototype – (PW925, PW929 & PW932)
1/72nd: Airfix Lancaster B Mk I/III & Paragon Conversion (#72051)
1/48th: Tamiya Lancaster B Mk I/III & Paragon Conversion (#48057)

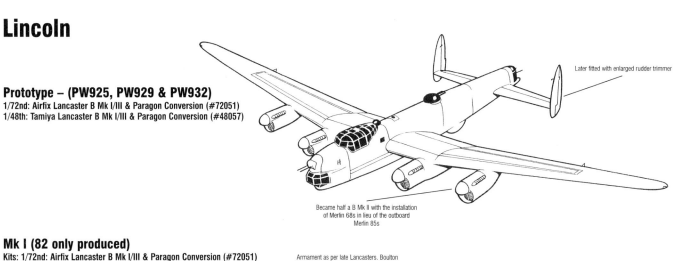

Later fitted with enlarged rudder trimmer

Became half a B Mk II with the installation of Merlin 68s in lieu of the outboard Merlin 85s

## Mk I (82 only produced)
Kits: 1/72nd: Airfix Lancaster B Mk I/III & Paragon Conversion (#72051)
1/48th: Tamiya Lancaster B Mk I/III & Paragon Conversion (#48057)

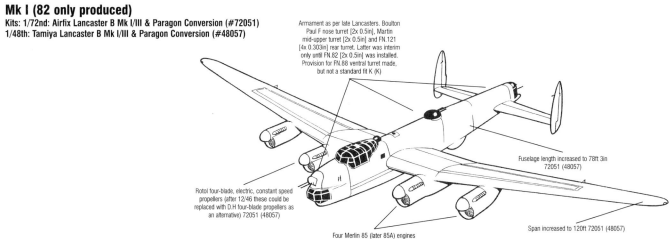

Armament as per late Lancasters. Boulton Paul F nose turret [2x 0.5in], Martin mid-upper turret [2x 0.5in] and FN.121 [4x 0.303in] rear turret. Latter was interim only until FN.82 [2x 0.5in] was installed. Provision for FN.88 ventral turret made, but not a standard fit K (K)

Fuselage length increased to 78ft 3in 72051 (48057)

Rotol four-blade, electric, constant speed propellers (after 12/46 these could be replaced with D.H four-blade propellers as an alternative) 72051 (48057)

Span increased to 120ft 72051 (48057)

Four Merlin 85 (later 85A) engines 72051 (48057)

## B Mk II (B.2)
Kits: 1/72nd: Airfix Lancaster B Mk I/III & Paragon Conversion (#72051)
1/48th: Tamiya Lancaster B Mk I/III & Paragon Conversion (#48057)

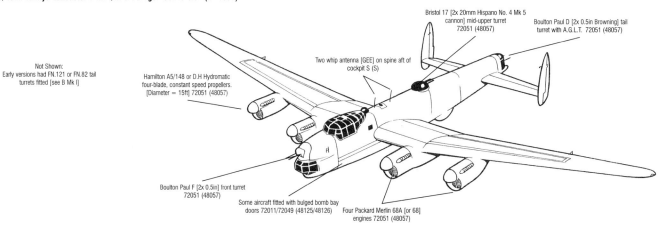

Bristol 17 [2x 20mm Hispano No. 4 Mk 5 cannon] mid-upper turret 72051 (48057)

Boulton Paul D [2x 0.5in Browning] tail turret with A.G.L.T. 72051 (48057)

Two whip antenna [GEE] on spine aft of cockpit S (S)

Not Shown:
Early versions had FN.121 or FN.82 tail turrets fitted [see B Mk I]

Hamilton A5/148 or D.H Hydromatic four-blade, constant speed propellers. [Diameter = 15ft] 72051 (48057)

Boulton Paul F [2x 0.5in] front turret 72051 (48057)

Some aircraft fitted with bulged bomb bay doors 72011/72049 (48125/48126)

Four Packard Merlin 68A [or 68] engines 72051 (48057)

## B.2/3A

**Kits: 1/72nd:** Airfix Lancaster B Mk I/III & Paragon Conversion (#72051)
**1/48th:** Tamiya Lancaster B Mk I/III & Paragon Conversion (#48057)
Note: As per B.2 except:

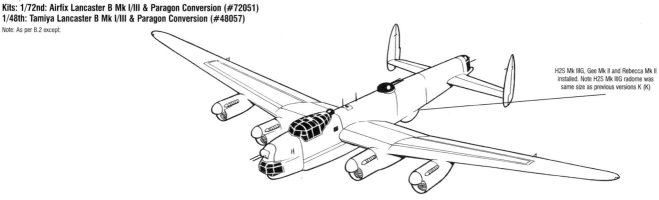

H2S Mk IIIG, Gee Mk II and Rebecca Mk II installed. Note H2S Mk IIIG radome was same size as previous versions K (K)

## B.2/4A

**Kits :1/72nd:** Airfix Lancaster B Mk I/III & Paragon Conversion (#72051)
**1/48th:** Tamiya Lancaster B Mk I/III & Paragon Conversion (#48057)
Note: As per B.2 except:

Mid-upper turret often deleted & nose turret faired over M (M)

No whip aerials on the spine

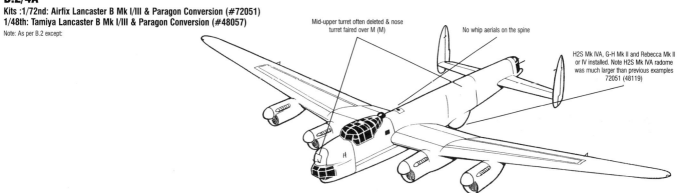

H2S Mk IVA, G-H Mk II and Rebecca Mk II or IV installed. Note H2S Mk IVA radome was much larger than previous examples 72051 (48119)

## B Mk IV

**Kits: 1/72nd:** Airfix Lancaster B Mk I/III & Paragon Conversion (#72051)
**1/48th:** Tamiya Lancaster B Mk I/III & Paragon Conversion (#48057)
Note: Similar to Lincoln B.2 except;

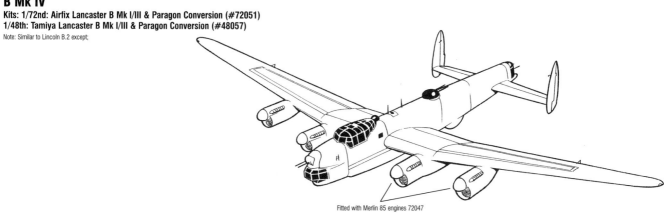

Fitted with Merlin 85 engines 72047

# Air-Sea Rescue

## Lancaster – ASR.3 (all conversions)
**Kits: 1/72nd:** Airfix Lancaster B Mk I/III
**1/48th:** Tamiya Lancaster B Mk I/III

Not Shown:
Two whip antenna forward of the cockpit, off-set to starboard S (S)

Packard Merlin 224 engines standard K (K)

Airborne Lifeboat Mk II [superseded by the Mk IIA in September 1946] carried on outside of bomb bay doors S (S)

Armament sometimes removed [especially post-1948] M (M)

Mid-upper turret removed and faired over M (M)

Windows added either side of rear fuselage, just forward of the tailplanes [starboard side one was in the access door] S (S)

Some aircraft had Lincoln style rudders, with 'squared-off' bottom edge S (S)

H2S radar retained K (K)

Three dipole antenna aft of radome S (S)

Usually not fitted with exhaust dampers 72013 (48122)

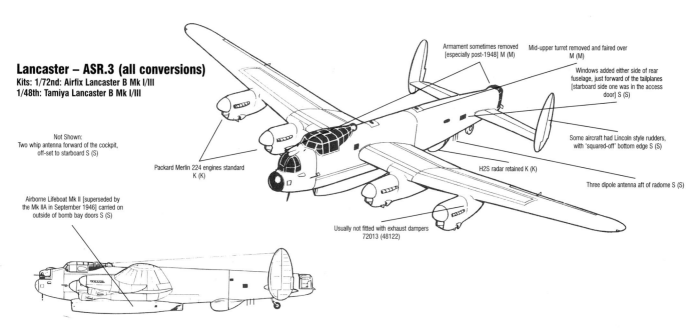

# General Reconnaissance

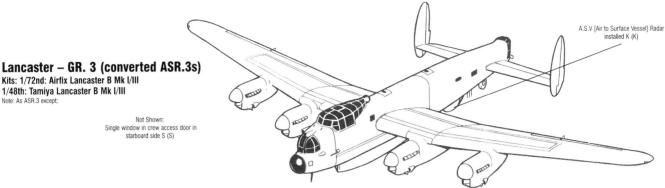

## Lancaster – GR. 3 (converted ASR.3s)
Kits: 1/72nd: Airfix Lancaster B Mk I/III
1/48th: Tamiya Lancaster B Mk I/III
Note: As ASR.3 except;

A.S.V [Air to Surface Vessel] Radar
installed K (K)

Not Shown:
Single window in crew access door in
starboard side S (S)

# Special Duties

## Lincoln – U.5
Kits: 1/72nd: Airfix Lancaster B Mk I/III & Paragon Conversion #72051 (48057)
1/48th: Tamiya Lancaster B Mk I/III
Note: Converted B.2 into drone aircraft. Only two (RF395 & RF366) ever converted. [No external modifications required]

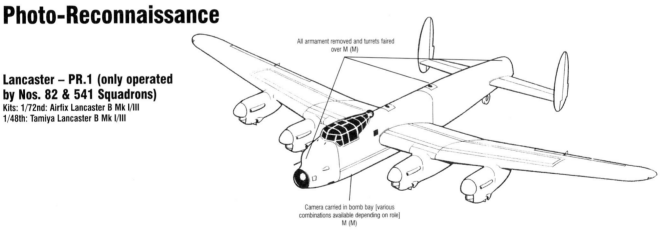

## Lincolnian
Kits: 1/72nd: Airfix Lancaster B Mk I/III
1/48th: Tamiya Lancaster B Mk I/III
Note: Unofficial name for the two Lincolns converted by the
Central Navigational School (RE364 [Aries II] and RE367 [Aries III])

Six windows added either side of rear
fuselage, aft of the wing trailing edge S
(S)

Rear section of canopy faired over
[RE364 only] M (M)

Not Shown:
RE364 was silver overall, while RE367
retained its wartime camouflage over
black scheme.

Lancastrian style tail and nose cones fitted
Magna #6272 (N/A)

# Photo-Reconnaissance

All armament removed and turrets faired
over M (M)

## Lancaster – PR.1 (only operated
by Nos. 82 & 541 Squadrons)
Kits: 1/72nd: Airfix Lancaster B Mk I/III
1/48th: Tamiya Lancaster B Mk I/III

Camera carried in bomb bay [various
combinations available depending on role]
M (M)

# Foreign

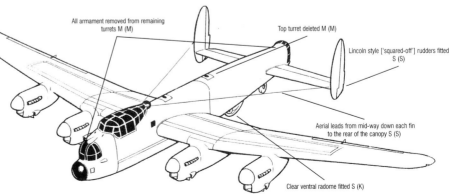

All armament removed from remaining
turrets M (M)

Top turret deleted M (M)

Lincoln style ['squared-off'] rudders fitted
S (S)

## Service & Conversion – France
Lancaster – B Mk VII (French Civil)
[S/No FCL-01 to 05, ex-RT693, 689,
673, 679 and NX738]
Kits: 1/72nd: Airfix Lancaster B Mk I/III
1/48th: Tamiya Lancaster B Mk I/III
Note: As per standard B Mk VII except;

Aerial leads from mid-way down each fin
to the rear of the canopy S (S)

Not Shown:
Rescue equipment installed internally
Decca navigation equipment installed
I.L.S [Instrument Landing System] fitted

Clear ventral radome fitted S (K)

## Canadian Built – Lancaster

Please note that all modified Lancasters in the 10 series were usually fitted with de-icing boots on the wings, tailplane and fin leading edges. If fuel tanks were fitted in the bomb bay, this usually resulted in a fuel dump tube being installed. When one tank was installed, this had its tube on the fuselage side, just below the wing leading edge. When the second (aft) tank was installed, its overflow/dump tube was fitted on the fuselage side, below the wing and at a point in line with the flap hinge line.

Designations: Please note that in line with RAF practice, the RCAF changed their aircraft numbering system in 1950 from Roman to Arabic, therefore after this point all Mk Xs became Mk 10s. For the purpose of this book, we have chosen to retain the early mark for the first (basic) versions of the Lancaster and Lincoln, but the Arabic series for all subsequent versions

## B Mk X
**Kits: 1/72nd:** Airfix Lancaster B Mk I/III
**1/48th:** Tamiya Lancaster B Mk I/III

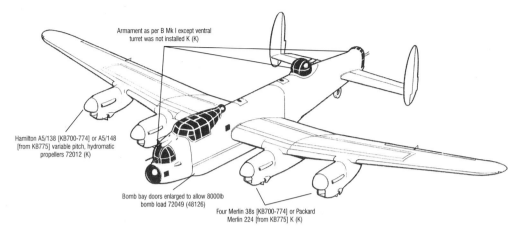

Armament as per B Mk I except ventral turret was not installed K (K)

Hamilton A5/138 [KB700-774] or A5/148 [from KB775] variable pitch, hydromatic propellers 72012 (K)

Bomb bay doors enlarged to allow 8000lb bomb load 72049 (48126)

Four Merlin 38s [KB700-774] or Packard Merlin 224 [from KB775] K (K)

## Mk 10 'S&R'
**Kits: 1/72nd:** Airfix Lancaster B Mk I/III
**1/48th:** Tamiya Lancaster B Mk I/III
Note: Converted B Mk Xs (The designation above is the only one ever referred to in official documents. There was no 'Mk 10ASR', as that role was initially envisaged for the Mk 10BR, and later, 10MR)

Not Shown:
Equipped for Air Sea Rescue duties

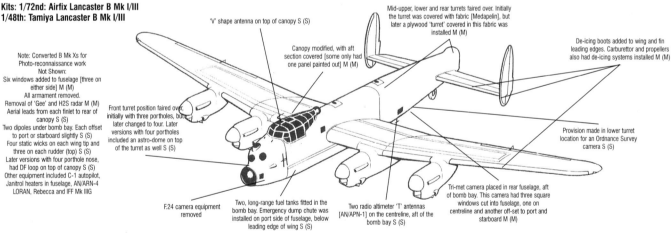

Mid-upper removed and faired over M (M)

Rear turret faired over M (M)

Two antenna on dorsal spine, equally spaced between rear of canopy and mid-upper turret location S (S)

De-icing boots added to wing, tailplane and fin leading edges S (S)

All armament removed M (M)

Ventral radome retained K (K)

Two radio altimeter 'T' antennas [AN/APN-1] on the centreline, aft of the bomb bay S (S)

## Mk 10P
**Kits: 1/72nd:** Airfix Lancaster B Mk I/III
**1/48th:** Tamiya Lancaster B Mk I/III

Note: Converted B Mk Xs for Photo-reconnaissance work
Not Shown:
Six windows added to fuselage [three on either side] M (M)
All armament removed. M (M)
Removal of 'Gee' and H2S radar M (M)
Aerial leads from each finlet to rear of canopy S (S)
Two dipoles under bomb bay. Each offset to port or starboard slightly S (S)
Four static wicks on each wing tip and three on each rudder (top) S (S)
Later versions with four porthole nose, had DF loop on top of canopy S (S)
Other equipment included C-1 autopilot, Janitrol heaters in fuselage, AN/ARN-4 LORAN, Rebecca and IFF Mk IIIG

'V' shape antenna on top of canopy S (S)

Canopy modified, with aft section covered [some only had one panel painted out] M (M)

Mid-upper, lower and rear turrets faired over. Initially the turret was covered with fabric [Medapelin], but later a plywood 'turret' covered in this fabric was installed M (M)

De-icing boots added to wing and fin leading edges. Carburettor and propellers also had de-icing systems installed M (M)

Front turret position faired over, initially with three portholes, but later changed to four. Later versions with four portholes included an astro-dome on top of the turret as well S (S)

Provision made in lower turret location for an Ordnance Survey camera S (S)

F.24 camera equipment removed

Two, long-range fuel tanks fitted in the bomb bay. Emergency dump chute was installed on port side of fuselage, below leading edge of wing S (S)

Two radio altimeter 'T' antennas [AN/APN-1] on the centreline, aft of the bomb bay S (S)

Tri-met camera placed in rear fuselage, aft of bomb bay. This camera had three square windows cut into fuselage, one on centreline and another off-set to port and starboard M (M)

## Mk 10BR (Interim) [Four Mk 10ASR converted to bomber-reconnaissance role]
Note: FM221 acted as series prototype, FM222 had a mid-upper turret fitted, FM228 did not and KB961 was fitted with a removable cover that allowed the turret to be fitted and removed as required
**Kits: 1/72nd:** Airfix Lancaster B Mk I/III
**1/48th:** Tamiya Lancaster B Mk I/III

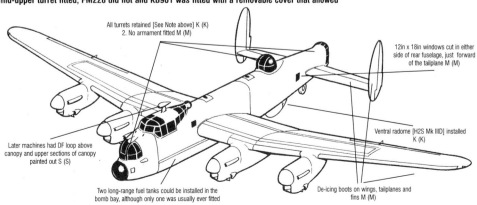

All turrets retained [See Note above] K (K)
2. No armament fitted M (M)

12in x 18in windows cut in either side of rear fuselage, just forward of the tailplane M (M)

Not Shown:
High and low-level bomb sights installed
Bomb bay retained all bomb carriers enabling bombs, depth charges, a torpedo, sonobuoys and flares to be carried. The latter two items were carried in a Light Series bomb carrier within the bomb bay.
Rear-facing F.24 camera installed S (S)
Some machines fitted with dual controls S (S)

Ventral radome [H2S Mk IIID] installed K (K)

Later machines had DF loop above canopy and upper sections of canopy painted out S (S)

Two long-range fuel tanks could be installed in the bomb bay, although only one was usually ever fitted

De-icing boots on wings, tailplanes and fins M (M)

## Mk 10BR (Bomber-Reconnaissance)
**Kits:** 1/72nd: Airfix Lancaster B Mk I/III
1/48th: Tamiya Lancaster B Mk I/III

Note
Nine B Mk Xs latter converted to same standard as Mk 10BR
(Interim) [KB907, 919, 925, 946, 957, 965, 973, 995 & 996]

Initially all these machines were delivered with a mid-upper
turret installed, but a change in the role of this type soon
saw these removed M (M)

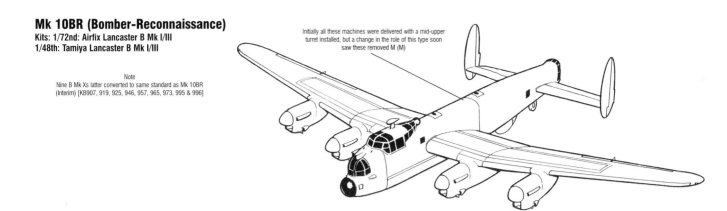

## Mk 10MR/MP (Converted B Mk Xs [approx 70 to 75])
**Kits:** 1/72nd: Airfix Lancaster B Mk I/III
1/48th: Tamiya Lancaster B Mk I/III

Not Shown:
No armament fitted, although photos of
KB892 show front and rear turrets fully
armed M (M)
Dipole underneath rear fuselage, off-set to
starboard S (S)
Whip antenna under chin S (S)
Late in their service life, once APS-33
installed, the front turret was often painted
out, and an astro-dome added
above it S (S)
Rear-facing camera fitted in fairing under
rear fuselage, aft of the tail wheel S (S)
Redesignated Mk 10MP in 1950.

'V' antenna above canopy
(not always fitted) S (S)

Two blisters (one on canopy, one aft of it)
that are most likely navigational aids or DF
loops S (S)

Two masts on fuselage spine. One at
mid-chord, the other approx 6ft forward of
rear access door S (S)

Basically a further conversion of the
Mk 10BR into a dedicated reconnaissance
role. Mid-upper turret removed, faired over
and strengthening plates added to either
side of the fuselage M/S (M/S)

12in x 18in windows cut in either side of
rear fuselage, just forward of the tailplane
M (M)

Initially fitted with H2S radome, although
later this was replaced with the APS-33
search radar 'dustbin' K/72006 (K/48050)

De-icing boots on wings,
tailplanes and fins M (M)

Two dipoles underneath fuselage, on
bomb doors, each slightly off-set either
side S (S)

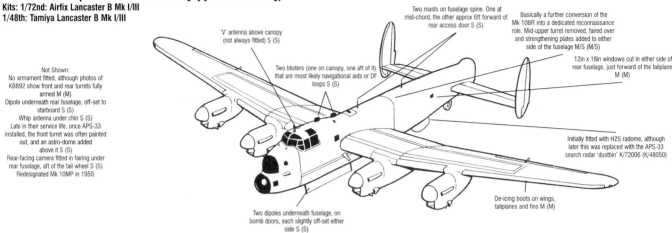

## Mk 10N (five converted B Mk Xs: FM208, FM211, FM206, KB826, KB986)
**Kits:** 1/72nd: Airfix Lancaster B Mk I/III
1/48th: Tamiya Lancaster B Mk I/III
Note: Similar to Mk 10P except.

Not Shown:
Initially a standard astro-dome (*) was to
replace the mid-upper turret, but these
were soon removed in service *S (*S)
A 12in x 18in lookout window was added
to the starboard fuselage side, well
forward of the leading edge of the
tailplane M (M)
Dual controls installed in cockpit M (M)

Front turret fairing only had three
portholes and there was no astro-dome
on top S (S)

Only standard F.24 camera
ports were retained

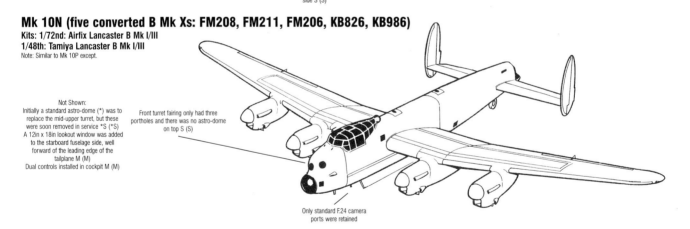

## Mk 10DC (Drone-carrying) [KB848 & KB851]
**Kits:** 1/72nd: Airfix Lancaster B Mk I/III
1/48th: Tamiya Lancaster B Mk I/III

Not Shown:
As per the Mk 10MR, except all operational
equipment for Maritime Reconnaissance
role removed
Mast and lead on starboard fuselage side,
just below rear edge of canopy. Lead going
to starboard tailplane endplate S (S)
Two sets of antenna and leads under bomb
bay. Units off-set to port, but combined into
one, so as to create a 'step' from front to
back S (S)
Drone controller system installed in rear
fuselage. Drone controller was seated at
windows in rear fuselage
N-9 movie camera could be fitted forward
of the above windows, on either side of the
fuselage S (S)
Later photos of Mk 10DCs show a small
blade antenna fitted
under the rear fuselage, about mid-way
between the rear of the bomb bay and the
tailwheel. This is almost certainly relating to
a 'modern' navigational system S (S)

Four static wicks added to each control
surface S (S)

12in x 18in window [with curved glass]
cut in either side of rear fuselage, forward
of tailplanes M (M)

Ryan KDA-4A Firebee drone carried on a
pylon under the tip of each wing S (S)

Ryan KDA-4A Firebee drone carried on a
pylon under the tip of each wing S (S)

No armament fitted, front and rear turrets
retained, mid-upper removed and faired
over M (M)

## Mk 10AR (Area Reconnaissance) [KB839, KB882 & KB976]
Kits: 1/72nd: Airfix Lancaster B Mk I/III
1/48th: Tamiya Lancaster B Mk I/III
Note: Similar to Mk 10P except;

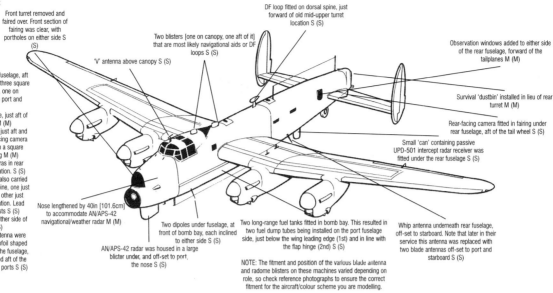

Front turret removed and faired over. Front section of fairing was clear, with portholes on either side S (S)

DF loop fitted on dorsal spine, just forward of old mid-upper turret location S (S)

Two blisters [one on canopy, one aft of it] that are most likely navigational aids or DF loops S (S)

Observation windows added to either side of the rear fuselage, forward of the tailplanes M (M)

'V' antenna above canopy S (S)

Not Shown:
Tri-met camera placed in rear fuselage, aft of bomb bay. This camera had three square windows cut into fuselage, one on centreline and one off-set to port and starboard M (M)
Forward-facing camera in nose, just aft of bomb aimer's glazing M (M)
Low-level stereo-strip camera just aft and to starboard of the forward-facing camera (see above). This resulted in a square glazed panel in the skinning M (M)
Two vertical high-level cameras in rear fuselage, aft of Tri-met installation. S (S)
Two hand-held cameras were also carried
Two mast antenna on dorsal spine, one just aft of the above DF loop, the other just forward of the rear turret location. Lead running between these masts S (S)
Aerial leads from each fin to either side of cockpit canopy S (S)
When the latter style blade antenna were installed [see above], two aerofoil shaped blisters were also fitted under the fuselage, just forward of the antenna and aft of the bomb bay and Tri-met camera ports S (S)

Survival 'dustbin' installed in lieu of rear turret M (M)

Rear-facing camera fitted in fairing under rear fuselage, aft of the tail wheel S (S)

Small 'can' containing passive UPD-501 intercept radar receiver was fitted under the rear fuselage S (S)

Nose lengthened by 40in [101.6cm] to accommodate AN/APS-42 navigational/weather radar M (M)

Two dipoles under fuselage, at front of bomb bay, each inclined to either side S (S)

AN/APS-42 radar was housed in a large blister under, and off-set to port, the nose S (S)

Two long-range fuel tanks fitted in bomb bay. This resulted in two fuel dump tubes being installed on the port fuselage side, just below the wing leading edge (1st) and in line with the flap hinge (2nd) S (S)

Whip antenna underneath rear fuselage, off-set to starboard. Note that later in their service this antenna was replaced with two blade antennas off-set to port and starboard S (S)

NOTE: The fitment and position of the various blade antenna and radome blisters on these machines varied depending on role, so check reference photographs to ensure the correct fitment for the aircraft/colour scheme you are modelling.

## Lincoln – B Mk XV
Kits: 1/72nd: Airfix Lancaster B Mk I/III & Paragon Conversion 72051
1/48th: Tamiya Lancaster B Mk I/III & Paragon Conversion 48057
Note: As per B.2 except

## Australia Built
## Lincoln – B.30
Kits: 1/72nd: Airfix Lancaster B Mk I/III & Paragon Conversion 72051
1/48th: Tamiya Lancaster B Mk I/III & Paragon Conversion 48057
Note: First five built from components sent from UK. Like B.2 except;

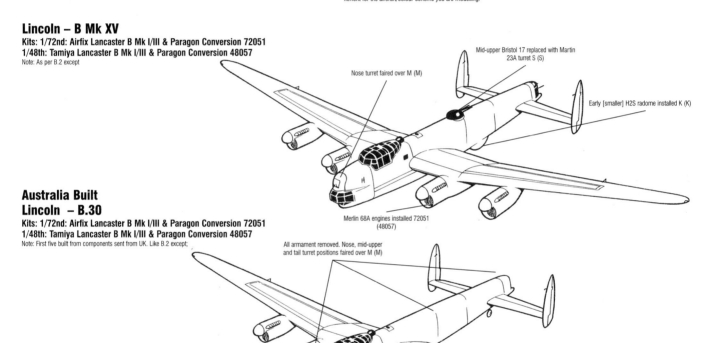

Mid-upper Bristol 17 replaced with Martin 23A turret S (S)

Nose turret faired over M (M)

Early [smaller] H2S radome installed K (K)

Merlin 68A engines installed 72051 (48057)

All armament removed. Nose, mid-upper and tail turret positions faired over M (M)

Initial fifty had Merlin 85 engines fitted 72051 (48057)
Subsequent aircraft had Merlin 102s installed [becoming B.30A]

## MR.31
Kits: 1/72nd: Airfix Lancaster B Mk I/III & Paragon Conversion 72051
1/48th: Tamiya Lancaster B Mk I/III & Paragon Conversion 48057
Note: Same as B.30 except;

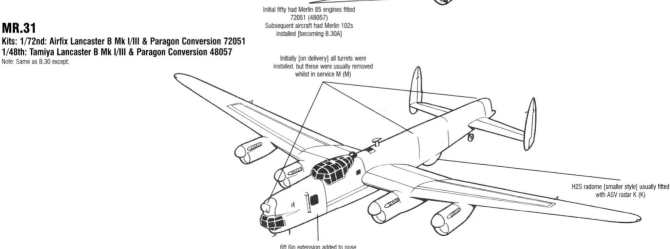

Initially [on delivery] all turrets were installed, but these were usually removed whilst in service M (M)

6ft 6in extension added to nose 72052 (48118)

H2S radome [smaller style] usually fitted with ASV radar K (K)

# Civil Conversions

## Lancaster/Lancastrian
## Lancaster (Civil) Mk I
Kits:1/72nd: Airfix Lancaster B Mk I/III
1/48th: Tamiya Lancaster B Mk I/III

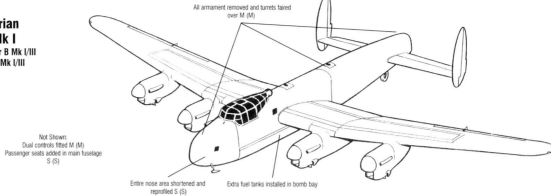

All armament removed and turrets faired over M (M)

Not Shown:
Dual controls fitted M (M)
Passenger seats added in main fuselage
S (S)

Entire nose area shortened and reprofiled S (S)

Extra fuel tanks installed in bomb bay

## Lancastrian I
Kits: 1/72nd: Airfix Lancaster B Mk I/III
1/48th: Tamiya Lancaster B Mk I/III

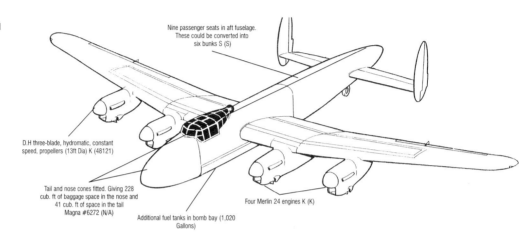

Nine passenger seats in aft fuselage. These could be converted into six bunks S (S)

Not Shown:
Six windows fitted to starboard side of rear fuselage only M (M)

D.H three-blade, hydromatic, constant speed, propellers (13ft Dia) K (48121)

Tail and nose cones fitted. Giving 228 cub. ft of baggage space in the nose and 41 cub. ft of space in the tail
Magna #6272 (N/A)

Additional fuel tanks in bomb bay (1,020 Gallons)

Four Merlin 24 engines K (K)

## Lancastrian C.2
Kits: 1/72nd: Airfix Lancaster B Mk I/III
1/48th: Tamiya Lancaster B Mk I/III
Note: As Lancastrian I except;

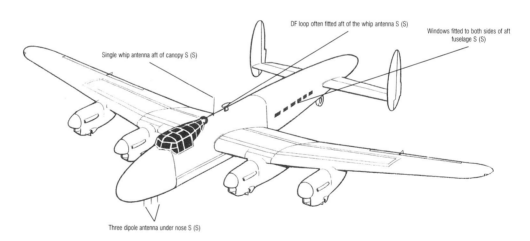

DF loop often fitted aft of the whip antenna S (S)

Single whip antenna aft of canopy S (S)

Windows fitted to both sides of aft fuselage S (S)

Not Shown:
One dipole antenna underneath rear fuselage S (S)

Three dipole antenna under nose S (S)

## Lancastrian Mk III
Kits: 1/72nd: Airfix Lancaster B Mk I/III
1/48th: Tamiya Lancaster B Mk I/III
Note: As Lancastrian C.2 except;

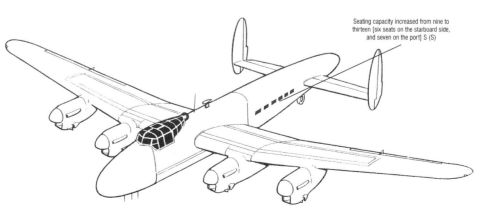

Seating capacity increased from nine to thirteen [six seats on the starboard side, and seven on the port] S (S)

## Lancastrian C.IV
Kits: 1/72nd: Airfix Lancaster B Mk I/III
1/48th: Tamiya Lancaster B Mk I/III
Note: As Lancastrian Mk III, but operated by RAF. Passed to civil operators in 1947 [See Lancastrian Mk III]

## Lincoln
### Freighter (B.2, RE290 [G-ALPF])
Kits: 1/72nd: Airfix Lancaster B Mk I/III & Paragon Conversion 72051
1/48th: Tamiya Lancaster B Mk I/III & Paragon Conversion 48057

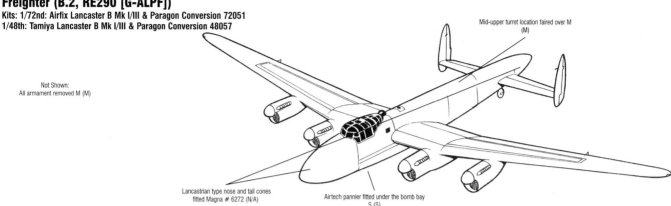

Mid-upper turret location faired over M
(M)

Not Shown:
All armament removed M (M)

Lancastrian type nose and tail cones
fitted Magna # 6272 (N/A)

Airtech pannier fitted under the bomb bay
S (S)

### Freighter {Meat} (RF419, RE376 & RF419)
Kits: 1/72nd: Airfix Lancaster B Mk I/III & Paragon Conversion 72051
1/48th: Tamiya Lancaster B Mk I/III & Paragon Conversion 48057

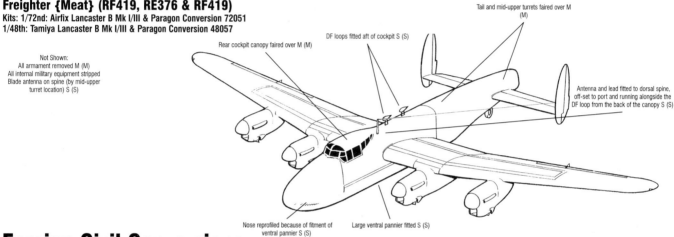

Tail and mid-upper turrets faired over M
(M)

DF loops fitted aft of cockpit S (S)

Rear cockpit canopy faired over M (M)

Not Shown:
All armament removed M (M)
All internal military equipment stripped
Blade antenna on spine (by mid-upper
turret location) S (S)

Antenna and lead fitted to dorsal spine,
off-set to port and running alongside the
DF loop from the back of the canopy S (S)

Nose reprofiled because of fitment of
ventral pannier S (S)

Large ventral pannier fitted S (S)

# Foreign Civil Conversions

## Lancaster
### Lancaster Mailplane (R5727)
Kits: 1/72nd: Airfix Lancaster B Mk I/III
1/48th: Tamiya Lancaster B Mk I/III

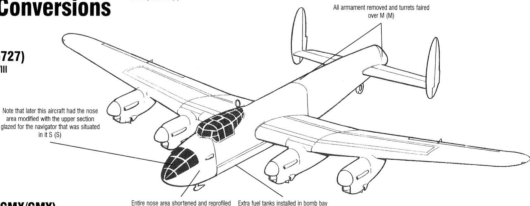

All armament removed and turrets faired
over M (M)

Note that later this aircraft had the nose
area modified with the upper section
glazed for the navigator that was situated
in it S (S)

Not Shown:
Dual controls fitted M (M)

Entire nose area shortened and reprofiled
S (S)

Extra fuel tanks installed in bomb bay

### B Mk X (FM184-185/CF-CMX/CMY)
Kits: 1/72nd: Airfix Lancaster B Mk I/III
1/48th: Tamiya Lancaster B Mk I/III

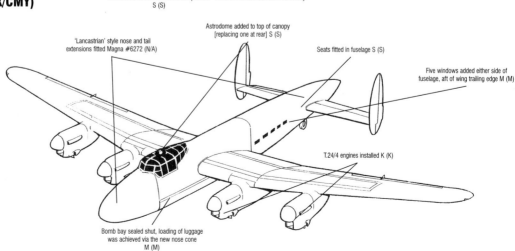

Astrodome added to top of canopy
[replacing one at rear] S (S)

'Lancastrian' style nose and tail
extensions fitted Magna #6272 (N/A)

Seats fitted in fuselage S (S)

Not Shown:
All armament removed M (M)

Five windows added either side of
fuselage, aft of wing trailing edge M (M)

T.24/4 engines installed K (K)

Bomb bay sealed shut, loading of luggage
was achieved via the new nose cone
M (M)

## B Mk X (FM186-187/CF-CMZ/CNA)
**Kits: 1/72nd: Airfix Lancaster B Mk I/III**
**1/48th: Tamiya Lancaster B Mk I/III**
Note: As per FM184 & 185 except;

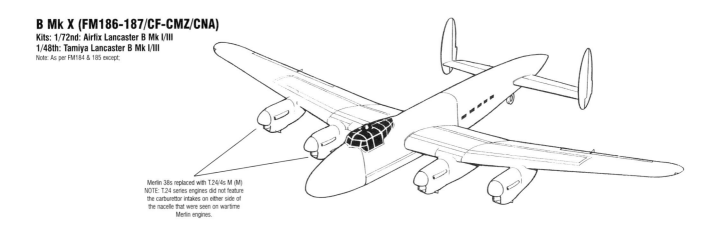

Merlin 38s replaced with T.24/4s M (M)
NOTE: T.24 series engines did not feature
the carburettor intakes on either side of
the nacelle that were seen on wartime
Merlin engines.

## B.10 (Spartan Air Services)
**Kits: 1/72nd: Airfix Lancaster B Mk I/III**
**1/48th: Tamiya Lancaster B Mk I/III**
Note: Same as 10.ASR except:

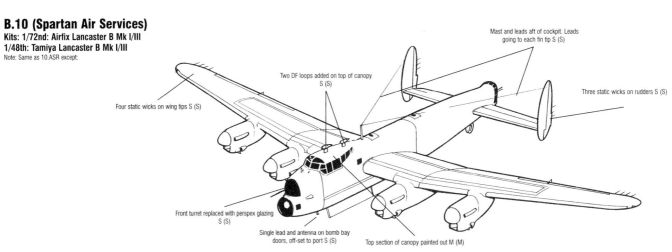

Mast and leads aft of cockpit. Leads
going to each fin tip S (S)

Two DF loops added on top of canopy
S (S)

Three static wicks on rudders S (S)

Four static wicks on wing tips S (S)

Front turret replaced with perspex glazing
S (S)

Single lead and antenna on bomb bay
doors, off-set to port S (S)

Top section of canopy painted out M (M)

# Test Beds (All Nations)

## Lancaster
## Python
**Kits: 1/72nd: Airfix Lancaster B Mk I/III**
**1/48th: Tamiya Lancaster B Mk I/III**

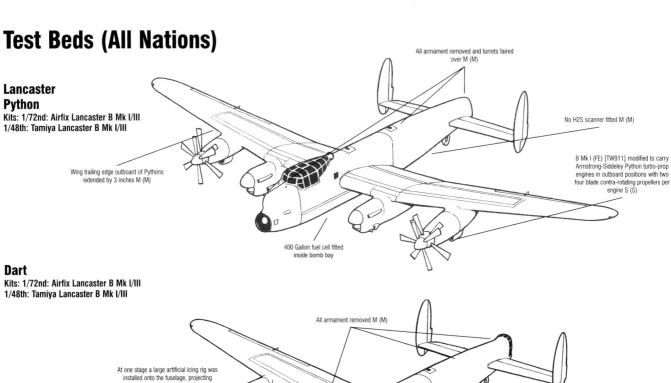

All armament removed and turrets faired
over M (M)

No H2S scanner fitted M (M)

B Mk I (FE) [TW911] modified to carry
Armstrong-Siddeley Python turbo-prop
engines in outboard positions with two
four blade contra-rotating propellers per
engine S (S)

Wing trailing edge outboard of Pythons
extended by 3 inches M (M)

400 Gallon fuel cell fitted
inside bomb bay

## Dart
**Kits: 1/72nd: Airfix Lancaster B Mk I/III**
**1/48th: Tamiya Lancaster B Mk I/III**

All armament removed M (M)

At one stage a large artificial icing rig was
installed onto the fuselage, projecting
forward of the Dart. Water jets were
supplied via two 100 gallon water tanks
mounted inside the fuselage S (S)

B Mk I [NG465] fitted with Rolls-Royce
Dart turbo-prop in nose S (S)

## Dovern (Swedish S/No = 80001)
**Kits: 1/72nd: Airfix Lancaster B Mk I/III**
**1/48th: Tamiya Lancaster B Mk I/III**

Not shown:
B Mk I [RA805] modified for Swedish Air
Force tests of Dovern engine with
afterburner.

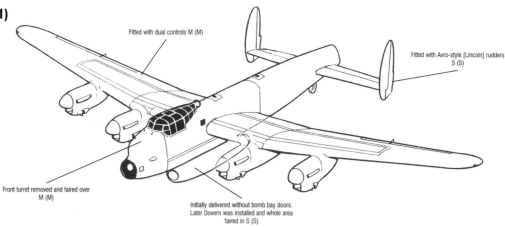

Fitted with dual controls M (M)

Fitted with Avro-style [Lincoln] rudders
S (S)

Front turret removed and faired over
M (M)

Initially delivered without bomb bay doors.
Later Dovern was installed and whole area
faired in S (S)

## Mk II (Universal Test Bed)
**Kits: 1/72nd: Airfix Lancaster B Mk I/III**
**1/48th: Tamiya Lancaster B Mk I/III**

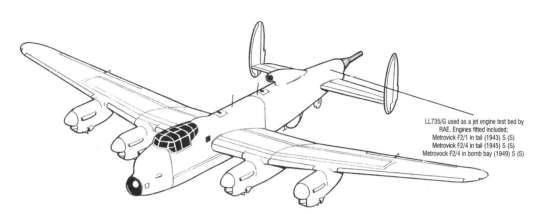

LL735/G used as a jet engine test bed by
RAE. Engines fitted included;
Metrovick F2/1 in tail (1943) S (S)
Metrovick F2/4 in tail (1945) S (S)
Metrovock F2/4 in bomb bay (1949) S (S)

## Gust Alleviation Research B Mk III (ME540 used by Boulton Paul in 1950 for research)
**Kits: 1/72nd: Airfix Lancaster B Mk I/III**
**1/48th: Tamiya Lancaster B Mk I/III**

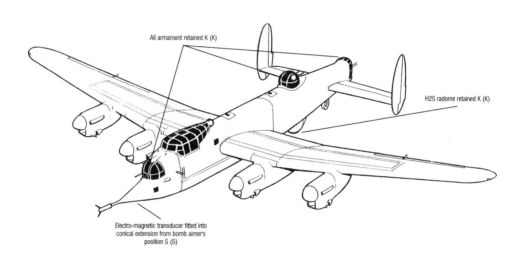

All armament retained K (K)

H2S radome retained K (K)

Electro-magnetic transducer fitted into
conical extension from bomb aimer's
position S (S)

## Armstrong-Siddeley A.S.X test bed (B Mk VI)
**Kits: 1/72nd: Airfix Lancaster B Mk I/III**
**1/48th: Tamiya Lancaster B Mk I/III**

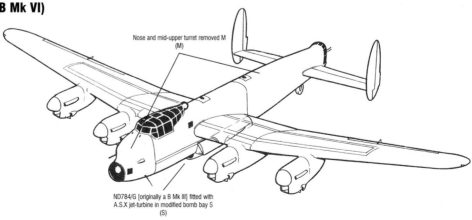

Nose and mid-upper turret removed M
(M)

ND784/G [originally a B Mk III] fitted with
A.S.X jet-turbine in modified bomb bay S
(S)

## Mamba/Adder/Viper B Mk VI
## 1st Test Bed
Kits: 1/72nd: Airfix Lancaster B Mk I/III
1/48th: Tamiya Lancaster B Mk I/III

Not shown:
Observer's compartment ['Boffin cell']
installed in rear fuselage

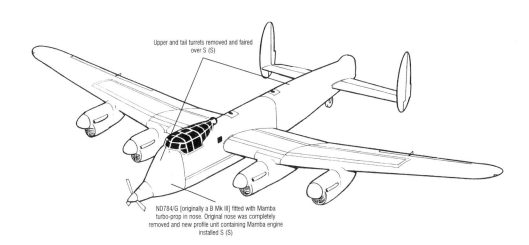

Upper and tail turrets removed and faired
over S (S)

ND784/G [originally a B Mk III] fitted with Mamba
turbo-prop in nose. Original nose was completely
removed and new profile unit containing Mamba engine
installed S (S)

## 2nd Test Bed
Kits: 1/72nd: Airfix Lancaster B Mk I/III
1/48th: Tamiya Lancaster B Mk I/III

Not shown:
Finally fitted with Viper in place of Adder in
tail S (S)

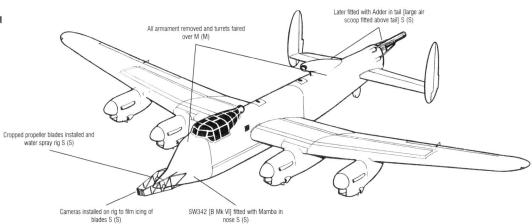

All armament removed and turrets faired
over M (M)

Later fitted with Adder in tail [large air
scoop fitted above tail] S (S)

Cropped propeller blades installed and
water spray rig S (S)

Cameras installed on rig to film icing of
blades S (S)

SW342 [B Mk VI] fitted with Mamba in
nose S (S)

## Orenda Mk 100 (B Mk X): FM209
Kits: 1/72nd: Airfix Lancaster B Mk I/III
1/48th: Tamiya Lancaster B Mk I/III

Not shown:
De-icing boots retained on wing, tailplane
and fin leading edges M (M)
All armament removed M (M)
Internal seating was revised with two
engine test observers seated behind the
pilot and navigator relocated to a position
aft of the bomb bay [as in the Mk 10N]

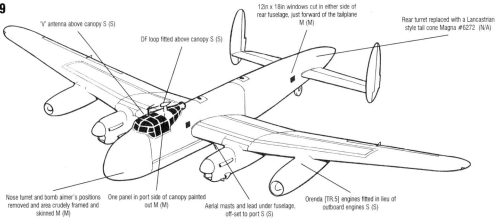

'V' antenna above canopy S (S)

DF loop fitted above canopy S (S)

12in x 18in windows cut in either side of
rear fuselage, just forward of the tailplane
M (M)

Rear turret replaced with a Lancastrian
style tail cone Magna #6272  (N/A)

Nose turret and bomb aimer's positions
removed and area crudely framed and
skinned M (M)

One panel in port side of canopy painted
out M (M)

Aerial masts and lead under fuselage,
off-set to port S (S)

Orenda [TR.5] engines fitted in lieu of
outboard engines S (S)

## Lincoln
## Phoebus (RA643)
Kits: 1/72nd: Airfix Lancaster B Mk I/III & Paragon Conversion 72051
1/48th: Tamiya Lancaster B Mk I/III & Paragon Conversion 48057
Note: Standard B Mk I except;

Nose and mid-upper turrets removed and
faired over M (M)

No armament fitted M (M)

Phoebus engine installed in bomb bay
with exhaust projecting down into
airstream S (S)

## Theseus (B Mk I, RA716/G)
**Kits: 1/72nd: Airfix Lancaster B Mk I/III & Paragon Conversion 72051**
**1/48th: Tamiya Lancaster B Mk I/III & Paragon Conversion 48057**

Not shown:
Later tests carried out with B.2 RE418 and
ex-Python test bed RE339/G

Mid-upper turret location faired over
M (M)

All armament removed M (M)

Front turret faired over M (M)

H2S radome retained K (K)

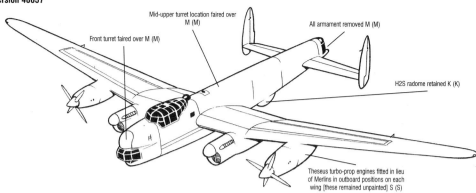

Theseus turbo-prop engines fitted in lieu
of Merlins in outboard positions on each
wing [these remained unpainted] S (S)

## Avon (B.2, RA716/G)
**Kits: 1/72nd: Airfix Lancaster B Mk I/III & Paragon Conversion 72051**
**1/48th: Tamiya Lancaster B Mk I/III & Paragon Conversion 48057**

Single whip antenna aft of canopy S (S)

All armament removed M (M)

Mid-upper turret location faired over
M (M)

H2S radome removed M (M)

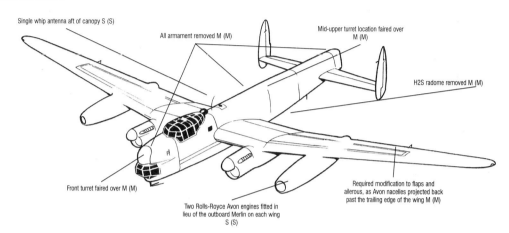

Front turret faired over M (M)

Two Rolls-Royce Avon engines fitted in
lieu of the outboard Merlin on each wing
S (S)

Required modification to flaps and
ailerous, as Avon nacelles projected back
past the trailing edge of the wing M (M)

## Python (B.2, RE339/G)
**Kits: 1/72nd: Airfix Lancaster B Mk I/III & Paragon Conversion 72051**
**1/48th: Tamiya Lancaster B Mk I/III & Paragon Conversion 48057**

Not shown:
All armament removed M (M)

Front turret faired over M (M)

Mid-upper turret location faired over
M (M)

H2S radome removed M (M)

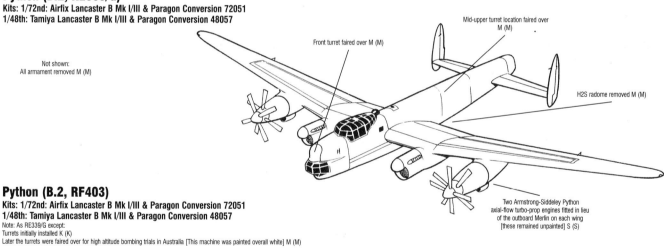

Two Armstrong-Siddeley Python
axial-flow turbo-prop engines fitted in lieu
of the outboard Merlin on each wing
[these remained unpainted] S (S)

## Python (B.2, RF403)
**Kits: 1/72nd: Airfix Lancaster B Mk I/III & Paragon Conversion 72051**
**1/48th: Tamiya Lancaster B Mk I/III & Paragon Conversion 48057**
Note: As RE339/G except:
Turrets initially installed K (K)
Later the turrets were faired over for high altitude bombing trials in Australia [This machine was painted overall white] M (M)

## Proteus (B.2, SX972)
**[Note: Initial trial installation was in B.2, RF398]**
**Kits: 1/72nd: Airfix Lancaster B Mk I/III & Paragon Conversion 72051**
**1/48th: Tamiya Lancaster B Mk I/III & Paragon Conversion 48057**

Not shown:
All armament removed M (M)

Mid-upper turret location faired over
M (M)

H2S radome removed M (M)

Front turret faired over M (M)

Two Proteus turbo-prop engines fitted.
Installed under each wing in lieu of
outboard Merlin engines [these remained
unpainted] S (S)

## Derwent (B.2, SX971)

Kits: 1/72nd: Airfix Lancaster B Mk I/III &
Paragon Conversion 72051
1/48th: Tamiya Lancaster B Mk I/III & Paragon
Conversion 48057

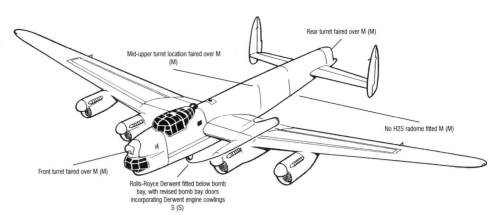

Not shown:
Retractable tail wheel fitted M (M)
All armament removed M (M)
Aircraft finished silver overall

Rear turret faired over M (M)

Mid-upper turret location faired over M
(M)

No H2S radome fitted M (M)

Front turret faired over M (M)

Rolls-Royce Derwent fitted below bomb
bay, with revised bomb bay doors
incorporating Derwent engine cowlings
S (S)

## Tyne (B.2, [RF530] G-37-1)

Kits: 1/72nd: Airfix Lancaster B Mk I/III & Paragon Conversion 72051
1/48th: Tamiya Lancaster B Mk I/III & Paragon Conversion 48057

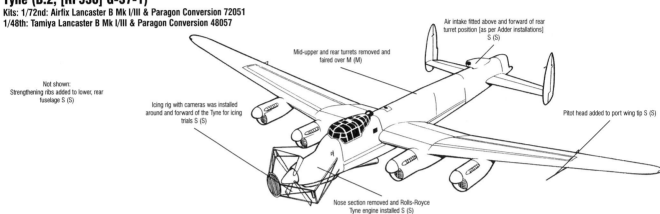

Not shown:
Strengthening ribs added to lower, rear
fuselage S (S)

Mid-upper and rear turrets removed and
faired over M (M)

Air intake fitted above and forward of rear
turret position [as per Adder installations]
S (S)

Icing rig with cameras was installed
around and forward of the Tyne for icing
trials S (S)

Pitot head added to port wing tip S (S)

Nose section removed and Rolls-Royce
Tyne engine installed S (S)

## Naiad (B.2, RF530)

Kits: 1/72nd: Airfix Lancaster B Mk I/III & Paragon Conversion 72051
1/48th: Tamiya Lancaster B Mk I/III & Paragon Conversion 48057

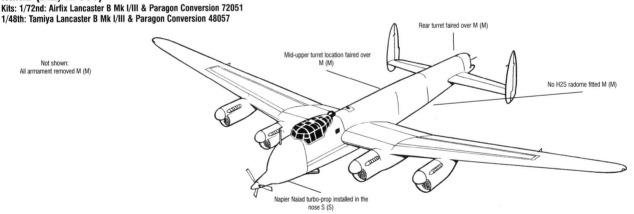

Not shown:
All armament removed M (M)

Rear turret faired over M (M)

Mid-upper turret location faired over
M (M)

No H2S radome fitted M (M)

Napier Naiad turbo-prop installed in the
nose S (S)

## Naiad (B.2, RF402)

Kits: 1/72nd: Airfix Lancaster B Mk I/III & Paragon Conversion 72051
1/48th: Tamiya Lancaster B Mk I/III & Paragon Conversion 48057
Note: As above except:

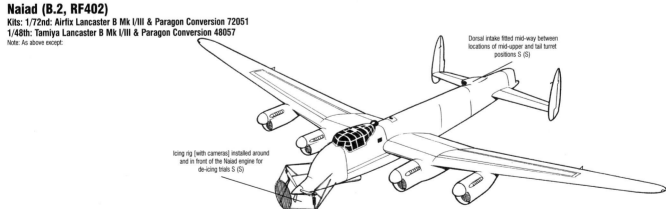

Dorsal intake fitted mid-way between
locations of mid-upper and tail turret
positions S (S)

Icing rig [with cameras] installed around
and in front of the Naiad engine for
de-icing trials S (S)

## Double Naiad (B.2, RF402)

Kits: 1/72nd: Airfix Lancaster B Mk I/III & Paragon Conversion 72051
1/48th: Tamiya Lancaster B Mk I/III & Paragon Conversion 48057
Napier Double Naiad turbo-prop installed in the nose S (S)
All armament removed M (M)
Mid-upper turret location faired over M (M)
Rear turret faired over M (M)
No H2S radome fitted M (M)

# Napier Test Airframe
## No. 1 (Lincoln B.2, RF402)
**Kits: 1/72nd: Airfix Lancaster B Mk I/III & Paragon Conversion 72051**
**1/48th: Tamiya Lancaster B Mk I/III & Paragon Conversion 48057**
Note: After the above tests with the Naiad, this aircraft undertook a number of tests for the Ministry of Supply.

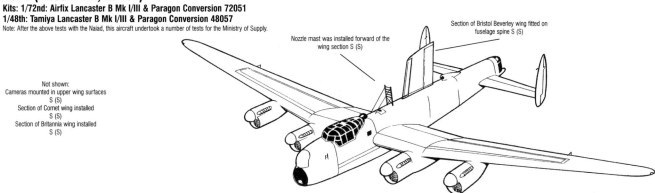

Nozzle mast was installed forward of the wing section S (S)

Section of Bristol Beverley wing fitted on fuselage spine S (S)

Not shown:
Cameras mounted in upper wing surfaces
S (S)
Section of Comet wing installed
S (S)
Section of Britannia wing installed
S (S)

## No.2 (B.2, RF342)
**Kits: 1/72nd: Airfix Lancaster B Mk I/III & Paragon Conversion 72051**
**1/48th: Tamiya Lancaster B Mk I/III & Paragon Conversion 48057**

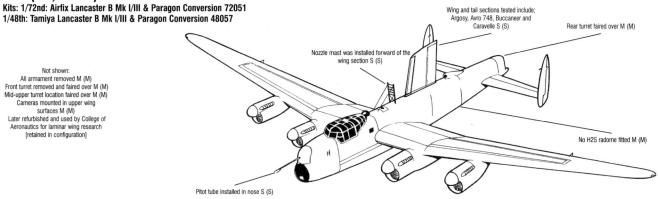

Wing and tail sections tested include;
Argosy, Avro 748, Buccaneer and
Caravelle S (S)

Rear turret faired over M (M)

Nozzle mast was installed forward of the
wing section S (S)

Not shown:
All armament removed M (M)
Front turret removed and faired over M (M)
Mid-upper turret location faired over M (M)
Cameras mounted in upper wing
surfaces M (M)
Later refurbished and used by College of
Aeronautics for laminar wing research
[retained in configuration]

No H2S radome fitted M (M)

Pitot tube installed in nose S (S)

## Nomad (B.2, SX973)
**Kits: 1/72nd: Airfix Lancaster B Mk I/III & Paragon Conversion 72051**
**1/48th: Tamiya Lancaster B Mk I/III & Paragon Conversion 48057**

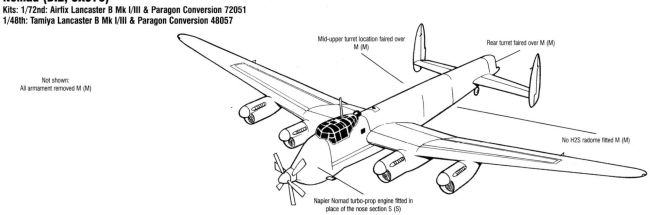

Mid-upper turret location faired over
M (M)

Rear turret faired over M (M)

Not shown:
All armament removed M (M)

No H2S radome fitted M (M)

Napier Nomad turbo-prop engine fitted in
place of the nose section S (S)

## Flight Refuelling (B.s, SX993 & RE293)
**Kits: 1/72nd: Airfix Lancaster B Mk I/III & Paragon Conversion 72051**
**1/48th: Tamiya Lancaster B Mk I/III & Paragon Conversion 48057**

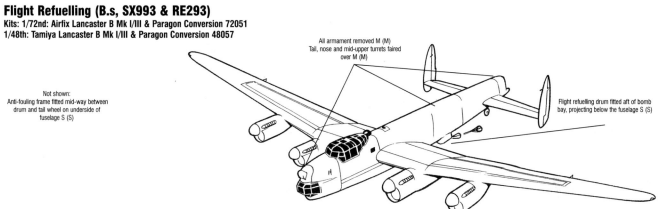

All armament removed M (M)
Tail, nose and mid-upper turrets faired
over M (M)

Not shown:
Anti-fouling frame fitted mid-way between
drum and tail wheel on underside of
fuselage S (S)

Flight refuelling drum fitted aft of bomb
bay, projecting below the fuselage S (S)

## Lancastrian
### Avon (Lancastrian C.2, VM732)
**Kits: 1/72nd: Airfix Lancaster B Mk I/III**
**1/48th: Tamiya Lancaster B Mk I/III**
Note: As per Lancastrian C.2 except:

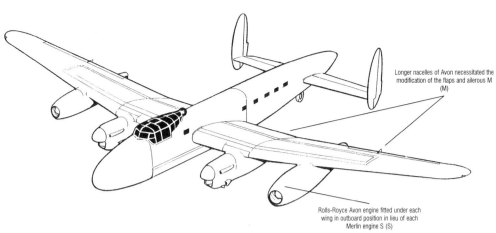

Longer nacelles of Avon necessitated the modification of the flaps and ailerons M (M)

Rolls-Royce Avon engine fitted under each wing in outboard position in lieu of each Merlin engine S (S)

### Avon (Lancastrian C.2, VL970)
**Kits: 1/72nd: Airfix Lancaster B Mk I/III**
**1/48th: Tamiya Lancaster B Mk I/III**
Note: As per Lancastrian C.2 except:

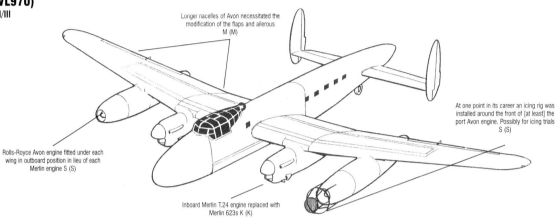

Longer nacelles of Avon necessitated the modification of the flaps and ailerons M (M)

At one point in its career an icing rig was installed around the front of [at least] the port Avon engine. Possibly for icing trials S (S)

Rolls-Royce Avon engine fitted under each wing in outboard position in lieu of each Merlin engine S (S)

Inboard Merlin T.24 engine replaced with Merlin 623s K (K)

### Clyde (Lancastrian C.2, VM704)
**Kits: 1/72nd: Airfix Lancaster B Mk I/III**
**1/48th: Tamiya Lancaster B Mk I/III**

Note: As per Lancastrian C.2 except:
Merlin 24s installed instead of T.24s inboard K (K)
Was intended that outboard engines would be replaced with Clyde turbo-props, but never installed

### Griffon (Lancastrian C.2, VM704)
**Kits: 1/72nd: Airfix Lancaster B Mk I/III**
**1/48th: Tamiya Lancaster B Mk I/III**
Note: As per Lancastrian C.2 except:

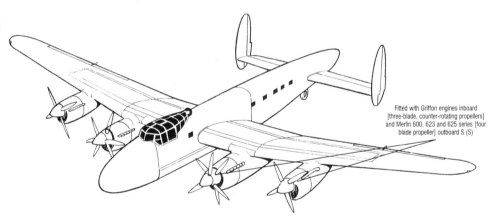

Fitted with Griffon engines inboard [three-blade, counter-rotating propellers] and Merlin 600, 623 and 625 series [four blade propeller] outboard S (S)

### Sapphire (Lancastrian C.2, VM733)
**Kits: 1/72nd: Airfix Lancaster B Mk I/III**
**1/48th: Tamiya Lancaster B Mk I/III**
Note: As per Lancastrian C.2 except:

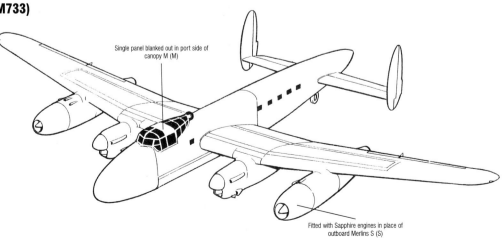

Single panel blanked out in port side of canopy M (M)

Fitted with Sapphire engines in place of outboard Merlins S (S)

## Ghost (Lancastrian C.2, VM703)
### Kits: 1/72nd: Airfix Lancaster B Mk I/III
### 1/48th: Tamiya Lancaster B Mk I/III
Note: As per Lancastrian C.2 except:

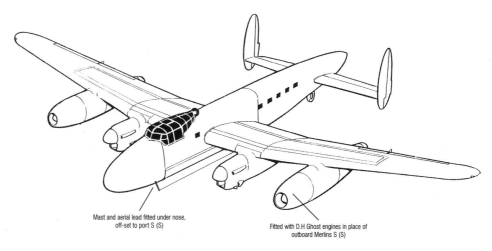

Mast and aerial lead fitted under nose,
off-set to port S (S)

Fitted with D.H Ghost engines in place of
outboard Merlins S (S)

## Ghost (Lancastrian C.2, VM749)
### Kits: 1/72nd: Airfix Lancaster B Mk I/III
### 1/48th: Tamiya Lancaster B Mk I/III
Note: As per Lancastrian C.2 except:

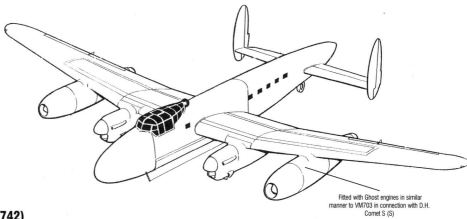

Fitted with Ghost engines in similar
manner to VM703 in connection with D.H.
Comet S (S)

## Nene (Lancastrian C.IV, VH737 & VH742)
### Kits: 1/72nd: Airfix Lancaster B Mk I/III
### 1/48th: Tamiya Lancaster B Mk I/III
Note: As per Lancastrian C.IV except;

Not shown:
Fuselage modification to increase fuel load
to 2,385 Gal (Kerosene) and 740 Gal
(Petrol)

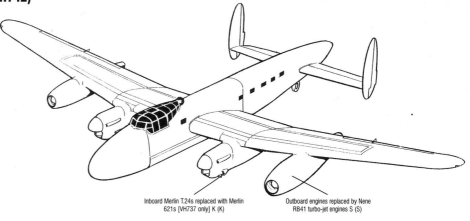

Inboard Merlin T.24s replaced with Merlin
621s [VH737 only] K (K)

Outboard engines replaced by Nene
RB41 turbo-jet engines S (S)

## Propeller Test Bed (Lancastrian C.2, VM733)
### Kits: 1/72nd: Airfix Lancaster B Mk I/III
### 1/48th: Tamiya Lancaster B Mk I/III

Note: As per Lancastrian C.2 except:
Originally intended for Clyde test programme, but these engines were never installed. Later used for;
1. Testing of paddle-blade de Havilland and Rotol propellers

Note:
All modifications that are not followed by the appropriate code letter and/or number are things which are internal, and therefore do not change the 'look' of the
model. They are listed here for completeness and in case modellers wish to add these internal items to their models.

KEY
K = Use components supplied in the kit
M = Modify existing kit components
S = Scratchbuild
Note: All conversion parts, e.g. '72150', refer to Paragon Design products unless otherwise stated.

# Detailing

O ne of the most complex areas to deal with in any modelling project is that of interior (and exterior) detail. What precisely is in the cockpit? What do the interior of the wheel wells look like? etc. All are questions which modellers ask. It can be a time-consuming process gathering all the information you need to attempt to detail any subject, so what we are offering in this chapter is a concise (ish!) section dealing with all those areas of the subject that you will want to know about.

## Manchester

### Cockpit Interior

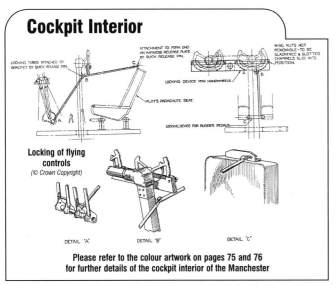

**Locking of flying controls**
(© Crown Copyright)

DETAIL 'A'    DETAIL 'B'    DETAIL 'C'

**Please refer to the colour artwork on pages 75 and 76 for further details of the cockpit interior of the Manchester**

### Fuselage

**Location of flares and chute in the rear fuselage, aft of the bomb bay**
(© Crown Copyright)

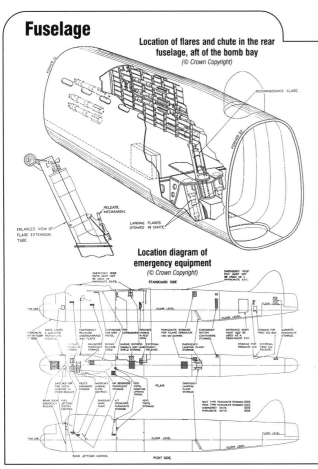

**Location diagram of emergency equipment**
(© Crown Copyright)

### Engine & Propellar

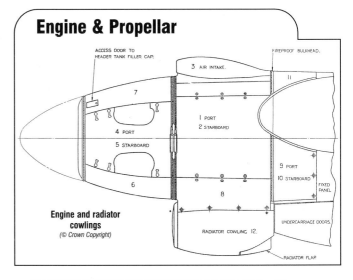

**Engine and radiator cowlings**
(© Crown Copyright)

### Wings

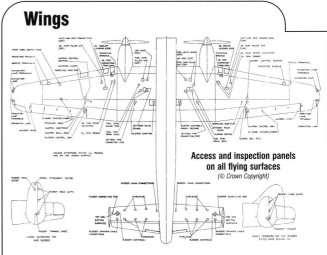

**Access and inspection panels on all flying surfaces**
(© Crown Copyright)

### Undercarriage • 1

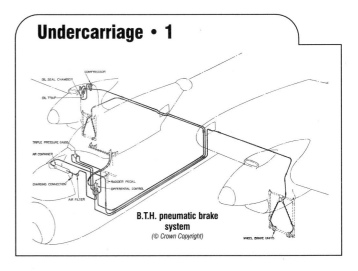

**B.T.H. pneumatic brake system**
(© Crown Copyright)

# Undercarriage • 2

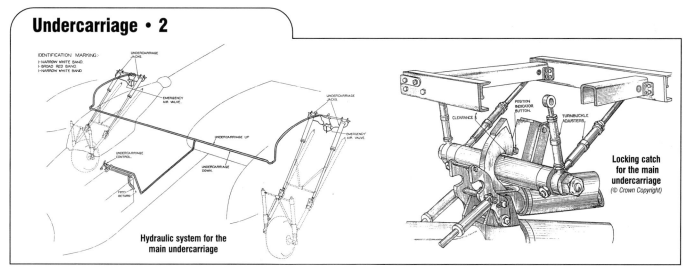

Hydraulic system for the main undercarriage

Locking catch for the main undercarriage
(© Crown Copyright)

# Turrets

The ventral F.N.21 turret
(© Crown Copyright)

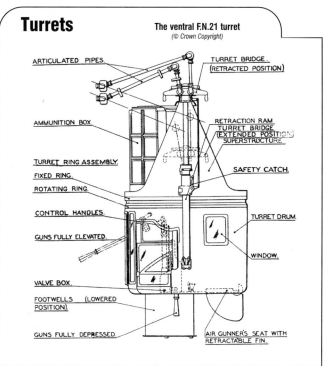

# Bombs & Bomb Load

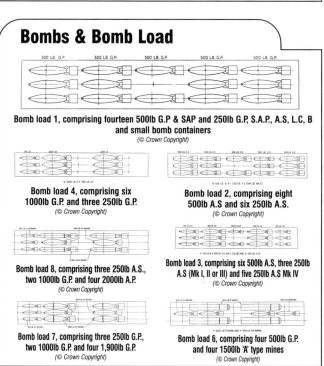

Bomb load 1, comprising fourteen 500lb G.P & SAP and 250lb G.P, S.A.P., A.S, L.C, B and small bomb containers
(© Crown Copyright)

Bomb load 4, comprising six 1000lb G.P. and three 250lb G.P.
(© Crown Copyright)

Bomb load 2, comprising eight 500lb A.S and six 250lb A.S.
(© Crown Copyright)

Bomb load 8, comprising three 250lb A.S., two 1000lb G.P. and four 2000lb A.P.
(© Crown Copyright)

Bomb load 3, comprising six 500lb A.S, three 250lb A.S (Mk I, II or III) and five 250lb A.S Mk IV
(© Crown Copyright)

Bomb load 7, comprising three 250lb G.P., two 1000lb G.P. and four 1,900lb G.P.
(© Crown Copyright)

Bomb load 6, comprising four 500lb G.P. and four 1500lb 'A' type mines
(© Crown Copyright)

# Miscellaneous

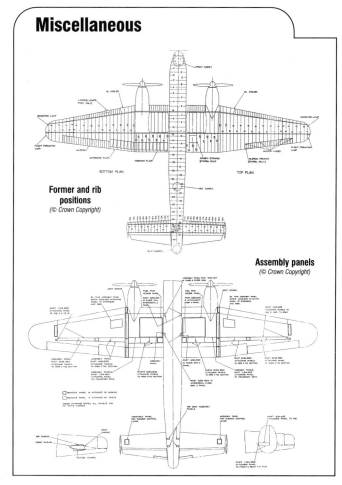

Former and rib positions
(© Crown Copyright)

Assembly panels
(© Crown Copyright)

# Radio Equipment

T.1154 & R.1155 (HF) installations
(© Crown Copyright)

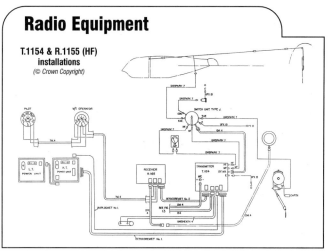

## Cockpit • 1

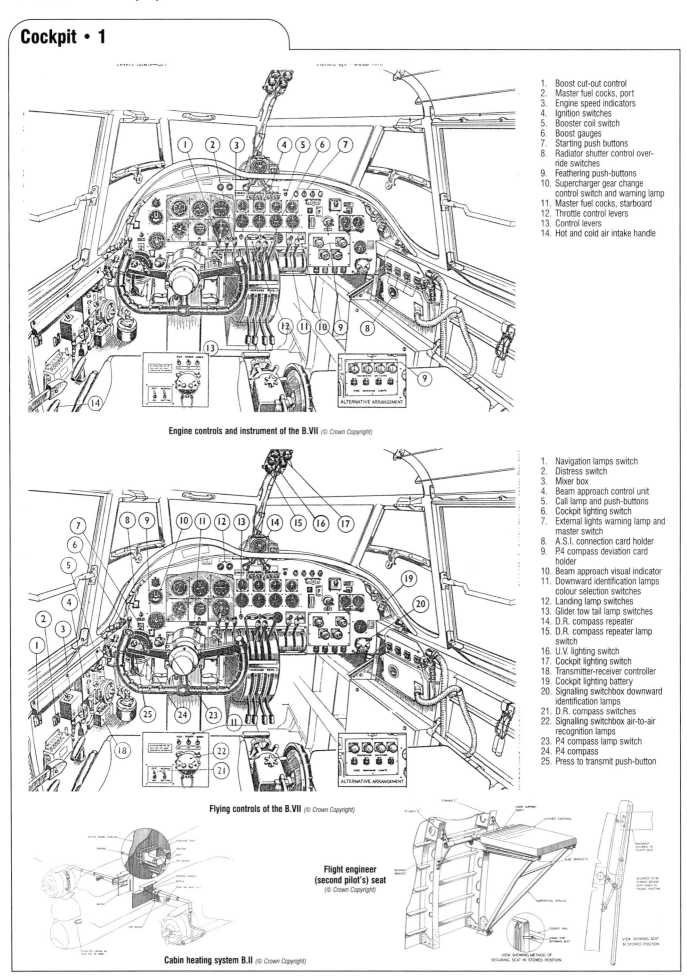

1. Boost cut-out control
2. Master fuel cocks, port
3. Engine speed indicators
4. Ignition switches
5. Booster coil switch
6. Boost gauges
7. Starting push buttons
8. Radiator shutter control over-ride switches
9. Feathering push-buttons
10. Supercharger gear change control switch and warning lamp
11. Master fuel cocks, starboard
12. Throttle control levers
13. Control levers
14. Hot and cold air intake handle

**Engine controls and instrument of the B.VII** (© Crown Copyright)

1. Navigation lamps switch
2. Distress switch
3. Mixer box
4. Beam approach control unit
5. Call lamp and push-buttons
6. Cockpit lighting switch
7. External lights warning lamp and master switch
8. A.S.I. connection card holder
9. P4 compass deviation card holder
10. Beam approach visual indicator
11. Downward identification lamps colour selection switches
12. Landing lamp switches
13. Glider tow tail lamp switches
14. D.R. compass repeater
15. D.R. compass repeater lamp switch
16. U.V. lighting switch
17. Cockpit lighting switch
18. Transmitter-receiver controller
19. Cockpit lighting battery
20. Signalling switchbox downward identification lamps
21. D.R. compass switches
22. Signalling switchbox air-to-air recognition lamps
23. P4 compass lamp switch
24. P4 compass
25. Press to transmit push-button

**Flying controls of the B.VII** (© Crown Copyright)

**Cabin heating system B.II** (© Crown Copyright)

**Flight engineer (second pilot's) seat** (© Crown Copyright)

# Cockpit • 2

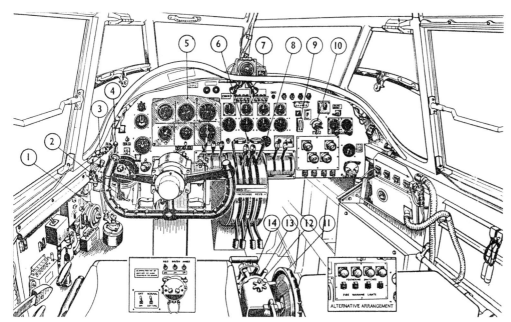

1. Pitch control
2. Air pressure and trim gauge
3. Cock
4. Clutch lever
5. Instrument flying panel
6. Flaps position indicator switch
7. Selector lever
8. Flaps position indicator
9. Suction gauge
10. Vacuum change-over cock lever
11. Elevator trimming tab control handwheel
12. Rudder trimming tab control handwheel
13. Aileron trimming tab control handwheel
14. Flaps control handle

Flying controls of the B.VII (© Crown Copyright)

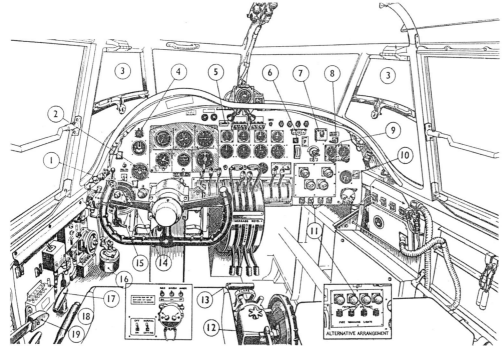

1. Bomb release button
2. Alighting gear position indicator
3. Direct-vision windows
4. Time clock
5. Alighting gear position indicator switch
6. Destrctor ON-OFF switch and buttons
7. Containers jettison push-button
8. Bomb jettison handle
9. Oxygen flow and contents gauges
10. Triple air-pressure gauge
11. Fire extinguisher push-button
12. Alighting gear control lever
13. Glider release handle
14. Brake lever parking catch
15. Brake lever
16. Windscreen de-icing pump
17. Fuel jettison handle
18. Seat adjusting lever
19. Bomb door lever

Operational and miscellaneous controls of the B.VII (© Crown Copyright)

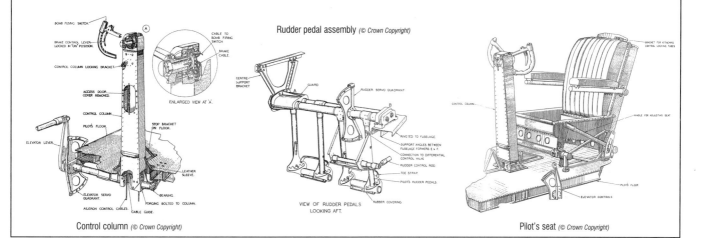

Control column (© Crown Copyright)

Rudder pedal assembly (© Crown Copyright)

Pilot's seat (© Crown Copyright)

WINDSCREEN SPRAY

PILOTS GLYCOL PUMP

PILOTS FLOOR

BOMB AIMERS
WINDOW SPRAY

CONTROL COCK.

GLYCOL TANK

BOMB AIMERS
GLYCOL PUMP

**Flare stowage and chute aft of the bomb bay [note ventral turret location]** (© Crown Copyright)

RELEASE
MECHANISM

ENLARGED VIEW OF
FLARE EXTENSION TUBE

PUMP

TO WINDSCREEN SPRAYS

WOOD BLOCK

PILOTS FLOOR
TOP SKIN

PILOTS FLOOR
BOTTOM SKIN

DISTANCE TUBE.

FROM GLYCOL TANK

ARRANGEMENT OF BOMB AIMER'S
GLYCOL PUMP.

**Windscreen de-icing system** (© Crown Copyright)

CONTROL COCKS

AIR VENT PIPE

NON-RETURN
VALVE

DELIVERY PIPES FROM
FUSELAGE AUXILIARY
TANK TO Nº1 TANKS

FUSELAGE AUXILIARY
TANK

ONE AUXILIARY TANK

OIL RESERVOIR
PT. No. Q.870.
DISTRIBUTOR
BLOCK
PT. No. Q.891

VENT PIPE TO ATMOSPHERE

HAND PUMP PT No C 7103

ACCUMULATOR PT No C 7104

RETURN

FEED

ONE DRIVEN
MP.-ST 80
OARD

GROUND TEST
CONNECTIONS
PT. No. C 7168

AUTOMATIC CUT-
OUT PT No C 7105

RETURN

FEED

HIGH PRESSURE
OIL FILTER
PT. No. 7ZL//79359

GROUND TEST
CONNECTIONS
PT. No. C 7168

BOMB DOOR
CONTROL VALVE.

MAIN WHEELS
CONTROL
VALVE

BOMB DOOR
CONTROL PIPES.

MAIN WHEELS
CONTROL PIPES

PILOTS FLOOR

FLAP
CONTROL
PIPES

FLAP CONTROL
VALVE

HOT & COLD AIR INTAKE
CONTROL VALVE.

ENGINE DRIVEN PUMP
PORT-INBOARD
PT. No. C 3589 L.H

JETTISON SYSTEM
CONTROL VALVE.

**The hydraulic supply system** (© Crown Copyright)

AIR VENT PIPE

CONTROL COCKS

FUSELAGE AUXILIARY
TANK Nº2

AIR VENT PIPE

NON-RETURN
VALVE

DELIVERY PIPES FROM
FUSELAGE AUXILIARY
TANKS TO Nº1 TANKS

FUSELAGE AUXILIARY
TANK Nº1

TWO AUXILIARY TANKS

**Single and twin overload tank fitment in the B.VII** (© Crown Copyright)

TANK SELECTOR COCK

FUSELAGE OVERLOAD TANKS
CONTROL COCKS

AIR VENT PIPE

TANK SELECTOR COCK

NON-RETURN
VALVE

DELIVERY PIPE FROM
FUSELAGE OVERLOAD
TANK TO Nº1 TANKS

FUSELAGE OVERLOAD TANK

THIS TANK CAN ONLY BE FITTED IN
AEROPLANES INCORPORATING MOD. Nº 431

**Overload fuel system (B.II) - one tank** (© Crown Copyright)

TANK SELECTOR COCK

FUSELAGE OVERLOAD TANKS
CONTROL COCKS

DELIVERY PIPE FROM
FUSELAGE OVERLOAD
TANKS TO Nº1 TANKS

AIR VENT PIPE

FUSELAGE OVERLOAD TANK Nº2

NON-RETURN VALVES

FUSELAGE OVERLOAD TANK Nº1

AIR VENT PIPE

TANK SELECTOR COCK

THESE TANKS CAN ONLY BE FITTED IN
AEROPLANES INCORPORATING MOD. Nº 431

**Overload fuel system (B.II) - two tanks** (© Crown Copyright)

# Engine • 1

Oil system for the outboard engines B.I/III *(© Crown Copyright)*

Engine cowlings for inboard engines of B.II with revised cowling after Mod.520 [inset] *(© Crown Copyright)*

Engine and radiator cowlings B.I/III, inboard [main] and outboard [inset] *(© Crown Copyright)*

Engine cowlings for inboard engines of B.II *(© Crown Copyright)*

Oil system outboard engines B.II *(© Crown Copyright)*

Oil system for the inboard engines *(© Crown Copyright)*

Main engine installation for B.II *(© Crown Copyright)*

The inboard engine sub-frame of the B.II *(© Crown Copyright)*

The inboard and outboard sub-frames of the B.II *(© Crown Copyright)*

Oil system inboard engines B.II *(© Crown Copyright)*

The outboard engine sub-frame of B.II *(© Crown Copyright)*

# Wings & Control Surfaces • 1

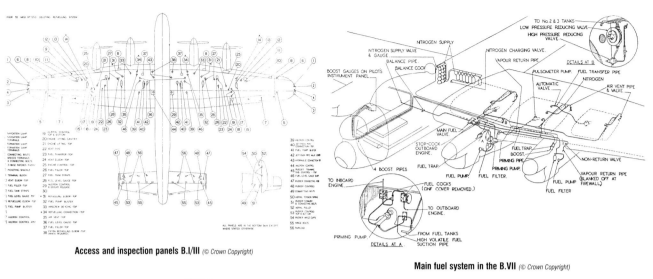

Access and inspection panels B.I/III *(© Crown Copyright)*

Main fuel system in the B.VII *(© Crown Copyright)*

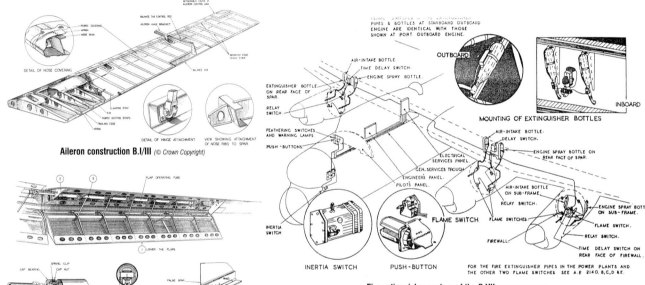

Aileron construction B.I/III *(© Crown Copyright)*

Fire extinguisher system of the B.VII *(© Crown Copyright)*

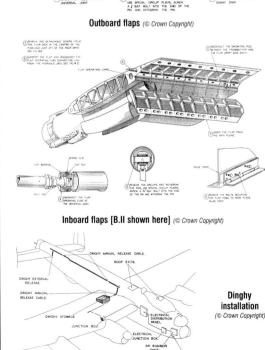

Outboard flaps *(© Crown Copyright)*

Inboard flaps [B.II shown here] *(© Crown Copyright)*

Dinghy installation *(© Crown Copyright)*

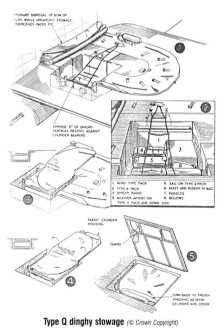

Type Q dinghy stowage *(© Crown Copyright)*

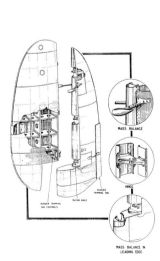

The enlarged 'Lincoln type' rudder and endplates of the B Mk VII *(© Crown Copyright)*

# Lancaster B Mk X

## Interior • 1

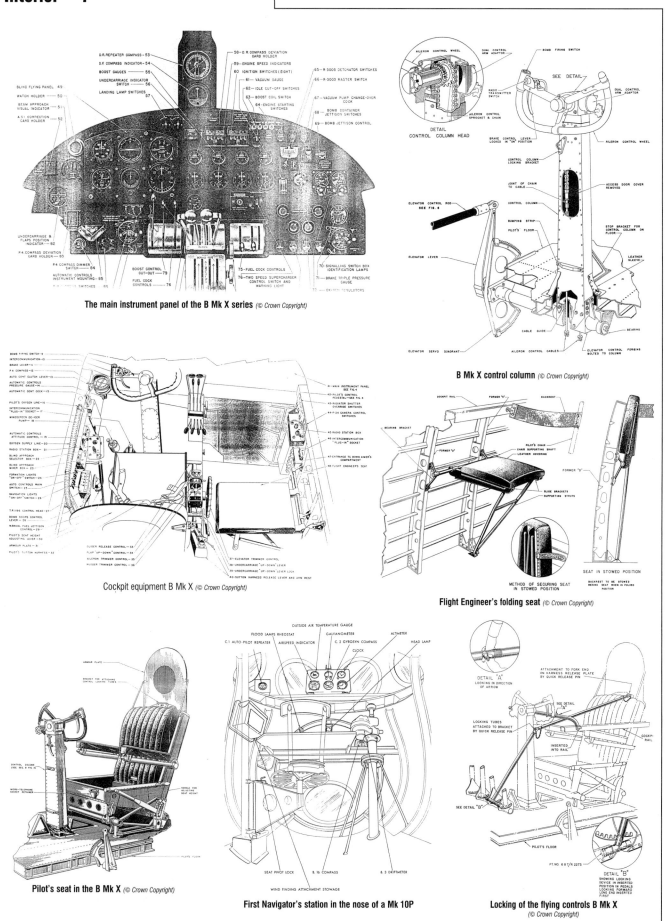

The main instrument panel of the B Mk X series *(© Crown Copyright)*

B Mk X control column *(© Crown Copyright)*

Cockpit equipment B Mk X *(© Crown Copyright)*

Flight Engineer's folding seat *(© Crown Copyright)*

Pilot's seat in the B Mk X *(© Crown Copyright)*

First Navigator's station in the nose of a Mk 10P

Locking of the flying controls B Mk X
*(© Crown Copyright)*

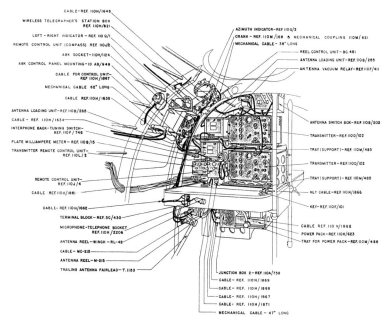

CABLE-REF. 110H/1648
WIRELESS TELEGRAPHER'S STATION BOX-REF. 110H/821
LEFT - RIGHT INDICATOR - REF. 110 Q/1
REMOTE CONTROL UNIT (COMPASS) REF. 110J/2
ABK SOCKET-110H/1124
ABK CONTROL PANEL MOUNTING-10 A9/949
CABLE FOR CONTROL UNIT-REF. 110H/1067
MECHANICAL CABLE 62" LONG
CABLE. REF. 110H/1635
ANTENNA LOADING UNIT-REF. 110B/265
CABLE - REF. 110H/1634
INTERPHONE BACK-TUNING SWITCH-REF. 110F/748
PLATE MILLIAMPERE METER - REF. 110B/15
TRANSMITTER REMOTE CONTROL UNIT-REF. 110L/2
REMOTE CONTROL UNIT-REF. 110J/4
CABLE- REF.110H/1661
CABLE-REF. 110H/1662
TERMINAL BLOCK-REF. 5C/430
MICROPHONE-TELEPHONE SOCKET REF. 110H/2206
ANTENNA REEL-WINCH - RL-42
CABLE- MC-215
ANTENNA REEL-M-215
TRAILING ANTENNA FAIRLEAD-T. 1153

AZIMUTH INDICATOR-REF.110Q/2
CRANK - REF. 110M/169 & MECHANICAL COUPLING 110M/621
MECHANICAL CABLE - 38" LONG
REEL CONTROL UNIT-BC 461
ANTENNA LOADING UNIT-REF.110B/265
ANTENNA VACUUM RELAY-REF.110F/411
ANTENNA SWITCH BOX-REF. 110B/202
TRANSMITTER-REF.110D/102
TRAY (SUPPORT)-REF. 110M/485
TRANSMITTER-REF.110D/102
TRAY (SUPPORT)-REF. 110M/485
KEY CABLE-REF. 110H/1866
KEY-REF.110H/101
CABLE REF. 110H/1862
POWER PACK-REF. 110K/623
TRAY FOR POWER PACK-REF.110M/486
JUNCTION BOX 2-REF.110A/738
CABLE- REF. 110H/1869
CABLE- REF. 110H/1868
CABLE- REF. 110H/1867
CABLE- REF. 110H/1871
MECHANICAL CABLE - 47" LONG

**Radio equipment at the radio operator's station in a B Mk X** *(© Crown Copyright)*

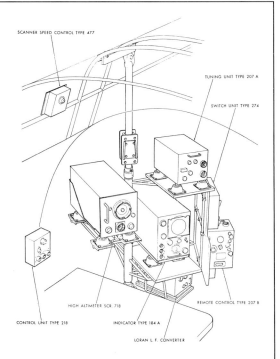

SCANNER SPEED CONTROL TYPE 477
TUNING UNIT TYPE 207 A
SWITCH UNIT TYPE 274
HIGH ALTIMETER SCR. 718
REMOTE CONTROL TYPE 207 B
CONTROL UNIT TYPE 218
INDICATOR TYPE 184 A
LORAN L. F. CONVERTER

**Radar equipment at the Navigator's station in a Mk 10P and Mk 10N**

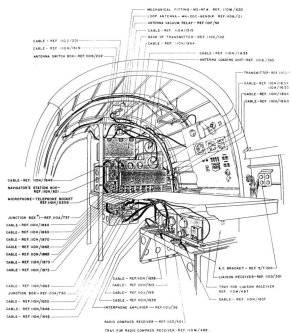

MECHANICAL FITTING - MS-47 A REF. 110M/620
LOOP ANTENNA - MN-20C-BENDIX REF.110B/21
ANTENNA VACUUM RELAY - REF 110F/411
CABLE - REF. 110H/1513
BACK OF TRANSMITTER - REF.110D/102
CABLE - REF. 110H/1864
CABLE - REF. 110J/201
CABLE - REF. 110H/1513
ANTENNA SWITCH BOX-REF.110B/202
CABLE- REF.110H/1633
ANTENNA LOADING UNIT-REF. 110B/265
TRANSMITTER-REF.110D/
CABLE- REF. 110H/1634 110H/1635
CABLE-REF. 110H/1864
CABLE-REF. 110H/1860

CABLE - REF. 110H/1649
NAVIGATOR'S STATION BOX-REF.110H/821
MICROPHONE-TELEPHONE SOCKET REF.110H/2206
JUNCTION BOX "1-REF.110A/737
CABLE-REF. 110H/1866
CABLE-REF. 110H/1863
CABLE-REF. 110H/1870
CABLE-REF. 110H/1862
CABLE-REF. 110H/1865
CABLE-REF. 110H/1873
CABLE-REF. 110H/1872
CABLE - REF. 110H/1863
JUNCTION BOX-REF.110A/736
CABLE - REF. 110H/1650
CABLE - REF. 110H/1648
CABLE - REF. 110H/1645

CABLE - REF.110H/1638
CABLE- REF.110H/1513
CABLE - REF.110J/199
CABLE - REF.110H/1639
INTERPHONE AMPLIFIER - REF.110U/36
RADIO COMPASS RECEIVER - REF.110D/401
TRAY FOR RADIO COMPASS RECEIVER - REF.110M/488

A.C BRACKET - REF. 5/T1310
LIAISON RECEIVER-REF.110D/301
TRAY FOR LIAISON RECEIVER REF. 110M/487
CABLE-REF.110H/1637

**Radio equipment at the navigator's station in a B Mk X** *(© Crown Copyright)*

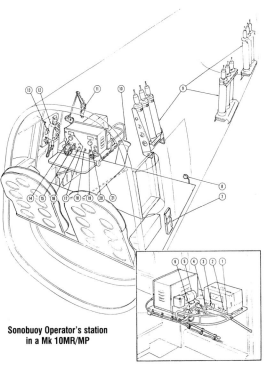

13 12 11 10 9

14 15 16 17 18 19 20 21 8 7

6 5 4 3 2 1

**Sonobuoy Operator's station in a Mk 10MR/MP**

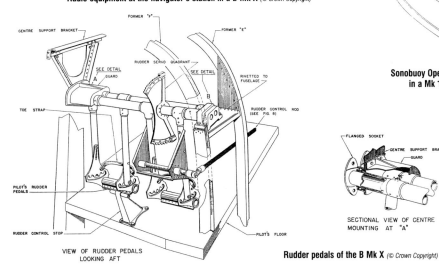

FORMER "F"
FORMER "E"
GENTRE SUPPORT BRACKET
RUDDER SERVO QUADRANT
SEE DETAIL A
GUARD
SEE DETAIL B
RIVETTED TO FUSELAGE
TOE STRAP
RUDDER CONTROL ROD (SEE FIG. 8)
PILOT'S RUDDER PEDALS
RUDDER CONTROL STOP
PILOT'S FLOOR
VIEW OF RUDDER PEDALS LOOKING AFT

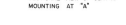

FLANGED SOCKET
CENTRE SUPPORT BRACKET
GUARD
SECTIONAL VIEW OF CENTRE MOUNTING AT "A"
SECTIONAL VIEW OF END MOUNTING AT "B"

**Rudder pedals of the B Mk X** *(© Crown Copyright)*

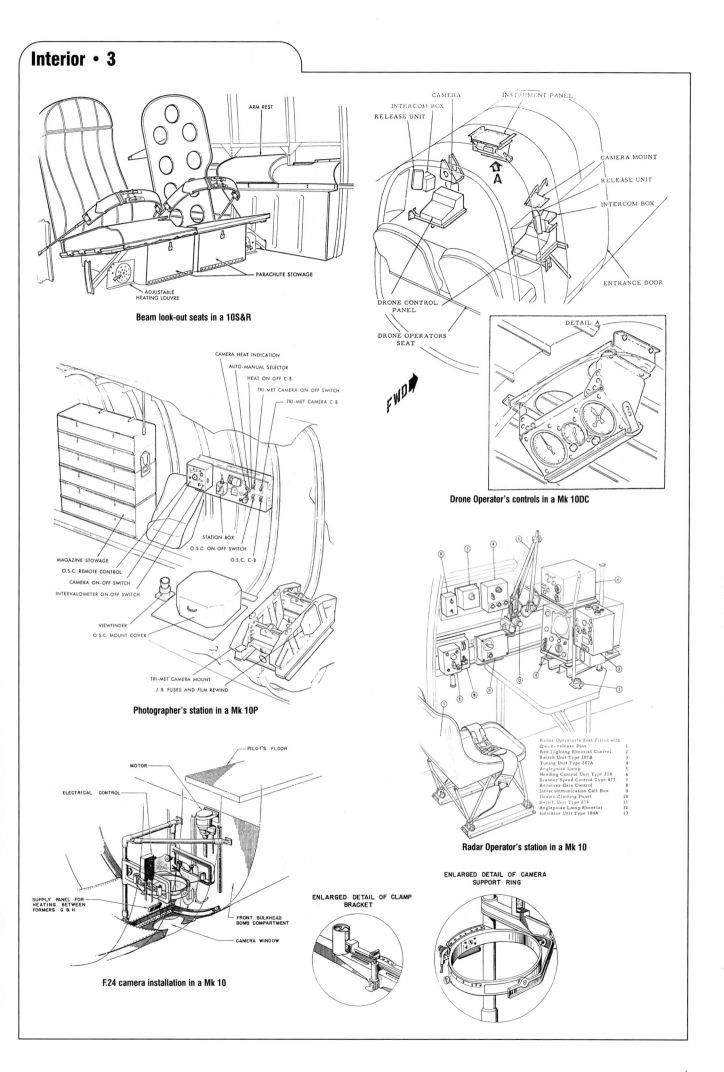

**Beam look-out seats in a 10S&R**

ARM REST

PARACHUTE STOWAGE

ADJUSTABLE HEATING LOUVRE

CAMERA

INTERCOM BOX
RELEASE UNIT

INSTRUMENT PANEL

A

CAMERA MOUNT

RELEASE UNIT

INTERCOM BOX

ENTRANCE DOOR

DRONE CONTROL PANEL

DRONE OPERATORS SEAT

FWD

DETAIL A

**Drone Operator's controls in a Mk 10DC**

CAMERA HEAT INDICATION
AUTO-MANUAL SELECTOR
HEAT ON-OFF C-B
TRI-MET CAMERA ON-OFF SWITCH
TRI-MET CAMERA C-B

STATION BOX
O.S.C. ON-OFF SWITCH
O.S.C. C-B

MAGAZINE STOWAGE
O.S.C. REMOTE CONTROL
CAMERA ON-OFF SWITCH
INTERVALOMETER ON-OFF SWITCH

VIEWFINDER
O.S.C. MOUNT COVER

TRI-MET CAMERA MOUNT
J. B. FUSES AND FILM REWIND

**Photographer's station in a Mk 10P**

Radar Operator's Seat Fitted with
Quick-release Pins                              1
Red Lighting Rheostat Control               2
Switch Unit Type 207B                          3
Tuning Unit Type 207A                          4
Anglepoise Lamp                                 5
Heading Control Unit Type 218              6
Scanner Speed Control Type 477           7
Receiver Gain Control                          8
Intercommunication Call Box                 9
Heated Clothing Panel                         10
Switch Unit Type 274                          11
Anglepoise Lamp Rheostat                   12
Indicator Unit Type 184A                     13

**Radar Operator's station in a Mk 10**

PILOT'S FLOOR

MOTOR

ELECTRICAL CONTROL

SUPPLY PANEL FOR HEATING BETWEEN FORMERS G & H

FRONT BULKHEAD BOMB COMPARTMENT

CAMERA WINDOW

**F.24 camera installation in a Mk 10**

ENLARGED DETAIL OF CLAMP BRACKET

ENLARGED DETAIL OF CAMERA SUPPORT RING

# Lancaster B Mk I, II, III & VII

## Turrets • 1

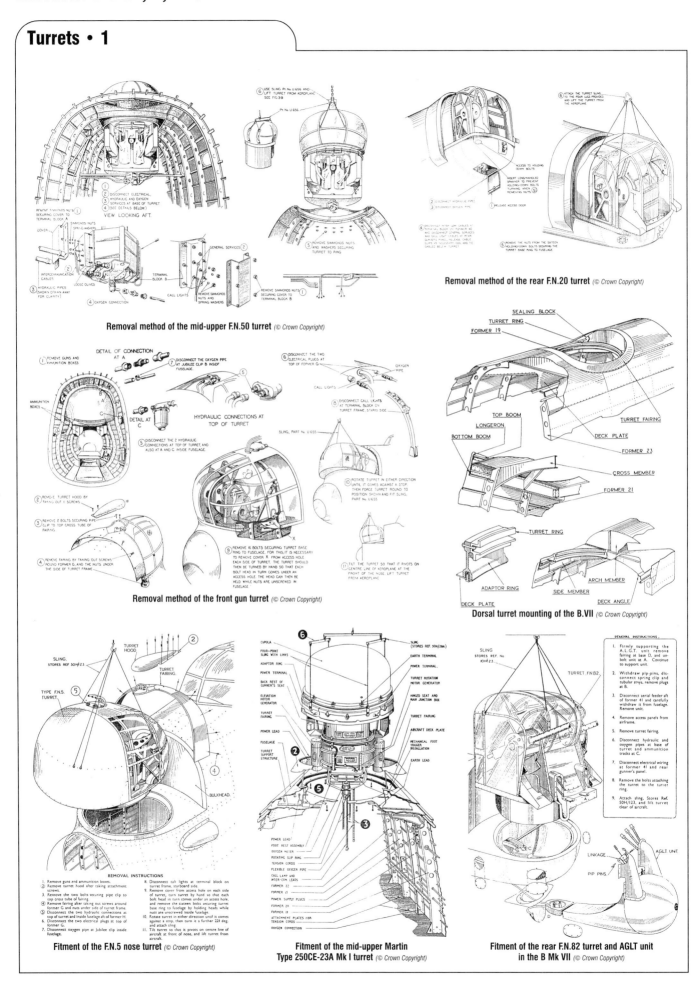

Removal method of the mid-upper F.N.50 turret *(© Crown Copyright)*

Removal method of the rear F.N.20 turret *(© Crown Copyright)*

Removal method of the front gun turret *(© Crown Copyright)*

Dorsal turret mounting of the B.VII *(© Crown Copyright)*

Fitment of the F.N.5 nose turret *(© Crown Copyright)*

Fitment of the mid-upper Martin Type 250CE-23A Mk I turret *(© Crown Copyright)*

Fitment of the rear F.N.82 turret and AGLT unit in the B Mk VII *(© Crown Copyright)*

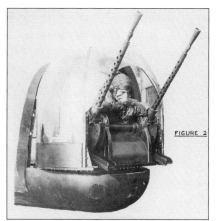

This official shot shows the Rose rear turret, and how (in theory) the gunner could vacate it via the front *(Author's Collection)*

Wartime shot of a gunner in the standard F.N. 20 rear turret of a Lancaster *(Author's Collection)*

Nice wartime shot into an F.N.82 rear turret *(Author's Collection)*

Wartime shot of the AGLT radar fitted under an F.N.82 rear turret of a Lancaster *(Author's Collection)*

• **1** Clear shot of the construction of the lower sections of an F.N. 82 turret, as well as the curved glazing panels in this B Mk VII *(© R.A.Franks)*

• **2** Unlike a B Mk I/II/III, the F.N.82 in a B Mk VII has very little in the way of an aerodynamic fairing, as can be seen here *(© R.A.Franks)*

• **3** This is the bulge above the front turret which protects the power and hydraulic cables that power the turret *(© R.A.Franks)*

• **4** Overall side view of the F.N.5 turret used in all marks of the Lancaster *(© R.A.Franks)*

• **5** The perforated barrel jackets and muzzle blast dampers on the Browning 0.303in machine guns in the front turret *(© R.A.Franks)*

• **6** View up into the front turret, showing all the framework inside the turret and the beading on the outside that retains the glazing *(© R.A.Franks)*

• **7** The rear identification lamp usually fitted below the turret on a Lancaster can't be installed in the AGLT radome is in place, so two new lamps are fitted either side of the turret, as seen here on a B Mk VII *(© R.A.Franks)*

• **8** Overall view of the F.N.82 turret in a B Mk VII *(© R.A.Franks)*

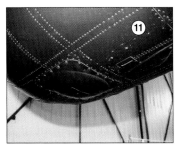

- **9** The side profile of an F.N.82 turret is very different from an F.N.20 or 121, as can be seen here (© R.A.Franks)

- **10** Close-up of the gun barrel and the cartridge chutes on an F.N.82 turret (© R.A.Franks)

- **11** Under the rear turret of the BBMFs B Mk III is this domed access panel. Unlike the RAFMs B Mk I, which has a flat panel here (© R.A.Franks)

- **12** This is the faring that was added forward of the rear turret to reduce the buffeting caused by transversing the turret in flight (© R.A.Franks)

- **13** Close-up of the machine gun barrels exiting the rear turret housing (© R.A.Franks)

- **14** Muzzle blast dampers on the rear turret machine guns of the BBMF machine (© R.A.Franks)

- **15** Side view of the rear turret (F.N.20) in the BBMF machine clearly showing the structure inside this unit (© R.A.Franks)

- **16** If you stick you head out the hatch in the dorsal spine, and look aft, this is the view of the mid-upper turret and its associated fairing (© R.A.Franks)

- **17** Inside the fuselage this is the view from on top of the bomb bay aft. You can see what a huge obstacle the mid-upper turret is to the crew! (© R.A.Franks)

- **18** View up into the front of the mid-upper turret. You can see the lap straps and the simple seat (© R.A.Franks)

- **19** Viewed from further away, the 'can' of the turret can be seen. Note the cartridge collection bags at the back (© R.A.Franks)

- **20** It is impossible to photograph the interior of a turret, but here you can see the electrical control panel between the breeches of the guns n the mid-upper turret (© R.A.Franks)

- **21** Another view inside the mid-upper turret, this time showing the port side (© R.A.Franks)

- **22** This view inside the F.N.82 rear turret in B Mk VII, NX622 shows the control column/trigger unit in the centre and the breeches of the guns (© Jim Grant)

# Bomb Bay, Bombs & Bomb Loads

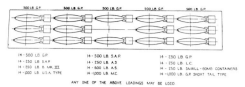

14 - 500 LB. G.P.
14 - 250 LB. S.A.P.
14 - 250 LB. B. MK. III
14 - 1000 LB. U.S.A. TYPE

14 - 500 LB. S.A.P.
14 - 250 LB. A.S.
14 - 600 LB. A.S.
14 - 1000 LB. G.P.

14 - 250 LB. G.P.
14 - 250 LB. L.C.
14 - 250 LB. SMALL-BOMB CONTAINERS
14 - 1000 LB. G.P. SHORT TAIL TYPE

ANY ONE OF THE ABOVE LOADINGS MAY BE USED.

**Bomb load 1, comprising fourteen of any of the types listed**
**[B.I/II/III/VII/X] (© Crown Copyright)**

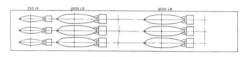

8 - 500 LB. & 6 - 250 LB. A.S. (MK. IV ONLY)

**Bomb load 2, comprising eight 500lb G.P. and six 250lb A.S. Mk IVs**
**[B.I/II/III/VII/X]** *(© Crown Copyright)*

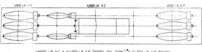

6 - 500 LB. & 3 - 250 LB. A.S. (MK. I, II & III) AND 5 - 250 LB. S.A.P.

**Bomb load 3, comprising six 500lb G.P., three 250lb A.S Mk I, II or III**
**and five 250lb A.S [B.I/II/III/VII/X]** *(© Crown Copyright)*

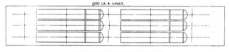

6 - 1000 LB. & 3 - 250 LB. G.P.

**Bomb load 4, comprising three 250lb G.P and six 1000lb G.P.**
**[B.I/II/III/VII/X]** *(© Crown Copyright)*

1 - 4,000 LB. H.C. & 6 - 1,000 LB. G.P. (SHORT TAIL TYPE) & 2 - 250 LB. G.P. BOMBS
OR 6 - 1,000 LB. U.S.A. BOMBS OR 1,000 LB. M.C. BOMBS

**Bomb load 5, comprising six 1000lb G.P (with short tails), two 250lb**
**G.P. and one 4000lb H.C. The 1000lb G.Ps could be replaced with**
**1000lb American or M.C. bombs [B.I/II/III/VII/X]** *(© Crown Copyright)*

6 - 1500 LB. A MINES OR 6 - 2000 LB. H.C. BOMBS

**Bomb load 6, comprising six 1500lb Type A mines or six 2000lb**
**H.C. bombs [B.I/II/III/VII/X]** *(© Crown Copyright)*

6 - 1900 LB. & 3 - 250 LB. G.P.

**Bomb load 7, comprising three 250lb G.P. and six 1900lb G.P**
**[B.I/II/III/VII/X]** *(© Crown Copyright)*

6 - 2000 LB. A.P. & 3 - 250 LB.S.A.P.

**Bomb load 8, comprising three 250lb S.A.P. and six 2000lb A.P.**
**[B.I/II/III/VII/X]** *(© Crown Copyright)*

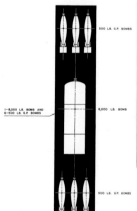

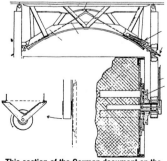

**Bomb load 9, comprising six 500lb G.P and one 8000lb H.C**
**(or six 500lb G.P.) bombs [B Mk X]** *(© Crown Copyright)*

- **1** The forward bulkhead of the bomb bay in a B Mk VII. Note the two inspection panels *(© R.A.Franks)*

- **2** Overall view of an Upkeep mine. Note the prominent rivets and bolts on the casing *(© R.A.Franks)*

- **3** Just to prove that the tail fins on a Grand Slam are off-set to induce spin, here is a view of the example at the RAFM *(© R.A.Franks)*

- **4** Close-up of a bomb rack in the bomb bay. Note the mass of pipes on the side of the bomb bay *(© R.A.Franks)*

- **5** Overall view, looking aft, in the BBMF Lancaster. The red units in the middle are crutches for H.C bombs *(© R.A.Franks)*

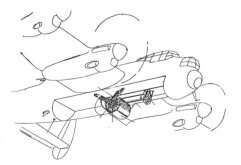

Extract from a German document showing the Upkeep installation in the Dams Raids Lancasters

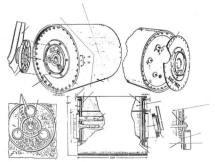

This section of the German document on the Upkeep mine shows how it was suspended under the Lancaster

Another extract from the German documentation on the Upkeep, this one shows the bombs construction

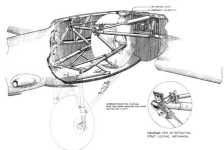

Main undercarriage B.I/III & B.II *(© Crown Copyright)*

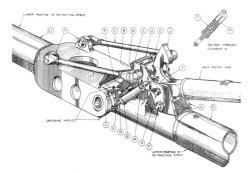

Retracting strut locking mechanism B.I/III & B.II *(© Crown Copyright)*

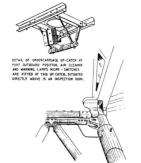

The main undercarriage of the B.VII *(© Crown Copyright)*

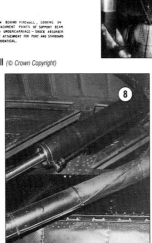

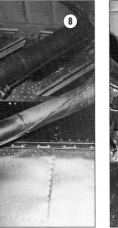

• **1** View up inside the front section of the wheel well. The two bottle at the top are fire extinguishers, while all the equipment further forward is associated with the hydraulic systems *(© R.A.Franks)*

• **2** View of the main hub and oleo leg on a B Mk VII. Note the brake pipe entering the hub. The silver section remains still, while the black section of the hub rotates around it *(© R.A.Franks)*

• **3** The tailwheel on a B Mk VII with the towing arm attached. This machine is a F.E. standard and one of the items that always seems to be changed on these machines is the tailwheel, which as seen here, is a Lincoln, anti-shimmy type. Note the lack of twin-contact anti-shimmy tyre and the damper unit on the front of the oleo *(© R.A.Franks)*

• **4** Overall view of the plain hub style and checked tyre pattern on a B Mk VII. The wire running off to the right is a ground earthing lead *(© R.A.Franks)*

• **5** Viewed from the back, and with the tail in 'flight' attitude, this B Mk Is twin-contact anti-shimmy tyre is clearly visible *(© R.A.Franks)*

• **6** Being airworthy, the BBMFs machine features modern fire extinguishers in the wheel wells. Note the exposed inboard fuel cell to the right *(© R.A.Franks)*

• **7** On the rear bulkhead of the main wheel wells are these blocks. I presume they are either 'scuff' blocks for the main wheels, or just stoppers for the undercarriage doors *(© R.A.Franks)*

• **8** This is the main retraction jack and strut *(© R.A.Franks)*

• **9** Looking into the back of the main wheel well, you can see these hydraulic connectors and valves associated with the retraction jacks *(© R.A.Franks)*

• **10** Attached to the cross-braces on the main oleo leg is this hydraulic pipe for the brakes *(© R.A.Franks)*

# Undercarriage • 2

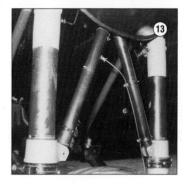

• **11** A look back along the undercarriage door, showing its profile as well as the linkage rod that is attached to it (© R.A.Franks)

• **12** Here you can see the substantial locking mechanism in the middle of the retraction arms of the main undercarriage. The red rod is a ground lock (© R.A.Franks)

• **13** Overall view of the main oleo legs and their cross-members (© R.A.Franks)

• **14** Highly cluttered view of the forward bulkhead in the undercarriage bay (© R.A.Franks)

• **15** Rear view of the undercarriage doors, showing their profile and the linkage arm at the front (© R.A.Franks)

• **16** Forward of the lock on the main retraction arm is this step, which allows the ground crew a safe platform on which to stand whilst working up inside the well (© R.A.Franks)

• **17** This is a clear view of the Lincoln style anti-shimmy tailwheel unit fitted to the BBMF Lancaster. Late-series Lancasters and F.E conversions all seem to have this unit fitted and this does away with the need for the twin-contact anti-shimmy tyre on the tailwheel (© R.A.Franks)

• **18** The tailwheel of the B Mk VII (NX622) in Australia is fitted with this odd diamond pattern treaded tyre. The yoke looks OK, but I am not sure about either the tyre or the hub (© Jim Grant)

# Miscellaneous

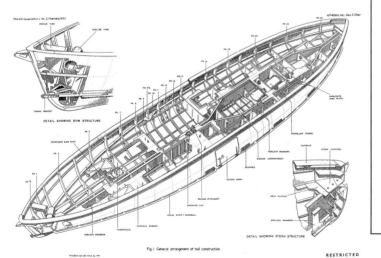

Fig.I. General arrangement of hull construction

The overall diagram of the Airborne Lifeboat Mk IIA. The Mk II carried by the Lancaster is very similar (© Crown Copyright)

CH11-301. Although this does not refer to the Lancaster ASR/GR (this is the Shackleton MR.2), this diagram does show the linkage system used to secure the Airborne Lifeboat under the Lancaster's bomb bay (© Crown Copyright)

# Radio

• **1** This is the SCR series radio transmitter/receiver that was used in Lancasters operated by the RAF in the Middle East, as well as by the Aéronavale and post-war Canadian machines (© R.A.Franks)

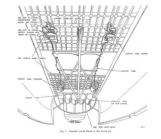

Diagram showing installation and equipment stowed inside an ASR/GR Lancaster bomb bay (© Crown Copyright)

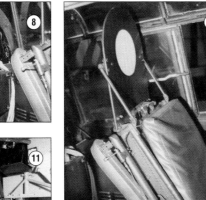

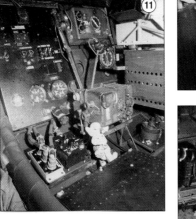

• **1** View down into the nose of a B Mk VII (© R.A.Franks)

• **2** Close-up of the kneeling pad over the oval panel in the nose of the B Mk VII (© R.A.Franks)

• **3** The gauges associated with the beam approach system, seen here in a B Mk VII (© R.A.Franks)

• **4** Overall view of the B Mk VII instrument panel (© R.A.Franks)

• **5** Shot of the pilot's seat as well as the trim wheel that is located alongside it in the B Mk VII (© R.A.Franks)

• **6** Overall view of the navigator's station in a B Mk VII. The two boxes at the top are tuners, behind and below that is an Air Mileage unit and the large indicator at the back is associated with Gee (© R.A.Franks)

• **7** Above the navigator's station is the bulkhead, which is padded in this B Mk VII. The item on top is an Aldis Lamp (© R.A.Franks)

• **8** Overall view of the navigator's station in a B Mk VII. Note the pilot's seat back to the right (© R.A.Franks)

• **9** Pilot's seat. The reason for the dot is often questioned. All I can suggest is does is show that the armours is in the up position, or if the pilot is still upright! (© R.A.Franks)

• **10** View of the control column and port sidewall in a B Mk VII (© R.A.Franks)

• **11** Overall view of the navigator's station in the BBMF machine. The box on the wall at right is the Air Mileage unit, below which is the repeater from the Master Compass and the circular switch on the deck is the DR Compass controller (© R.A.Franks)

• **12** On the left side of the navigator's table is the indicator for the Gee system (© R.A.Franks)

• **13** Opposite the navigator is the Astro Compass, plus an oxygen economiser (© R.A.Franks)

• **14** Looking back inside the canopy you can see the DF loop (and Snoopy!) (© R.A.Franks)

• **15** Overall view of the ex-Aéronavale (duel-control) B Mk VII (NX622) in Australia (© Jim Grant)

# Fuselage • 2

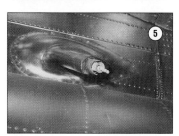

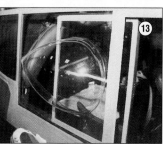

- **1** The de-icer jets in front of the windscreen [B Mk VII shown] *(© R.A.Franks)*

- **2** The astro-dome at the rear of the canopy *(© R.A.Franks)*

- **3** Aerial leads attached to the canopy framework and fuselage side on a B Mk VII *(© R.A.Franks)*

- **4** Aerial lead-in on the port fuselage side, below and slightly aft of the mid-upper turret *(© R.A.Franks)*

- **5** Trailing aerial fairlead on the port lower fuselage side, just above the bomb bay doors and slightly aft of the wing leading edge *(© R.A.Franks)*

- **6** Nice shot of the shape of the ventral H₂S radome when viewed from the bomb bay *(© R.A.Franks)*

- **7** This is one of the three downward ident lights in the lower rear fuselage. The aft section of the H2S radome should be clear, as this exposes the two other lights units that are currently obscured by it *(© R.A.Franks)*

- **8** The rear access door. As this B Mk VII is an ex-Aéronavale machine, the door has had the window in it covered over to look more 'war-like', but you can still see its location *(© R.A.Franks)*

- **9** Overall view of the later series [B Mk VII shown] bomb aimer's blister *(© R.A.Franks)*

- **10** The main antenna unit seen on either side of the nose *(© R.A.Franks)*

- **11** Close-up view of the windscreen, showing the hinged panel in the centre *(© R.A.Franks)*

- **12** Overall view of the windscreen *(© R.A.Franks)*

- **13** The sliding panel and the blister in the canopy. Not all Lancasters had the blisters *(© R.A.Franks)*

- **14** This outlet appears on a number of Lancasters. I suspect it is either a vent or a charging point, but its precise use is unknown *(© R.A.Franks)*

- **15** This guard protects the outlet of the flare dispenser in the rear fuselage. It is to port and aft of the H₂S radome *(© R.A.Franks)*

- **16** Here you can see the two aerial leads attached to the vertical fin endplate *(© R.A.Franks)*

- **17** Lower section of the endplate. Note the leading edge de-icer boots on this B Mk VII *(© R.A.Franks)*

- **18** Overall side view of the H₂S radome. Usually the rear section was clear and in some cases (especially post-war) the entire radome was clear *(© R.A.Franks)*

- **18a** The flat optical panel in the larger style bomb aimer's blister has the de-icing pipework you can see here fitted to it *(© R.A.Franks)*

# Fuselage • 3

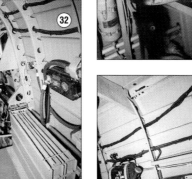

• **19** The pitot static head is situated on the port fuselage side, just below the canopy (© R.A.Franks)

• **20** Being an F.E. machine, this B Mk VII features the oval panel aft of the bomb aimer's blister. Aft of this is the escape hatch and further aft and to the right is the tactical camera (© R.A.Franks)

• **21** These are the two rear idents lights on a B Mk I. The circular access panels to either side are relating to the turret mechanism, while the larger one underneath is for access to the centre pivot point of the rear turret (© R.A.Franks)

• **22** The antenna either side of the nose on a B Mk I, as well as the outlets below it which are associated with the cabin heater system (© R.A.Franks)

• **23** At the rear of the fuselage, on the port side aft of the access door is this cover and pull handle that contains a first aid kit and dinghy (© R.A.Franks)

• **24** This is the rear fuselage transit joint on the BBMF machine and as you can see it leads to quite a pronounced step at this point (© R.A.Franks)

• **25** With neither a ventral turret or $H_2S$ radar installed, this is the shape of the surround that is exposed on the underside (© R.A.Franks)

• **26** The window fitted to the port fuselage side to give light in the radio operator's station (© R.A.Franks)

• **27** This is the bulkhead and step in the bulkhead in the bomb aimer's compartment. Note the parachute stowage and the frame to the side of it that is around the tactical camera (© R.A.Franks)

• **28** This is the hydraulic reservoir inside the fuselage above the aft spar (© R.A.Franks)

• **29** The crew rest bunk in the fuselage mid-section. On certain types (like the B Mk VII) this area was packed with electronic equipment (© R.A.Franks)

• **30** You can see the rear spar in the background, but what you see here is the worm jack for the flaps (© R.A.Franks)

• **31** This is the port side of the fuselage, just at the extreme back of the bomb bay, looking aft (© R.A.Franks)

• **32** This is the starboard side of the fuselage, at the extreme rear of the bomb bay, looking aft. The rear turret ammunition boxes can be clearly seen (© R.A.Franks)

• **33** The starboard fuselage side, just aft of the rear bomb bay bulkhead. Here you can see the hydraulic reservoir for the mid-upper turret as well as its electrical distribution box (© R.A.Franks)

• **34** In the back bulkhead of the bomb bay, you get inspection portholes. In the B Mk I and III these usually consist of two on the port side [as shown] and one on the starboard. Later marks [B Mk VII etc] have just one either side of the step in the middle (© R.A.Franks)

• **35** Overall view of the bomb bay rear bulkhead. Note the steps (this was where the flare chute was in earlier machines) and the two portholes (© R.A.Franks)

• **36** This is the starboard fuselage side directly forward of the mid-upper turret. Here you can see a fire extinguisher, a wire mesh container with a portable oxygen bottle in it and an oxygen economiser for the gunner (© R.A.Franks)

• **37** The port fuselage side, forward of the mid-upper turret. Here you can see a hydraulic reservoir and a stowed parachute (© R.A.Franks)

• **38** Aft of the mid-upper turret, on the port fuselage side is the DR compass. As you can see this fragile item is protected by a metal frame (© R.A.Franks)

• **39** The flare dispenser fitted on the port fuselage side opposite the rear access door (© R.A.Franks)

• **40** With the step for the rear access door visible in the left hand corner, here you can see the Elsen toilet and the spar for the tailplane (© R.A.Franks)

• **41** The rear fuselage section viewed from about where the Elsen is (© R.A.Franks)

• **42** Moving further aft, here you can see the inner doors just aft of the rear turret and the interior of the turret itself (© R.A.Franks)

• **43** A closer shot of the port side of the last few feet of the fuselage. Here you can see the doors, the portable oxygen bottle in the mesh cage and a stowed parachute (© R.A.Franks)

• **44** This is the starboard side of the aft fuselage. Here you can see the doors, a storage crate, electrical distribution box and fire extinguisher (© R.A.Franks)

• **45** This is the bomb sight sighting head (© R.A.Franks)

• **46** This is the electrical distribution panel on the port side of the bomb aimer's station (© R.A.Franks)

• **47** The starboard side of the bomb aimer's station in the later marks includes the T-1 bombing computer. The small grey box above and behind it is a controller for the tactical camera (© R.A.Franks)

• **48** A strange shot I know, but this is what the pilot's rudder pedals look like when viewed from the bomb aimer's station (© R.A.Franks)

• **49** Overall view into the nose of the BBMF Lancaster. The yellow grab rails are modern concessions for safety (© R.A.Franks)

• **50** The BBMF Lancaster is an F.E. version with dual controls. Here you can see the dual yoke as well as the rudder pedals (© R.A.Franks)

• **51** Overall view of the canopy framework on the port side. Note the grab rail for the sliding section (© R.A.Franks)

• **52** The flight engineer's panel opposite the pilot. Note his seat stowed to the left (© R.A.Franks)

• **53** The BBMF Lancaster has had the navigator's table truncated, so here you get a look at the starboard sidewall, aft of the pilot' seat that would usually be behind various bits of electronic equipment (© R.A.Franks)

• **54** Overall view of the some-what abridged navigator's table in the BBMF machine (© R.A.Franks)

• **55** Overall view back in the cockpit. You can see the padded bulkhead as well as the DF loop towards the rear and the sun screens stowed in the top of the canopy (© R.A.Franks)

• **56** This is the front section of the canopy. You can see the frame of the escape hatch at the extreme top and the cluster of dimmer switches further forward (© R.A.Franks)

• **57** Nice overall view of the instrument panel and the dual controls in the BBMF machine (© R.A.Franks)

• **58** The radio operator's station in the mid-section. Here you can see the standard 1154/155 Transmitter/receiver combination, as well as the H2S indicator to the left. Note the access to the astrodome above (© R.A.Franks)

• **59** If the radio operator turns round, this is the view. Here you can see the hydraulic reservoir on the spar, the signal pistol attached in the roof and the oxygen economiser on the side. Note that all the cockpit area and nose right back to the radio operators compartment are black, while aft of this is Interior Grey/Green.

• **60** A closer look at the signal pistol in the roof

• **61** Opposite the radio operator is this electrical distribution panel on the port fuselage side

# Engine • 2

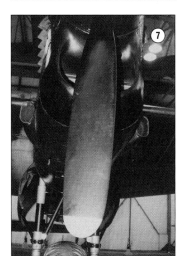

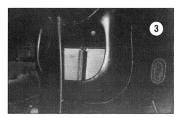

• **1** The single-stack exhaust stacks on the B Mk VII. Note that they are bifurcated, as on the engine block each outlet per cylinder is split. Some earlier Lancasters had two-into-one stacks, while others had non-bifurcated stacks *(© R.A.Franks)*

• **2** The rear section of the inboard engine nacelles are split, so that as the flaps drop [as shown here] they can tuck inside the fixed section of the nacelle *(© R.A.Franks)*

• **3** View into the front of the radiator. The unit is split vertically for oil and coolant elements *(© R.A.Franks)*

• **4** This B Mk I has the wartime flame dampers fitted over the exhaust stacks *(© R.A.Franks)*

• **5** View into the back of the radiator unit in a B Mk I *(© R.A.Franks)*

• **6** The profile and blade cut-outs in the spinner of the Lancaster can be seen here. These are for 'paddle' blades *(© R.A.Franks)*

• **7** Clear view of the profile of a 'paddle' blade *(© R.A.Franks)*

• **8** A view down onto one of the carburettor intakes on the side of the nacelle, showing the ice guard that is fitted *(© R.A.Franks)*

• **9** Nice close-up of the bifurcated style of exhaust stack *(© R.A.Franks)*

• **10** View into the rear section of the inboard engine, showing the frames that supports the cowlings and the engine bearer *(© R.A.Franks)*

• **11** This is the aft section of the radiator outlet on the engine nacelle. Note the vent pipe protruding from the cowl on the left *(© R.A.Franks)*

• **12** With the flaps up, here you can see the step and gap that is at the back of the inboard engine nacelles *(© R.A.Franks)*

• **13** Close-up of the engine panels, showing the fire extinguisher access panel used by ground crews *(© R.A.Franks)*

• **14** A look into the radiator cowling, showing the linkage arms that operate the outlet flap *(© R.A.Franks)*

• **15** Overall shot of the outboard starboard engine with the main cowling removed *(© R.A.Franks)*

• **16** A closer look inside the exposed outboard engine nacelle *(© R.A.Franks)*

• **17** This shot shows a totally exposed engine on a B Mk VII (NX622) in Australia *(© Jim Grant)*

• **18** A top view of the starboard inner engine of a B Mk VII *(© Jim Grant)*

• **19** This complete engine unit (probably a late 224 series) is displayed with the radiator, header tank and engine bearers *(© Dave Frowen)*

• **20** Close-up of the non-bifurcated exhaust stacks on a later series engine *(© Dave Frowen)*

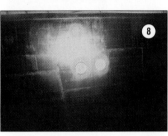

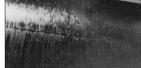

• **1** All Lancaster flaps are slipt into two sections, as seen here. The flaps operate on the bar you can see at the top, which rotates and pulls all the rods upwards thereby closing the flap *(© R.A.Franks)*

• **2** A closer look at the rod and linkage system for the flaps *(© R.A.Franks)*

• **3** The inboard section of the flaps. Note the fixed section at the extreme inboard area and the corresponding cut-out in the flaps *(© R.A.Franks)*

• **4** Nice overall shot of the construction of the flaps on this B Mk VII *(© R.A.Franks)*

• **5** Trim tab linkage on a B Mk VII *(© R.A.Franks)*

• **6** One of the many static discharge wicks fitted on the control surfaces of late-series Lancasters [B Mk VII shown] *(© R.A.Franks)*

• **7** Not an easy shot, this nevertheless shows the overall profile of a B Mk VII wing *(© R.A.Franks)*

• **8** Under the outboard wing panel on the port side are these two downward ident lamps *(© R.A.Franks)*

• **9** These are the counter balance weights on the trim tabs of a B Mk I *(© R.A.Franks)*

• **10** This shot shows the inboard outer edge of the flap, as well as the section that moves inside the nacelle *(© R.A.Franks)*

• **11** Due to buffeting, caused by the rear turret, a fairing was added behind it and this required this section to be removed from the inboard section of the elevators, as seen here on the BBMFs example *(© R.A.Franks)*

• **12** because of its varied career the BBMF Lancaster has been locally modified with this single rear light unit *(© R.A.Franks)*

• **13** Close-up of the mass balance weights on the rudder of the BBMF Lancaster *(© R.A.Franks)*

• **14** This is the outboard vent for the fuel tanks in the BBMF machine. The white stains form the exhaust that are visible to the left are quite common *(© R.A.Franks)*

• **15** These are the three outboard cable-cutter on the leading edge of the wing on the BBMF machine *(© R.A.Franks)*

• **16** This vent is under the starboard wing leading edge, just outboard of the root *(© R.A.Franks)*

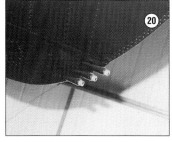

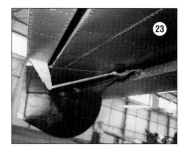

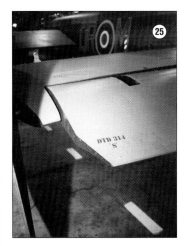

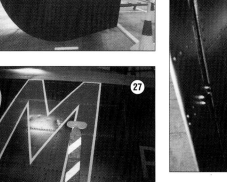

• **17** Here you can see the inboard fuel tank vent and its bulged cover, plus the access door to its right (© R.A.Franks)

• **18** The BBMF machine does not have the cabin heating system installed, so this intake in the inboard wing leading edge has been filled, but usually this would be open (© R.A.Franks)

• **19** Prominent control horns and linkage can be seen on the upper surface of each wing for the trim tabs (© R.A.Franks)

• **20** The trailing edge of the wing tip has these three lights fitted, although on the BBMF machine here, these have been capped (© R.A.Franks)

• **21** This is the prominent control surface hinge that can be seen on the underside of the tailplane (© R.A.Franks)

• **22** Here is the linkage and actuator horn of the trim tab on the elevators (© R.A.Franks)

• **23** This is the outboard trim tab linkage under the starboard elevator (© R.A.Franks)

• **24** The cut-out on the inside of the endplates, showing the linkage inside of it for the rudder (© R.A.Franks)

• **25** Overall view of the extreme end of the tailplane as well as the elevator on the starboard side. Note the cut-out in both to allow for the full movement of the rudder (© R.A.Franks)

• **26** The 'Lincoln style' later rudder. The increased trim tab area resulted in the lower edge of the endplate being simply squared-off to give this revised profile. Many of the post-war Lancasters (ASR/GR IIIs) had these fitted (© R.A.Franks)

• **27** Often officially called the 'static source', this static vent can be found on either side of the rear fuselage, just forward of the rear transit joint (© R.A.Franks)

• **28** The trailing aerial fairlead on the starboard fuselage side, just below the leading edge of the wing (© R.A.Franks)

• **29** Up under the nose of the BBMF machine you will find the tell-tale oval panel that identifies this machine as a Far East (F.E.) conversion (© R.A.Franks)

• **30** The tactical F.24 camera mounted in the back of the nose (© R.A.Franks)

• **31** Just so you know what is inside, this shot shows the inboard leading edge panels hinged open to expose all the pipework etc that is inside (© Jim Grant)

# Lancaster B Mk X

## Fuselage

Emergency equipment and exits in a B Mk X *(© Crown Copyright)*

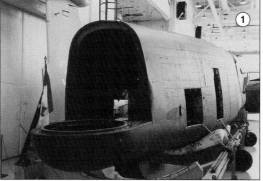

• **1** With the rear turret and tailplanes removed from the TAM machine, here you can see the resulting holes including the massive 'box' opening for the tailplane spar *(© Bill Coffman)*

Windscreen de-icing system in the B Mk X *(© Crown Copyright)*

Installation diagram for the T-1 bomb sight *(© Crown Copyright)*

## Bomb Bay, Bombs & Bomb Loads

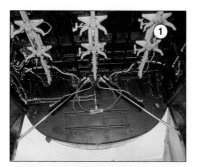

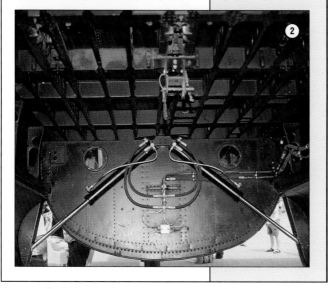

• **1** View up into the bomb bay, looking forward, of the CWHs B Mk X *(© A. Cline)*

• **2** The view towards the back of the CWH B Mk Xs bomb bay *(© A. Cline)*

## Turrets

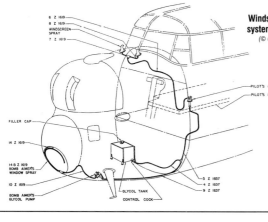

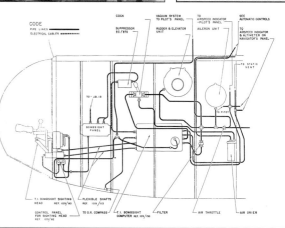

• **1** The Martin 250 mid-upper turret *(© A. Cline)*

• **2** Another view of the Martin 250 mid-upper turret *(© A. Cline)*

• **3** The rear F.N. 20 turret of the Mk X *(© A. Cline)*

• **4** Side view of the F.N. 20 turret showing the internal structure *(© A. Cline)*

# Undercarriage

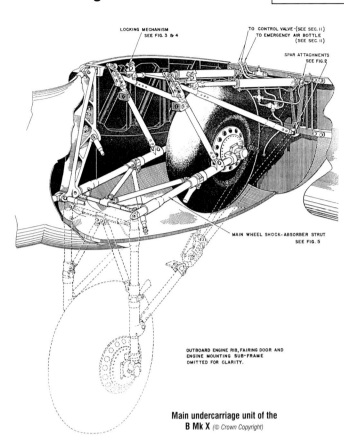

LOCKING MECHANISM
SEE FIG. 3 & 4

TO CONTROL VALVE-(SEE SEC. 11)
TO EMERGENCY AIR BOTTLE
(SEE SEC. 11)

SPAR ATTACHMENTS
SEE FIG. 2

MAIN WHEEL SHOCK-ABSORBER STRUT
SEE FIG. 5

OUTBOARD ENGINE RIB, FAIRING DOOR AND
ENGINE MOUNTING SUB-FRAME
OMITTED FOR CLARITY.

**Main undercarriage unit of the
B Mk X** *(© Crown Copyright)*

• **1** Overall shot of the main undercarriage leg of a Mk X *(© A. Cline)*

• **2** The CWH's airworthy B Mk X is fitted with these tyres that have a checked tread pattern *(© A. Cline)*

• **3** The TAM Lancasters main undercarriage has been retracted for many years, so at least the wheels seem OK! *(© Bill Coffman)*

• **4** The centre section, viewed from the back. Here you can see the rear spar web and the linkage for the controls. The massive H section is not original, it was used to support the aircraft on a pylon for many years *(© Bill Coffman)*

• **5** The inner side of the starboard inboard engine. Note the mass of pipework in the wing leading edge (all nicely wrapped in asbestos!) *(© Bill Coffman)*

• **6** The main wheels fitted to the B Mk X at the NAM in Canada. Note the different style of hub fitted to this machine. This seems to be more in keeping with Maritime Lancasters *(© Bill Coffman)*

• **7** This view from the rear of the NAMs Lancaster show the extent at which the tyres bulge under weight, as well as the shape and position of the undercarriage doors *(© Bill Coffman)*

# Engines, Wings & Control Surfaces

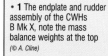

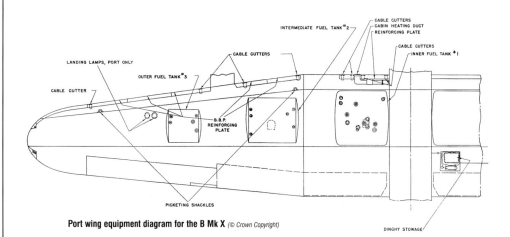

Port wing equipment diagram for the B Mk X *(© Crown Copyright)*

**Labels on diagram:**
- CABLE CUTTERS
- CABIN HEATING DUCT
- REINFORCING PLATE
- INTERMEDIATE FUEL TANK #2
- CABLE CUTTERS
- CABLE CUTTER
- INNER FUEL TANK #1
- LANDING LAMPS, PORT ONLY
- OUTER FUEL TANK #3
- CABLE CUTTER
- B.B.P. REINFORCING PLATE
- PICKETING SHACKLES
- DINGHY STOWAGE

INBOARD ENGINE

- 3
- 10
- 1 PORT
- 2 STARBOARD
- 8 PORT
- 9 STARBOARD
- 7
- 6
- 11
- 4 PORT
- 5 STARBOARD

**Engine and radiator cowlings of the B Mk X** *(© Crown Copyright)*

- 3
- 10
- 1 PORT
- 2 STARBOARD
- 8 PORT
- 9 STARBOARD
- 11

OUTBOARD ENGINE

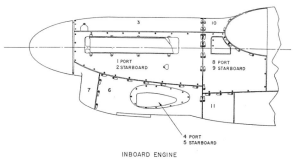

- **1** The endplate and rudder assembly of the CWHs B Mk X, note the mass balance weights at the top *(© A. Cline)*

- **2** You don't often get to see a Lancaster in bits, so this shot of TAM B Mk Xs engine bearers is very useful *(© Bill Coffman)*

- **3** The TAM Lancaster again, this time you can see all the ribs of the inner wing section as well as the oil tank, bulkhead and engine bearers. The air bottles are for the emergency undercarriage and flap extension *(© Bill Coffman)*

- **4** The starboard side of the centre section of the TAM airframe. Note the lack of air bottles on this side

- **5** The exhaust stacks of the B Mk X in the NAM in Canada. Note that these stacks are not bifurcated, they are single units with a fish-tail outlet *(© Bill Coffman)*

- **6** This view of the tip of a B Mk X wing shows the three lights at the trailing edge and the single light on the leading edge *(© Bill Coffman)*

## Bomb doors, and construction
*(© Crown Copyright)*

PORT DOOR
RUBBER SEALING STRIP
END RIB
BOMB DOOR INNER SKIN
STIFFENER
JACK ATTACHMENT
HINGE AT "A"
HINGE CHANNEL
INTERMEDIATE RIB
SPAR
BOMB DOOR OUTER SKIN
EDGE CHANNEL

DETAIL OF BOMB DOOR CONSTRUCTION (FORWARD END)

VIEW OF HINGE AT "A"

## Canopy framing construction *(© Crown Copyright)*

JOINT "A" WINDSCREEN FRAME TO STEEL TUBES
JOINT "C" SPRUCE FRAME TO STEEL TUBES
JOINT "E" SPRUCE FRAME TO FUSELAGE
JOINT "B" WINDSCREEN FRAME TO STEEL TUBES
SPRUCE
WELDED STEEL TUBES
TOP GUIDE FOR SLIDING WINDOW
JOINT "D", JOINTS IN SPRUCE FRAME
SLIDING WINDOW AT "Y"
BOTTOM GUIDE FOR SLIDING WINDOW SECURED TO COCKPIT RAIL
FROM INSIDE LOOKING OUT
FROM INSIDE LOOKING IN
WINDSCREEN FRAME DIE-CAST
FRAME SCREWED TO GUIDE
DIRECT VISION WINDOW AT "X"

## F.24 tactical camera mount *(© Crown Copyright)*

CAMERA MOTOR
BULKHEAD AT FORMER E
TYPE A MAGAZINE
TYPE 25 MOUNT
INSTALLATION OF F24 CAMERA
FLEXIBLE DRIVE
F24 CAMERA
MOUNTING ASSEMBLY

## Elevator construction
*(© Crown Copyright)*

TRIMMING TAB
BALANCE TAB
HINGE
MASS BALANCE LEVER
RIB WELDED STEEL TUBE
HARDWOOD SIDE MEMBERS
SERATED FABRIC STRIPS
FABRIC COVER
TRIMMER OPERATING GEAR
SEE DETAIL "A"
BALANCE WEIGHT WELDED TO RIBS
ELEVATOR SPAR
SLOTS FOR HINGE BRACKETS
FABRIC COVERING

DETAILS OF HINGE ATTACHMENT

HARDWOOD
CONNECTING ROD TO BALANCE TAB
DETAIL "A" BALANCE TAB CONNECTIONS
HINGE BRACKET

## Aileron construction [B Mk X shown]
*(© Crown Copyright)*

AILERON SPAR
HINGE ARM
HINGE ATTACHMENT FITTING
AILERON HINGE POSITION

DETAIL OF HINGE ATTACHMENT TO AILERON SPAR

METAL APRON
AILERON CONTROL ARM ATTACHED HERE (SEE SECT. 8 FIG 5)
BALANCE TAB CONTROL ROD
BALANCE TAB
FABRIC COVERING
FABRIC CLAMPING-STRIP
TRIMMER CONTROL GEAR FABRIC SEATING STRIP INSPECTION HOLES
AILERON SPAR
TRIMMER CONTROL CABLE (SEE SECT. 8 FIG. 14)
TRIMMER TAB

NOSE RIB
FABRIC COVERING
METAL APRON
AILERON SPAR
METAL COVERING

VIEW SHOWING ATTACHMENT NOSE RIB TO SPAR

DETAIL OF NOSE COVERING SHOWING CLAMPING STRIPS

## Tailplane construction [B Mk X shown] *(© Crown Copyright)*

ENLARGED DETAIL SHOWING ATTACHMENT OF NOSE RIBS
ENLARGED DETAIL SHOWING ATTACHMENT OF STRINGERS
STRINGER ATTACHMENT BRACKET
STRINGER
STIFFENER

REAR JOINT OF PORT & STARBD HALVES OF TAILPLANE (SEE FIG. 1)
FRONT JOINT OF PORT & STARBD HALVES OF TAILPLANE (SEE FIG. 1)
"A"
"B"

## Fuel jettison system
*(© Crown Copyright))*

IDENTIFICATION MARKING ONE BROAD WHITE BAND
CUT AWAY OF JETTISON VALVE SHOWING CLOSED POSITION
JETTISON VALVE OPEN
AIR VALVE PT. NO.F 4007
JETTISON VALVE PT. NO.P 5061
FUEL TANK
AIR VALVE PT. NO.F 4007
JETTISON PT. NO.P 5061
HYDRAULIC FEED (REF.)
JETTISON CONTROL VALVE PT. NO.C 5603
TO ATMOSPHERE

ENLARGED DETAIL OF RUDDER CONTROL LEVER AT "A"

BALL BEARING HOUSING
ENLARGED DETAIL OF RUDDER CONTROL OPERATING LEVER AT "B"

# Miscellaneous • 2

## Wing leading edge cable cutters
*(© Crown Copyright)*

ENLARGED DETAIL OF CONTAINER FOR CABLE CUTTER

DOUBLE CUTTER

STEEL REINFORCING PLATE

STEEL REINFORCING PLATE

RETAINING NUT

WELD

₡ OF ENGINE

₡ OF ENGINE

## Main undercarriage locking mechanism *(© Crown Copyright)*

LOWER PORTION - RETRACTING STRUT
2 LUGS—LOWER PORTION RETRACTING STRUT
3 SIDE STRUT ASSEMBLY
4 SWITCH OPERATING PIN
5 DOWN CATCH LOCKS
17 SPRING IN PLUNGER
18 SPRING IN PLUNGER
SECTION THROUGH CYLINDER 13
6 UP CATCH LOCK
7 LATCH SPRING PIN
JACK PISTON ROD
3 SIDE STRUT ASSEMBLY
GREASING NIPPLE
16 SHAFT
15 LEVERS
14 SPRING UNIT PLUNGER
13 SPRING UNIT ASSEMBLY
12 ARRESTOR BLOCK
11 LATCH HINGE PIN
10 JACK FORK PIN
9 UPPER PORTION - RETRACTING STRUT
8 LUGS—UPPER PORTION RETRACTING STRUT

## Main undercarriage legs
*(© Crown Copyright)*

TOP END FITTING 1
INFLATION VALVE 2
TOP OUTER CYLINDER 3
20 BALANCE PIPE
BALANCE PIPE 19 CONNECTION
STACK PIPE 18
PISTON NUT ATTACHMENT 17
GLAND NUT 16
GLAND RING 15
BOTTOM CYLINDER 14
CYLINDER SEATING 13
STEEL SEALING WASHER 12
SPECIAL NUT 11
ATTACHMENT SLEEVE 4
U/C DOOR TUBE PICK UP 5
LOCKING CLIP TECALAMITE FITTING 6
ATTACHMENT SLEEVE 7
LOCKING CLIP TECALAMITE FITTING 6
SCREWED ROD 8
CIRCLIP LOCKING END CAP 10
9 AXLE
21 SET SCREW
22 TOP INTERNAL CYLINDER
23 PISTON
24 RECOIL DAMPING VALVE
25 GLAND RING
26 RUBBER PERCUSSION RINGS
27 DISTANCE PIECE
28 PISTON ROD
29 DISTANCE PIECE
30 LOCKING SCREW
31 BRONZE LINER
32 SPLIT BEARING
33 BOTTOM SLIDING TUBE
34 BRAKE TORQUE ARM
35 AXLE ATTACHMENT FITTING

## Rear turret ammunition tracks *(© Crown Copyright)*

AMMUNITION TRACK COVER PLATES

RESERVE AMMUNITION BOXES

AMMUNITION BOXES REAR TURRET

AMMUNITION CHUTES CUT AWAY FOR CLARITY

FORMER

FORMER

DETAIL OF ATTACHMENT OF AMMUNITION CHUTE AT FORMER 22

DETAIL OF ATTACHMENT OF AMMUNITION CHUTE AT FORMER 23

DETAIL OF ATTACHMENT OF AMMUNITION CHUTE AT FORMERS 28, 30, 31, 32, 33, 34, 35, 36, & 40

## Crutching and fusing of an 800lb H.C bomb *(© Crown Copyright)*

FRONT CENTRE SECTION FLOOR
FRONT SPAR
CENTRE SECTION FLOOR
REAR SPAR
REAR CENTRE SECTION FLOOR
FLOOR INTERCOSTALS
BOMB CRUTCHING GEAR - REAR (SEE FIG 16)
SIDE FUSING UNITS
BOMB CRUTCHING GEAR - FRONT (SEE FIG 16)
FRONT FUSING UNITS
BOMB SLIP TYPE "G"
QUICK RELEASE BUTTONS
FUSING UNIT
FUSING CABLE TO BOMB
ENLARGED VIEW OF FRONT FUSING UNITS

## Crutching and fusing a 4000lb H.C. bomb *(© Crown Copyright)*

FRONT CENTRE SECTION FLOOR
FRONT SPAR
CENTRE SECTION FLOOR
REAR SPAR
REAR CENTRE SECTION FLOOR
FLOOR INTERCOSTALS
SIDE FUSING UNITS
FRONT FUSING UNITS (SEE FIG 19)
BOMB SLIP TYPE "F"
QUICK - RELEASE PIN
TURNBUCKLE
TIE MEMBER
QUICK - RELEASE PINS
ENLARGED VIEW OF CRUTCHING UNIT

# Lincoln B.I/II

## Cockpit • 1

### Engine controls and instruments
(© Crown Copyright)

1. Engine speed indicator
2. Boost gauges
3. Ignition switches
4. Supercharger M.S.-AUTO switch, warning lamps and test push-button
5. Slow running cut-off switches protected by guard rail.
6. Starting push-buttons
7. Booster coil push-buttons
8. Engine priming push-buttons
9. Primer master switch and warning lamp
10. Air cleaner switch
11. Hot and cold air-intake switch
12. Feathering push-buttons
13. Radiator shutter control over-ride switches
14. Master fuel cocks, starboard
15. Oil pressure gauges
16. Throttle control levers
17. Propeller control levers
18. Master fuel cocks, port
19. Boost cut-out control

### Flying controls and instruments
(© Crown Copyright)

1. Instrument-flying panel
2. Suction gauge
3. Vacuum change-over switch
4. Flaps position indicator
5. Flaps control handle
6. Aileron trimming tab control handwheel
7. Rudder trimming tab control handwheel
8. Elevator trimming tab control handwheel
9. Clutch lever
10. Air pressure gauge
11. Cock
12. Pitch control
13. Selection lever

### Navigational, signalling and lighting equipment
(© Crown Copyright)

1. A.S.I. correction card holder
2. Beam approach visual indicator
3. P4 compass lamp switch
4. Downward identification lamp colour selection switch
5. P4 compass
6. D.R. compass repeater
7. Repeater compass lamp switch
8. Cockpit floodlight switches
9. Signalling switchbox
10. Glider tow tail lamp switch
11. Landing lamps switch
12. Navigation lamps switch
13. Resin lamps Off-ON switch
14. External lamps warning lamp and master switch
15. Beam approach control unit
16. Distress switch
17. Isolation switch for navigators telephone
18. Call lamp and push-button

### Operational and miscellaneous controls and instruments
(© Crown Copyright)

1. Alighting gear position indicator
2. Triple air-pressure gauge
3. Camera warning lamp
4. Time clock
5. Bomb jettison handle
6. Containers jettison push-button
7. Oxygen flow and contents gauges
8. Direct-vision windows
9. Destructor OFF-ON switch and push-buttons
10. Fire warning lamps
11. Fire extinguisher push buttons
12. Alighting gear control lever
13. Glider release handle
14. Windscreen de-icing pump
15. Mixer box
16. Fuel jettison handle
17. Transmitter-receiver controller
18. Seat-adjusting lever
19. Bomb door lever
20. Brakes lever
21. Press-to-transmit push-button
22. Bomb release button
23. Brakes lever parking catch

### Tactical camera installation
(© Crown Copyright)

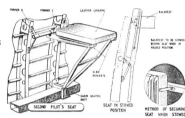

1. Camera heater switch
2. Camera control switches
3. Electrical control
4. Air bombers panel (port)
5. Camera mounting
6. Camera - type F 24
7. Motor mounted on bulkhead
8. Main floor front centre section
9. Terminal block No 55
10. Terminal block No 57
11. Terminal block No 51
12. Terminal block No 56
13. Camera heater supply panel

### Mk VIII auto-pilot installation
(© Crown Copyright)

Please refer to the colour artwork on page XXX for further details of the cockpit interior of the Lincoln

### Flight engineer's seat
(© Crown Copyright)

### Rudder pedals
(© Crown Copyright)

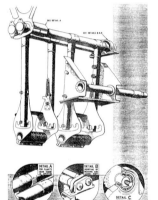

### Control column
(© Crown Copyright)

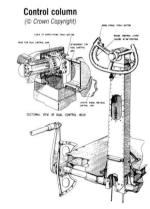

## Fuselage • 1

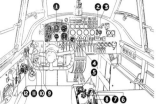

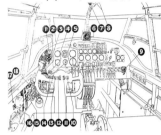

•1 An overall look at the Lincoln currently preserved in Argentina (© P. Calcutera)

•2 View from the back of the Argentinian Lincoln (© P. Calcutera)

•3 The port side, mid-section of the preserved Argentine Lincoln (© P. Calcutera))

•4 Overall shot of the rear fuselage, note the 'squared-off' rudder bottoms (© P. Calcutera)

•5 Overall view of the mid-section, note the intake on this side and the DF loop fitted behind the canopy on Argentine examples (© P. Calcutera)

# Fuselage • 2

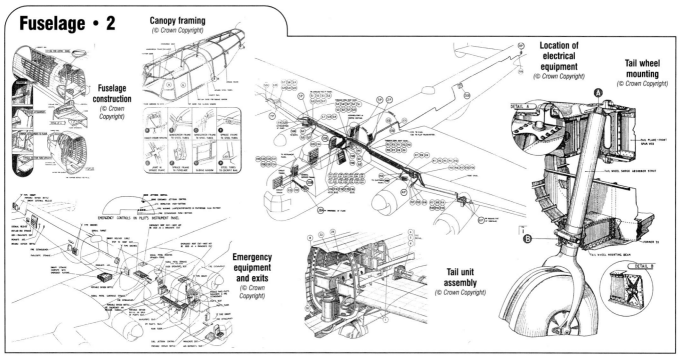

**Canopy framing**
*(© Crown Copyright)*

**Fuselage construction**
*(© Crown Copyright)*

**Emergency equipment and exits**
*(© Crown Copyright)*

EMERGENCY CONTROLS ON PILOTS INSTRUMENT PANEL

**Location of electrical equipment**
*(© Crown Copyright)*

**Tail wheel mounting**
*(© Crown Copyright)*

**Tail unit assembly**
*(© Crown Copyright)*

DETAIL A

DETAIL B

# Engine & Propellar • 1

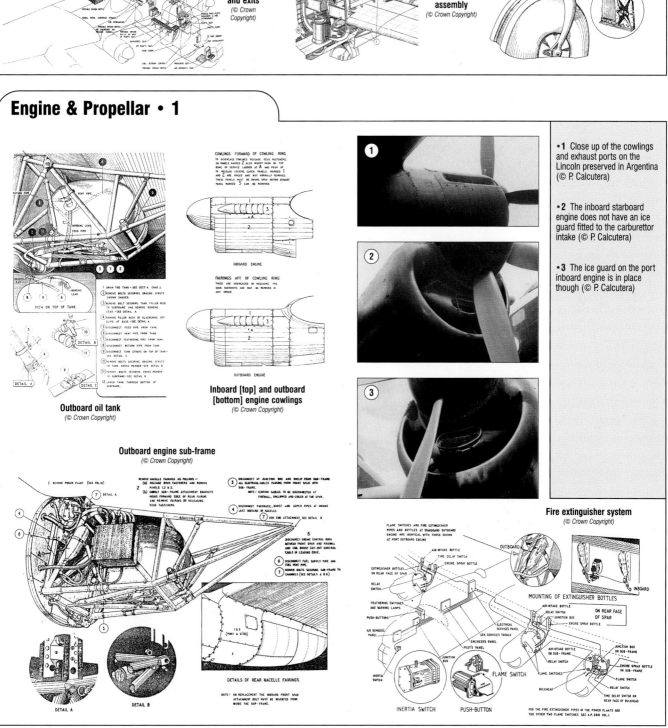

**Outboard oil tank**
*(© Crown Copyright)*

VIEW ON TOP OF TANK

DETAIL A    DETAIL B    DETAIL C

**Inboard [top] and outboard [bottom] engine cowlings**
*(© Crown Copyright)*

INBOARD ENGINE

OUTBOARD ENGINE

**Outboard engine sub-frame**
*(© Crown Copyright)*

DETAIL A    DETAIL B

DETAILS OF REAR NACELLE FAIRINGS.

•**1** Close up of the cowlings and exhaust ports on the Lincoln preserved in Argentina (© P. Calcutera)

•**2** The inboard starboard engine does not have an ice guard fitted to the carburettor intake (© P. Calcutera)

•**3** The ice guard on the port inboard engine is in place though (© P. Calcutera)

**Fire extinguisher system**
*(© Crown Copyright)*

MOUNTING OF EXTINGUISHER BOTTLES

INERTIA SWITCH    PUSH-BUTTON    FLAME SWITCH

# Turrets

### The front B.P. Type F turret installation
*(© Crown Copyright)*

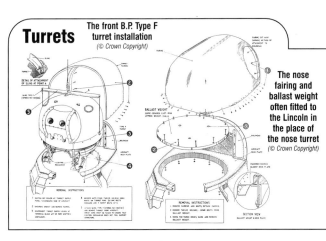

The nose fairing and ballast weight often fitted to the Lincoln in the place of the nose turret
*(© Crown Copyright)*

•1 The nose B.P. Type F turret fitted in the Lincoln preserved in Argentina (© P. Calcutera)

# Miscellaneous

### The MK XIVA bomb sight installation
*(© Crown Copyright)*

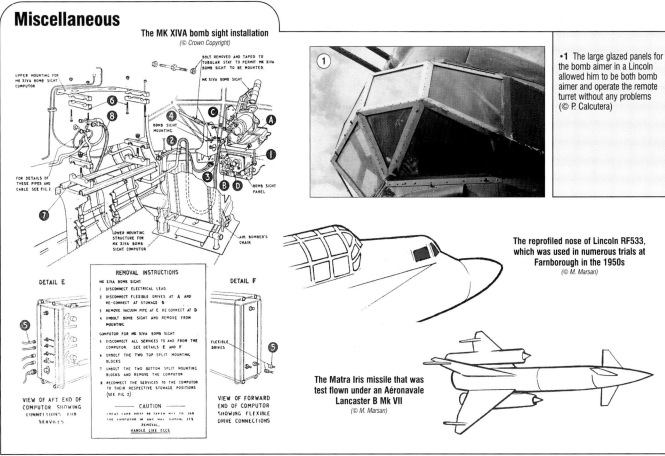

•1 The large glazed panels for the bomb aimer in a Lincoln allowed him to be both bomb aimer and operate the remote turret without any problems (© P. Calcutera)

The reprofiled nose of Lincoln RF533, which was used in numerous trials at Farnborough in the 1950s
*(© M. Marsan)*

The Matra Iris missile that was test flown under an Aéronavale Lancaster B Mk VII
*(© M. Marsan)*

# Undercarriage

### Main undercarriage unit
*(© Crown Copyright)*

### Main undercarriage doors etc
*(© Crown Copyright)*

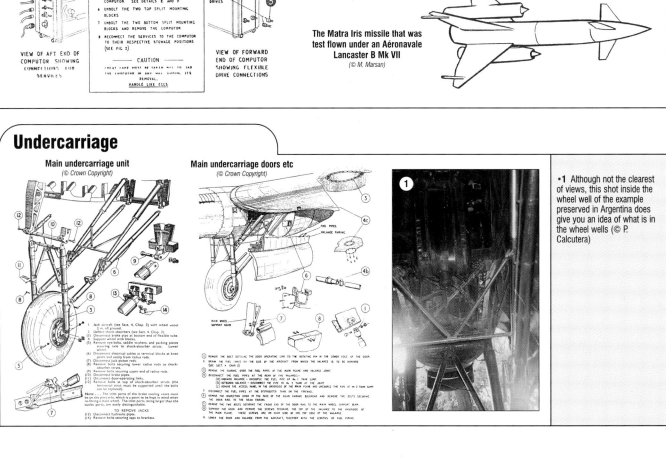

•1 Although not the clearest of views, this shot inside the wheel well of the example preserved in Argentina does give you an idea of what is in the wheel wells (© P. Calcutera)

# Wings & Control

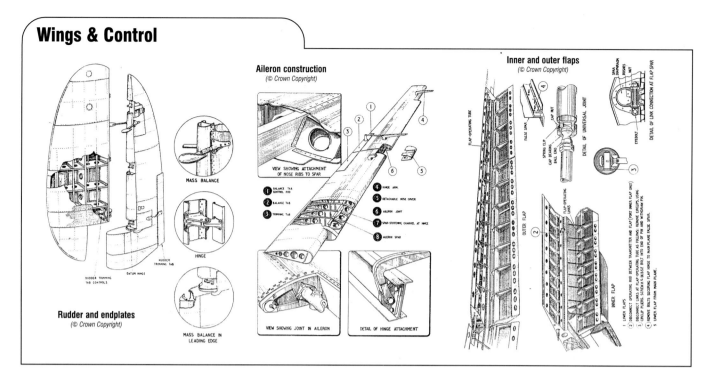

**Rudder and endplates**
(© Crown Copyright)

MASS BALANCE

HINGE

MASS BALANCE IN LEADING EDGE

RUDDER TRIMMING TAB CONTROLS

DATUM HINGE

**Aileron construction**
(© Crown Copyright)

VIEW SHOWING ATTACHMENT OF NOSE RIBS TO SPAR

1 BALANCE TAB CONTROL ROD
2 BALANCE TAB
3 TRIMMING TAB
4 HINGE ARM
5 DETACHABLE NOSE COVER
6 AILERON JOINT
7 SPAR-STIFFENING CHANNEL AT HINGE
8 AILERON SPAR

VIEW SHOWING JOINT IN AILERON

DETAIL OF HINGE ATTACHMENT

**Inner and outer flaps**
(© Crown Copyright)

# Bombs

**Bomb compartment data**
(© Crown Copyright)

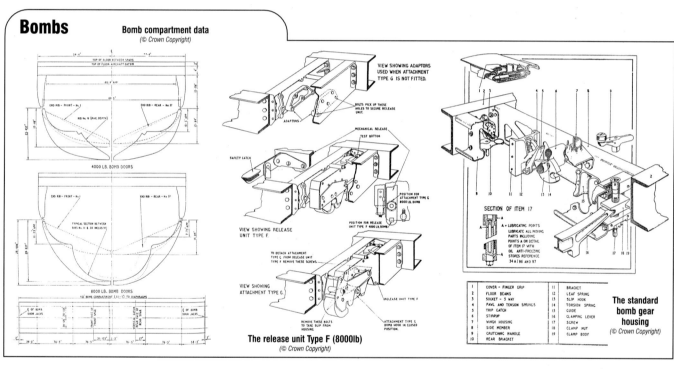

VIEW SHOWING ADAPTORS USED WHEN ATTACHMENT TYPE G IS NOT FITTED.

VIEW SHOWING RELEASE UNIT TYPE F.

VIEW SHOWING ATTACHMENT TYPE G.

**The release unit Type F (8000lb)**
(© Crown Copyright)

SECTION OF ITEM 17

| 1 | COVER - FINGER GRIP | 11 | BRACKET |
| 2 | FLOOR BEAMS | 12 | LEAF SPRING |
| 3 | SOCKET - 5 WAY | 13 | SLIP HOOK |
| 4 | PAWL AND TENSION SPRINGS | 14 | TORSION SPRING |
| 5 | TRIP CATCH | 15 | GUIDE |
| 6 | STIRRUP | 16 | CLAMPING LEVER |
| 7 | WINCH HOUSING | 17 | SCREW |
| 8 | SIDE MEMBER | 18 | CLAMP NUT |
| 9 | CRUTCHING HANDLE | 19 | CLAMP BODY |
| 10 | REAR BRACKET | | |

**The standard bomb gear housing**
(© Crown Copyright)

# Bombs & Mines • 1

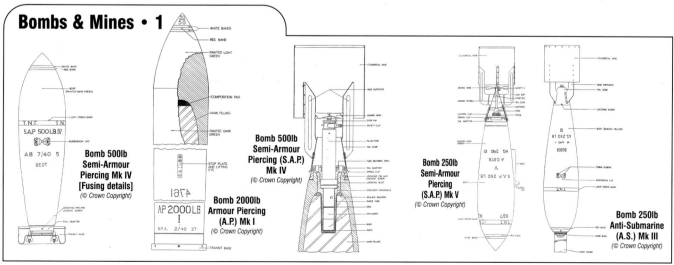

**Bomb 500lb Semi-Armour Piercing Mk IV [Fusing details]**
(© Crown Copyright)

**Bomb 2000lb Armour Piercing (A.P.) Mk I**
(© Crown Copyright)

**Bomb 500lb Semi-Armour Piercing (S.A.P.) Mk IV**
(© Crown Copyright)

**Bomb 250lb Semi-Armour Piercing (S.A.P.) Mk V**
(© Crown Copyright)

**Bomb 250lb Anti-Submarine (A.S.) Mk III**
(© Crown Copyright)

**Bomb 8000lb High Capacity (H.C.) Mk II**
*(© Crown Copyright)*

**Bomb 4000lb High Capacity (H.C.) Mk II**
*(© Crown Copyright)*

**Bomb 4000lb High Capacity (H.C.) Mk I**
*(© Crown Copyright)*

**Bomb 250lb Medium Capacity (M.C.) Mk I [with No. 2 Mk II Tail]**
*(© Crown Copyright)*

**Bomb 1000lb Medium Capacity (M.C.) Mk III [with transit base, transit plus and protecting rings fitted]**
*(© Crown Copyright)*

**Bomb 500lb Medium Capacity (M.C.) Mk II [with No. 25 Mk II Tail]**
*(© Crown Copyright)*

**Bomb 500lb Medium Capacity (M.C.) Mk I [with No. 25 Mk II Tail]**
*(© Crown Copyright)*

**Bomb 500lb Medium Capacity (M.C.) Mk VII [with No. 25 Mk II Tail]**
*(© Crown Copyright)*

**Bomb 1000lb Medium Capacity (M.C.) Mk I [with transit base, transit plus and protecting rings fitted]**
*(© Crown Copyright)*

**Bomb 12000lb Medium Capacity (M.C.) Mk I as drawn by German bomb disposal in July 1944**

Top beam

Suspension lug

Tail

Nose cover

Fuze

Tensioning strap

Incendiary bombs

**Cluster Projectile 500lb No. 14**

**Thanks**
The aircraft featured in this section are the Lancaster B Mk I from the RAF Museum, Hendon, B Mk III (F.E.) of the Battle of Britain Memorial Flight, RAF Coningsby and the B Mk VII of the Lincolnshire Aviation Heritage Centre, East Kirkby. Also featured are a number of Mk 10 variants currently on show in Canada, the Canadian Warplane Heritage's (CWH) airworthy example and the AWM and MOTAT examples in Australia. The Lincoln featured is the example currently on display in Argentina. Our thanks to all these organisations for allowing us access to these airframes, as well as to Andy Cline, Dave Frowen and Pablo Calcatera for the use of their photographs.

**Museum Owners and Representatives**
If you own or represent an aviation museum anywhere in the world, and would be willing to allow me (or my representative) access to your airframes for photography, please write to the author c/o SAM Publications. I am currently working on a mass of new titles for this series, so would be delighted to hear from you regardless of the aircraft types in your care.

# Building the Lancaster

**W**hat follows is a selection of reviews of the currently available Lancaster kits in 1/44th and 1/72nd scales.

## • 1/144th Minicraft

At the time of writing (June 2000), this kit is marketed by Minicraft, but its roots can be traced back to the 1970s when this model was originally produced by the Japanese Crown company. In 1993 this kit was under the Academy label, and it may have appeared under other labels in the last 30 years. Just remember that this is the only injection moulded mainstream kit of the Lancaster ever produced in 1/144th scale, so if you see one listed as 'new', just make sure it is not this one!

The small size of this model also means that it is very simple, comprising just forty-five parts, plus five in clear plastic. In our example, the plastic is dark green. Panel lines are all raised and limited to the larger/main ones. The interior is devoid of any detail except a plain flat 'floor' and although this is fine with a kit this small, you can easily make up some 'seats' with plasticard (especially the armoured pilot's seat which sits up high into the canopy). None of the turrets need to be added before the main fuselage halves are cemented together, as they all sit on 'ledges' in their respective positions and can therefore be installed after assembly and painting. The wings are moulded in two halves, the lower one not being full span, as the upper half has the tip moulded complete. The tailplanes come as a single unit that fits into a slot in the rear fuselage. This is very reminiscent of older kits (e.g. Lindberg) and does show the kit's age, but it seems to work fine in this scale. Just keep the fuselage halves parallel, otherwise the tailplanes will be twisted. The engine nacelles are in two parts, split vertically, and the propellers fit via shafts that are trapped between them. Glue the shafts (Pt No. 26) into the nacelle and fit the props onto them later. Propeller shape seems to be a problem in all Lancaster kits, and this one is no exception as the blade shape depicted in it is neither standard nor 'paddle' version. Being a product of the 1970s, the kit has 'features' like the

ability to fit the undercarriage in the 'up' position and replace the propellers with just the spinners, so it looks like they are turning. The undercarriage units themselves are not bad for a kit of this scale, but they are at least 3mm too long. Once this is coupled with the oversized wheels included in the kit, the model gains a distinctive 'leggy' look. Shortening the oleos will not be too hard, but finding replacement wheels may cause a few problems. The fit of the nacelles to the wing is OK, but filler is required on all major joints.

Once all the filling and sanding is complete, you can start applying the overall colour scheme. This

current edition only offers one scheme, which is W4794, PH•V, a machine that was operated by No. 12 Squadron. As with all wartime bombers it is Dark Green and Dark Earth over Night (Black). The simplest approach with a model of this scale is to leave off all the turrets and canopy, and spray the entire model black. Once this has dried install all the turrets etc, mask them off and then apply the Dark Earth and Dark Green camouflage to the upper surfaces. Once dry the decals were applied, and these are quite well printed for their small size, although the carrier film is quite prominent. Once all of the

**Minicraft 1/144th scale
B Mk I**

decals were dry the model was sprayed with a semi-gloss varnish. Once that has dried the canopy and turret frames can be painted in with a fine brush and the gun barrels painted Gunmetal.

### Conclusion

The only game in town I am afraid, and although it is not bad for its age, the various inaccuracies listed elsewhere coupled with those long undercarriage legs make this model 'look' all wrong, which really spoils it.

## • 1/72nd Scale Airfix B Mk I/III

Many of you will recall the original Lancaster B Mk I released by Airfix way back in 1958. By the late 1970s that tooling had seen better days, and as the subject was still as popular as ever, Airfix retooled; releasing the all-new

B Mk I/III in 1979. This kit is still (2000) available, and it has been around in many special markings and boxed sets over the years. The current version (#08002) is listed as a 'B Mk I' on the box and a 'B Mk III' on the instructions - confused! No problem really as they are externally identical, but as many of you will know the

Airfix 1/72nd scale B Mk I

bomb aimer's glazing of a B Mk I was much shallower than that of the B Mk III, and I am afraid that this kit has a B Mk I version. The kit is moulded in grey plastic with raised panel lines and rivets. The instructions start you off with assembly of the front, mid-upper and rear turrets, as these need to be trapped in the fuselage halves before they can be assembled. You don't actually have to add the glass (Pt No. 17) to the rear turret, as the back will be the bit trapped in the fuselage halves. You do have to assemble the front one and the mid-upper, the latter item being split vertically and therefore impossible to assemble 'cleanly'.

Cockpit interior consists of a stepped section on which a basic seat, pilot figure and control yoke fit. Cockpit sidewall details, or any other interior details are non-existent and the Flightpath detail set is a real 'must' if you want more inside your Lanc. The bomb bay roof is supplied and there is a lovely 4,000lb 'Cookie' included (complete with all its stencils in decal form). The other bombs included are a bit non-descript though. Once the fuselage halves were joined, I skipped some stages and moved on to assemble the engine nacelles and wings. There is no need to fit the undercarriage legs into the inboard engine nacelles, as this can be done at the final stages after painting etc. The propellers don't need to be added either, as I just cut off the shafts of the tabs (Pt Nos 73, 77, 81 & 85) and glue them into the back of the propellers (Pt Nos 74, 78, 82 & 86). The fit of the engine fronts (Pt Nos 72, 76, 80 & 84) is very poor, and I also found that once the nacelles were offered up to the wings, they did not fit all that well either. The inboard nacelles are the worst and filler was required on all the main joints in this kit. The wings feature movable ailerons and the tailplanes have movable elevators, so these compromise truly accurate representation in those areas.

With the bulk of the model assembled and all the filler sanded back (removing all the raised detail in the process!), the model can now be painted. Once again I just sprayed the whole model black, then once this was dry, the turrets and canopy were tacked in place and masked, before the upper camouflage scheme of Dark Green and Dark Earth was applied. Once this is dry you can choose from one of the four schemes offered in the box, and then apply the appropriate decals. These are up to Airfix's usual standard and are therefore quite thick with prominent carrier film. A great deal of careful masking will be required for the turret and canopy frames if you choose to spray them, alternatively you need a steady hand if you intend to brush paint them on. Once the paint scheme and decals are all dry the model was toned down with a coat of semi-gloss varnish and the smaller parts plus the undercarriage and propellers were added.

### Conclusion

Still the best 1/72nd scale Lancaster you can get, although

those raised panel lines and rivets look horrible. The fit of the main parts could be better and the total lack of interior detail makes it less appealing than I remember it when I made it back in 1979! Probably the most annoying thing for a modeller, is that none of the BBMF PA474 options can truly be made from this kit, as PA474 has Lincoln tailplane endplates and tail wheel, plus an oval glazed panel below the bomb aimer's blister (which, by the way is the B Mk I style in the kit of course!). Still, that said, this is the best you can currently get and is the basis of all the conversions you will find in this scale.

## • Airfix B Mk III Dambuster

Basically, this kit is a modified version of the standard kit and it was released in 1993. The 'modifications' take the form of a new sprue (in white plastic) that offers the Dambuster style revised bomb bay and Upkeep mine and supports.

All the comments I made about the assembly of the standard kit apply here also. The new bomb bay insert is not a good fit I am afraid, especially at its forward edge, and if you are not careful a 'step' will be apparent there. The Upkeep mine is depicted with wooden shutters fitted around it, and there always seems to be various interpretations of the struts that

support it, this kit being no exception. The main shortfalls of this kit in Dambuster guise is that there is no ventral turret depicted, and although many will dispute that they were fitted for the raid, most photos seem to show a gun in that position, and nothing is included in this kit. The final omission is the two lights fitted underneath these machines to assist in the aircraft attaining the correct altitude prior to the release of the mine.

Two colour schemes are offered in this kit, the first being a true Dams Raid (Operation Chastise) machine; AJ•G, flown by Wg Cdr Guy Gibson and the other being an ex-Dams Raid machine (AJ•S) as it was in December 1943 when it had acquired nose art. With the model finished as per the B Mk I/III kit previously, it was sprayed black overall, followed by the Dark Green and Dark Earth upper camouflage scheme. The decals are well printed, albeit a little thick with prominent carrier film, and once they are on and dry the whole model can be sprayed with semi-gloss varnish. Once again, when all of this is dry, the undercarriage etc can be fitted and then all you have to do

is paint in the canopy frames and add any additional touches you require.

### Conclusion

This is certainly a better specimen of a Dams Raid machine than the old Revell® example, but at least that one had the ventral turret in it. Oddly the 'modifications' to the mould have meant that where the blank has been installed to fill the mid-upper turret location, the raised panel lines and rivets on it don't match those on the surrounding fuselage! If you deal with all the problems in the kit, and can get everything to fit OK, this kit makes up into a nice Dambuster for your collection, but it needs quite

**Airfix 1/72nd scale B Mk III Dambuster**

a bit of work to do this and after 21 years, it is starting to look a bit old (aren't we all!)

## • Revell B Mk I

This kit has a copyright logo dated 1964 on it, and because it is a product of this era, it features lots of 'movable' gimmicks, like turrets, control surfaces and flaps. The current example is moulded in a disgusting brown plastic, but the panel lines are surprisingly engraved and all the rivets raised.

Assembly starts with the cockpit interior. This comprises a very simple 'shelf' depicting the floor, onto which goes the pilot's seat and a pilot and engineer figures. Both of these are very poor mouldings, as they are both shown holding fighter type control columns. That is it for the interior, which is bad news considering that big canopy! All the turrets are made up of a base, into which fits a truncated figure whose base is the lug for the turret's fitment into the fuselage half. Don't worry about fitting any of the turrets now, as they can all be glued in place once all the painting etc is complete. The bomb bay includes representations of the bomb load moulded very unconvincingly in half-relief. The bomb doors were also intended to open and close, so they have very large and inaccurate lugs on which they 'hinge'. The tailplanes feature movable control surfaces, and these need to be carefully assembled to ensure you don't spill glue on them. The undercarriage was also designed to go up and down, so there are no lugs to secure it to; instead there is a groove

**Revell 1/72nd scale B Mk I**

that allows the unit to be extended or retracted. It is best to leave the undercarriage off until last and then glue the whole lot in situ. The engine nacelles are split vertically, with the usual propeller lugs trapped between the halves. The fit of these assemblies to the wings is not very good, and the wings themselves feature not only moving control surfaces, but separate (movable) flaps. These are so slack in their fitment to mean that they just keep falling out, so leave them until last or cement them in the up position at this stage. Because this model went on to be a Dambuster version, the ventral turret's location is covered with a blanking plate. The surround for the mid-upper turret is separate, which is nice if you want to use the kit as the basis of a conversion, but the shape is incorrect.

By this stage it is time to paint the model and once more the good old, Night (Black), Dark Earth and Dark Green

scheme was applied. The current kit comes with two decal options; PG•J, LM378 of No. 619 Squadron, and CA•R, EE136, 'Spirit of Russia' of No. 189 Squadron. Although the kit claims to be a B Mk I, the instructions clearly state both these options are for B Mk IIIs! The decals are well printed and settle down onto the model quite well. The carrier film is a bit excessive, so some trimming prior to their application is advisable. Once all the painting and decals are dry, the model was sprayed with semi-gloss varnish and the undercarriage, canopy etc were added.

**Conclusion**

This is a really old kit, with lots of gimmicks, and as a result, poor fit. The level of detail is worse than the Airfix examples, and that one is not that good either. The age of the mouldings coupled with those moving parts, the inaccuracies and lack of detail, mean that this kit really does not deserve the amount of input required to make it presentable. I am sure Revell® will keep on reissuing this one, as it has sold well over the past 36 years, but you are better off with the Airfix examples.

There you have it, a brief overview of the current kits in 1/144th and 1/72nd scales. For those of you wanting to create other variants, I would direct your attention to Chapter 10, which lists all the modifications and accessories you will need to build any Manchester, Lancaster or Lincoln variant

Thanks to Airfix Ltd and Toyway (Minicraft) for supplying models for use in this section.

# Camouflage and Markings

## • The Manchester

### Royal Air Force Bomber Command

When the first prototype of the Manchester flew it was painted in the usual Dark Earth and Dark Green disruptive camouflage over Night (Black). This camouflage was applied in the 'A' and 'B' schemes, the latter being a mirror image of the former. Serials were applied in white under each wing and A1 roundels were used on the fuselage and upper wings. Once war was declared this machine had the underwing serials painted out and B Type roundels replaced the Type A1s. By the Summer of 1940 the prototypes had gained yellow under surfaces more in keeping with their status.

With production Mk Is, and up until L7300, alternate A and B pattern camouflage schemes were applied to each machine on the production line. This practice was stopped in early 1941 and the A scheme was subsequently applied to all Manchesters after L7300. The demarcation point was a straight line from the leading edge of the tailplanes to the trailing edge of the wing, and it projected forward of the wing at the same level. Roundels on the fuselage were Type A1 of 66½in diameter, although later these were revised to 49in diameter. Codes were in Medium Sea Grey (36in), serial numbers (8in) were Roundel (Dull) Red and the fin flashes were usually 24in x 27in with the red, white and blue segments in equal (8in) parts. Sometimes the fin flash was changed to the 24in x 24in type, but was still equally split into three 8in segments. By February 1941 the demarcation line was extended up the fuselage sides and terminated in a wavy line and this line swept up to meet at the leading edge of

Lancaster B Mk III, RE172 in flight and showing the camouflage pattern applied to all Lancasters

the central fin. Codes remained Medium Sea Grey, and the serial numbers, although remaining at 8in, were now either Dull (Roundel) Red or Medium Sea Grey. With the introduction of the wavy line demarcation, the fuselage roundel was reduced to 42in diameter. Often the starboard roundel was sited further forward than the port, and this was because the squadron codes (two numbers) were applied ahead of the roundels on the port side and aft on the starboard. This is not a 'hard and fast' rule, as you will see combinations including two letters forward or two behind the roundel, so careful study of period photographs is advisable. No. 97 Squadron machines

More colourful nose art, this time on Lancaster B Mk I, AR·H² of No. 460 Squadron at RAF Binbrook
(©RAFM P016119)

Lancaster B Mk I, R5868 of No 467 Squadron visiting a USAF base. Note the aircraft call-sign on the endplate, it is red with a yellow outline
(©RAFM P007009)

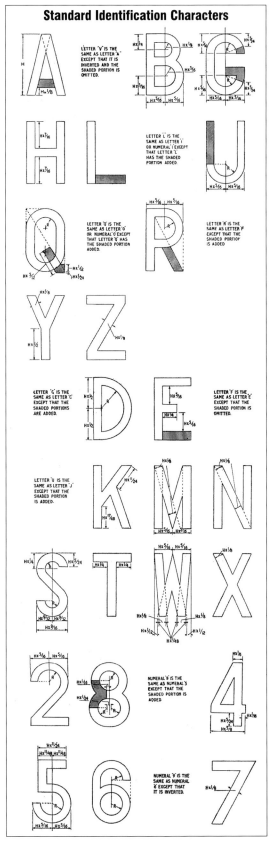

## Standard Identification Characters

seemed to feature strokes that were much thinner than those seen on other Manchesters, and this was a practice also seen on No. 83 Squadron machines. By November the demarcation line changed once again; this time the point was ¹/₃rd of the way down the fuselage side and it swept up to meet the leading edge of the vertical fin. Codes remained in Medium Sea Grey with grey or red serials

# • The Lancaster

### Royal Air Force
### Bomber Command

When the Lancaster entered service it featured a camouflage pattern inherited from the Manchester. the demarcation between the lower (Black) and upper (Dark Green and Dark Earth) was at the same point (¹/₃rd of the way down the fuselage side) as the Manchester. The roundels were at first 42in Type A1 and the fin flash was 24in x 27in. Squadron codes were Medium Sea Grey, with the serial in Dull (Roundel) Red. Upper wing roundels were 102in diameter Type B. Later the roundels on the fuselage were changed to the 60in diameter Type C1 and

A very well known shot of Lancaster B Mk I, R5689, VN•N of No. 50 Squadron in flight, but this does serve to show the demarcation of the upper and lower colours, as well as the 'standard' roundels, codes and serials

the fuselage codes were now applied in Dull (Roundel) Red. The style of the letters for the fuselage codes varied greatly, and many styles will be seen if you study photographs. A large number of Lancasters feature yellow-bordered red serials.

The only real exception to the rules was No.83 Squadron who added the codes of each aircraft above the tailplanes. Usually they were in the same size and format as those on the fuselage and were thus red outlined in yellow.

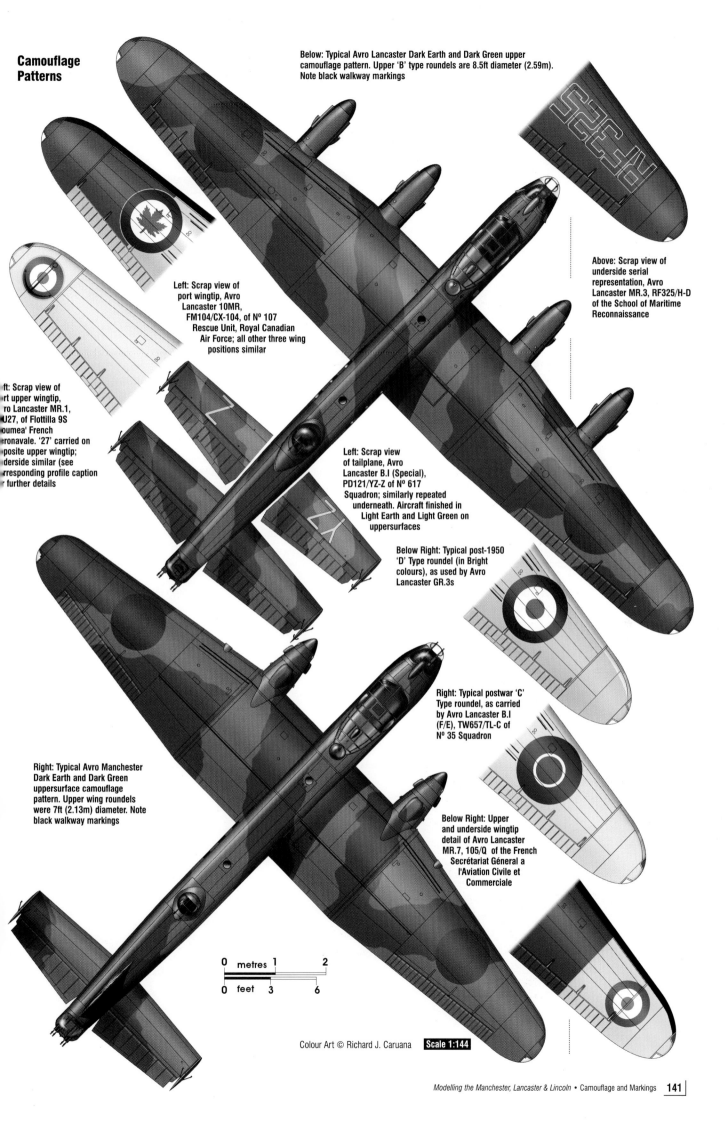

**Camouflage Patterns**

Below: Typical Avro Lancaster Dark Earth and Dark Green upper camouflage pattern. Upper 'B' type roundels are 8.5ft diameter (2.59m). Note black walkway markings

Above: Scrap view of underside serial representation, Avro Lancaster MR.3, RF325/H-D of the School of Maritime Reconnaissance

Left: Scrap view of port wingtip, Avro Lancaster 10MR, FM104/CX-104, of Nº 107 Rescue Unit, Royal Canadian Air Force; all other three wing positions similar

ft: Scrap view of
rt upper wingtip,
ro Lancaster MR.1,
U27, of Flottilla 9S
oumea' French
éronavale. '27' carried on
posite upper wingtip;
derside similar (see
rresponding profile caption
r further details

Left: Scrap view of tailplane, Avro Lancaster B.I (Special), PD121/YZ-Z of Nº 617 Squadron; similarly repeated underneath. Aircraft finished in Light Earth and Light Green on uppersurfaces

Below Right: Typical post-1950 'D' Type roundel (in Bright colours), as used by Avro Lancaster GR.3s

Right: Typical postwar 'C' Type roundel, as carried by Avro Lancaster B.I (F/E), TW657/TL-C of Nº 35 Squadron

Right: Typical Avro Manchester Dark Earth and Dark Green uppersurface camouflage pattern. Upper wing roundels were 7ft (2.13m) diameter. Note black walkway markings

Below Right: Upper and underside wingtip detail of Avro Lancaster MR.7, 105/Q of the French Secrétariat Géneral a l'Aviation Civile et Commerciale

0  metres  1        2

0  feet  3        6

Colour Art © Richard J. Caruana    Scale 1:144

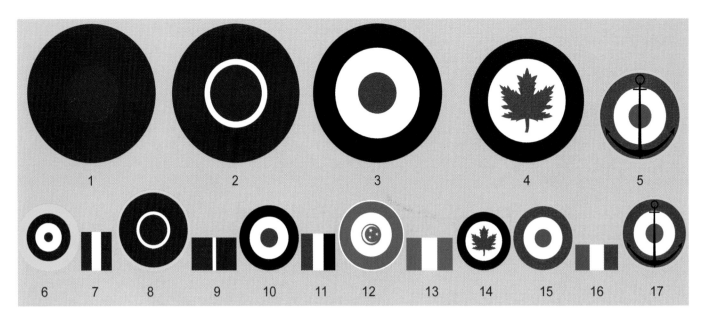

## LANCASTER MARKINGS

### Wing Markings

1 Standard Type B roundel, 102" diameter
2 Standard post-1945 Type C roundel, 102" diameter
3 Standard post-May 1947 Type D roundel, 102" diameter (Bright colours)
4 Canadian Air Force roundels, 90" diameter
5 French Aéronavale roundel, 78" diameter; French Secrétariat Géneral a l'Aviation Civile et Commerciale roundels same size, but without yellow outline and anchor

### Fuselage Markings

6 Early Type A1 roundel, 49" diameter; rather rare
7 Fin flash 8"x8"x8"x27"; combined with '6' above
8 Standard Type C1 roundel, 60" diameter; some size and proportion variations are known to exist
9 Fin flash 36"x24"' combined with '8' above
10 Type D roundel, 48" diameter (Bright colours)
11 Fin flash 9"x9"x9"x27" (Bright colours)
12 Royal Egyptian Air Force roundel, 52" diameter
13 Fin flash 12"x12"x12"x24"; combined with '12' above
14 Royal Canadian Air Force roundel, 42" diameter
15 French Secrétariat Géneral a l'Aviation Civile et Commerciale roundel, 48" diameter
16 Fin flash, 12"x12"x12"x18"; combined with '15' above
17 French Aéronavale roundel, 54" diameter

*Colour Art © Richard J. Caruana*

**Lancaster B Mk I, PD328, 'Aries' of the Empire Central Navigation School at Reykjavik in May 1945**
(©RAFM P014762)

### Tallboy & Grand Slam

The Grand Slam Lancasters of No. 617 Squadron were finished in Light Earth and Light Green over Ocean Grey. Roundels were the 60in diameter Type C1 and the aircraft featured fuselage codes that were either white or yellow bordered in red. The practice of putting the codes above and below the vertical tailplanes that had existed for daylight operations meant that these machines had codes in this fashion, albeit usually just produced in yellow. It was normal for these codes to be painted in such a manner that they were read from the leading edge under the port tailplane and the trailing edge under the starboard. The serial number was usually applied in white under each wing, and the serial number on the aft fuselage was Dull (Roundel) Red.

### Post-War Coastal Command

Lancasters operated in the maritime reconnaissance role during the post-war period were painted in white with the extreme upper sections of the fuselage and upper surface of the wings in Medium Sea Grey. Type C roundels and fin flashes were applied, and the fuselage codes were usually in Light Slate Grey. Many of these machines featured the serial number high up on the fuselage sides, just above the leading edge of the tailplane. Squadrons all adopted specific colours, and these were often reproduced on the spinners of the GR/MR.IIIs. Red, white and blue were quite common, with No. 120 Squadron having these colours in bands around the spinners of their Lancasters in 1949. Roundels up to May 1947 were usually (102in) Type C, and after this time they were (102in) Type D. The School of Maritime Reconnaissance later finished their remaining MR Mk IIIs in a scheme that was also adopted by the Shackleton. This was Dark Sea Grey overall with 50in diameter Type D roundels on the fuselage. The serial was applied in 8in Dull (Roundel) Red on the fuselage and under each wing in red with a white border. Once again these codes were read from the leading edge of the port and trailing edge of the starboard. A 27in x 27in Type D fin flash was applied to each vertical fin

### Tiger Force

The Lancasters for this operation were finished with white uppersurfaces and black underneath. Usually these aircraft

# Camouflage Patterns

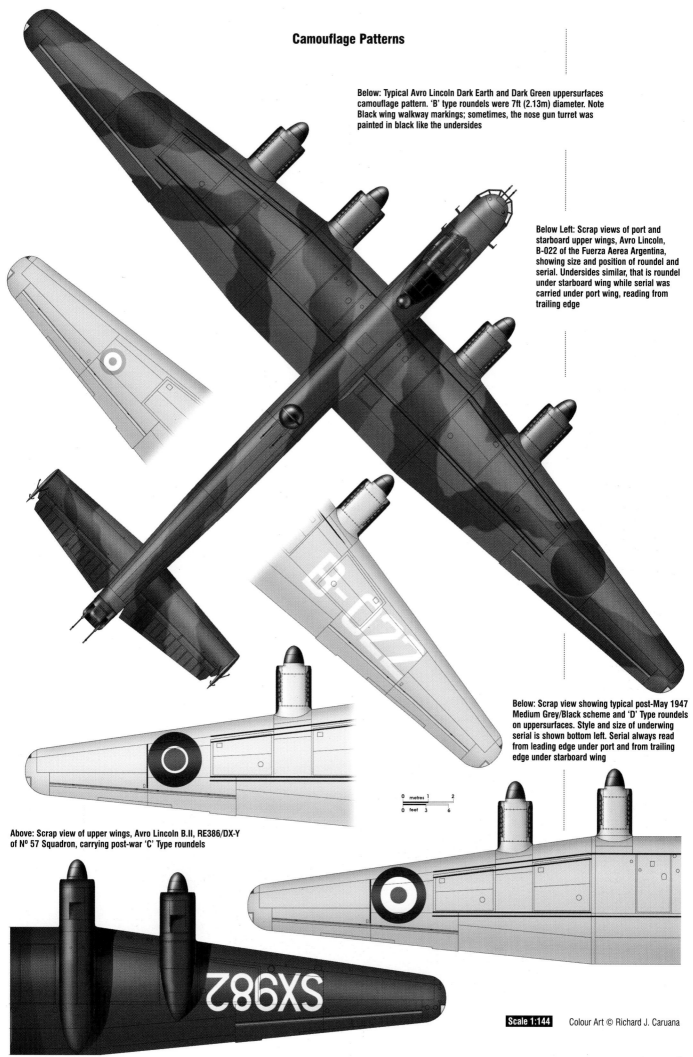

Below: Typical Avro Lincoln Dark Earth and Dark Green uppersurfaces camouflage pattern. 'B' type roundels were 7ft (2.13m) diameter. Note Black wing walkway markings; sometimes, the nose gun turret was painted in black like the undersides

Below Left: Scrap views of port and starboard upper wings, Avro Lincoln, B-022 of the Fuerza Aerea Argentina, showing size and position of roundel and serial. Undersides similar, that is roundel under starboard wing while serial was carried under port wing, reading from trailing edge

Below: Scrap view showing typical post-May 1947 Medium Grey/Black scheme and 'D' Type roundels on uppersurfaces. Style and size of underwing serial is shown bottom left. Serial always read from leading edge under port and from trailing edge under starboard wing

Above: Scrap view of upper wings, Avro Lincoln B.II, RE386/DX-Y of Nº 57 Squadron, carrying post-war 'C' Type roundels

Scale 1:144    Colour Art © Richard J. Caruana

## MANCHESTER MARKINGS

1 Wing Type B roundel, 85" diameter
2 Early fuselage Type A1 roundel, 66.5" diameter (9.5" bars)
3 Standard fuselage Type A1 roundel, 49" diameter (7" bars); later reduced to 42" on some aircraft
4 Fin flash, 8"x8"x8"x24"
5 Fin flash variation (more common) 8"x8"x8"x27"
6 Fuselage Type C1 roundel, carried by very few aircraft, 60" diameter
7 Late style fin flash carried in combination with '6' above, 14"x2"x14"x24"

*Colour Art © Richard J. Caruana*

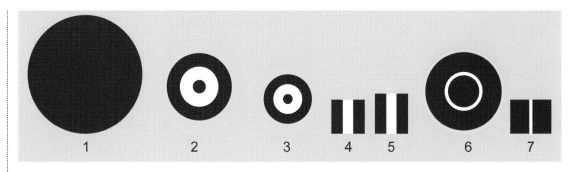

### Squadron Code Letters

Scale 1:48

Left to right: 27in MSG; 38in MSG; 30in MSG; 24in Sky; 24in Dull Red; 25in Black; note that the design style practically varied from squadron to squadron

## LINCOLN MARKINGS

**Wing Markings**
1 Standard Type B roundel, 84" diameter
2 Standard Type C roundel, 84" diameter
3 Standard Type D roundel, 84" diameter (Bright colours)
4 Fuerza Aerea Argentina roundel, 40" diameter

**Fuselage Markings**
5 Type C1 roundel, 58" diameter
6 Fin flash, 36"x24", combined with '5' above
7 Type D roundel, 50" diameter (Bright colours)
8 Fin flash, 30"x24"; combined with '7' above
9 Royal Australian Air Force roundel, 58" diameter; combined with '3' and '8' above
10 Fuerza Aerea Argentina roundel, 48" diameter
11 FAA fin flash, 32"x16"

*Colour Art © Richard J. Caruana*

featured (60in) Type C1 roundels, although many were seen with Type C on the upper surface of the wings. Codes, although of the same size as those used in wartime, were usually black, as were the serial numbers. The serial was repeated in white under each wing, being red from the leading edge of the port wing, and trailing edge of the starboard. The fin flashes were usually 30in x 24in Type C.

### Government Establishments

The Empire Flying School's Lancasters in the post-war period featured the serial in white on the rear fuselage and under each wing. The fuselage roundels were often Type D, while those on the wing upper surface remained Type B. The example shown in the colour profiles in this title features the fuselage codes in black and the entire fuselage codes and roundel combination applied over a Trainer Yellow rectangle.

### Civil Lancaster & Lancastrian

Much has been said about BOAC colours during the war years and it is best to think of the 'civil' Lancasters used during the war period as being in standard Bomber Command colours with only the addition of civil registrations on the fuselage and wings. Usually all roundels were removed, as were the RAF squadron codes. These were replaced with the civil registrations that were

usually in white. Many of these machines retained their RAF serial in 8in high black numerals though.

Later in the war, and during the post-war period most civil operated Lancaster/Lancastrians were stripped of all paint and flew in bare metal. Black anti-dazzle panels were added forward of the canopy and the civil registration was re-applied in black (or blue) on the fuselage and wings.

### Flight Refuelling

It seems as if this operator actually repainted their fleet of Lancaster tankers in aluminium. Registrations and 'Flight Refuelling' legends were added in dark blue, the former running across the entire span, top and bottom.

## Foreign

### Argentina

The basic camouflage applied to all FAA Lancasters was that which had been applied in the UK for RAF service. This scheme comprised Night (Matt Black) for all the under surfaces, fuselage sides and fin endplates (and interior), plus Dark Green (FS 34079) and Dark Earth (FS 30118) in a disruptive camouflage pattern on the upper surface. Later machines were delivered in a brown (?) and black scheme (Note: This may have been Medium Sea Grey or a darker hue, possibly Dark Slate Grey) that still utilised the same upper/lower demarcation. These colours were all applied with masks and as a result all demarcations lines are 'hard'. Registration markings also came in two forms. The first one saw the serial number on the tailplane endplates (above the flag), outer wing leading edges, outer engine panels and on either side of the nose in 12in high white characters. Roundels (28in diameter) were restricted above and below the wings and on either fuselage side, below where the mid-upper turret would be. An Argentinian flag was applied to the lower section

of the fin endplates with the aircraft serial number in white above it. These markings remained unchanged until 1955, as photos of B-037 in this form are seen right up to this date. Although it is not known at what precise date the markings changed, it was certainly shortly after 1955. These changes comprised a much larger white serial number (30in white characters) behind a larger (48in) roundel on each fuselage side and a larger flag higher up on the fin endplates. The serial was no longer applied to the endplates, but is was retained on either side of the nose (12in). Serial numbers were also added below the port and above the starboard wings, with roundels above the port and below the starboard.

## Royal Australian Air Force (RAAF)
The Lancasters operated by RAAF units only did so whilst they were attached to the RAF during wartime. Please refer to the Bomber Command section for the RAF Lancasters camouflage and marking notes.

## Royal Canadian Air Force (RCAF)
## WWII
The Lancasters operated by RCAF during wartime did so whilst they were attached to the RAF. Please refer to the Bomber Command section for the RAF Lancasters camouflage and marking notes.

## Post-War
## Maritime Reconnaissance
Initially the machines used in the maritime reconnaissance role (10MR) were natural metal on the upper sections of the fuselage, fin and rudder and upper forward sections of the engine nacelles, while the rest of the airframe was Gloss Light Grey. The demarcation for these areas is made via a red lightning bolt that extends from the nose blister to just underneath the trailing edge of the vertical fin. Without the extension of this 'flash' beyond this point, the demarcation follows an imaginary line that could be projected all the way to the back. Because these machines had de-icing boots on the wing, vertical fin and tailplane leading edges these areas were also black (in fact, they were rubber coated). The upper

and lower tips of each wing were Artic Red, as were the non-movable sections of the tailplanes. The control surfaces on the tailplanes remained Gloss Light Grey. The fuselage roundel was 42in diameter, while those on the wings were 90in diameter. The codes either side of the fuselage roundels were also 42in high and were black, while the 'rescue' legend was in Artic Red in 36in high letters on the lower portion of the fuselage side. The serial number was applied in 8in high black characters above the fin flash on the vertical fins, and the numeric elements (e.g. '104' for FM104) were repeated aft of the bomb aimer's glazing. Although official plans were considered to paint the MR Lancasters in Dark Blue overall, this scheme was never sanctioned or applied to these aircraft.

## Air-Sea Rescue
The S&R Lancasters operated by the RCAF were initially bare metal overall with a black anti-dazzle panel on the nose and Artic Red panels on the upper and lower surfaces of each wing tip. Later these machines were painted in line

All these Lancasters, including B Mk I, KM•N, ex-No. 44 Squadron in the foreground, are awaiting disposal at an MU after the war, but this shot serves to show the diversity of schemes and markings applied to the type in service
(©RAFM P016433)

Lancaster B Mk III, PB509, OJ•C of No. 149 Squadron
(©RAFM P014542)

Lancaster B Mk I, AR•A² of No. 460 Squadron, RAF Binbrook, sporting some nice nose art and bombing missions noted in the form or kangaroo silhouettes
(©RAFM P016120)

Lancaster B Mk I, AR•K2 of No. 460 Squadron, RAF Binbrook
(©RAFM P016118)

Obviously Joe flew this Lancaster B Mk III [FZ•C of No. 100 Squadron] !
(©RAFM P014345)

with the MR versions, gaining aluminium engine nacelles, a Gloss Light Grey lower fuselage and red lightning bolt separating the grey from the bare metal sections. Spinners were usually red and a wide Artic Red band was applied around the fuselage. Although the maple flag roundels were carried by these machines in later life, there are clear colour photos showing machines with a Type B roundel on the starboard wing, and just the blue and white section of a Canadian roundel on the port! Obviously colour and marking changes could be quite drawn out, so check your references.

## Special Duties

The Orenda test bed (Mk 10O) remained bare metal throughout its life. 90in diameter roundels were applied above the wings and a standard fin flash plus codes in 6in black characters were applied to each endplate. The upper nose had a black anti-dazzle panel. The Drone Controller (Mk 10DC) machines were in the same bare metal/Gloss Light Grey scheme as the MR, although the cheatline between these two colours was a thin (2in) blue line. The entire nose, right back past the mid-section of the canopy, plus the wing tips, rear fuselage and fixed sections of the tail endplates were all Artic Red. The undersurface of the wings and the engine nacelle lower surfaces aft of the

removeable engine cowlings were Gloss Light Grey, as were the special wing pylons. The upper nose anti-dazzle panel was black and 90in roundels were carried above and below each wing. The fuselage roundels were 42in diameter and 50in black codes were applied fore and aft of them. The Ryan Firebee drones were a deep red colour (the same colour as the Lancaster's spinners), with their codes in 6in white letters on either side of the tail. Usually a small maple leaf roundel was also carried on either side of the drone.

### Notes

Most RCAF post-war Lancasters went from bare metal to bare metal and Gloss Light Grey. The Artic Red panels were usually applied under the wings, as well as in bands around the fuselage, but the latter do seem to vary in width and some were also edged in blue. Spinners have been seen in black, red, light blue and grey. Fuselage roundels are usually 42in, with 50in codes, but very small (less than 20in) versions have also been seen late in the type's service. It seems that the smaller diameter fuselage roundel is seen once the roundels have been added below each wing, but as always, there are exceptions. The above notes can only be offered as a basic guide, and the modeller is advised to undertake more research with regard to the scheme of the specific aircraft modelled.

## Egypt

The Lancasters supplied to Egypt in the post-war period were refurbished before delivery and received the 'current' camouflage of the period. This comprised Medium Sea Grey upper surfaces with black underneath. The demarcation was identical to the wartime scheme and 52in diameter Egyptian roundels were applied either side of the

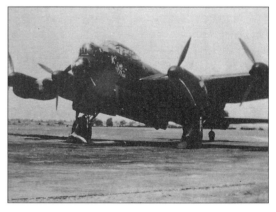

fuselage and above and below each wing. The serial was applied in white on the rear fuselage and under each wing and the fin flash was 36in x 24in.

## France

The Lancasters supplied under the Western Union agreement in the post-war period were Dark Blue with a 24in wide yellow band running down the centre of each fuselage side. In the centre of these bands, just aft of the roundel, was the title 'SAR'. The wing tips and rudders were also painted yellow. The fuselage roundels were 48in diameter, as were those above and below the wings. A 24in x 18in fin flash was applied to each fin, along with the aircraft letter (e.g. Q) in 18in high white characters above it. The numerical element of the serial number (e.g. '105' for WU-105) was applied in 8in white characters under the fin flash and the aircraft letters on the tail were repeated in 8in high white characters aft of the bomb aimer's glazing.

By the latter stages of the Lancaster's service with the

Lancaster B Mk I, PD328, 'Aries' of the CNS at RNZAF Wigram, New Zealand in 1944
(©RAFM P015681)

Aéronavale, many of the aircraft had been repainted white overall. A black anti-dazzle panel was added forward of the cockpit, and as you will see from the colour profile elsewhere in this title, it was not uncommon for the exhaust stained areas of the nacelles to be painted black. A 78in diameter roundel was applied to each fuselage side and on each upper wing. The lower wing featured the aircraft number (e.g. 27) in black very close to the tip. This number was also repeated in 8in black characters on the lower section of the vertical fins.

## • The Lincoln

### Royal Air Force
### Bomber Command

The initial colour scheme for the Lincoln was similar to that applied to the Lancaster. Dark Earth and Dark Green

camouflaged upper surface, with black underneath and a demarcation point ¹/₃rd of the way down the fuselage sides. The fuselage roundels were 58in diameter Type C1, while 84in Type B roundels were applied on top of the wings. Codes were applied in white on either side of the fuselage. The serial number was in Dull (Roundel) Red on the rear fuselage and in large white characters under each wing (read from the leading edge of the port and trailing edge of the starboard). 36in x 24in Type C fin flashes were also applied.

By the 1950s the Lincoln was seen in a Medium Sea Grey over Night (black) scheme, although the demarcation between these two colours stayed the same as that seen in the previous scheme. Roundels remained the same, although the upper wing Type C was later replaced with a similar sized Type D. Fuselage codes were now white, but the serial number remained Dull (Roundel) Red. The radome of the Lincoln during this period was either painted in Medium Sea Grey, or left clear, so check your references.

Lancaster B Mk I, PD328, 'Aries' of the Empire Air Navigation School, RAF Shawbury, 10th May 1945
(©RAFM P015682)

# Modeller's Cross-reference Colour Chart

## ARGENTINA

Initially the machines supplied to this country were in the standard RAF scheme.

| COLOUR | FS595A | BS or RAL | USE | AVAILABLE PAINTS |
|---|---|---|---|---|
| Dark Green | ~4079 | | Topside camouflage | See entry under 'Royal Air Force' section |
| Dark Earth | ~0118 | | Upper surface camouflage | See entry under 'Royal Air Force' section |
| Night | ~7038 | | Under surfaces | See entry under 'Royal Air Force' section |
| Light Blue | ~5240 | | Roundels | N/A |
| Identification White | ~7875 | | Roundels & Codes | See entry under 'Royal Air Force' section |
| Identification Yellow | ~3538 | | Propeller Tips | See entry under 'Royal Air Force' section |
| Aluminium | ~7178 | | Overall colour | See entry under 'Royal Air Force' section |

## ROYAL AIR FORCE

| COLOUR | FS595A | BS or RAL | USE | AVAILABLE PAINTS |
|---|---|---|---|---|
| Dark Earth | | | Topside camouflage with Dark Green | AeroMaster Warbird Enamel: 9110 Dark Earth |
| | | | | AeroMaster Warbird Acrylic: 1110 Dark Earth |
| | ~0118 | | | Floquil M189: Field Drab 30118 |
| | ~0118 | | | Floquil 145: Dark Earth 30118 |
| | | | | Gunze Sangyo: H072 Dark Earth |
| | | | | Humbrol Authentic: HU02, Dark Earth |
| | | | | Humbrol Authentic: HF03, Terre Fonce |
| | ~0118 | 450 | | Humbrol Authentic: HU18, Brown 30118 |
| | | | | Humbrol Super Enamel: No.29 Dark Earth |
| | ~0118 | | | Lifecolor UA0116 Dark Earth |
| | | | | ModelMaster: 1702 Field Drab |
| | ~0118 | | | Pactra Acrylics: A24, Brown Drab FS 30118 |
| | | | | Polly-S 830: Field Drab |
| | ~0118 | 450 | | Polly-S Acrylic 5252: British Dark Earth 30118 |
| | | | | Xtracolor: X2 Dark Earth BS450 |
| | ~0118 | | | Xtracolor: X101 Earth 30118 |
| Light Earth | ~0257 | | Topside camouflage 'Grand Slam' | N/A |
| Dark Green | ~4079 | | Topside camouflage with Dark Earth | AeroMaster Warbird Enamel: 9111 Dark Green |
| | | | | AeroMaster Warbird Acrylic: 1111 Dark Green |
| | | | | Compucolor: CAC2, Forest Green |
| | ~4079 | | | Floquil: M196, Dark Green 34079 |
| | ~4079 | | | Floquil: 3143, British Dark Green (34079) |
| | | | | Humbrol Authentic: HG02, Dark Green RLM71 |
| | ~4079 | | | Humbrol Authentic: HU07, Green 34079 |
| | ~4079 | | | Lifecolor UA001 Dark Green |
| | | | | ModelMaster: 1710, Dark Green |
| | ~4079 | | | Mr Color: 309, Dark Green FS34079 |
| | | | | Pactra: M5 |
| | ~4079 | | | Pactra Acrylics: A29, Jungle Green FS34079 |
| | | | | Polly-S: 835, Forest Green |
| | | | | Polly-S: 814 Dark Green |
| | ~4079 | | | Polly-S Acrylic: Dark Green (34079) |
| | ~4079 | | | Polly-S Enamel: Dark Green 34079 |
| | | | | Tamiya: XF58, Olive Green |
| | ~4079 | | | Xtracolor: X110, Forest Green FS14079 |
| | | 451 | | Xtracolor: X1 Dark Green (BS451) |
| Light Green | ~4096 | | Topside camouflage 'Grand Slam' | N/A |
| Medium Sea Grey | | | Early code letters, Upper Surface on GR.III | AeroMaster Warbird Enamel: 9113 |
| | | | | AeroMaster Warbird Acrylic: 1113 |
| | ~6270 | | | Compucolor: CAC28, Neutral Grey |
| | ~6270 | | | Floquil: M206, Neutral Grey |
| | ~6270 | | | Floquil Enamel: 3151, Sea Grey, Medium |
| | | 640 | | Gunze Sangyo Acrylic: Medium Sea Grey |
| | ~6270 | | | Gunze Sangyo Acrylic: Grey |
| | ~6270 | | | Humbrol Authentic: HF04 Gris Bleu Clair |
| | ~6440 | | | Humbrol Authentic: HB06 Sea Grey Medium |
| | ~6270 | | | Humbrol Authentic: USN2, Medium Gray |
| | | 637 | | Humbrol Super Enamel: No.165 |
| | ~6270 | | | Lifecolor UA094 Medium Sea Grey |
| | | | | ModelMaster: 1725, Neutral Grey |
| | ~6293 | | | Polly Scale: 505258, Sea Grey, Medium |
| | ~6293 | | | Polly-S Acrylic: British Sea Grey, Medium |
| | ~6270 | | | Replicolor: Grey |
| | ~6424 | | | Tamiya: XF20 Medium Grey |
| | ~6270 | | | Xtracolor: X133, Neutral Gray (FS 16270) |
| | | 637 | | Xtracolor: X3, Medium Sea Grey |
| Ocean Grey | | | Under surface 'Grand Slam' | AeroMaster Warbird Enamel: 9112, Ocean Grey |
| | | | | AeroMaster Warbird Acrylic: 1112, Ocean Grey |
| | ~6152 | | | Floquil: 3149, Ocean Grey |
| | ~6152 | | | Humbrol Authentic: HN02 Dark Grey |
| | | | | Humbrol Super Enamels: No.106 Ocean Grey |
| | ~6187 | | | Lifecolor UA093 Ocean Grey |
| | ~6187 | | | Polly-S: 823, Ocean Grey |
| | ~5237 | | | Polly-S: 5256, Ocean Grey |
| | ~5237 | | | Polly-S: 5256, Ocean Grey |
| Light Slate Grey | ~4159 | BS639 | Code letters post-war | Xtracolor: X037 Light Slate Grey |
| | ~4159 | | | LifeColor: UA059, RLM 62 |
| Dark Slate Grey | ~4096 | | Upper surface colour on ASR.IIIs | AeroMaster Warbird Acrylic: 1119, Slate Grey |
| | ~4091 | | | Floquil Classic: 3159, Dark Slate Grey |
| | ~4091 | | | Gunze Sangyo Acrylic: H036, Dark Green |
| | ~4091 | | | Gunze Sangyo Acrylic: H052, Olive Drab |
| | ~4096 | | | Gunze Sangyo Acrylic: H320, Dark Green |
| | ~4096 | | | Humbrol Authentic: HB01, Dark Green |
| | ~4091 | | | Humbrol Authentic: HI03, Overall Green |
| | ~4096 | | | Humbrol Authentic: HG17, Dark Green |
| | ~4096 | | | Humbrol Authentic: HJ01, Green N1 |
| | ~4091 | | | Humbrol Authentic: HI01, Mottle Green |
| | ~4127 | | | Humbrol Authentic: HM07, Khaki Drab |
| | | | | Humbrol Super Enamel: No.102 Dark Slate Grey |
| | ~4127 | | | Humbrol Super Enamel: No.150 Forest Green |
| | ~4127 | | | Lifecolor UA006 Green |
| | ~4096 | | | Pactra: MG54, Sherwood Green |
| | ~4127 | | | Pactra Acrylic: A34, Artillery Olive |
| | ~4096 | | | Polly-S Acrylic: 5266, Dark Slate Grey |
| | ~4127 | | | Floquil: M200, Forest Green |
| | ~4127 | | | ModelMaster: 1714, Forest Green |
| | | | | Xtracolor: X25, Dark Slate Grey |
| Extra Dark Sea Grey | | | Upper surface colour on ASR.IIIs | AeroMaster Warbird Acrylic: 1118 |
| | ~6118 | | | Compucolor: CAC16, Gunship Grey |
| | ~6118 | | | Floquil: M204, Sea Grey |
| | ~6118 | | | Floquil Classic: 3157, Extra Dark Sea Grey |
| | ~6118 | | | Gunze Sangyo Acrylic: H032, Field Grey |
| | ~6118 | | | Gunze Sangyo Acrylic: H072, Dark Sea Grey |
| | ~6118 | | | Gunze Sangyo Acrylic: H305, Grey |
| | ~6118 | 638 | | Gunze Sangyo Acrylic: H331, Dark Sea Grey |
| | ~6118 | | | Humbrol Authentic: HF02, Gris Blue Fonce |
| | ~6118 | | | Humbrol Authentic: HM04, German Panzer Grey |
| | ~6118 | | | Humbrol Authentic: HU03, Neutral Grey |
| | ~6118 | | | Humbrol Authentic: HU22, Blue Grey ANA 603 |
| | ~6118 | | | Humbrol Authentic: USN1, Dark Grey |
| | | 638 | | Humbrol Super Enamel: No.123, Extra Dark Sea Grey |
| | ~6118 | | | Lifecolor UA0022 Dark Grey |
| | ~6118 | | | ModelMaster: 1723, Gunship Gray |
| | ~6118 | | | Mr Color: 305, Grey |
| | ~6118 | | | Polly-S, 822, Sea Grey |
| | ~6118 | | | Poly-S Acrylic: 5264, Extra Dark Sea Grey |
| | ~6118 | | | Xtracolor: X130, Gunship Gray |
| Sky | | | Undersurface colour on ASR.IIIs | AeroMaster Warbird Enamel: 9114 |
| | | | | AeroMaster Warbird Acrylic: 1114 |
| | ~4424 | | | Compucolor: CAS10, Light Grey Green |
| | ~4424 | | | Gunze Sangyo Acrylic: H074, Sky |
| | | 210 | | Humbrol Authentic: HB05, Sky Type S |
| | ~4424 | | | Lifecolor: UA095 Sky |
| | ~4424 | | | Monogram-Promodeler Acrylic: 88-0038 |
| | ~4424 | | | Polly Scale Acrylic: 505254 |
| | ~4424 | | | Polly-S Acrylic: 500108 |
| | ~4454 | | | Tamiya: XF21, Sky |
| | | 210 | | Xtracolor: X7, Sky |
| Night | ~7038 | | Under surfaces | AeroMaster Warbird Enamel: 9001, Black |
| | ~7038 | | | Floquil Classic: 3010, Black |
| | ~7038 | | | Gunze Sangyo Acrylic: H002, Black |
| | ~7038 | | | Gunze Sangyo Acrylic: H012, Flat Black |
| | ~7038 | | | Humbrol Authentic: HB1, Night Black |
| | ~7038 | | | Humbrol Authentic: HU12, Night Black |
| | | 624 | | Humbrol Super Enamels: No.33, Black |
| | ~7038 | | | Lifecolor LC02 Matt Black |
| | ~7038 | | | ModelMaster: 1747, Gloss Black |
| | ~7038 | | | ModelMaster: 1749, Flat Black |
| | ~7038 | | | Pactra: MG61, Ebony Black |
| | ~7038 | | | Pactra Acrylic: A46, Black |
| | ~7038 | | | Polly-S: PF-10, Black |
| | ~7038 | | | Polly-S: 5214, Night Black |
| | | RAL 9005 | | Revell: 07, Black |
| | | RAL 9011 | | Revell: 08, Black |
| | ~7038 | | | Tamiya: X01, Black |
| | ~7038 | | | Tamiya: X18, Semigloss Black |
| | ~7038 | | | Tamiya: XF01, Flat Black |
| | ~7038 | | | Testors: 1749, Black |
| | ~7038 | | | Testors: 1747, Black |
| | | 624 | | Xtracolor: X12, Night Black |
| Black | ~7038 | | Codes Post-war | See entries under 'Night' heading |
| Identification Blue (Dull) | ~5044 | | Roundels | Gunze Sangyo Acrylic: H326, Blue |
| | ~5044 | | | ModelMaster: 1719, Insignia Blue |
| | ~5044 | | | Mr Color: 326, Blue |
| | ~5044 | | | Tamiya: XF17, Sea Blue |
| | ~5044 | | | Xtracolor: X122, Insignia Blue |
| | | 110 | | Xtracolor: X30, RAF Roundel Blue |
| Identification Blue (Bright) | ~5056 | | Post war Roundels | Compucolour: CIS7, Insignia Blue |
| Identification Red (Dull) | ~0109 | | Roundel centre & codes | N/A |
| Identification White | ~7875 | | Roundels, Post war codes, Undersurface colour on GR.IIIs, Pre-war Serials (under wings) | AeroMaster Warbird Enamel: 9002, White |
| | ~7875 | | | Compucolor: CAC12, White |
| | ~7875 | | | Humbrol Super Enamel: No.22, White |
| | ~7925 | | | Humbrol Super Enamel: No.34, Matt White |
| | | | | Lifecolor LC01 Matt White |
| | ~7778 | | | Gunze Sangyo Acrylic: H021, Off White |
| | ~7875 | | | Gunze Sangyo Acrylic: H001, White |
| | ~7875 | | | Gunze Sangyo Acrylic: H011, Flat White |
| | ~7875 | | | Humbrol Authentic: USN6, White |
| | ~7875 | | | ModelMaster: 1745, Insignia White |
| | ~7875 | | | ModelMaster: 1768, Flat White |
| | ~7875 | | | Mr Color: 316, White |
| | ~7875 | | | Pactra: MG52, Alpine White |
| | ~7875 | | | Pactra Acrylic: A47, White |
| | ~7875 | | | Polly-S: PG-10, White |
| | ~7875 | | | Polly-S: II-33, White |
| | ~7875 | | | Polly-S: PF-11, White |
| | ~7875 | | | Tamiya: X02, White |
| | ~7875 | | | Tamiya: XF02, Flat White |
| | ~7875 | | | Testors: 1168, White |
| | ~7875 | | | Xtracolor: X141, White |

Lancaster WU-41 of Escadrille 9S based at Nouméa
(©Coll. J.J. Petit)

| COLOUR | FS 595A | BS or RAL | USE | AVAILABLE PAINTS |
|---|---|---|---|---|
| Aluminium | ~7178 | | Overall Post-war Canadian & Test-beds | Compucolor: CIS12, Aluminium |
| | | | | Halford Acrylic: Aluminium |
| | | | | Halford Acrylic: Nissan Silver (Met) |
| | | | | Humbrol Super Enamel: No.11, Silver |
| | | | | Humbrol Super Enamel: No.191, Chrome Silver |
| | ~7178 | | | Lifecolor LC24 Natural Metal |
| | ~7178 | | | ModelMaster: 1790, Chrome Silver |
| | | | | ModelMaster Metalizer: 1401 Aluminium Plate |
| | ~7178 | | | Polly-S, IJ-17 |
| | ~7178 | | | Tamiya: XF16, Flat Aluminium |
| | ~7178 | | | Testors: 1146 Aluminium |
| | ~7178 | | | Xtracolor: X142, Aluminium |

### ROYAL AUSTRALIAN AIR FORCE
Wartime Lancasters were operated in the UK in standard RAF schemes (See Dark Green, Dark Earth and Night in Royal Air Force section).

| | | | | |
|---|---|---|---|---|
| Aluminium | ~7178 | | Overall Post-war (Lincoln) | See entry under 'Royal Air Force' section |
| Identification (Trainer) Yellow | ~3538 | | Markings Propeller Tips etc. | See entry under 'Royal Air Force' section |
| Identification Blue (Bright) | ~5056 | | Post war Roundels | See entry under 'Royal Air Force' section |
| (Identification) Bright Red | ~1105 | | Post war Roundels | N/A |
| Identification White | ~7875 | | Roundels | See entry under 'Royal Air Force' section |
| Black | ~7038 | | Codes Post-war | See entry under 'Royal Air Force' section |

### ROYAL CANADIAN AIR FORCE
Wartime Lancasters were delivered from this country in standard RAF schemes (See Dark Green, Dark Earth and Night in Royal Air Force section).

| | | | | |
|---|---|---|---|---|
| Aluminium | ~7178 | | Overall Post-war | See entry under 'Royal Air Force' section |
| Identification Yellow | ~3538 | | Markings Wing Leading Edges etc. | See entry under 'Royal Air Force' section |
| Identification Blue (Bright) | ~5056 | | Post war Roundels | See entry under 'Royal Air Force' section |
| Identification Red (Dull) | ~0109 | | Roundel centre & codes | See entry under 'Royal Air Force' section |
| Identification White | ~7875 | | Roundels Post war codes | See entry under 'Royal Air Force' section |
| Black | ~7038 | | Codes Post-war | See entry under 'Royal Air Force' section |
| Gloss Light Grey (Sky Grey) | ~6373 | | Lower fuselage & wings | LifeColor: UA036, Grey Reflectance High/Low |
| (Arctic) Red | ~1086 | | SAR and Hi-vis Markings | N/A |

### ROYAL EGYPTIAN AIR FORCE
Lancasters were delivered to this country in standard RAF schemes.

| | | | | |
|---|---|---|---|---|
| Dark Earth | ~0118 | | Upper surface camouflage | See entry under 'Royal Air Force' section |
| Dark Green | ~4079 | | Topside camouflage | See entry under 'Royal Air Force' section |
| Aluminium | ~7178 | | Overall colour | See entry under 'Royal Air Force' section |
| Identification White | ~7875 | | Codes & Roundels | See entry under 'Royal Air Force' section |

### AÉRONAVALE (FRANCE)
Initially the machines supplied to this country were in the standard RAF scheme.

| | | | | |
|---|---|---|---|---|
| Dark Green | ~4079 | | Topside camouflage | See entry under 'Royal Air Force' section |
| Dark Earth | ~0118 | | Upper surface camouflage | See entry under 'Royal Air Force' section |
| Aluminium | ~7178 | | Overall colour | See entry under 'Royal Air Force' section |
| Gris Bleu Clair | ~6473 ~6473 | | Code Letters | AeroMaster Warbird Acrylic: 1101 |
| | | | | Lifecolor Acrylic: UA141 French Blue-Grey |
| | | | | ModelMaster Enamel: 2109 |
| | | | | Poly Scale Acrylic: 505242 |
| | | | | Xtracolor: X389 French WWII Gris Bleu Clair |
| (Glossy Sea) Blue | ~5042 | | Overall | AeroMaster Warbird Enamel: 9057, US Sea Blue |
| | | | | AeroMaster Warbird Acrylic: 1044, US Sea Blue |
| | | | | Humbrol Super Enamel: 182, Sea Blue |
| | | | | LifeColor: UA044, Non-specular Sea Blue |
| | | | | ModelMaster Acylic: 50118, Flat Sea Blue |
| | | | | ModelMaster Enamel: 1718, Flat Sea Blue |
| | | | | Poly-S Acrylic: 505092, Sea Blue (ANA 607) |
| | | | | Tamiya: XF17, Sea Blue |
| Identification White | ~7875 | | Codes & Roundels | See entry under 'Royal Air Force' section |

NOTE:
The above lists references to Federal Standard (FS 595A) numbers do not include the prefix number. This just denotes the sheen of the colour e.g. 1 = Gloss, 2=Semi-gloss and 3 =Matt.
The above list has been compiled using manufacturers' paint lists and in conjunction with the 'IPMS Color Cross-Reference Guide' by David Klaus. Although every care has been taken to offer modellers the broadest spectrum of appropriate colours, further research for each scheme is advisable.
AeroMaster Warbird Enamel & Acrylic - At the time of writing (June 2000) AeroMaster announced that both their enamel and acrylic Warbird Color ranges would be discontinued. These colours are listed above for completeness only.

## Australia

The Lincolns supplied and built in Australia were left in bare metal overall. A black anti-dazzle panel was applied forward of the cockpit. Australian roundels of 58in diameter were applied to either side of the fuselage, but RAF Type D roundels of 84in diameter were applied above and below the wings. RAF Type D 30in x 24in fin flashes were also applied and the serial was in 6in black characters on the aft fuselage. Usually the aircraft number (e.g. '36' of A73-36) would be applied in 6in black letters under the bomb aimer's glazing.

## Argentina

The Lincolns supplied to Argentina were refurbished prior to being delivered, and therefore obtained the 'current' RAF camouflage scheme. This meant that these machines were Medium Sea Grey over Black, with the 1/3rd demarcation point. Some of you will note that a 'brown' was mentioned elsewhere in this title, and this may highlight that these machines were actually supplied in a darker hue (maybe Dark Slate Grey?) Initially the fuselage roundels were small (28in dia) and the fin flashes (12in x 32in) were applied only to the outside of the endplates, below the serial number in white. The serials (all 12in high) were also applied to either side of the nose and on the leading edge of each wing, outboard of the outer engine. Later the fuselage roundel was increased

Close-up of the nose of a Lancaster at East Kirkby. This is either DX•U (57 Squadron), AR•U (460 Squadron) or LE•U (630 Squadron)

Lincoln B Mk II, RE367, 'Aries II' of the RAF Flying College, prior to the North Pole Flight in 1951
(©RAFM P0018975)

in size to 48in diameter and the fin flash was 16in x 32in, placed mid-way up the fin endplate. The serial number was in white aft of the fuselage roundel (both sides), under the port and above the starboard wings and aft of the bomb aimer's glazing on the fuselage sides. The latter one remained 12in high, while the wing and fuselage ones were 30in white characters.

The Lincolns operated by the Fuerza Aerea del Tareas Antarticas had high-visibility orange panels added around the fuselage and above and below the wing tips. Usually nose art in the form of a Penguin was also carried by these machines.

The aircraft used in the maritime role had their wing leading edges and the entire outer face of each fin endplate painted in high-visibility orange, while the airframes converted to the transport role were usually Gloss White on the upper fuselage, and polished metal underneath. The inner and outer tips and bottoms of the fin endplates were in high-visibility orange and serial numbers were applied in black aft of the fuselage roundel and above the starboard and below the port wings. The mothership for the PAT-1 missile was Gloss Red overall with the 'Military Production' roundels under the tailplanes only.

Lincoln B Mk II, RE369, 'Aries III' of the RAF Flying College, Heany, 1950
(©RAFM P015545)

Lincoln B Mk II, RE367, 'Aries II' of the RAF Flying College, at Eielson AFB after the Trans-Polar Flight, 24th July 1951
(©RAFM P0019752)

# Kit Listing

| MANUFACTURER | SCALE | TYPE | SUBJECT | RELEASED | NOTES |
|---|---|---|---|---|---|
| Academy | 1/144th | IM | Lancaster B Mk I | 1993 | Ex-Crown |
| Advent | 1/72nd | IM | Lancaster 'Dambuster' | 1979 | Ex-Revell |
| Aircraft in Miniature | 1/72nd | VF/WM | Manchester | 1980s | Ex-Contrail |
| Airfix | 1/72nd | IM | Lancaster B Mk I | 1958 | First Mould |
| Airfix | 1/72nd | IM | Lancaster B Mk I/III | 1979 | & issued BofB 50th Anniversary set |
| Airfix | 1/72nd | IM | Lancaster 'Dambuster' | 1993 | Modified Tooling |
| Airfix Corporation | 1/72nd | IM | Lancaster B Mk I | 1963 | Ex-Airfix |
| Airfix Craftmaster | 1/72nd | IM | Lancaster B Mk I | 1965 | Ex-Airfix |
| Atlantic | 1/100th | N/K | Lancaster B Mk I | 1980 | |
| Contrail | 1/72nd | VF | Manchester | 1970s | |
| Contrail | 1/72nd | VF | Lincoln B Mk 2 | 1970s | Retooled and reissued in 1988 |
| Crown | 1/144th | IM | Lancaster B Mk I | 1970s | |
| DFI | 1/96th | IM | Lancaster B Mk I | 1980s | Ex-Frog |
| Formaplane | 1/72nd | VF | Manchester | 1980s | |
| Frog | 1/72nd | IM | Lancaster B Mk I | 1976 | |
| Frog | 1/96th | IM | Lancaster B Mk I | 1959 | |
| Gunze Sangyo | 1/72nd | IM | Lancaster B Mk I/III | 1980s | Ex-Airfix |
| ID Models | 1/32nd | VF | Lancaster B Mk I/III | 1983 | Limited Edition |
| International Modeling | 1/125th | IM | Lancaster | 1970s | Ex-Lincoln |
| Kader | 1/125th | IM | Lancaster | 1970s | Ex-Lincoln |
| Lincoln International | 1/125th | IM | Lancaster | 1950s | |
| Matchbox | 1/72nd | IM | Lancaster B Mk I/III | 1980 | |
| Minicraft | 1/144th | IM | Lancaster B Mk I | 1998 | Ex-Crown |
| MPC | 1/72nd | IM | Lancaster B Mk I | 1972 | Ex-Airfix |
| Novo | 1/96th | IM | Lancaster B Mk I | 1978 | Ex-Frog |
| Novo Export | 1/96th | IM | Lancaster B Mk I | 1982 | May never have been issued |
| Revell | 1/72nd | IM | Lancaster 'Dambuster' | 1964 | |
| Revell | 1/72nd | IM | Lancaster | 1960s | |
| Tamiya | 1/48th | IM | Lancaster B Mk I/III | 1976 | |
| Tamiya | 1/48th | IM | Lancaster 'Dambuster' | 1976 | |
| Tri-ang | 1/96th | IM | Lancaster B Mk I | 1970s | Ex-Frog |
| USAirfix | 1/72nd | IM | Lancaster B Mk I/III | 1979 | Ex-Airfix |
| UPC | 1/96th | IM | Lancaster B Mk I | 1969 | Ex-Frog |

Note: *This list contains all known Manchester, Lancaster and Lincoln kits, along with their original release date (if known). Subsequent reissue details are not included.*

**KEY**

IM = Injection Moulded Plastic (Inc Limited-Run Injection Moulded Plastic)
R = Resin
VF = Vac-formed Plastic
WM = White Metal (Inc Pewter)

| MANUFACTURER | SCALE | TYPE | PRODUCT NO | ITEM | DESIGNED FOR/NOTES | |
|---|---|---|---|---|---|---|
| Aeroclub | 1/72nd | VF | C042 | Lancaster Early Nose Blister | |
| Aeroclub | 1/72nd | IM/WM | E030 | Bristol Hercules & Cowlings | Lancaster B Mk I |
| Aeroclub | 1/72nd | WM | E052 | Rolls-Royce Merlin VIII/X/22 | |
| Aeroclub | 1/72nd | WM | P020 | D.H. 3 Blade Propeller | Lancaster B Mk II |
| Aeroclub | 1/72nd | WM | P030 | D.H. Hydromatic 4 Blade Propellers | Lincoln |
| Aeroclub | 1/72nd | WM | V031 | Lancaster 3 Blade Paddle Propellers | Lancaster |
| Aeroclub | 1/72nd | WM | V035 | Hercules Hedgehog Exhaust Stacks | Lancaster B Mk II |
| Aeroclub | 1/72nd | WM | V040 | Lancaster 6-stack Exhausts | |
| Aeroclub | 1/72nd | IM/VF/WM | VA51 | Lancaster B Mk II Conversion | Airfix B Mk I/III |
| Airkit | 1/72nd | A | C017 | Lancaster Cockpit Placards | |
| Airwaves | 1/72nd | EB | 72193 | Lancaster Detail Set | Airfix B Mk I/III |
| BMW Models | 1/72nd | P | 0772 | Paper Instrument Panels | inc Lancaster |
| Cutting Edge | 1/48th | M | BM48127 | Lancaster Wheel Hub Masks | True Detail set 48049 |
| Cutting Edge | 1/48th | M | BM48128 | Lancaster Wheel Hub Masks | True Detail set 48079 |
| Engines & Things | 1/72nd | R | 72028 | Bristol Hercules | Lancaster B Mk II |
| Engines & Things | 1/72nd | R | 72080 | Rolls-Royce Merlin 61/68 | Lincoln B.2 |
| Engines & Things | 1/72nd | R | 72102 | Bristol Hercules | Lancaster B Mk II |
| Engines & Things | 1/72nd | R | 72107 | Rolls-Royce Merlin XX/21 | Lancaster B Mk II/VII/VII |
| Engines & Things | 1/48th | R | 48016 | Bristol Hercules | Lancaster B Mk II |
| Engines & Things | 1/48th | R | 48036 | Rolls-Royce Merlin 61/68 | Lincoln B.2 |
| Engines & Things | 1/48th | R | 48103 | Rolls-Royce Merlin XX/21 | Lancaster B Mk I/II/VII |
| Engines & Things | 1/48th | R | 48117 | Bristol Hercules | Lancaster B Mk II |
| Falcon | 1/72nd | VF | CV22 | RAF Bombers Pt.4 | Inc Lancaster |
| Flightpath | 1/72nd | EB | 72021 | Avro Lancaster Detail Set | Airfix B Mk I/III |
| Flightpath | 1/48th | EB | | Avro Lancaster Detail Set | Tamiya B Mk I/III |
| Magna Models | 1/72nd | R/WM/VF | 7262 | Avro Lancastrian Conversion | Airfix B Mk I/III |
| M&E Models | 1/72nd | IM | | Avro Lancastrian Conversion | Airfix B Mk I/III |
| Paragon Designs | 1/72nd | R | 72009 | Lancaster 'Tallboy' | Airfix B Mk I/III |
| Paragon Designs | 1/72nd | R | 72010 | Lancaster 'Grand Slam' | Airfix B Mk I/III |
| Paragon Designs | 1/72nd | R | 72011 | Lancaster Bulged Bomb Bay Doors | Airfix B Mk I/III |
| Paragon Designs | 1/72nd | R | 72012 | Lancaster Paddle Blade Propellers | |
| Paragon Designs | 1/72nd | R | 72013 | Lancaster 6-stack Exhaust Stacks | |
| Paragon Designs | 1/72nd | R | 72014 | Lancaster Flaps | |
| Paragon Designs | 1/72nd | R/VF/EB | 72041 | 100 Group (Inc Lancaster) | Airfix B Mk I/III |
| Paragon Designs | 1/72nd | R | 72047 | Lancaster Merlin 85 Nacelles | Airfix B Mk I/III |
| Paragon Designs | 1/72nd | R | 72048 | Lancaster Mk II Conversion | Airfix B Mk I/III |
| Paragon Designs | 1/72nd | R | 72049 | Lancaster Bulged Bomb Bay Doors | Airfix B Mk I/III |
| Paragon Designs | 1/72nd | R/VF | 72050 | Manchester Mk I/IA Conversion | Airfix B Mk I/III |
| Paragon Designs | 1/72nd | R/VF | 72051 | Lincoln Conversion | Airfix B Mk I/III |
| Paragon Designs | 1/72nd | R | 72052 | Lincoln MR.31 Nose Extension | Airfix B Mk I/III |
| Paragon Designs | 1/72nd | R | 72055 | Lancaster Bulged Wheels | |
| Paragon Designs | 1/72nd | R/VF | 72065 | Lancaster Prototype Conversion | Tamiya B Mk I/III |
| Paragon Designs | 1/48th | R/VF | 48057 | Lincoln Conversion | Tamiya B Mk I/III |
| Paragon Designs | 1/48th | R/VF/EB | 48092 | 100 Group Lancaster | Tamiya B Mk I/III |
| Paragon Designs | 1/48th | R | 48108 | Lancaster Merlin 85 Nacelles | Tamiya B Mk I/III |
| Paragon Designs | 1/48th | R | 48118 | Lincoln MR.31 Nose Extension | Tamiya B Mk I/III |
| Paragon Designs | 1/48th | R/VF | 48119 | Lincoln 'Saddle' Radome& Scanner | Tamiya B Mk I/III |
| Paragon Designs | 1/48th | RVF | 48120 | Lancaster Mk II Conversion | Tamiya B Mk I/III |
| Paragon Designs | 1/48th | R | 48121 | Lancaster Narrow Blade Propellers | |
| Paragon Designs | 1/48th | R | 48122 | Lancaster 6-stack Exhaust Stacks | |
| Paragon Designs | 1/48th | R | 48123 | Lancaster 'Tallboy' Conversion | Tamiya B Mk I/III |
| Paragon Designs | 1/48th | R | 48124 | Lancaster Flaps | |
| Paragon Designs | 1/48th | R | 48125 | Lancaster Bulged Bomb Bay Doors | Tamiya B Mk I/III |
| Paragon Designs | 1/48th | R | 48126 | Lancaster Bomb Bay Doors (8,000lb) | Tamiya B Mk I/III |
| Paragon Designs | 1/48th | R/VF | 48127 | Manchester Mk I/IA Conversion | Tamiya B Mk I/III |
| Paragon Designs | 1/48th | R | 48129 | Lancaster Bulged Wheels | |
| Paragon Designs | 1/48th | R/VF | 48140 | Lancaster Prototype Conversion | Tamiya B Mk I/III |
| Pavla | 1/72nd | VF | | Lancaster Canopy & Gun Turrets | Revell B Mk I |
| True Details | 1/48th | R | 48049 | Lancaster Main Wheels | |

Engines & Things (48016) Bristol Hercules

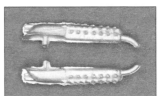
Aeroclub (V035) Hercules Hedgehog Exhuast Stacks

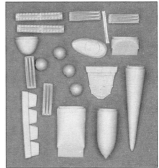
Paragon Designs (72010) Lancaster 'Grand Slam' Conversion

Paragon Designs (72013) Lancaster 6-stack Exhaust Stacks

Aeroclub (C042) Lancaster Early Nose Blister

Aeroclub (P030) D.H. Hydromatic 4 Blade Propellers

Aeroclub (E052) Rolls-Royce Merlin VIII/X/22

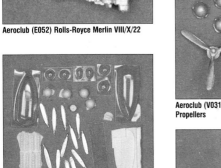
Magna Models (7262) Avro Lancastrian Conversion

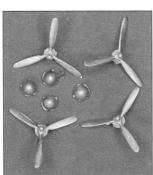
Aeroclub (V031) Lancaster 3 Blade Paddle Propellers

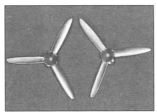
Aeroclub (P020) D.H. 3 Blade Propeller

Paragon Designs (72048) Lancaster Mk II Conversion

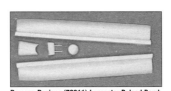
Paragon Designs (72011) Lancaster Bulged Bomb Bay Doors

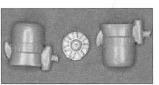
Aeroclub (E030) Bristol Hercules & Cowlings

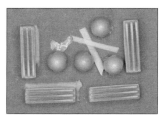

Paragon Designs (72012) Lancaster Paddle Blade Propellers

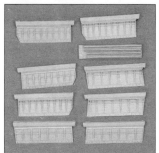

Paragon Designs (72014) Lancaster Flaps

Paragon Designs (72041) 100 Group (Inc Lancaster)

Paragon Designs (72055) Lancaster Bulged Wheels

Paragon Designs (48125) Lancaster Bulged Bomb Bay Doors

Aeroclub (V040) Lancaster 6-stack Exhausts

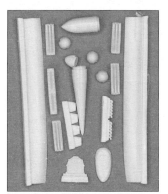

Paragon Designs (72009) Lancaster 'Tallboy' Conversion

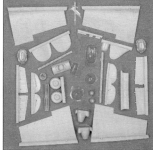

Paragon Designs (72050) Manchester Mk I/IA Conversion

Paragon Designs (72051) Lincoln Conversion

Paragon Designs (72052) Lincoln MR.31 Nose Extension

Paragon Designs (72047) Lancaster Merlin 85 Nacelles

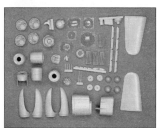

Paragon Designs (48057) Lincoln Conversion

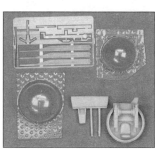

Paragon Designs (48092) 100 Group Lancaster

Paragon Designs (48118) Lincoln MR.31 Nose Extension

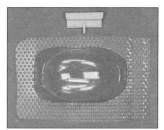

Paragon Designs (48119) Lincoln 'Saddle' Radome & Scanner

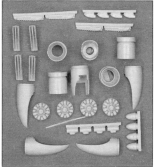

Paragon Designs (48120) Lancaster Mk II Conversion

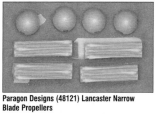

Paragon Designs (48121) Lancaster Narrow Blade Propellers

Paragon Designs (48122) Lancaster 6-stack Exhaust Stacks

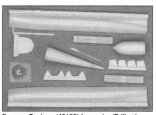

Paragon Designs (48123) Lancaster 'Tallboy' Conversion

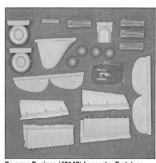

Paragon Designs (48140) Lancaster Prototype Conversion

Paragon Designs (48124) Lancaster Flaps

Paragon Designs (48108) Lancaster Merlin 85 Nacelles

Paragon Designs (48127) Manchester Mk I/IA Conversion

Paragon Designs (48129) Lancaster Bulged Wheels

Paragon Designs (48126) Lancaster Bomb Bay Doors (8,000lb)

Pavla Lancaster Canopy & Gun Turrets

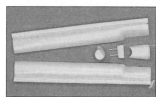

Paragon Designs (72049) Lancaster Bulged Bomb Bay Doors

# Decals

| MANUFACTURER | SCALE | SHEET NO. | TITLE |
|---|---|---|---|
| **ADS** | **1/72nd** | **011-72** | **Avro Lancaster Part 1** |
| B Mk II, DS842, JI•F, 'Fanny Firkin', No. 514 Squadron | | | |
| B Mk III, LM739, HW•Z, 'Grogs the Shot', No. 100 Squadron | | | |
| B Mk III, ED989, DX•F, 'Frederick III', No. 57 Squadron | | | |
| B Mk I (Special), PD119, YZ•J, No. 617 Squadron | | | |
| B Mk I (Special), PD121, YZ•Z, No. 617 Squadron | | | |
| **ADS** | **1/48th** | **011-48** | **Avro Lancaster Part 1** |
| B Mk II, DS842, JI•F, 'Fanny Firkin', No. 514 Squadron | | | |
| B Mk III, LM739, HW•Z, 'Grogs the Shot', No. 100 Squadron | | | |
| B Mk III, ED989, DX•F, 'Frederick III', No. 57 Squadron | | | |
| B Mk I (Special), PD119, YZ•J, No. 617 Squadron | | | |
| B Mk I (Special), PD121, YZ•Z, No. 617 Squadron | | | |
| **AeroMaster** | **1/72nd** | **72-156** | **Lancaster Bombers Pt.1** |
| EE176, QR•M, 'Mickey the Moocher', No. 61 Squadron | | | |
| LL757, SR•W, 'Oor Willie', No. 100 Squadron | | | |
| LM550, AS•B, No. 166 Squadron | | | |
| LM624, DX•A, No. 57 Squadron | | | |
| **AeroMaster** | **1/72nd** | **72-157** | **Lancaster Bombers Pt.2** |
| W4118, ZN•Y, 'Admiral Prune', No. 106 Squadron | | | |
| MB499, AS•D, No. 66 Squadron | | | |
| PR150, CV•F, No. 625 Squadron, RCAF | | | |
| KB772, VR•R, No. 419 (RCAF) Squadron | | | |
| **AeroMaster** | **1/48th** | **48-451** | **Lancaster Bombers Pt.1** |
| EE176, QR•M, 'Mickey the Moocher', No. 61 Squadron | | | |
| LL757, SR•W, 'Oor Willie', No. 100 Squadron | | | |
| LM550, AS•B, No. 166 Squadron | | | |
| **AeroMaster** | **1/48th** | **48-452** | **Lancaster Bombers Pt.2** |
| W4118, ZN•Y, 'Admiral Prune', No. 106 Squadron | | | |
| MB499, AS•D, No. 66 Squadron | | | |
| PR150, CV•F, No. 625 Squadron, RCAF | | | |
| **AeroMaster** | **1/48th** | **48-453** | **Lancaster Bombers Pt.3** |
| KB772, VR•R, No. 419 (RCAF) Squadron | | | |
| LM624, DX•A, No. 57 Squadron | | | |
| **Albatros Modelworks** | **1/72nd** | **ALC-72003** | **Sexy Lancs** |
| B Mk I, P8817/G, IQ•Q, No. 105 Squadron, RAF Hemswell | | | |
| B Mk X, KB864, NA•S, 'Sugar's Blues', No. 428 (Ghost) Squadron | | | |
| RAF Middleton St. George, June 1945. | | | |
| B Mk I, LL814, BH•F, No. 300 (Masovian) Squadron, RAF Faldingworth | | | |
| B Mk I, NG374, QB•P, 'Piccadilly Princess', No. 424 (City of Hamilton) | | | |
| Sqn (RCAF), RAF Skipton-on-Swale | | | |
| B Mk I, B-033, Argentinian Air Force, 1948. | | | |
| **Albatros Modelworks** | **1/48th** | **ALC-48003** | **Sexy Lancs** |
| B Mk I, P8817/G, IQ•Q, No. 105 Squadron, RAF Hemswell | | | |
| B Mk X, KB864, NA•S, 'Sugar's Blues', No. 428 (Ghost) Squadron | | | |
| RAF Middleton St. George, June 1945. | | | |
| B Mk I, LL814, BH•F, No. 300 (Masovian) Squadron, RAF Faldingworth | | | |
| B Mk I, NG374, QB•P, 'Piccadilly Princess', No. 424 (City of Hamilton) | | | |
| Sqn (RCAF), RAF Skipton-on-Swale | | | |
| B Mk I, B-033, Argentinian Air Force, 1948. | | | |
| **Almarks** | **1/72nd** | **S7203** | |
| inc Lancaster B Mk I | | | |
| **Arrow Graphics** | **1/72nd** | **E-3** | **'Mynarski Memorial'** |
| Lancaster, VR•R, No. 419 (Moose) Squadron | | | |
| **Arrow Graphics** | **1/72nd** | **F-7** | **Avro Lancaster Mk 10** |
| 10ASR, No. 123 Search & Rescue Flight, RCAF, Sea Island, 1948. | | | |
| **Arrow Graphics** | **1/72nd** | **J-1** | **Avro Lancaster Mk 10** |
| FM213, Display aircraft of the Goderich Chapter, | | | |
| Royal Canadian Legion 1968-1977 | | | |
| **Arrow Graphics** | **1/48th** | **G-1** | **'Mynarski Memorial'** |
| Lancaster, VR•R, No. 419 (Moose) Squadron | | | |
| **Arrow Graphics** | **1/72nd** | **A-4** | **RCAF Lancaster** |
| Early style Roundels (48in & 84in) | | | |
| **Australian Military Models** | **1/48th** | **AMMD001** | **617 Squadron** |
| ED909/G, AJ•P, 'P-Popsi', No. 617 Squadron, | | | |
| flown by Flt Lt H.B. Martin (Dams Raid) | | | |
| **Australian Military Models** | **1/48th** | **AMMD002** | **617 Squadron** |
| ED912/G, AJ•N, 'N-Nun', No. 617 Squadron, | | | |
| flown by Flt Lt L.G. Knight (Dams Raid) | | | |
| **Australian Military Models** | **1/48th** | **AMMD003** | **617 Squadron** |
| ED929/G, AJ•L, 'L-Leather', No. 617 Squadron, | | | |
| flown by Flt Lt D.J. Shannon (Dams Raid) | | | |
| **Australian Military Models** | **1/48th** | | **Australian War Memorial** |
| W4783, AR•G, 'G-George' No. 460 Squadron | | | |
| (Preserved AWM, Canberra, A.C.T.) | | | |
| **Kits at War** | **1/72nd** | **K7/3** | |
| Manchester Mk I, L7316, EM•U, No. 207 Squadron | | | |
| Lancaster B Mk I, L7533, KM•K, No. 44 Squadron | | | |
| **Kits at War** | **1/72nd** | **K4/5** | |
| Manchester Mk I, L7316, EM•U, No. 207 Squadron | | | |
| Lancaster B Mk I, L7533, KM•K, No. 44 Squadron | | | |
| **RAFDEC** | **1/72nd** | **7203** | **No. 5 Group** |
| 48" Red Codes with Yellow Outlines | | | |
| **RAFDEC** | **1/72nd** | **7204** | **No. 5 Group** |
| 36" Red Codes with Yellow Outlines | | | |
| **RAFDEC** | **1/72nd** | **7205** | **RAF 1940-47** |
| Inc; Lancaster ASR.III, RF310, RL•A, No. 279 Squadron, | | | |
| RAF Beccles, Detached to Pegu, Burma, early 1946. | | | |
| **RAFDEC** | **1/72nd** | **7206** | **RAF 1949-54** |
| Inc; Lancaster GR Mk III, RE164, H•U, School of Maritime Reconnaissance, | | | |
| RAF St. Mawgan, July 1953. | | | |
| **SkyModel** | **1/72nd** | **72006** | **Lancaster** |
| LM220, WS•Y, 'Getting Younger Everyday', No. 9 Squadron | | | |
| RF141, JO•U, 'Uncle Joe Again', No. 463 Squadron | | | |
| R5868, PO•S, No. 467 Squadron | | | |
| LL757, SR•W, 'Oor Willie', No. 100 Squadron | | | |
| W4118, ZN•Y, 'Admiral Prune', No. 106 Squadron | | | |
| PA474, 'City of Lincoln', BBMF, RAF Coningsby | | | |

**Note:** Some of the above listed manufacturers are no longer in business. Please check with your local hobby shop regarding availability.

**Kits at War** – These decals are produced by Dutch Decals.

ADS (011-72) Avro Lancaster Part 1

AeroMaster (72-156) Lancaster Bombers Pt.1

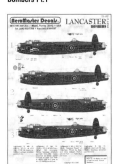
AeroMaster (72-157) Lancaster Bombers Pt.2

AeroMaster (48-451) Lancaster Bombers Pt.1

AeroMaster (48-453) Lancaster Bombers Pt.3

SkyModel (72006) Lancaster

Albatros Modelworks (ALC-48003) Sexy Lancs

RAFDEC (7204) No. 5 Group

Australian Military Models (AMMD001)

ED912/G    ED912/G
Australian Military Models (AMMD002)

RAFDEC (7205) RAF 1940-47

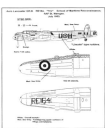
Australian Military Models (AMMD003)

RAFDEC (7206) RAF 1949-54

Kits at War (K7/3)

Kits at War (K4/5)

RAFDEC (7203) No. 5 Group

Australian Military Models 'G-George'

# Powerplants

## The Rolls-Royce Vulture & Merlin Manchester, Lancaster (Lancastrian) and Lincoln Usage

### Manchester

#### Vulture I

This 1,800hp engine resembled two Peregrine engines with a common crankshaft mounted in a common crankcase. This 24-cylinder, 90°, X-format engine used a 70-30% water/etylene-glycol coolant. The two-speed, single-stage supercharger had a compression ratio of 6:1. Fuel used was 87 Octane.

Fitted to: Manchester Prototype, Mk I and Mk IA

Production: 538 Derby

Total Production: 538

Production Period:1939-42

**Rolls-Royce Vulture I**

#### Vulture II

This engine was an update of the previous one and was in the same 24-cylinder, 90°, X-format. Coolant was once again 70-30% water/etylene-glycol and the two-speed, single-stage supercharger had a compression ratio of 6:1. Fuel used was 100 Octane.

Fitted to: Manchester Prototype, Mk I and Mk IA

Production: (See Vulture I above)

Total Production: (See Vulture I above)

Production Period:1939-42

### Lancaster, Lancastrian & Lincoln

#### Merlin X

This was the first two-speed supercharged engine with a propeller reduction of 0.42:1. Pressurised water-glycol cooling was installed and power at the rated altitude was 2,250hp. Medium supercharger M Gear with +5.75lb/sq in boost, fully supercharged S Gear with +5.75lb/sq in and 87 Octane fuel.

Fitted to: Manchester B Mk III (Lancaster B Mk I)

Production: 312 Derby, 4,589 Crewe

Total Production: 4,901

Production Period: 1938-42

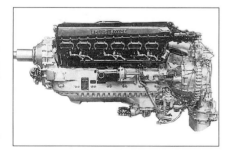

**Rolls-Royce Merlin X**

#### Merlin XX

This two-speed supercharged engine was a modified version of the Mk X, for which it was the replacement. A 70-30% ethylene-glycol pressure cooling system was used (like the Mk XII) and a propeller reduction gear of 0.42:1. Maximum boost was +12lb/sq. in. and 100 octane fuel was used. The maximum power output of this engine was 1,390hp.

Fitted to: Lancaster B Mk I, III & VII

Production: 2,592 Derby, 3,391 Crewe, 9,500 Glasgow, 12,538 Ford

Total Production: 28,021

Production Period: 1940-44

#### Merlin 22

This 1,390hp two-speed supercharged engine was a modified version of the Mk XX and 21. A propeller reduction gear of 0.42:1 and maximum boost was +16lb/sq. in. 100 octane fuel was used and the maximum power output of this engine was 1,480hp (full-throttle in MS gear).

Fitted to: Lancaster B Mk I & VII

Production: 1,478 (Mk 22) & 8 (Mk 22Ys) Derby, 1,387 Crewe, 2,164 Glasgow, 5,590 Ford

Total Production: 10,627

Production Period: 1942-43

**Rolls-Royce Merlin 22**

#### Merlin 22A

This engine was similar to the Merlin 22, which in turn was a development of the XX. It featured a two-piece cylinder block. All 22As were modified Ford built examples that had the two-piece block installed but retained the nickel-steel cylinder studs. The '22A' title was applied because the different material used for the studs resulted in the need to have different torque settings. Power outputs etc are identical to the Mk XX

Fitted to: Lancaster B Mk I & VII

Production: N/K Ford

Total Production: N/K

Production Period: 1940-44

#### Merlin 24

This 1,610hp engine was similar to the Merlin XX and 22, but had an RAE anti-G carburettor. It also featured double-girder pistons which allowed +18lb.sq.in boost.

Fitted to: Lancaster B Mk I & VII

Production: 542 Derby, 229 Crewe, 2,550 Glasgow, 10,400 Ford

Total Production: 13, 721

Production Period: 1944-45

#### Merlin T-24-1 & 2

This 1,610hp engine was similar to the Merlin 24, but was modified to improve its service life. This became the Merlin 500 in civil guise.

Fitted to: Lancaster B Mk I & Lancastrian I

Production: 903 Derby, 35 Glasgow, 1,000 Ford

Total Production: 1,938

Production Period: 1944-45

#### Merlin T-24-4

This 1,610hp engine was similar to the Merlin T-24-2, but with after-heating. The civil version became the Merlin 501.

Fitted to: Lancastrian I

Production: N/K

Total Production: N/K

Production Period: 1944-45

#### Merlin 65

This 1,315hp engine was similar to the Merlin 63 with a two-speed, two-stage supercharger. 100 Octane fuel was used.

Fitted to: Lancaster B Mk I

Production: 2 Derby

Total Production: 2

Production Period: 1943

#### Merlin 68A

This two-speed, two-stage supercharged engine was similar to the Merlin 68, but had a charge-temperature control scheme. Propeller reduction was once again 0.420:1

Fitted to: Lincoln B Mk II (B.2)

Production: N/K

Total Production: N/K

Production Period: 1945

#### Merlin 85

This 1,635hp engine offered a similar rating to the Merlin 66 & 68. It was equivalent to the Packard Merlin 68 and the propeller reduction was 0.420:1

Fitted to: Lancaster B Mk VI, Lincoln B Mk I, II & IV

Production: 34 Derby, 1,400 Glasgow

Total Production: 1,434

Production Period: 1944-5

#### Merlin 86

This 1,635hp engine was similar to the Merlin 85, but was fitted with anti-surge diffusers. It was equivalent to the Packard V-1650-9.

Fitted to: Lincoln B Mk II & Lincolnian

Production: N/K

Total Production: N/K

Production Period: 1944-5

#### Merlin 102

This 1,635hp engine was an experimental type, which was generally strengthened for civil use. It featured end-feed lubrication.

Fitted to: Lincoln B II & Lincolnian

Production: 169 Glasgow

Total Production: 169

Production Period: 1944-6

#### Merlin 102A

This 1,635hp engine was also an experimental type, and was similar to the Merlin 102. It featured an after-heater.

Fitted to: Lancastrian I

Production: N/K

Total Production: N/K

Production Period: 1944-6

#### Merlin 500

This 1,660hp engine was basically a civil version of the Mk T.24/2. It had a two-stage, single-speed supercharger and propeller reduction was 0.42:1.

Fitted to: Lancastrian I

Production: 10 (500-3), 2 (500-4), 20 (500-5), 1 (500-6) & 2 (500-20) Derby

Total Production: See Above

Production Period: 1947-9

### Merlin 501

This 1,660hp engine was based on the Mk T.24/4. It had a two-stage, single-speed supercharger and offered an after-heater to reduce spark plug-leading.

| | |
|---|---|
| Fitted to: Lancastrian I |
| Production: N/K |
| Total Production: N/K |
| Production Period: 1947-9 |

### Merlin 604

This 1,720hp engine was basically a military version of the Merlin 621. It had a two-stage, single-speed supercharger and propeller reduction was 0.42:1.

| | |
|---|---|
| Fitted to: Lincoln B.2 (Argentina) |
| Production: N/K |
| Total Production: N/K |
| Production Period: 1947-9 |

## The Bristol Hercules
## Lancaster Usage

### Hercules VI

This 1,615hp sleeve-valve radial two-speed, single-stage supercharged engine was a development based on the HE-6SM. It featured 7:1 compression ratio and could operate on 87 or 100 Octane fuel.

| | |
|---|---|
| Fitted to: Lancaster B Mk II |
| Production: N/K |
| Total Production: N/K |
| Production Period:1941-43 |

### Hercules XVI

This 1,615hp sleeve-valve radial two-speed, single-stage supercharged engine was similar to the VI. It featured 7:1 compression ratio, epicyclic reduction of 0.444:1 and it could operate on 87 or 100 Octane fuel.

| | |
|---|---|
| Fitted to: Lancaster B Mk II |
| Production: N/K |
| Total Production: N/K |
| Production Period:1941-43 |

**Bristol Hercules VI**
**(shown here installed in a Beaufighter Mk VIc)**

## The Rolls Royce Merlin
## The American Connection

### Merlin 28

This 1,390hp engine was a two-speed, single-stage supercharged unit, similar to the Merlin 22A, but built by Packard for RAF use. This engine featured a two-piece block (as per the V-1650-1) and a British propeller shaft. They featured Bendix carburettors (except later fuel-injected versions) and had a propeller reduction ratio of 0.42:1.

| | |
|---|---|
| Fitted to: Lancaster B Mk III & Mk X |
| Production: N/K |
| Total Production: N/K |
| Production Period: 1944-45 |

### Merlin 38

This 1,390hp engine had a two-speed, single-stage supercharger and was basically a Packard-built Merlin 22. Propeller reduction was 0.42:1.

| | |
|---|---|
| Fitted to: Lancaster B Mk III & Mk X |
| Production: N/K |
| Total Production: N/K |
| Production Period: 1942-5 |

**Rolls-Royce Merlin 28 installation in the**
**prototype B Mk III (R5849)**

### Merlin 68

This two-speed, two-stage supercharged engine was similar to the Merlin 66, and was basically a Packard-built version of the Merlin 85. Propeller reduction 0.420:1.

| | |
|---|---|
| Fitted to: Lincoln B Mk II (B.2) |
| Production: N/K |
| Total Production: N/K |
| Production Period: 1945 |

### Merlin 224

This 1,610hp two-speed, single-stage supercharged engine was a Packard-built Merlin 24. It was fitted with a Bendix carburettor instead of an RAE anti-G unit.

| | |
|---|---|
| Fitted to: Lancaster B Mk I & III |
| Production: N/K |
| Total Production: N/K |
| Production Period: 1944-6 |

**A cutaway of the Bristol Hercules 'power egg'** *(© BAe)*

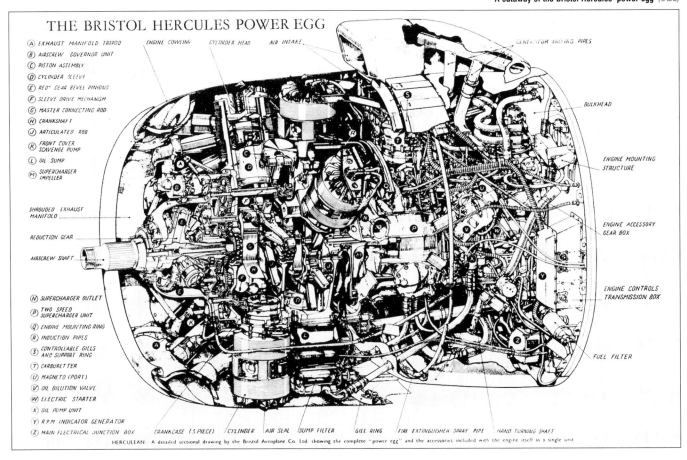

THE BRISTOL HERCULES POWER EGG

(A) EXHAUST MANIFOLD TRIPOD
(B) AIRSCREW GOVERNOR UNIT
(C) PISTON ASSEMBLY
(D) CYLINDER SLEEVE
(E) RED" GEAR BEVEL PINIONS
(F) SLEEVE DRIVE MECHANISM
(G) MASTER CONNECTING ROD
(H) CRANKSHAFT
(J) ARTICULATED ROD
(K) FRONT COVER SCAVENGE PUMP
(L) OIL SUMP
(M) SUPERCHARGER IMPELLER
(N) SUPERCHARGER OUTLET
(P) TWO SPEED SUPERCHARGER UNIT
(Q) ENGINE MOUNTING RING
(R) INDUCTION PIPES
(S) CONTROLLABLE GILLS AND SUPPORT RING
(T) CARBURETTER
(U) MAGNETO (PORT)
(V) OIL DILUTION VALVE
(W) ELECTRIC STARTER
(X) OIL PUMP UNIT
(Y) R.P.M. INDICATOR GENERATOR
(Z) MAIN ELECTRICAL JUNCTION BOX

ENGINE COWLING   CYLINDER HEAD   AIR INTAKE   GENERATOR LAGGING PIPES   BULKHEAD   ENGINE MOUNTING STRUCTURE   ENGINE ACCESSORY GEAR BOX   ENGINE CONTROLS TRANSMISSION BOX   FUEL FILTER

SHROUDED EXHAUST MANIFOLD   REDUCTION GEAR   AIRSCREW SHAFT

CRANKCASE (3 PIECE)   CYLINDER   AIR SEAL   SUMP FILTER   GILL RING   FIRE EXTINGUISHER SPRAY PIPE   HAND TURNING SHAFT

HERCULEAN  A detailed sectional drawing by the Bristol Aeroplane Co. Ltd. showing the complete "power egg" and the accessories included with the engine itself as a single unit

# Manchester, Lancaster & Lincoln Variants

## Manchester

**Designation:** **Prototype (L7246)**
Specification: P.13/36
Avro Type No.: 679
First Flight: 24th July 1939
Span: 82ft 2in (32.36m)
Length: 68ft 10in (20.98m) [tail down]
Height: 19ft 6in (5.94m)
Engine: Two 1,760hp (1,312kW) Rolls-Royce Vulture I, 24-cylinder, X-type
Crew: Test Crew Only (Designed for a crew of 7)
Weight: Empty 29,432lb (13,186kg), Loaded 56,000lb (25,088kg)
Max Speed: 265mph (427km/h) at 17,000ft (5,180m)
Service Ceiling: 19,200ft (5,850m)
Armament: None
Max Bomb Load: 10,350lb (4,637kg)
Propeller: Three-blade, de Havilland D.I.S. 27 Type 6/3, Variable Pitch, Hydromatic

**Designation:** **Prototype (L7247)**
Specification: P.13/36
Avro Type No.: 679
First Flight: 26th May 1940
Span: 82ft 2in (25.04m) [later modified to B Mk I standard]
Length: 68ft 4 1/2in (20.84m)
Height: 19ft 6in (5.94m)
Engine: Two 1,760hp (1,312kW) Rolls-Royce Vulture I, 24-cylinder, X-type
Crew: Test Crew Only (Designed for a crew of 7)
Weight: Empty 25,959lb (11,630kg), Gross 45,000lb (29,120kg)
Max Speed: 265mph (427km/h) at 17,000ft (5,180m)
Service Ceiling: 19,200ft (5,850m)
Armament: 2x 0.303 in Browning machine guns in front, rear (F.N.4) and ventral (F.N.21) turrets
Bomb Load: Provision to carry 8x 1,000lb (455kg) bombs
Propeller: Three-blade, de Havilland D.I.S. 27 Type 6/3, Variable Pitch, Hydromatic

**Designation:** **Mk I**
Avro Type No.: 679
Span: 90ft 1in (27.46m)
Length: 69ft 4 1/4in (22.88m) [tail up] 68ft 10in (20.98m) [tail down]
Height: 19ft 6in (5.94m) [tail down]
Tailplane Span: (initially) 28ft (8.93m) (later modified to 33ft [10.06m])
Engine: Two 1,760hp (1,312kW) Rolls-Royce Vulture I, 24-cylinder, X-type, Two-speed, Supercharged [these engines were in fact derated to 1,480-1,500hp]
Crew: 7
Weight: Loaded 56,000lb (25,088kg), Tare 29,432lb (13,186kg). Note that the type was never authorised for operations above 50,00lb (22,400kg)
Max Speed: 265mph (426km/h) at 17,000ft (5,180m) with 8,100lb (3,629kg) bomb load
Cruising Speed: 185mph (297km/h) at 15,000ft (4,571m)
Range: 1,630 miles (2,623km) with 8,000lb (3,584kg) bomb load and 1,160 gallons of fuel. 1,200 miles with 10,350lb (4,367kg) bomb load and

Fuel Capacity: 882 gallons of fuel 1,190 Imp Gal (Note initial production versions had the fuel tanks forming part of the wing centre section)
Oil Capacity: Total 57 Imp Gal (Note initial production versions had oil tanks built intergrally with the fuel tanks).
Service Ceiling: 19,200ft (5,850m)
Armament: 2x 0.303in Browning Mk II machine guns in nose (F.N.5) and ventral and 4x 0.303in Browning Mk III machine guns in tail (F.N.20) turret.
Bomb Load: Initial provision for 250lb, 500lb, 2,000lb bombs & small bomb containers. Later modified to carry 4,000lb bombs
Max Bomb Load: 10,350lb (4,367kg)
Propeller: Three-blade, de Havilland D.I.S. 27 Type 6/3, Variable Pitch, Hydromatic
Radio Equipment: T.1083 (Transmitter), R1082 (Receiver) & TR.9F (Transmitter/Receiver Remotely Controlled)
Production: 20

**Designation:** **Mk IA**
Avro Type No.: 679
Span: 90ft 1in (27.46m)
Length: 69ft 4 1/4in (22.88m) [tail up] 68ft 10in (20.98m) [tail down]
Height: 19ft 6in (5.94m)
Tailplane Span: (initially) 28ft (8.93m) [later modified to 33ft (10.06m)]
Engine: Two 1,760hp (1,312kW) Rolls-Royce Vulture I, 24-cylinder, X-type, Two-speed, Supercharged (these engines were in fact derated to 1,480-1,500hp)
Crew: 7
Weight: Loaded 56,000lb (25,088kg), Tare 29,432lb (13,186kg)
Max Speed: 265mph (426km/h) at 17,000ft (5,180m) with 8,100lb (3,629kg) bomb load
Cruising Speed: 185mph (298km/h) at 15,000ft (4,571m)
Range: 1,630 miles (2,623km) with 8,000lb (3,584kg) bomb load and 1,160 gallons of fuel. 1,200 miles (1,931km) with 10,350lb (4,367kg) bomb load and 882 gallons of fuel
Fuel Capacity: 1,190 Imp Gal (Note initial production versions had the fuel tanks forming part of the wing centre section).
Oil Capacity: Total 57 Imp Gal (Note initial production versions had oil tanks built integrally with the fuel tanks).
Service Ceiling: 19,200ft (5,850m)
Armament: 2x 0.303in Browning Mk II machine guns in nose (F.N.5) and dorsal (F.N.7) turrets and 4x 0.303in Browning Mk III machine guns in tail (F.N.20) turret
Bomb Load: Initial provision for 250lb (112kg), 500lb (224kg), 2,000lb (896kg) bombs & small bomb containers. Later modified to carry 4,000lb (1,792kg) bombs
Max Bomb Load: 10,350lb (4,367kg)
Propeller: Three-blade, de Havilland D.I.S. 27 Type 6/3, Variable Pitch, Hydromatic
Radio Equipment: T.1083 (Transmitter), R1082 (Receiver) & TR.9F (Transmitter/Receiver Remotely Controlled)

**Manchester L7248, 1940** (©Real Photos)

**Designation:** **Mk IIA**
Avro Type No.: 679
Span: 90ft 1in (27.46m)
Length: 69ft 4 1/4in (22.88m) [tail up] 68ft 10in (20.98m) [tail down]
Height: 19ft 6in (5.94m)
Tailplane Span: 33ft (10.06m)
Engine: Two 2,000hp (1,490kW) Napier Sabre I, 24-cylinder, horizontally-opposed, H-shaped, Sleeve-valve, Supercharged
Crew: 7
Armament (Likely): 2x 0.303in Browning Mk I machine guns in nose (F.N.5) and dorsal (F.N.7) turrets and 4x 0.303in Browning Mk III machine guns in tail (F.N.20) turret
Max Bomb Load: N/K
Propeller: N/K
Production: Design only, never put into production

**Designation:** **Mk IIB**
Avro Type No.: 679
Span: 90ft 1in (27.46m)
Length: 69ft 4 1/4in (22.88m) [tail up] 68ft 10in (20.98m) [tail down]
Height: 19ft 6in (5.94m)
Tailplane Span: 33ft (10.06m)
Engine: Two 2,000hp (1,490kW) Bristol Centaurus, 18-cylinder, Two-row, Air-cooled, Sleeve-valve, Two-speed, Single-stage Supercharged, Radial
Crew: 7
Armament (Likely): 2x 0.303in Browning Mk II machine guns in nose (F.N.5) and dorsal (F.N.7) turrets and 4x 0.303in Browning Mk III machine guns in tail (F.N.20) turret
Production: Design only, never put into production

## Lancaster

**Designation:** **Prototype (BT308) [originally designated 'Manchester Mk III']**
Avro Type No.: 683
Span: 100ft (30.47m)
Length: 68ft 10in (20.98m)
Height: 19ft 6in (5.94m)
Tailplane Span: 33ft (10.06m)
Engine: Four 1,145hp (854kW) Rolls-Royce Merlin X, 12-cylinder, V, Single-stage, Supercharged
Crew: 7
Weight: Tare 37,000lb (16,576kg), AUW 65,000lb (29,120kg)
Max Speed: 275mph (443km/h) at 15,000ft (4,571m)
Range: 2,530 miles (4,071km) with 7,000lb (3,136kg) load
Service Ceiling: 19,000ft (5,790m)
Armament: 2x 0.303in Browning Mk II machine guns in nose (F.N.5) turret and 4x 0.303in Browning Mk II machine guns in the tail (F.N.20) turret
Max Bomb Load: 22,000lb (9,856kg)
Propeller: Three-blade, de Havilland D.H.5/40, Constant-speed, Variable Pitch.

**Designation:** **Prototype (DG595) [originally designated 'Manchester Mk III']**
Avro Type No.: 683
Span: 100ft (30.47m)
Length: 68ft 10in (2Q.98m)

Height: 19ft 6in (5.94m)
Tailplane Span: 33ft (10.06m)
Engine: Four 1,640hp (1,223kW) Rolls-Royce Merlin XX
Crew: 7
Weight: Tare 37,000lb (16,576kg), AUW 65,000lb (29,120kg)
Max Speed: 275mph (443km/h) at 15,000ft (4,571m)
Range: 2,530 miles (4,071km) with 7,000lb (3,136kg) load
Service Ceiling: 19,000ft (5,790m)
Fuel Capacity: 1,710 gallons
Armament: 2x 0.303in Browning Mk II machine guns in nose (F.N.5) and dorsal (F.N.7) turrets and 4x 0.303in Mk II machine guns in tail (F.N.20) turret
Max Bomb Load: 22,000lb (9,856kg)
Propeller: Three-blade, de Havilland D.H.5/40, Constant-speed, Variable Pitch.

**Designation:** **B Mk I**
Avro Type No.: 683
Span: 102ft (31.09m)
Length: 69ft 6in (21.18m) [tail up], 68ft 10in (20.98m) [tail down]
Height: 20ft 6in [top of fin with tail up] (6.25m)
Tailplane Span: 33ft (10.06m)
Engine: Four 1,640hp (1,223kW) Rolls-Royce Merlin XX, 22 or 24, 12-cylinder, V, Two-Speed, Supercharged.
Crew: 7
Weight: Tare 37,000lb (16,576kg), AUW 65,000lb (29,120kg)
Max Speed: 275mph (443km/h) with full load at 15,000ft (4,571m), 245mph (394km/h) at Sea Level. Cruising speed 200mph (322km/h) at 15,000ft (4,571m).
Range: 2,530 miles (4,071km) with 7,000lb (3,136kg) bomb load, 1,730 miles (2,784km) with 12,000lb (5,455kg) bomb load and 1,550 miles (2,494km) with 22,000lb (9,856kg) bomb load
Service Ceiling: 19,000ft (5,790m)
Fuel Capacity: 2x 580, 2x 383 and 2x 144 Imp Gal tanks in wings. One or two 400 Imp Gal overload fuel tanks could be installed in the bomb bay.
Fuel Capacity: 2,154 Imp Gal in six tanks (Note first six a/c [L7527 to L7532] were limited to 1,710 Imp Gal capacity in four tanks).
Oil Capacity: 150 Imp Gal
Armament: 2x 0.303in Browning Mk II machine guns in nose (F.N.5) and mid-upper (F.N.50) turrets and 4x 0.303in Browning Mk II machine guns in rear (F.N.20) turret. Early production models had 2x 0.303in Browning Mk II machine gun in a ventral (F.N.64) turret [sometimes one was removed at station level]. By January 1943 the F.N.79 (2x 20mm Hispano cannon) or F.N.150 (2x 0.303in Browning Mk II machine guns) mid-upper turret was being installed, and in late production aircraft the rear turret was replaced by 2x 0.5in Browning Mk 2 machine guns in an F.N.82 or F.N.121 turret
Max Bomb Load: 22,000lb (9,856kg)
Propeller: de Havilland D.H.5/40 constant speed, variable pitch, three-blade. Later fitted

**Manchester Mk Ia, L7427, QL•Q of No. 83 Squadron** (via R. Sturtivant)

**Lancaster B Mk VI** (©*RAFM P005191*)

with Hamilton A5/138 variable speed, hydromatic three-blade.
Radio Equipment: T.1154 (Transmitter), R.1155 (Receiver), TR.9F (Transmitter/Receiver Remotely Controlled by Pilot). Also fitted with ARI.5033 & 5000.
Production: 3,444 (896 Avro, 944 Metropolitan-Vickers, 535 Vickers-Armstrong, 150 Austin Motors & 919 Armstrong-Whitworth)

**Designation:** **B Mk I (Special)**
Avro Type No.: 683
Span: 102ft (31.09m)
Length: 69ft 6in (21.18m) [tail up], 68ft 10in (20.98m) [tail down]
Height: 20ft 6in [top of fin with tail up] (6.25m)
Tailplane Span: 33ft (10.06m)
Engine: Four 1,610hp (1,223kW) Rolls-Royce Merlin 24, 12-cylinder, V, Two-speed Supercharged
Crew: 5
Weight: Tare 35,457lb (15,885kg), Loaded 72,000lb (32,256kg)
Max Speed: 287mph (462km/h)
Cruising Speed: 200mph (322km/h) at 15,000ft (4,571m).
Range: 1,550 miles (2,494km) at 15,000ft (4,571m) at 200mph (322km/h)
Service Ceiling: 19,000ft (5,790m) with 22,000lb (9,856kg) bomb load
Fuel Capacity: 1,675 Imp Gal
Oil Capacity: 150 Imp Gal
Armament: 4x 0.303in Browning Mk II machine guns in tail (F.N.20 or 121) turret.
Bomb Load: One 22,000lb (9,856kg) 'Grand Slam' bomb in semi-internal bomb bay.
Max Bomb Load: 22,000lb (9,856kg)
Propeller: de Havilland D.H.5/40 constant speed, variable pitch, three-blade. Later fitted with Three-blade, Hamilton A5/138 Variable Speed, Hydromatic
Production: 33

**Designation:** **B Mk I 'Saddle Tank'**
Avro Type No.: 683
Span: 102ft (31.09m)
Length: 69ft 6in (21.18m) [tail up], 68ft 10in (20.98m) [tail down]
Height: 20ft 6in [top of fin with tail up] (6.25m)
Tailplane Span: 33ft (10.06m)
Engine: Four 1,640hp (1,223kW) Rolls-Royce Merlin 24, 12-cylinder, V, Two-speed Supercharged
Crew: 7
Weight: AUW 72,000lb (32,256kg)
Max Speed: 287mph (462km/h)
Cruising Speed: 200mph (322km/h) at 15,000ft (4,571m).
Range: N/K
Fuel Capacity: 3,354 Imp Gal
Oil Capacity: 150 Imp Gal
Armament: 2x 0.303in Browning Mk II machine guns in nose (F.N.5) and 2x 0.5in Browning Mk 2 machine guns in an F.N.82 or F.N.121 rear turret.
Max Bomb Load: 12,000lb (5,376kg)
Propeller: de Havilland D.H.5/40 constant speed, variable pitch, three-blade. Later fitted with Hamilton A5/138 variable speed, hydromatic three-blade.
Production: 2

**Designation:** **B Mk I (F.E.)**
Avro Type No.: 683
Span: 102ft (31.09m)
Length: 69ft 6in (21.18m) [tail up], 68ft 10in (20.98m) [tail down]
Height: 20ft 6in [top of fin with tail up] (6.25m)
Tailplane Span: 33ft (10.06m)
Engine: Four 1,640hp (1,223kW) Rolls-Royce Merlin 24 (tropicalised), 12-cylinder, V, Two-speed, Two-stage Supercharged
Crew: 7
Weight: Tare 37,000lb (16,576kg), AUW 65,000lb (29,120kg)
Max Speed: 275mph (443km/h) with full load at 15,000ft (4,571m), 245mph (394km/h) at Sea Level. Cruising

speed 200mph (322km/h) at 15,000ft (4,571m).
Range: 2,530 miles with 7,000lb (3,136kg) bomb load, 1,730 miles (2784km) with 12,000lb (5,376kg) bomb load and 1,550 miles (2,494km) with 22,000lb (9,856kg) bomb load
Service Ceiling: 19,000ft (5,790m)
Fuel Capacity: 2x 580, 2x 383 and 2x 144 gall. tanks in wings. One or two 400 Imp Gal overload fuel tanks could be installed in the bomb bay
Fuel Capacity: 2,154 Imp Gal in six tanks
Oil Capacity: 150 Imp Gal
Armament: 2x 0.303in Browning Mk II machine guns in nose (F.N.5) and mid-upper (F.N 150) turret, or 2x 20mm Hispano cannon in (F.N.79) mid-upper turret. Plus 2x 0.5in Browning Mk 2 machine guns in an F.N.82 or F.N.121 rear turret
Max Bomb Load: 22,000lb (9,856kg)
Propeller: de Havilland D.H.5/40 constant speed, variable pitch, three-blade. Later fitted with Hamilton A5/138 variable speed, hydromatic three-blade
Radio Equipment: Rebecca Mk II, LORAN Mk I, Gee & H2S Mk IIIG.
Production: N/K (All conversions)

**Designation:** **B Mk II**
Avro Type No.: 683
Span: 102ft (31.09m)
Length: 69ft 6in (21.18m) [tail up], 68ft 10in (20.98m) [tail down]
Height: 20ft 6in [top of fin with tail up] (6.25m)
Tailplane Span: 33ft (10.06m)
Engine: Four 1,650hp (1,231kW) Bristol Hercules VI or 1,735hp (1,294kW) Bristol Hercules XVI. 14-cylinder, Two-row, Sleeve-valve, Air-cooled, Two-speed, Supercharged, Radial
Crew: 7
Weight: Tare 36,449lb (16,329kg), AUW 63,000lb (28,224kg)
Max Speed: 270mph (435km/h) at 16,000ft (4,876m)
Range: 1,550 miles (2,494km) at 15,000ft (4,571m) at 200mph (322km/h)
Fuel Capacity: 2,154 Imp Gals (2x 580, 2x 383 and 2x 114 Imp Gal tanks in the wings). Also had provision to carry one or two 400 Imp Gal overload tanks in the bomb bay
Fuel Capacity: 2,954 Imp Gal
Oil Capacity: 150 Imp Gal.
Armament: 2x 0.303in Browning Mk II machine guns in nose (F.N.5) and mid-upper (F.N.50) turrets and 4x 0.303in Browning Mk II machine guns in rear (F.N.20) turret. Early production models had 2x 0.303in Browning Mk II machine gun in a ventral (F.N.64) turret.
Max Bomb Load: 23,095lb (10,347kg)
Propeller: Three-blade, Rotol Series R.E.6, Constant-speed, Left-hand (Tractor) Rotation.
Radio Equipment: TR.9F [replaced by TR.1196 in Feb. 1943] (Transmitter/Receiver Remotely

Controlled by Pilot), R.1155 (Receiver) [removed after Mod. No. 676] & TR.1335 (Transmitter/Receiver) at Navigator's Station and T.1154 (Transmitter) and R.1155 (Receiver) at Radio Operator's Station. Also fitted with Beam Approach (R.1124A), ARI.5033, ARI.5000 and R.3003 Equipment.
Production: 302 [inc 2 prototypes] (all Armstrong-Whitworth built)

**Designation:** **B Mk III**
Avro Type No.: 683
Span: 102ft (31.09m)
Length: 69ft 6in (21.18m) [tail up], 68ft 10in (20.98m) [tail down]
Height: 20ft 6in [top of fin with tail up] (6.25m)
Tailplane Span: 33ft (10.06m)
Engine: Four Packard Merlin 28, 38 (1,390hp) or 224 (1,610hp), 12-cylinder, V, Two-speed, Supercharged.
Crew: 7
Weight: AUW 65,000lb (29,120kg), Tare 37,000lb (16,576kg)
Max Speed: 287mph (462km/h)
Range: 1,730 miles (2,784kg) with 12,000lb (5,376kg) bomb load.
Service Ceiling: 19,000ft (5,790m)
Fuel Capacity: 2x 580, 2x 383 and 2x 144 gall. tanks in wings. One or two 400 Imp Gal overload fuel tanks could be installed in the bomb bay
Fuel Capacity: 2,154 Imp Gal in six tanks
Oil Capacity: 150 Imp Gal
Armament: 2x 0.303in Browning machine guns in nose (F.N.5), mid-upper (F.N.50) turrets and ventral (F.N.64) turrets plus 4x 0.303in Browning machine guns in rear (F.N.20) turret
Max Bomb Load: 22,000lb (9,856kg)
Internal Bomb Load: 18,000lb (8,064kg)
Propeller: de Havilland D.H.5/40 constant speed, variable pitch, three-blade. Later fitted with Hamilton A5/138 variable speed, hydromatic three-blade
Production: 3,020 (2,774 Avro, 136 Metropolitan-Vickers, 110 Armstrong-Whitworth)

**Designation:** **B Mk III (Special)**
Avro Type No.: 683
Modification No.: 1693
Span: 102ft (31.09m)
Length: 69ft 6in (21.18m) [tail up], 68ft 10in (20.98m) [tail down]
Height: 20ft 6in [top of fin with tail up] (6.25m)
Tailplane Span: 33ft (10.06m)
Engine: Four 1,640hp (1,223kW) Rolls-Royce Merlin 24, 12-cylinder, V, Two-speed Supercharged
Crew: 6
Weight: Tare 35,457lb (15,885kg), Loaded 72,000lb (32,256kg)
Max Speed: 287mph (462km/h)
Cruising Speed: 200mph (322km/h) at 15,000ft (4,571m).
Range: 1,550 miles (2,494km) at 15,000ft (4,571m) at 200mph (322km/h)
Service Ceiling: 19,000ft (5,790m)
Fuel Capacity: 1,675 Imp Gal
Oil Capacity: 150 Imp Gal
Armament: 2x 0.303in Browning machine guns in nose (F.N.5), one 0.303in Vickers K machine gun in ventral and 4x 0.303in Brownings in rear (F.N. 20) turret
Bomb Load: One 8,599lb (3,900kg) 'Upkeep' mine in special cradle under bomb bay.
Max Bomb Load: 12,000lb (5,376kg)
Propeller: de Havilland D.H.5/40 constant speed, variable pitch, three-blade. Later fitted with Hamilton A5/138 variable speed, hydromatic three-blade

**Designation:** **B Mk IV**
**See Avro Lincoln B Mk I**

**Designation:** **B Mk V**
**See Avro Lincoln B Mk II**

**Lancaster ASR Mk III, RF310, RL•A of No. 38 Squadron** (via R. Sturtivant)

**Designation:** **B Mk VI**
Avro Type No.: 683
Span: 102ft (31.09m)
Length: 69ft 6in (21.18m) [tail up], 68ft 10in (20.98m) [tail down]
Height: 20ft 6in [top of fin with tail up] (6.25m)
Tailplane Span: 33ft (10.06m)
Engine: Four 1,640hp (1,223kW) Packard Merlin 85 or 87, 12-cylinder, V, Two-speed, Two-stage Supercharged
Crew: 5
Weight: Tare 35,457lb (15,885kg), Loaded 72,000lb (32,256kg)
Max Speed: 345mph (555km/h)
Cruising Speed: 200mph (322km/h) at 15,000ft (4,571m).
Range: 1,550 miles (2,494km) at 15,000ft (4,571m) at 200mph (322km/h)
Service Ceiling: 21,418ft (6,500m)
Fuel Capacity: 1,675 Imp Gal
Oil Capacity: 150 Imp Gal
Armament: 4x 0.303in Browning machine guns in rear (F.N.20 or 121) turret.
Max Bomb Load: 22,000lb (9,856kg)
Propeller: Four-blade Rotol
Production: 9 (All conversions; 2 from B Mk I and 7 from B Mk III)

**Designation:** **B Mk VII**
Avro Type No.: 683
Span: 102ft (31.09m)
Length: 69ft 6in (21.18m) [tail up], 68ft 10in (20.98m) [tail down]
Height: 20ft 6in [top of fin with tail up] (6.25m)
Tailplane Span: 33ft (10.06m)
Engine: Four 1,640hp (1,223kW) Rolls-Royce Merlin 24 (tropicalised), 12-cylinder, V, Two-speed, Two-stage Supercharged
Crew: 7
Weight: Tare 35,974lb (16,116kg), Loaded 72,000lb (32,256kg)
Max Speed: 287mph (462km/h)
Cruising Speed: 200mph (322km/h) at 15,000ft (4,571m).
Range: 1,550 miles (2,494km) at 15,000ft (4,571m) at 200mph (322km/h)
Service Ceiling: 19,000ft (5,790m)
Fuel Capacity: 2,154 Imp Gal (2x 580, 2x 383 & 2x 114 Imp Gal tanks in wings). Provision to carry one or two 400 Imp Gal overload fuel tanks in the bomb bay.
Fuel Capacity: 2,954 Imp Gal
Oil Capacity: 150 Imp Gal
Armament: 2x 0.303 Browning Mk II machine guns in front (F.N.5) turret, 2x 0.5in No 2 Mk II Browning machine guns in (Martin 250CE 23A) mid-upper turret & 2x 0.5in Browning Mk 2 machine guns in (F.N.82 or Rose) rear turret.
Max Bomb Load: 22,000lb (9,856kg)
Propeller: Three-blade Hamilton A5/148 or A5/159 Constant-speed, Hydromatic (13ft Dia)
Production: 180 (All Austin-Motors built)

**Designation:** **B Mk VII (F.E.)**
Avro Type No.: 683
Span: 102ft (31.09m)
Length: 69ft 6in (21.18m) [tail up], 68ft 10in (20.98m) [tail down]
Height: 20ft 6in [top of fin with tail up] (6.25m)
Tailplane Span: 33ft (10.06m)
Engine: Four 1,640hp (1,223kW) Rolls-Royce Merlin 24 (tropicalised), 12-cylinder, V, Two-speed, Two-stage Supercharged
Crew: 7
Weight: Tare 35,974lb (16,116kg), Loaded 72,000lb (32,256kg)
Max Speed: 287mph (462km/h)
Cruising Speed: 200mph (322km/h) at 15,000ft (4,571m).
Range: 1,550 miles (2,494km) at 15,000ft (4,571m) at 200mph (322km/h)
Service Ceiling: 19,000ft (5,790m)
Fuel Capacity: 2,154 Imp Gal (2x 580, 2x 383 & 2x 114 Imp Gal tanks in wings). Provision to carry one or two 400 Imp Gal overload fuel tanks in the bomb bay.
Fuel Capacity: 2,954 Imp Gal
Oil Capacity: 150 Imp Gal
Armament: 2x 0.303 Browning Mk II machine guns in front (F.N.5) turret, 2x 0.5in M2 Browning machine guns in (Martin 250CE-23) mid-upper turret & 2x 0.5in Browning Mk 2 machine guns in (Rose) rear turret.
Max Bomb Load: 22,000lb (9,856kg)
Propeller: de Havilland D.H.5/40, Constant-speed, Variable-pitch, Three-blade. Later fitted with Hamilton A5/138 Variable-speed, Hydromatic, Three-blade

# Air Sea Rescue (ASR)

**Designation:** **ASR Mk III (or ASR.3)**
Avro Type No.: 683
Span: 102ft (31.09m)
Length: 69ft 6in (21.18m) [tail up], 68ft 10in (20.98m) [tail down]

Height: 20ft 6in [top of fin with tail up] (6.25m)
Tailplane Span: 33ft (10.06m)
Engine: Four 1,610hp Packard Merlin 224, 12-cylinder, V, Two-speed, Supercharged.
Crew: 7
Armament: 2x 0.303 Browning Mk II machine guns in front (F.N.5) turret, 2x 0.5in M2 Browning machine guns in (Martin 250CE-23) mid-upper turret & 2x 0.5in Browning Mk 2 machine guns in (Rose) rear turret. Post-war machines had the mid-upper turret removed and all guns removed from the remaining two
Maximum Load: 22,000lb (9,856kg)
Propeller: de Havilland D.H.5/40 constant speed, variable pitch, three-blade. Later fitted with Hamilton A5/138 variable speed, hydromatic three-blade
Equipment: Airborne Lifeboat Mk IIIA
Production: All Conversions (by Cunliffe-Owen)

# Maritime Reconnaissance

Designation: GR Mk III (or GR.3)
Avro Type No.: 683
Span: 102ft (31.09m)
Length: 69ft 6in (21.18m) [tail up], 68ft 10in (20.98m) [tail down]
Height: 20ft 6in [top of fin with tail up] (6.25m)
Tailplane Span: 33ft (10.06m)
Engine: Four 1,610hp Packard Merlin 224, 12-cylinder, V, Two-speed, Supercharged.
Crew: 7
Armament: 2x 0.303 Browning Mk II machine guns in front (F.N.5) turret, 2x 0.5in M2 Browning machine guns in (Martin 250CE-23) mid-upper turret & 2x 0.5in Browning Mk 2 machine guns in (Rose) rear turret. Post-war machines had the mid-upper turret removed and all guns removed from the remaining two
Maximum Load: 22,000lb (9,856kg)
Propeller: de Havilland D.H.5/40, Constant-speed, Variable-pitch, Three-blade. Later fitted with Hamilton A5/138, Variable-speed, Hydromatic, Three-blade
Production: All Conversions from ASR.3s (later redesignated MR.3)

# Photo-Reconnaissance

Designation: PR Mk I
Avro Type No.: 683
Span: 102ft (31.09m)
Length: 69ft 6in (21.18m) [tail up], 68ft 10in (20.98m) [tail down]
Height: 20ft 6in [top of fin with tail up] (6.25m)
Tailplane Span: 33ft (10.06m)
Engine: Four 1,640hp (1,223kW) Rolls-Royce Merlin 24, 12-cylinder, V, Two-speed, Supercharged
Crew: 7
Weight: Tare 37,000lb (16,576kg), AUW 65,000lb (29,120kg)
Max Speed: 275mph (443km/h) with full load at 15,000ft (4,571m), 245mph (394km/h) at Sea Level. Cruising speed 200mph (322km/h) at 15,000ft (4,571m).
Range: 2,530 miles with 7,000lb bomb load, 1,730 miles (2784km) with 12,000lb (5,376kg) bomb load and 1,550 miles (2,494km) with 22,000lb (9,856kg) bomb load
Service Ceiling: 19,000ft (5,790m)
Fuel Capacity: 2x 580, 2x 383 and 2x 144 gall. tanks in wings. One or two 400 Imp Gal overload fuel tanks could be installed in the bomb bay.
Fuel Capacity: 2,154 Imp Gal in six tanks
Oil Capacity: 150 Imp Gal
Armament: None
Max Bomb Load: 22,000lb (9,856kg) [None carried]
Photographic Equipment: Various F.24 combinations in bomb bay
Propeller: de Havilland D.H.5/40, Constant-speed, Variable-pitch, Three-blade. Later fitted with Hamilton A5/138, Variable-speed, Hydromatic, Three-blade

# Foreign Production

## Bomber

Designation: B Mk X (Later redesignated Mk 10)
Avro Type No.: 683
Span: 102ft (31.09m)
Length: 69ft 6in (21.18m) [tail up], 68ft 10in (20.98m) [tail down]
Height: 20ft 6in [top of fin with tail up] (6.25m)
Tailplane Span: 33ft (10.06m)
Engine: 4x Packard Merlin 38 (a/c KB700-774)
or 224 (a/c KB775 onwards), 12-cylinder, V, Two-speed, Supercharged
Crew: 7
Weight: Tare 35,415lb (15,866kg), AUW 61,500lb (27,552kg)
Max Speed: 275mph (443km/h) with full load at 15,000ft (4,571m), 245mph (394km/h) at Sea Level. Cruising speed 200mph (322km/h) at 15,000ft (4,571m).
Range: 2,530 miles with 7,000lb (3,136kg) bomb load, 1,730 miles (2784km) with 12,000lb (5,376kg) bomb load and 1,550 miles (2,494km) with 22,000lb (9,856kg) bomb load
Service Ceiling: 19,000ft (5,790m)
Fuel Capacity: 2,154 Imp Gal (2x 580, 2x 383 & 2x 114 Imp Gal tanks in wings). Also provision to carry one or two 400 Imp Gal overload tanks in bomb bay.
Fuel Capacity: 2,954 Imp Gal
Oil Capacity: 150 Imp Gal
Armament: 2x 0.303in Browning Mk II machine guns in nose (F.N.5) and mid-upper (F.N.50) turrets and 4x 0.303in Browning Mk II machine guns in rear (F.N.20) turret. Early production models had 2x 0.303in Browning Mk II machine guns in a ventral (F.N.64) turret.
Max Bomb Load: 12,000lb (5,376kg)
Propeller: Three-blade Hamilton A5/138 (a/c KB700-774), A5/148 (a/c KB775-796) or A5/159 (a/c KB797 onwards), Constant-speed, Hydromatic (RH Tractor)
Radio Equipment: TR.1196 (Transmitter/Receiver Remotely Operated by Pilot), 2x Bendix TA.12C (Transmitter), Bendix 3611B Intercommunication Amplifier and Bendix RA10B (General Purpose Receiver) at Radio-operator's Station. Also fitted with ARI.5122, Blind Approach and R.3003 or R.3090.
Production: 430 (Victory Aircraft) [all subsequent 10 series airframes were conversions of a number of these machines].

# Reconnaissance

Designation: Mk 10AR (Area Reconnaissance)
Avro Type No.: 683
Span: 102ft (31.09m)
Length: 73ft (28.75m) [tail up], 72ft 8in (28.42m) [tail down]
Height: 20ft 6in [top of fin with tail up] (6.25m)
Tailplane Span: 33ft (10.06m)
Engine: 4x Packard Merlin 224, 12-cylinder, V, Two-speed, Supercharged
Crew: 10
Weight: Tare 35,415lb (15.866kg), AUW 61,500lb (27,552kg)
Max Speed: 275mph (443km/h) with full load at 15,000ft (4,571m), 245mph (394km/h) at Sea Level. Cruising speed 200mph (322km/h) at 15,000ft (4,571m).
Range: 2,530 miles with 7,000lb bomb load, 1,730 miles (2784km) with 12,000lb (5,376kg) bomb load and 1,550 miles (2,494km) with 22,000lb (9,856kg) bomb load
Service Ceiling: 19,000ft (5,790m)
Fuel Capacity: 2,154 Imp Gal (2x 580, 2x 383 & 2x 114 Imp Gal tanks in wings). Also provision to carry one or two 400 Imp Gal overload tanks in bomb bay.
Fuel Capacity: 2,954 Imp Gal
Oil Capacity: 150 Imp Gal
Armament: None
Maximum
Bomb Capacity: 12,000lb (5,376kg)
Propeller: Hamilton A5/138, Variable-speed, Hydromatic Three-blade
Production: 3 (All converted from B Mk 10s)

Designation: Mk 10BR (Bomber-reconnaissance)
Avro Type No.: 683
Span: 102ft (31.09m)
Length: 73ft (28.75m) [tail up], 72ft 8in (28.42m) [tail down]
Height: 20ft 6in [top of fin with tail up] (6.25m)
Tailplane Span: 33ft (10.06m)
Engine: 4x Packard Merlin 224, 12-cylinder, V, Two-speed, Supercharged
Crew: 10
Weight: Tare 35,415lb (15,866kg), AUW 61,500lb (27,552kg)
Max Speed: 275mph (443km/h) with full load at 15,000ft (4,571m), 245mph (394km/h) at Sea Level. Cruising speed 200mph (322km/h) at 15,000ft (4,571m).
Range: 2,530 miles with 7,000lb (3,136kg) bomb load, 1,730 miles (2784km) with 12,000lb (5,376kg) bomb load and 1,550 miles (2,494km) with 22,000lb (9,856kg) bomb load
Service Ceiling: 19,000ft (5,790m)
Fuel Capacity: 2,154 Imp Gal (2x 580, 2x 383 & 2x 114 Imp Gal tanks in wings). Also provision to carry one or two 400 Imp

**Lancaster GR Mk III, RF164, H•U of the School of Maritime Reconnaissance, 1953**
*(via R. Sturtivant)*

Gal overload tanks in bomb bay.
Fuel Capacity: 2,954 Imp Gal
Oil Capacity: 150 Imp Gal
Armament: None
Maximum
Bomb Capacity: 12,000lb (5,376kg)
Propeller: Hamilton A5/138, Variable-speed, Hydromatic, Three-blade
Production: 13 (All converted from B Mk 10s)

Designation: Mk 10MR (Maritime Reconnaissance)
Avro Type No.: 683
Span: 102ft (31.09m)
Length: 73ft (28.75m) [tail up], 72ft 8in (28.42m) [tail down]
Height: 20ft 6in [top of fin with tail up] (6.25m)
Tailplane Span: 33ft (10.06m)
Engine: 4x Packard Merlin 224, 12-cylinder, V, Two-speed, Supercharged
Crew: 10
Weight: Tare 35,415lb (15,866kg), AUW 61,500lb (27,552kg)
Max Speed: 275mph (443km/h) with full load at 15,000ft (4,571m), 245mph (394km/h) at Sea Level. Cruising speed 200mph (322km/h) at 15,000ft (4,571m).
Range: 2,530 miles with 7,000lb (3,136kg) bomb load, 1,730 miles (2784km) with 12,000lb (5,376kg) bomb load and 1,550 miles (2,494km) with 22,000lb (9,856kg) bomb load
Service Ceiling: 19,000ft (5,790m)
Fuel Capacity: 2,154 Imp Gal (2x 580, 2x 383 & 2x 114 Imp Gal tanks in wings). Also provision to carry one or two 400 Imp Gal overload tanks in bomb bay.
Fuel Capacity: 2,954 Imp Gal
Oil Capacity: 150 Imp Gal
Armament: None
Maximum
Bomb Capacity: 12,000lb (5,376kg)
Propeller: Hamilton A5/138, Variable-speed, Hydromatic, Three-blade
Production: 70+ (All converted from B Mk 10s). Later redesignated 10MP

Designation: Mk 10P (Photo-reconnaissance)
Avro Type No.: 683
Span: 102ft (31.09m)
Length: 73ft (28.75m) [tail up], 72ft 8in (28.42m) [tail down]
Height: 20ft 6in [top of fin with tail up] (6.25m)
Tailplane Span: 33ft (10.06m)
Engine: 4 x Packard Merlin 224, 12-cylinder, V, Two-speed, Supercharged
Crew: 10
Weight: Tare 35,415lb (15,866kg), AUW 61,500lb (27,552kg)
Max Speed: 275mph (443km/h) with full load at 15,000ft (4,571m), 245mph (394km/h) at Sea Level. Cruising speed 200mph (322km/h) at 15,000ft (4,571m).
Range: 2,530 miles with 7,000lb (3,136kg) bomb load, 1,730 miles (2784km) with 12,000lb (5,376kg) bomb load and 1,550 miles (2,494km) with 22,000lb (9,856kg) bomb load
Service Ceiling: 19,000ft (5,790m)
Fuel Capacity: 2,154 Imp Gal (2x 580, 2x 383 & 2x 114 Imp Gal tanks in wings). Also provision to carry one or two 400 Imp Gal overload tanks in bomb bay.

Fuel Capacity: 2,954 Imp Gal
Oil Capacity: 150 Imp Gal
Armament: None
Maximum
Bomb Capacity: 12,000lb (5,376kg)
Propeller: Hamilton A5/138, Variable-speed, Hydromatic, Three-blade
Camera
Equipment: 1x Ordnance & Tri-Metrogen System (3x Camera) aft of bomb bay in lower fuselage
Production: 11 (All converted from B Mk 10s)

# Air Sea Rescue

Designation: Mk 10SR
Avro Type No.: 683
Span: 102ft (31.09m)
Length: 73ft (28.75m) [tail up], 72ft 8in (28.42m) [tail down]
Height: 20ft 6in [top of fin with tail up] (6.25m)
Tailplane Span: 33ft (10.06m)
Engine: 4x Packard Merlin 224, 12-cylinder, V, Two-speed, Supercharged
Crew: 10
Weight: Tare 35,415lb (15,866kg), AUW 61,500lb (27,552kg)
Max Speed: 275mph (443km/h) with full load at 15,000ft (4,571m), 245mph (394km/h) at Sea Level. Cruising speed 200mph (322km/h) at 15,000ft (4,571m).
Range: 2,530 miles with 7,000lb (3,136kg) bomb load, 1,730 miles (2784km) with 12,000lb (5,376kg) bomb load and 1,550 miles (2,494km) with 22,000lb (9,856kg) bomb load
Service Ceiling: 19,000ft (5,790m)
Fuel Capacity: 2,154 Imp Gal (2x 580, 2x 383 & 2x 114 Imp Gal tanks in wings). Also provision to carry one or two 400 Imp Gal overload tanks in bomb bay.
Fuel Capacity: 2,954 Imp Gal
Oil Capacity: 150 Imp Gal
Armament: None
Maximum
Bomb Capacity: 12,000lb (5,376kg)
Propeller: Hamilton A5/138, Variable-speed, Hydromatic, Three-blade
Production: 8 (All converted from B Mk 10s)

# Special Duties

Designation: Mk 10DR (Drone Carrier)
Avro Type No.: 683
Span: 102ft (31.09m)
Length: 73ft (28.75m) [tail up], 72ft 8in (28.42m) [tail down]
Height: 20ft 6in [top of fin with tail up] (6.25m)
Tailplane Span: 33ft (10.06m)
Engine: 4x Packard Merlin 224, 12-cylinder, V, Two-speed, Supercharged
Crew: 10
Weight: Tare 35,415lb (15,866kg), AUW 61,500lb (27,552kg)
Max Speed: 275mph (443km/h) with full load at 15,000ft (4,571m), 245mph (394km/h) at Sea Level. Cruising speed 200mph (322km/h) at 15,000ft (4,571m).

**Lancaster B Mk X, KB700** *(©Real Photos)*

**Lincoln B Mk I, RA648 at RAF St. Mawgan** *(©RAFM P0018379)*

Range: 2,530 miles with 7,000lb (3,136kg) bomb load, 1,730 miles (2784km) with 12,000lb (5,376kg) bomb load and 1,550 miles (2,494km) with 22,000lb (9,856kg) bomb load
Service Ceiling: 19,000ft (5,790m)
Fuel Capacity: 2,154 Imp Gal (2x 580, 2x 383 & 2x 114 Imp Gal tanks in wings). Also provision to carry one or two 400 Imp Gal overload tanks in bomb bay.
Fuel Capacity: 2,954 Imp Gal
Oil Capacity: 150 Imp Gal
Armament: None
Maximum Bomb Capacity: 12,000lb (5,376kg)
Bomb Load: Carried 1x Ryan KDA-4 Firebee Drones on modified Type 51 Bomb Shackle under each wing
Propeller: Hamilton A5/138, Variable-speed, Hydromatic, Three-blade
Production: 2 (All converted from B Mk 10s)

## Lancastrian (Inc Civil Lancasters)

**Designation: Mailplane (Conversion)**
Avro Type No.: 683
Span: 102ft (31.09m)
Length: 73ft (28.75m) [tail up], 72ft 8in (28.42m) [tail down]
Height: 20ft 6in [top of fin with tail up] (6.25m)
Tailplane Span: 33ft (10.06m)
Engine: Four 1,610hp (1,223kW) Rolls-Royce Merlin T-24-1 or T-24-2, 12-cylinder, V, Two-speed Supercharged
Crew: 5
Weight: AUW 65,000lb (29,484kg), Tare 37,000lb (16,783kg)
Max Speed: 275mph (443km/h) at 15,000ft (4,571m)
Range: 4,100 miles (6,598km) at 230mph (370km/h) at 20,000ft (6,095m)
Service Ceiling: 19,000ft (5,790m)
Fuel Capacity: 2x 580, 2x 383 and 2x 144 gall. tanks in wings. One or two 400 Imp Gal overload fuel tanks could be installed in the bomb bay.
Fuel Capacity: 2,154 Imp Gal in six tanks
Oil Capacity: 150 Imp Gal
Armament: None
Maximum Load Capacity: 12,000lb (5,376kg)
Propeller: de Havilland D.H.5/40 constant speed, variable pitch, three-blade. Later fitted with Hamilton A5/138 variable speed, hydromatic three-blade
Production: 5 (All converted B Mk 10s for Trans-Canada Airlines)

**Designation: Lancastrian I (C Mk 1)**
Avro Type No.: 691
Span: 102ft (31.09m)
Length: 76ft (23.16m) [Tail Down] 76ft 10in (23.41m) [Tail Up]
Height: 20ft 6in [top of fin with tail up] (6.25m)
Engine: 4x 1,640hp (1,223kW) Rolls-Royce Merlin T-24, Two-Speed, Two-Stage Supercharged, V12
Crew: 5
Passengers: 9 (6 at night)
Weight: Empty 30,220lb (13,539kg), Loaded 65,000lb (29,120kg)
Max Speed: 315mph (507km/h) at 12,000ft (3,657m)
Cruising Speed: Maximum 290mph (467km/h) at 12,500ft (3,809m), Economical 230mph (370km/h) at 15,000ft (4,571m)
Range: 4,100 miles (6,598km) [with nine passengers and 230lb (103kg) of mail] at 230mph (370km/h) at 20,000ft (6,095m)
Service Ceiling: 24,300ft (7,405m)
Fuel Capacity: 3,174 Imp Gal
Propeller: de Havilland D.H.5/40, Constant-speed, Hydromatic, Three-blade (13ft diameter)
Production: 23

**Designation: Lancastrian C Mk II (or C.2)**
Avro Type No.: 691
Span: 102ft (31.09m)
Length: 76ft (23.16m) [Tail Down] 76ft 10in (23.41m) [Tail Up]
Height: 20ft 6in [top of fin with tail up] (6.25m)
Engine: 4x 1,640hp (1,223kW) Rolls-Royce Merlin T-24, Two-Speed, Two-Stage Supercharged, V12
Crew: 5
Passengers: 9 (6 at night)
Weight: Empty 30,426lb (13,631kg), Loaded 65,000lb (29,120kg)
Max Speed: 315mph (507km/h) at 12,000ft (3,657m)
Cruising Speed: Maximum 290mph (467km/h) at 12,500ft (3,809m), Economical 230mph (370km/h) at 15,000ft (4,571m)
Range: 4,100 miles (6,598km) [with nine passengers and 230lb (103kg) of mail] at 230mph (370km/h) at 20,000ft (6,095m)
Service Ceiling: 24,300ft (7,405m)
Fuel Capacity: 3,174 Imp Gal
Propeller: de Havilland D.H.5/40, Constant-speed, Hydromatic, Three-blade (13ft diameter)
Production: 33

**Designation: Lancastrian III**
Avro Type No.: 691
Span: 102ft (31.09m)
Length: 76ft (Tail Down) 76ft 10in (Tail Up)
Height: 20ft 6in [top of fin with tail up] (6.25m)
Engine: 4x 1,640hp (1,223kW) Rolls-Royce Merlin T-24, Two-Speed, Two-Stage Supercharged, V12
Crew: 5
Passengers: 13
Weight: Empty 36,190lb (16,213kg), Loaded 61,860lb (27,713kg) Maximum 65,000lb (29,120kg)
Max Speed: 315mph (507km/h) at 12,000ft (3,657m)
Cruising Speed: Maximum 290mph (467km/h) at 12,500ft (3,809m), Economical 230mph (370km/h) at 15,000ft (4,571m)
Range: 2,820 miles (4,538km) [with 7,500lb (3,360kg) of payload) at 230mph (370km/h) at 20,000ft (6,095m)
Fuel Capacity: 3,174 Imp Gal
Propeller: de Havilland D.H.5/40, Constant-speed, Hydromatic, Three-blade (13ft diameter)
Production: 18

**Crew members sit on top of Lincoln B Mk II, RF388, KM•C of No. 44 Squadron**
*(©RAFM P016434)*

**Designation: Lancastrian C Mk IV**
Avro Type No.: 691
Span: 102ft (31.09m)
Length: 76ft (Tail Down) 76ft 10in (Tail Up)
Height: 20ft 6in [top of fin with tail up] (6.25m)
Engine: 4x 1,640hp (1,223kW) Rolls-Royce Merlin T-24, Two-Speed, Two-Stage Supercharged, V12
Crew: 5
Passengers: 13
Weight: Empty 36,190lb (16,213kg), Loaded 61,860lb (27,713kg) Maximum 65,000lb (29,120kg)
Max Speed: 315mph (507km/h) at 12,000ft (3,657m)
Cruising Speed: Maximum 290mph (467km/h) at 12,500ft (3,809m), Economical 230mph (370km/h) at 15,000ft (4,571m)
Range: 2,820 miles (4,538km) [with 7,500lb (3,360kg) of payload) at 230mph (370km/h) at 20,000ft (6,095m)
Fuel Capacity: 3,174 Imp Gal
Propeller: de Havilland D.H.5/40, Constant-speed, Hydromatic, Three-blade (13ft diameter)
Production: 8

## Lincoln

**Designation: Lincoln B Mk I Prototype (originally designated 'Lancaster B Mk IV')**
Specification: B.14/43
Avro Type No.: 694
First Flight: 6th June 1943 (PW925)
Span: 120ft (36.57m)
Length: 78ft 3.5in (23.86m)
Height: 17ft 3.5in (5.27m)
Engine: Four 1,750hp (1,305kW) Rolls-Royce Merlin 85, 12-cylinder, V, Two-stage, Two-speed Supercharged
Weight: AUW 70,000lb (31,360kg) [Projected]
Max Speed: 310mph (499km/h) level flight. Cruising Speed 167mph (269km/h)
Range: 2,640 miles (4,248km) with 14,000lb (6,272kg) bomb load at 20,000ft (6,095m). 2,800 miles (4,506km) with 14,000lb (6,272kg) bomb load at 15,000ft (4,571m)
Fuel: 2,850 Imp Gal (2x 580, 2x 545 & 2x 300 Imp Gal tanks in wings) Also had provision to fit one or two 400 Imp Gal overload tanks in bomb bay.
Oil Capacity: 150 Imp Gal
Armament: 2x 0.5in Browning machine guns in Martin 250 mid-upper turret and 4x 0.303in Browning machine guns in F.N.121 rear turret
Propeller: Hamilton A5/138, Variable-speed, Hydromatic, Three-blade

**Designation: B Mk 1 (B.1)**
Avro Type No.: 694
Span: 120ft (36.57m)
Length: 78ft 3.5in (23.86m)
Height: 17ft 3.5in (5.27m)
Engine: Four 1,750hp (1,305kW) Rolls-Royce Merlin 85 or 85A, 12-cylinder, V, Two-stage, Two-speed Supercharged
Weight: Empty 23,112lb Total Maximum AUW 82,000lb
Max Speed: 310mph (499km/h) level flight. Cruising Speed 167mph (269km/h)
Range: 2,640 miles (4,248km) with 14,000lb (6,272kg) bomb load at 20,000ft (6,095m). 2,800 miles (4,506km) with 14,000lb (6,272kg) bomb load at 15,000ft (4,571m)
Fuel: 2,850 Imp Gal (2x 580, 2x 545 & 2x 300 Imp Gal tanks in wings) Also had provision to fit one or two 400 Imp Gal overload tanks in bomb bay.
Oil Capacity: 150 Imp Gal
Armament: 2x Browning 0.5in Browning No 2 Mk II machine guns in front (B.P. 'F' Mk I) turret, 2x 20mm Hispano No 4 Mk V cannon in mid-upper (Bristol Type 17 Mk I) turret and 2x Browning 0.5in No 2 Mk II machine guns in the tail (B.P. 'D' Mk I) turret. Note that a Glenn Martin 250CE 23A Mk I turret with 2x 05in Browning No 2 Mk II machine guns was initially installed in the mid-upper position for early production airframes.
Bomb Load: Maximum 14,000lb (6,272kg)
Propeller: Initially fitted with four-blade Rotol, then replaced by de Havilland version, finally replaced with Hamilton A5/148, Constant-speed, Variable-pitch (13ft Dia)
Production: 82

**Designation: B Mk II (or B.2)**
Avro Type No.: 694
Span: 120ft (36.57m)
Length: 78ft 3.5in (23.86m)
Height: 17ft 3.5in (5.27m)
Engine: Four 1,750hp (1,305kW) Packard Merlin 68A (68 & 300 also used), 12-cylinder, V, Two-stage, Two-speed Supercharged
Weight: Empty 23,112lb (10,354kg), Maximum AUW 82,000lb (36,736kg)
Max Speed: 310mph (499km/h) level flight. Cruising Speed 167mph (269km/h)
Range: 2,640 miles (4,248km) with 14,000lb (6,272kg) bomb load at 20,000ft (6,095m). 2,800 miles (4,506km) with 14,000lb (6,272kg) bomb load at 15,000ft (4,571m)
Fuel: 2,850 Imp Gal (2x 580, 2x 545 & 2x 300 Imp Gal tanks in wings). Also had provision to fit one or two 400 Imp Gal overload tanks in bomb bay.
Oil Capacity: 150 Imp Gal
Armament: 2x Browning 0.5in Browning No 2 Mk II machine guns in front (B.P. 'F' Mk I) turret, 2x 20mm Hispano No 4 Mk V cannon in mid-upper (Bristol Type 17 Mk I) turret and 2x Browning 0.5in No 2 Mk II machine guns in the tail (B.P. 'D' Mk I) turret. Note that a Glenn Martin 250CE 23A Mk I turret with 2x 05in Browning No 2 Mk II machine guns was initially installed in the mid-upper position for early production airframes.
Propeller: Four-blade Hamilton A5/148, Constant-speed, Variable-pitch. Or de Havilland D.20/445/1-5 after Mod No. 1469. Both 13ft Dia.
Note: After February 1947 these machines were referred to as B.2/3G or B.2/4A for the following equipment fits; B.2/3G = H2S Mk IIIG, Gee Mk II & Rebecca Mk II
B.2/4A = H2S Mk IVA, G-H Mk II & Rebecca Mk II or IV

## Foreign Production

### Bomber

**Designation: B Mk 30 (and early B Mk 31)**
Span: 120ft (36.57m)
Length: 78ft 3.5in (23.86m) [Mk 31: 85ft 4in (26m)]
Height: 17ft 3.5in (5.27m) [Mk 31: 19ft (5.79m)]
Engine: Four 1,750hp (1,305kW) Rolls-Royce Merlin 85B, 12-cylinder, V, Two-stage, Two-speed, Supercharged (Some B Mk 30s had two 1,580hp (1,178kW) Merlin 66s in the outboard positions)
Weight: Empty 23,112lb (10,354kg), Maximum AUW 82,000lb (36,736kg)
Max Speed: 310mph (499km/h) level flight. Cruising Speed 167mph (269km/h)
Range: 2,640 miles (4,248km) with 14,000lb (6,272kg) bomb load at 20,000ft (6,095m). 2,800 miles (4,506km) with 14,000lb (6,272kg) bomb load at 15,000ft (4,571m)
Armament: 2x Browning 0.5in Browning No 2 Mk II machine guns in front (B.P. 'F') turret, 2x 20mm Hispano Mk V cannon in mid-upper (Bristol Type 17) turret and 2x Browning 0.5in No 2 Mk II machine guns in the tail (B.P. 'D') turret
Propeller: Four-blade Hamilton A5/148, Constant-speed, Variable-pitch (13ft Dia)

**Designation: B Mk 30A and Mk 31**
Span: 120ft (36.57m)
Length: 78ft 3.5in (23.86m) [Mk 31: 85ft 4in (26m)]
Height: 17ft 3.5in (5.27m) [Mk 31: 19ft (5.79m)]
Engine: Four 1,750hp (1,305kW) Rolls-Royce Merlin 102 12-cylinder, V, Two-stage, Two-speed, Supercharged
Weight: Empty 23,112lb (10,354kg), Maximum AUW 82,000lb (36,736kg)
Max Speed: 310mph (499km/h) level flight. Cruising Speed 167mph (269km/h)
Range: 2,640 miles (4,248km) with 14,000lb (6,272kg) bomb load at 20,000ft (6,095m). 2,800 miles (4,506km) with 14,000lb (6,272kg) bomb load at 15,000ft (4,571m)
Armament: 2x Browning 0.5in Browning No 2 Mk II machine guns in front (B.P. 'F') turret, 2x 20mm Hispano Mk V cannon in mid-upper (Bristol Type 17) turret and 2x Browning 0.5in No 2 Mk II machine guns in the tail (B.P. 'D') turret (Note: All armament was often removed once in service)
Propeller: Four-blade Hamilton A5/148, Constant-speed, Variable-pitch (13ft Dia)

*N.B.*
*For test-beds and research aircraft, see Chapter 4*

# Manchester, Lancaster & Lincoln Genealogy

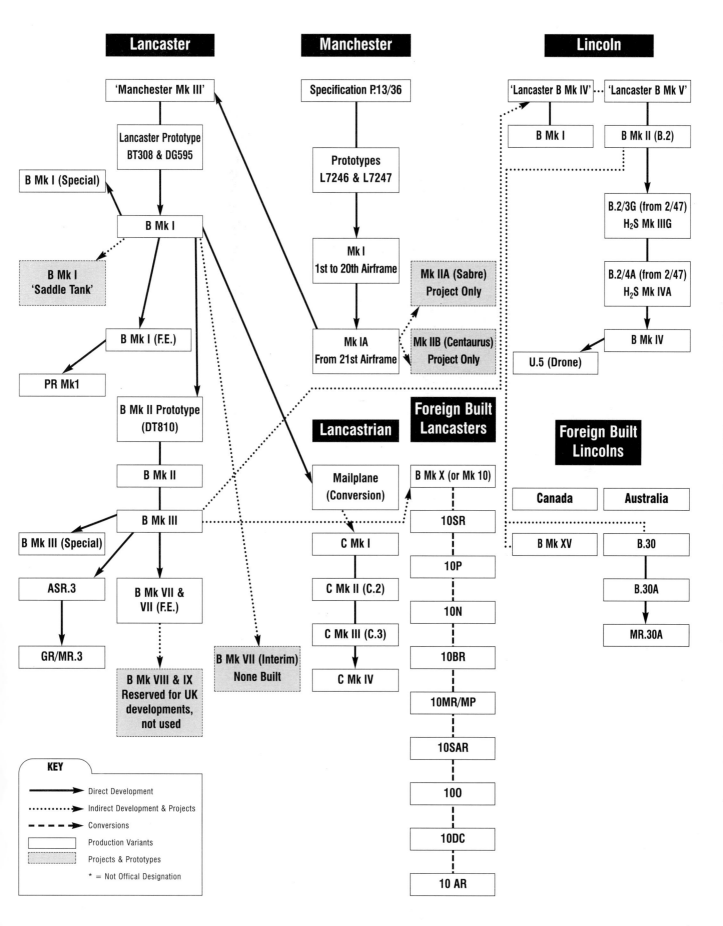

## Lancaster

- 'Manchester Mk III'
- Lancaster Prototype BT308 & DG595
- B Mk I (Special)
- B Mk I
- B Mk I 'Saddle Tank'
- B Mk I (F.E.)
- PR Mk1
- B Mk II Prototype (DT810)
- B Mk II
- B Mk III
- B Mk III (Special)
- ASR.3
- GR/MR.3
- B Mk VII & VII (F.E.)
- B Mk VIII & IX Reserved for UK developments, not used

## Manchester

- Specification P.13/36
- Prototypes L7246 & L7247
- Mk I 1st to 20th Airframe
- Mk IA From 21st Airframe
- Mk IIA (Sabre) Project Only
- Mk IIB (Centaurus) Project Only

## Lincoln

- 'Lancaster B Mk IV'
- 'Lancaster B Mk V'
- B Mk I
- B Mk II (B.2)
- B.2/3G (from 2/47) H₂S Mk IIIG
- B.2/4A (from 2/47) H₂S Mk IVA
- B Mk IV
- U.5 (Drone)

## Lancastrian

- Mailplane (Conversion)
- C Mk I
- C Mk II (C.2)
- C Mk III (C.3)
- C Mk IV
- B Mk VII (Interim) None Built

## Foreign Built Lancasters

- B Mk X (or Mk 10)
- 10SR
- 10P
- 10N
- 10BR
- 10MR/MP
- 10SAR
- 10O
- 10DC
- 10 AR

## Foreign Built Lincolns

### Canada
- B Mk XV

### Australia
- B.30
- B.30A
- MR.30A

## KEY

→ Direct Development

⋯⋯▸ Indirect Development & Projects

--→ Conversions

☐ Production Variants

▨ Projects & Prototypes

* = Not Offical Designation

# Squadrons
## Manchester (M), Lancaster (La) and Lincoln (Li)

### No.7 Squadron
Code: MG
Started Operations: (La) Oakington, July 1943, (Li) Upwod August 1949
UK Based: Oakington 7/43-7/45, Mepal 7/45-7/46, Upwood 7/46-12/55
Foreign Based: N/A
Detachments: Changi 1/47-2/47, Shallufa 1948 & 1949, Luqa 3/50, Habbaniya 11/53-12/53, Khormaksar 8/55-12/55, Bahrein 11/55-12/55
Reformed: N/A
Disbanded: Upwood January 1956
Re-equipped: N/A
Variants Operated: (La) B Mk I, B Mk III, B Mk VI, B Mk I (F.E.) and (Li) B.2

### No.9 Squadron
Code: WS
Started Operations: (La) Waddington August 1942, (Li) Binbrook July 1946
UK Based: Waddington 8/42-4/43, Bardney 4/43-7/45, Waddington 7/45-1/46, Binbrook 4/46-7/46, Lindholme 7/46-9/46, Binbrook 9/46-5/52
Foreign Based: Salbani [India] 1/46-4/46
Detachments: Yagodnik [Russia] 9/44, Lossiemouth 10/44 & 11/44, Luqa 1/47, Shallufa 1948 & 1949, Pakistan 10/49, Shallufa 8/51-10/51
Reformed: N/A
Disbanded: N/A
Re-equipped: Binbrook May 1952 (E.E. Canberra)
Variants Operated: (La) B Mk I, B Mk III and (Li) B.2

### No.12 Squadron
Code: PH
Started Operations: (La) Wickenby November 1942, (Li) Waddington August 1946
UK Based: Wickenby 11/42-9/45, Binbrook 9/45-7/46, Waddington 7/46-9/46, Binbrook 9/46-4/52
Foreign Based: N/A
Detachments: Hemswell 1/48-3/48, Shallufa [Egypt] various times during 1949-1951
Reformed: N/A
Disbanded: N/A
Re-equipped: Binbrook April 1952 (E.E. Canberra B.2)
Variants Operated: (La) B Mk I, B Mk III and (Li) B.2

### No.15 Squadron
Code: LS
Started Operations: (La) Mildenhall December 1943, (Li) Wyton February 1947
UK Based: Mildenhall 12/43-8/46, Wyton 8/46-11/50, Marham 11/50-2/51
Foreign Based: N/A
Detachments: Shallufa [Egypt] 3/48 and 11/49
Reformed: N/A
Disbanded: N/A
Re-equipped: Marham January 1951 (Boeing Washington)
Variants Operated: (La) B Mk I, B Mk I (Special), B Mk III and (Li) B.2

### No.18 Squadron
Code: None
Started Operations: (La) Ein Shemer 9/46
UK Based: N/A
Foreign Based: Ein Shemer (Palestine) 9/46
Detachments: N/A
Reformed: N/A
Disbanded: Ein Shemer 9/46
Re-equipped: N/A
Variants Operated: (La) GR Mk III

### No.35 (Madras Presidency) Squadron
Code: TL
Started Operations: (La) Graveley March 1944, (Li) Mildenhall September 1949
UK Based: Graveley 3/44-9/46, Stradishall 9/46-2/49, Mildenhall 2/49-2/50
Foreign Based: N/A
Detachments: Malta various times 1946-9, Shallufa [Egypt] various times 1946-9, Shallufa [Egypt] 1/50
Reformed: N/A
Disbanded: Mildenhall 23/2/50
Re-equipped: N/A
Variants Operated: (La) B Mk I, B Mk I (F.E.), B Mk III and (Li) B.2

### No.37 Squadron
Code: LF
Started Operations: (La) Fayid [Egypt] April 1946
UK Based: N/A
Foreign Based: Fayid [Egypt] 4/46-8/46, Kabrit [Egypt] 8/46-9/46, Shallufa [Egypt] 9/46-1/47

**Group shot of No. 12 Squadron by a Lincoln, 1949** (©RAFM P013785)

Detachments: N/A
Reformed: N/A
Disbanded: Shallufa [Egypt] 1/4/47
Re-equipped: N/A
Variants Operated: (La) B Mk III, B Mk VII (F.E.) & GR Mk III

### No.38 Squadron
Code: RL
Started Operations: (La) Luqa (Malta) 4/46
UK Based: N/A
Foreign Based: Luqa (Malta), Ein Shemer (Palestine), Shallufa (Egypt) & Ramut David (Palestine)
Detachments: N/A
Reformed: N/A
Disbanded: N/A
Re-equipped: Ramut David 12/53
Variants Operated: (La) ASR Mk III & GR Mk III

### No.40 Squadron
Code: BL
Started Operations: (La) Abu Sueir [Egypt] January 1946
UK Based: N/A
Foreign Based: Abu Sueir [Egypt] 1/46-9/46, Shallufa [Egypt] 9/46-4/47
Detachments: N/A
Reformed: N/A
Disbanded: Shallufa [Egypt] 1/4/47
Re-equipped: N/A
Variants Operated: (La) B Mk VII (F.E.)

### No.44 (Rhodesia) Squadron
Code: KM
Started Operations: (La) Waddington December 1941, (Li) Mildenhall October 1945
UK Based: Waddington 12/41-5/43, Dunholme Lodge 5/43-9/44, Spilsby 9/44-7/45, Mepal 7/45-8/45, Mildenhall 8/45-8/46, Wyton 8/4-1/51
Foreign Based: N/A
Detachments: Southern Rhodesia 6/48, Shallufa [Egypt] at various times 1946-8
Reformed: N/A
Disbanded: N/A
Re-equipped: Wyton January 1951 (Boeing Washington)
Variants Operated: (La) B Mk I, B Mk I (F.E.), B Mk III and (Li) B Mk I & B.2

### No.49 Squadron
Code: EA
Started Operations: (M) Scampton April 1942, (La) Scampton June 1942, (Li) Upwood October 1949
UK Based: Scampton 4/42-1/43, Fiskerton 1/43-10/44,

Fulbeck 10/44-4/45, Syerston 4/45-9/45, Mepal 9/45-7/46, Upwood 7/46-7/52, Waddington 7/52-8/53, Wittering 8/53-2/54, Upwood 2/54-8/55
Foreign Based: (See Below)
Detachments: Shallufa [Egypt] 11/53, Eastleigh [Kenya] 11/53-1/54, Eastleigh [Kenya] 1954/5, Khormaksar [Aden] 1954/5
Reformed: N/A
Disbanded: Upwood 1/8/55
Re-equipped: N/A
Variants Operated: (La) B Mk I, B Mk I (F.E.), B Mk III and (Li) B.2

### No.50 Squadron
Code: VN
Started Operations: (M) Skellingthorpe April 1942, (La) Swinderby June 1942, (Li) Waddington July 1946
UK Based: Skellingthorpe 4/42-6/42, Swinderby 6/42-10/42, Skellingthorpe 10/42-6/45, Sturgate 6.45-1/46, Waddington 1/46-1/51
Foreign Based: (See Below)
Detachments: Binbrook 8/47-12/47, Shallufa [Egypt] various times
Reformed: N/A
Disbanded: Waddington 31/1/51
Re-equipped: N/A
Variants Operated: (M) Mk I, (La) B Mk I, B Mk III & (Li) B.2

### No.57 Squadron
Code: DX
Started Operations: (La) Scampton September 1942, (Li) Lindholme 1946
UK Based: Scampton 9/42-8/43, East Kirkby 8/43-11/45, Elsham Wolds 11/45-12/45, Scampton 12/45-5/46, Lindholme 5/46-10/46, Waddington 10/46-5/51
Foreign Based: N/A
Detachments: Hemswell 11/47-12/47, Tengah [Singapore] 3/50-7/50, Marham 4/51-5/51, Luqa [Malta] & Shallufa [Egypt] at various times between 11/46-1/51
Reformed: Elsham Wolds 26/11/45 as No. 103 (B) Sqn, later renumbered No. 57 Squadron
Disbanded: East Kirkby 25/11/45
Re-equipped: Waddington May 1951 (Boeing Washington)
Variants Operated: (La) B Mk I, B Mk III and (Li) B Mk I & B.2

### No.61 Squadron
Code: QR
Started Operations: (M) North Luffenham October 1941, (La) Woolfox Lodge April 1942, (Li) Waddington May 1946

UK Based: North Luffenham 10/41, Woolfox Lodge 10/41-5/42, Syerston 5/42-11/43, Skellingthorpe 11/43-2/44, Coningsby 2/44-4/44, Skellingthorpe 4/44-6/45, Sturgate 6/45-1/46, Waddington 1/46-8/53, Wittering 8/53-8/54
Foreign Based: N/A
Detachments: St. Eval 7/42-8/42, Hemswell 7/47-12/47, Tengah [Singapore] 12/50-4/51, Shallufa [Egypt] & Khormaksar [Aden] at various times during 1949-53
Reformed: N/A
Disbanded: N/A
Re-equipped: Wittering August 1954 (E.E. Canberra B.2)
Variants Operated: (M) Mk I/IA, (La) B Mk I, B Mk II, B Mk III and (Li) B.2

### No.70 Squadron
Code: None
Started Operations: (La) Fayid [Egypt] April 1946
UK Based: N/A
Foreign Based: Fayid [Egypt] 4/46-8/46, Kabrit [Egypt] 8/46-9/46, Shallufa [Egypt] 9/46-4/47
Detachments: N/A
Reformed: N/A
Disbanded: Shallufa [Egypt] 1/4/47
Re-equipped: N/A
Variants Operated: (La) B Mk I (F.E.)

### No.75 (New Zealand) Squadron
Code: AA
Started Operations: (La) Mepal March 1944
UK Based: Mepal 3/44-7/45, Spilsby 7/45-10/45
Foreign Based: N/A
Detachments: N/A
Reformed: N/A
Disbanded: Spilsby 15/10/45
Re-equipped: N/A
Variants Operated: (La) B Mk I & B Mk III

### No.83 Squadron
Code: OL
Started Operations: (M) Scampton January 1942, (La) Scampton May 1942, (Li) Coningsby July 1946
UK Based: Scampton 1/42-8/42, Wyton 8/42-4/44, Coningsby 4/44-10/46, Hemswell 10/46-12/55
Foreign Based: N/A
Detachments: Luqa [Malta] 12/46, Shallufa [Egypt] 8/47, 8/48 * 2/51-3/51
Reformed: N/A
Disbanded: Renamed Antler Squadron 1/1/57
Re-equipped: N/A
Variants Operated: (M) B Mk I/IA, (La) B Mk I, B Mk III & (Li) B.2

### No.90 Squadron
Code: WP
Started Operations: (La) Tuddenham May 1944, (Li) Wyton April 1947
UK Based: Tuddenham 5/44-11/46, Wyton 11/46-9/50
Foreign Based: N/A
Detachments: Shallufa [Egypt] at various times during 1948-50
Reformed: N/A
Disbanded: Wyton 1/9/50
Re-equipped: N/A
Variants Operated: (La) B Mk I, B Mk I (F.E.), B Mk III & (Li) B.2

### No.97 (Straits Settlements) Squadron
Code: OF
Started Operations: (M) Waddington February 1941, (La) Coningsby January 1942, (Li) Coningsby July 1946
UK Based: Waddington 2/41-3/41, Coningsby 3/41-3/42, Woodhall Spa 3/42-4/43, Bourn 4/43-4/44, Coningsby 4/44-10/46, Hemswell 10/46-12/55
Foreign Based: N/A
Detachments: Gransden Lodge, Graveley & Oakington 8/43-9/43, Luqa [Malta] 12/46-1/47, Negombo [Ceylon] & Tengah [Singapore] 4/48-6/48, Shallufa [Egypt] at various times between 11/48-12/53
Reformed: N/A
Disbanded: Renamed Arrow Squadron 1/1/56
Re-equipped: N/A
Variants Operated: (M) Mk I/IA, (La) B Mk I, B Mk III & (Li) B.2

### No.100 Squadron
Code: HW
Started Operations: (La) Waltham January 1943, (Li) Lindholme May 1946
UK Based: Waltham 1/43-4/45, Elsham Wolds 4/45-12/45, Scampton 12/45-5/46, Lindholme 5/46-10/46, Hemswell 10/46-3/50, Waddington 3/50-6/50, Waddington 12/50-5/52, Waddington 8/52-8/53, Wittering 8/53-1/54, Wittering 3/54-4/54
Foreign Based: Tengah [Singapore] 6/50-12/50, Shellufa [Egypt] 5/52-8/52, Eastleigh [Kenya] 1/54-3/54
Detachments: Tengah [Singapore] 5/50
Reformed: N/A
Disbanded: N/A
Re-equipped: Wittering April 1954 (E.E. Canberra B.2)
Variants Operated: (La) B Mk I, B Mk III and (Li) B.2

### No.101 Squadron
Code: SR
Started Operations: (La) Holme-on-Spalding Moor October 1942, (Li) Binbrook August 1946
UK Based: Holme-on-Spalding Moor 10/42-6/43, Ludford Magna 6/43-10/45, Binbrook 10/45-6/51
Foreign Based: N/A
Detachments: Shallufa [Egypt], Butterworth [Malaya], Changi [Singapore] & Luqa [Malta] at various times
Reformed: N/A
Disbanded: N/A
Re-equipped: Binbrook June 1951 (E.E. Canberra B.2)
Variants Operated: (La) B Mk I, B Mk III and (Li) B.2

### No.103 Squadron
Code: PM
Started Operations: (La) Elsham Wolds October 1942
UK Based: Elsham Wolds 10/42-11/45
Foreign Based: N/A
Detachments: N/A
Reformed: N/A
Disbanded: Renumbered No. 57 (B) Squadron 26/11/45
Re-equipped: N/A
Variants Operated: (La) B Mk I & B Mk III

### No.104 Squadron
Code: EP
Started Operations: (La) Abu Sueir [Egypt] November 1945
UK Based: N/A
Foreign Based: Abu Sueir [Egypt] 11/45-6/46, Shallufa [Egypt] 6/46-3/47
Detachments: N/A
Reformed: N/A
Disbanded: Shallufa [Egypt] 1/4/47
Re-equipped: N/A
Variants Operated: (La) B Mk VII (F.E.)

### No.106 Squadron
Code: ZN
Started Operations: (M) Coningsby February 1942, (La) Coningsby May 1942
UK Based: Coningsby 2/42-9/42, Syerston 9/42-11/43, Metheringham 11/43-12/46
Foreign Based: N/A
Detachments: N/A
Reformed: N/A
Disbanded: Metheringham 18/2/46
Re-equipped: N/A
Variants Operated: (M) B Mk I/IA, (La) B Mk I & B Mk III

### No.115 Squadron
Code: IL & KO
Started Operations: (La) East Wretham March 1943, (Li) Mildenhall September 1949
UK Based: East Wretham 3/43-8/43, Little Snoring 8/43-11/43, Witchford 11/43-9/45, Graveley

9/45-9/46, Stradishall 9/46-2/49, Mildenhall 2/49-3/50
Foreign Based: N/A
Detachments: Shallufa [Egypt] various during 1946-9
Reformed: N/A
Disbanded: Mildenhall 1/3/50
Re-equipped: N/A
Variants Operated: (La) B Mk I, B Mk II, B Mk III & (Li) B.2

### No.120 Squadron
Code: BS
Started Operations: (La) Leuchars 11/46
UK Based: Leuchars & Kinloss
Foreign Based: N/A
Detachments: N/A
Reformed: N/A
Disbanded: N/A
Re-equipped: Kinloss 4/51
Variants Operated: (La) GR Mk III

### No.138 Squadron
Code: AC & NF
Started Operations: (La) Tuddenham March 1945, (Li) Wyton September 1947
UK Based: Tuddenham 3/45-11/46, Wyton 11/46-8/50
Foreign Based: N/A
Detachments: Shallufa [Egypt] and Aden at various times between 11/47 & 3/50.
Reformed: N/A
Disbanded: Wyton 1/9/50
Re-equipped: N/A
Variants Operated: (La) B Mk I, B Mk I (F.E.) & (Li) B.2

### No.148 Squadron
Code: AU
Started Operations: (La) Upwood November 1946, (Li) Upwood January 1950
UK Based: Upwood 11/46-7/55
Foreign Based: N/A
Detachments: Luqa [Malta], Shallufa [Egypt], Nicosia [Cyprus] & Tengah [Singapore] at various times
Reformed: N/A
Disbanded: Upwood 1/7/55
Re-equipped: N/A
Variants Operated: (La) B Mk I (F.E.) & (Li) B.2

### No.149 (East India) Squadron
Code: OJ and TK
Started Operations: (La) Methwold August 1944, (Li) Mildenhall October 1949
UK Based: Methwold 8/44-4/46, Tuddenham 4/46-11/46, Stradishall 11/46-2/49, Mildenhall 2/49-3/50.
Foreign Based: N/A
Detachments: Woodbridge 12/44, Pomigliano [Italy] between 4/46-11/46, Shallufa [Egypt] between 11/46-2/49 & 11/49-3/50
Reformed: N/A
Disbanded: Mildenhall 1/3/50
Re-equipped: N/A
Variants Operated: (La) B Mk I, B Mk III and (Li) B.2

### No.150 Squadron
Code: JN and IQ
Started Operations: (La) Fiskerton November 1944
UK Based: Fiskerton 11/44, Hemswell 11/44-11/45
Foreign Based: N/A
Detachments: N/A
Reformed: N/A
Disbanded: Hemswell 7/11/45
Re-equipped: N/A
Variants Operated: (La) B Mk I & B Mk III

A Flight, No. 207 Squadron by a Manchester at RAF Waddington, August 1941 (©RAFM P009995)

### No.153 Squadron
Code: P4
Started Operations: (La) Kirmington October 1944
UK Based: Kirmington 11/44, Scampton 11/44-9/45
Foreign Based: N/A
Detachments: N/A
Reformed: N/A
Disbanded: Scampton 28/9/45
Re-equipped: N/A
Variants Operated: (La) B Mk I & B Mk III

### No.156 Squadron
Code: GT
Started Operations: (La) Warboys January 1943
UK Based: Warboys 1/43-3/44, Upwood 3/44-6/45, Wyton 6/45-9/45
Foreign Based: N/A
Detachments: N/A
Reformed: N/A
Disbanded: Wyton 25/9/45
Re-equipped: N/A
Variants Operated: (La) B Mk I & B Mk III

### No.160 Squadron
Code: BS
Started Operations: (La) Leuchars 8/46
UK Based: Leuchars 8/46-9/46
Foreign Based: N/A
Detachments: N/A
Reformed: N/A
Re-equipped: Leuchars 9/46
Variants Operated: (La) GR Mk III

### No.166 Squadron
Code: AS
Started Operations: (La) Kirmington September 1943
UK Based: Kirmington 9/43-11/45
Foreign Based: N/A
Detachments: N/A
Reformed: N/A
Disbanded: Kirmington 18/11/45
Re-equipped: N/A
Variants Operated: (La) B Mk I & B Mk III

### No.170 Squadron
Code: TC
Started Operations: (La) Kelstern October 1944
UK Based: Kelstern 10/44-11/44, Dunholme Lodge 11/44-11/45
Foreign Based: N/A
Detachments: N/A
Reformed: N/A
Disbanded: Dunholme Lodge 14/11/45
Re-equipped: N/A
Variants Operated: (La) B Mk I & B Mk III

### No.178 Squadron
Code: N/K
Started Operations: (La) Ein Shemer [Palestine] November 1945
UK Based: N/A
Foreign Based: Ein Shemer [Palestine] 11/45, Fayid [Egypt] 11/45-4/46
Detachments: N/A
Reformed: N/A
Disbanded: Renumbered No. 70 Squadron 15/4/46
Re-equipped: N/A
Variants Operated: (La) B Mk III

### No.179 Squadron
*See Air-Sea Rescue*

### No.186 Squadron
Code: XY
Started Operations: (La) Tuddenham October 1944
UK Based: Tuddenham 10/44-12/44, Stradishall 12/44-7/45
Foreign Based: N/A
Detachments: N/A
Reformed: N/A
Disbanded: Stradishall 17/7/45
Re-equipped: N/A
Variants Operated: (La) B Mk I & B Mk III

Group shot of No 106 Squadron (including Guy Gibson) by Lancaster B Mk I, ED593 at RAF Syerston (©RAFM P016121)

**Lancaster B Mk III (FE), NX612, 9X• of No 1689 Flight, No 20MU Aston Down** *(via R. Sturtivant)*

### No.189 Squadron
Code: CA
Started Operations: (La) Bardney October 1944
UK Based: Bardney 10/44-11/44, Fulbeck 11/44-10/45, Metheringham 10/45-11/45
Foreign Based: N/A
Detachments: N/A
Reformed: N/A
Disbanded: Metheringham 20/11/45
Re-equipped: N/A
Variants Operated: (La) B Mk I & B Mk III

### No.195 Squadron
Code: A4 ( A & B Flt) JE ( C Flt)
Started Operations: (La) Witchford October 1944
UK Based: Witchford 10/44-11/44, Wratting Common 11/44-8/45
Foreign Based: N/A
Detachments: N/A
Reformed: N/A
Disbanded: Wratting Common 14/8/45
Re-equipped: N/A
Variants Operated: (La) B Mk I & B Mk III

### No.199 Squadron
Code: None
Started Operations: (Li) Watton July 1951
UK Based: Watton 7/51-4/52, Hemswell 4/52-10/52, Honington 10/52-11/57
Foreign Based: N/A
Detachments: N/A
Reformed: N/A
Disbanded: N/A
Re-equipped: Honington 11/57 (Vickers Valiant)
Variants Operated: (Li) B.2

### No.207 Squadron
Code: EM
Started Operations: (M) Waddington November 1940, (La) Bottesford March 1942, (Li) Mildenhall March 1949
UK Based: Waddington 11/40-11/41, Bottesford 11/41-9/42, Langar 9/42-10/43, Spilsby 10/43-10/45, Methwold 10/45-4/46, Tuddenham 4/46-11/46, Stradishall 11/46-2/49, Mildenhall 2/49-3/50
Foreign Based: N/A
Detachments: Shallufa [Egypt] 7/47, 12/48 & 1/50
Reformed: N/A
Disbanded: Mildenhall 1/3/50
Re-equipped: N/A
Variants Operated: (M) Mk I/IA, (La) B Mk I, B Mk I (F.E.), B Mk III and (Li) B.2

### No.214 (Federated Malay States) Sqn
Code: QN
Started Operations: (La) Fayid [Egypt] November 1945, (Li) Upwood February 1950
UK Based: Upwood 11/46-12/54
Foreign Based: Fayid [Egypt] 11/45-4/45
Detachments: Luqa [Malta], Shallufa [Egypt], Karachi [India], Idris [Libya], Negombo [Ceylon] & Eastleigh [Kenya] at various times
Reformed: N/A
Disbanded: Upwood 30/12/54
Re-equipped: N/A
Variants Operated: (La) B Mk I (F.E.) & (Li) B.2

### No.218 (Gold Coast) Squadron
Code: HA
Started Operations: (La) Methwold August 1944
UK Based: Methwold 8/44-12/44, Chedburgh 12/44-8/45
Foreign Based: N/A
Detachments: N/A
Reformed: N/A
Disbanded: Chedburgh 10/8/45
Re-equipped: N/A
Variants Operated: (La) B Mk I & B Mk III

### No.224 Squadron
Code: XB
Started Operations: (La) St. Eval 10/46
UK Based: St. Eval 10/46-11/47
Foreign Based: N/A
Detachments: N/A
Reformed: N/A
Disbanded: N/A
Re-equipped: St. Eval 11/47
Variants Operated: (La) GR Mk III

### No.279 Squadron
*See Air-Sea Rescue*

### No. 300 'Masovian' (Polish) Squadron
Code: BH
Started Operations: (La) Faldingworth April 1944
UK Based: Faldingworth 4/44-10/46
Foreign Based: N/A
Detachments: N/A
Reformed: N/A
Disbanded: Faldingworth 11/10/46
Re-equipped: N/A
Variants Operated: (La) B Mk I & B Mk III

### No.405 (Vancouver) Squadron, RCAF
Code: LQ
Started Operations: (La) Gransden Lodge August 1943
UK Based: Gransden Lodge 8/43-5/45, Linton-on-Ouse 5/45-6/45
Foreign Based: N/A
Detachments: N/A
Reformed: N/A
Disbanded: Linton-on-Ouse (returned to Canada) June 1945
Re-equipped: N/A
Variants Operated: (La) B Mk I, B Mk III & B Mk X

### No.408 (Goose) Squadron, RCAF
Code: EQ
Started Operations: (La) Linton-on-Ouse August 1943
UK Based: Linton-on-Ouse 9/43-8/44
Foreign Based: N/A
Detachments: N/A
Reformed: N/A
Disbanded: N/A
Re-equipped: Linton-on-Ouse July 1944 (Halifax B Mk III)
Variants Operated: (La) B Mk II

### No.419 (Moose) Squadron, RCAF
Code: VR
Started Operations: (La) Middleton St. George early 1944
UK Based: Middleton St. George 1/44-6/45
Foreign Based: N/A
Detachments: N/A
Reformed: N/A
Disbanded: Middleton St. George (returned to Canada) June 1945
Re-equipped: N/A
Variants Operated: (La) B Mk X

### No.420 (Snowy Owl) Squadron, RCAF
Code: PT
Started Operations: (La) Tholthorpe April 1945
UK Based: Tholthorpe 4/45-6/45
Foreign Based: N/A
Detachments: N/A
Reformed: N/A
Disbanded: Tholthorpe (returned to Canada) June 1945
Re-equipped: N/A
Variants Operated: (La) B Mk X

### No.424 (Tiger) Squadron, RCAF
Code: QB
Started Operations: (La) Skipton-on-Swale January 1945
UK Based: Skipton-on-Swale 1/45-10/45
Foreign Based: N/A
Detachments: N/A
Reformed: N/A
Disbanded: Skipton-on-Swale 15/10/45
Re-equipped: N/A
Variants Operated: (La) B Mk I

### No.425 (Alouette) Squadron, RCAF
Code: KW
Started Operations: (La) Tholthorpe May 1945
UK Based: Tholthorpe 5/45-6/45
Foreign Based: N/A
Detachments: N/A
Reformed: N/A
Disbanded: Tholthorpe (returned to Canada) June 1945
Re-equipped: N/A
Variants Operated: (La) B Mk X

### No.426 (Thunderbird) Squadron, RCAF
Code: OW
Started Operations: (La) Linton-on-Ouse June 1943
UK Based: Linton-on-Ouse 6/43-5/44
Foreign Based: N/A
Detachments: N/A
Reformed: N/A
Re-equipped: Linton-on-Ouse May 1944 (H.P. Halifax B Mk III)
Variants Operated: (La) B Mk II

### No.427 (Lion) Squadron, RCAF
Code: ZL
Started Operations: (La) Leeming March 1945
UK Based: Leeming 3/45-5/46
Foreign Based: N/A
Detachments: N/A
Reformed: N/A
Disbanded: Leeming 31/5/46
Re-equipped: N/A
Variants Operated: (La) B Mk I & B Mk III

### No.428 (Ghost) Squadron, RCAF
Code: NA
Started Operations: (La) Middleton St. George March 1945
UK Based: Middleton St. George 3/45-5/46
Foreign Based: N/A
Detachments: N/A
Reformed: N/A
Disbanded: Middleton St. George 31/5/46
Re-equipped: N/A
Variants Operated: (La) B Mk I & B Mk III

### No.431 (Iroquois) Squadron, RCAF
Code: SE
Started Operations: (La) Croft October 1944
UK Based: Croft 10/44-6/45
Foreign Based: N/A
Detachments: N/A
Reformed: N/A
Disbanded: Croft (returned to Canada) June 1945
Re-equipped: N/A
Variants Operated: (La) B Mk X

### No.432 (Leaside) Squadron, RCAF
Code: QO
Started Operations: (La) East Moor October 1943
UK Based: East Moor 10/43-2/44
Foreign Based: N/A
Detachments: N/A
Reformed: N/A
Disbanded: N/A
Re-equipped: East Moor (H.P. Halifax B Mk III) February 1944
Variants Operated: (La) B Mk II

### No.433 (Porcupine) Squadron, RCAF
Code: BM
Started Operations: (La) Skipton-on-Swale January 1945
UK Based: Skipton-on-Swale 1/45-10/45
Foreign Based: N/A
Detachments: N/A

Reformed: N/A
Disbanded: Skipton-on-Swale 15/10/45
Re-equipped: N/A
Variants Operated: (La) B Mk I

### No.434 (Bluenose) Squadron, RCAF
Code: IP
Started Operations: (La) Croft December 1944
UK Based: Croft 12/44-6/45
Foreign Based: N/A
Detachments: N/A
Reformed: N/A
Disbanded: Croft (returned to Canada) June 1945
Re-equipped: N/A
Variants Operated: (La) B Mk I & B Mk X

### No.460 Squadron, RAAF
Code: AR
Started Operations: (La) Breighton October 1942
UK Based: Breighton 10/42-5/43, Binbrook 5/43-7/45, East Kirkby 7/45-10/45
Foreign Based: N/A
Detachments: N/A
Reformed: N/A
Disbanded: East Kirby 10/10/45
Re-equipped: N/A
Variants Operated: (La) B Mk I & B Mk III

### No.463 Squadron, RAAF
Code: PO & JO
Started Operations: (La) Waddington November 1943
UK Based: Waddington 11/43-7/45, Skellingthorpe 7/45-9/45
Foreign Based: N/A
Detachments: N/A
Reformed: N/A
Disbanded: Skellingthorpe 25/9/45
Re-equipped: N/A
Variants Operated: (La) B Mk I & B Mk III

### No.467 Squadron, RAAF
Code: PO
Started Operations: (La) Scampton November 1942
UK Based: Scampton 11/42, Bottesford 11/42-11/43, Waddington 11/43-6/45, Metheringham 6/45-9/45
Foreign Based: N/A
Detachments: N/A
Reformed: N/A
Disbanded: Metheringham 30/9/45
Re-equipped: N/A
Variants Operated: (La) B Mk I & B Mk III

### No.514 Squadron
Code: JI & A2 (C Flt)
Started Operations: (La) Foulsham September 1943
UK Based: Foulsham 9/43-11/43, Waterbeach 11/43-8/45
Foreign Based: N/A
Detachments: N/A
Reformed: N/A
Disbanded: Waterbeach 22/8/45
Re-equipped: N/A
Variants Operated: (La) B Mk I, B Mk II & B Mk III

### No.550 Squadron
Code: BQ
Started Operations: (La) Waltham November 1943
UK Based: Waltham 11/43-1/45, North Killingholme 1/45-10/45
Foreign Based: N/A
Detachments: N/A
Reformed: N/A
Disbanded: North Killingholme 31/10/45
Re-equipped: N/A
Variants Operated: (La) B Mk I & B Mk III

### No.576 Squadron
Code: UL
Started Operations: (La) Elsham Wolds November 1943
UK Based: Elsham Wolds 11/43-10/44, Fiskerton 10/44-9/45
Foreign Based: N/A
Detachments: N/A
Reformed: N/A
Disbanded: Fiskerton 13/9/45
Re-equipped: N/A
Variants Operated: (La) B Mk I & B Mk III

### No.582 Squadron
Code: 60
Started Operations: (La) Little Staughton April 1944
UK Based: Little Staughton 4/44-9/45
Foreign Based: N/A
Detachments: N/A
Reformed: N/A
Disbanded: Little Staughton 10/9/45
Re-equipped: N/A
Variants Operated: (La) B Mk I & B Mk III

### No.617 Squadron
Code: AJ, YZ & KC
Started Operations: (La) Scampton May 1943, (Li) Binbrook September 1946
UK Based: Scampton 5/43-8/43, Coningsby 8/43-1/44, Woodhall Spa 1/44-6/45, Waddington 6/45-1/46, Binbrook 5/46-1/52
Foreign Based: Salbani [India] 1/46-5/46

Detachments: Tempsford 12/43, Yagodnik [Russia] 9/44, Lossiemouth 10/44 & 11/44
Reformed: N/A
Disbanded: N/A
Re-equipped: Binbrook January 1952 (E.E. Canberra)
Variants Operated: (La) B Mk I, B Mk I (Special), B Mk III, B Mk III (Special), B Mk VII (F.E.) & (Li) B.2

### No.619 Squadron
Code: PG
Started Operations: (La) Woodhall Spa April 1943
UK Based: Woodhall Spa 4/43-1/44, Coningsby 1/44-4/44, Dunholme Lodge 4/44-9/44, Strubby 9/44-6/45, Skellingthorpe 6/45-7/45
Foreign Based: N/A
Detachments: N/A
Reformed: N/A
Disbanded: Skellingthorpe 18/7/45
Re-equipped:
Variants Operated: (La) B Mk I & B Mk III

### No.621 Squadron
*See Air-Sea Rescue*

### No.622 Squadron
Code: GI
Started Operations: (La) Mildenhall December 1943
UK Based: Mildenhall 12/43-8/45
Foreign Based: N/A
Detachments: N/A
Reformed: N/A
Disbanded: Mildenhall 15/8/45
Re-equipped: N/A
Variants Operated: (La) B Mk I & B Mk III

### No.625 Squadron
Code: CF
Started Operations: (La) Kelstern October 1943
UK Based: Kelstern 10/43-4/45, Scampton 4/45-10/45
Foreign Based: N/A
Detachments: N/A
Reformed: N/A
Disbanded: Scampton 7/10/45
Re-equipped: N/A
Variants Operated: (La) B Mk I & B Mk III

### No.626 Squadron
Code: UM
Started Operations: (La) Wickenby November 1943
UK Based: Wickenby 11/43-10/45
Foreign Based: N/A
Detachments: N/A
Reformed: N/A
Disbanded: Wickenby 14/10/45
Re-equipped: N/A
Variants Operated: (La) B Mk I & B Mk III

### No.630 Squadron
Code: LE
Started Operations: (La) East Kirkby November 1943
UK Based: East Kirkby 11/43-7/45
Foreign Based: N/A
Detachments: N/A
Reformed: N/A
Disbanded: East Kirkby 18/7/45
Re-equipped: N/A
Variants Operated: (La) B Mk I & B Mk III

### No.635 Squadron
Code: F2
Started Operations: (La) Downham Market March 1944
UK Based: Downham Market 3/44-9/45
Foreign Based: N/A
Detachments: N/A
Reformed: N/A
Disbanded: Downham Market 1/9/45
Re-equipped: N/A
Variants Operated: (La) B Mk I, B Mk III & B Mk VI

# Other Units which have used the Manchester, Lancaster or Lincoln

Royal Air Force - Others

### Heavy Conversion Units
No. 1651 (La)
Woolfox Lodge Code: BS & QQ
No. 1653 (Ma/La)
Lindholme, North Luffenham, Lindholme Code: A3, H4 & M9
No. 1654 (La)
Swinderby, Wigsley Code: UG & JF
No. 1656 (La)
Lindholme  Code: EK & BL
No. 1660 (Ma/La)
Swinderby Code: YW & TV
No. 1661 (Ma/La)
Winthorpe Code: KB & GP
No. 1662 (La)
Blyton Code: KF & PE
No. 1666 [RCAF] (La)
Dalton Code: ND & QY
No. 1667 (La)
Lindholme, Faldingworth, Sandtoft  Code: GG & KR
No. 1668 (Ma/La)
Balderton, Syerston, Bottesford, Cottesmore Code: J9, CE & 2K

### Heavy Conversion Flights
No. 1678 (La)
East Wretham
No. 1679
Foulsham, Waterbeach Code: SW

### Operational Conversion Units
No. 230 OCU (La/Li)
Lindholme Code: A3 & SN
No. 236 OCU (La)
Kinloss Code: K7

### Lancaster Finishing Schools
No. 1 LFS Code: 3C
Formed by combining elements of No. 1656, 1662 and 1667 HCUs in November 1943. Consisted A Flt at Lindholme, B Flt at Blyton and C Flt at Faldingworth (later Hemswell). Disbanded July 1945.

No. 3 LFS Code: AS
Formed at Feltwell, with first course in December 1943. It Comprised three flights by its disbandment on 31/1/45.

No. 5 LFS Code: RC & CE
Formed from No. 1668 HCU at Syerston. Disbanded there 31/3/45.

No. 6 LFS
Formed for RCAF crews at Ossington in December 1944. Disbanded November 1945.

### Miscellaneous
No. 1323 AGLT Flight (La)
AGLT training flight operating from Warboys in co-operation with No 1696 Bomber Defence Training Flight. Disbanded 30/9/45.

No. 1577 (Special Duties) Flight
Bomber trials flight formed at Llandow on 9th August 1943. Flew to Salbani (India) via Cairo in October 1943. Moved to Chakeri on 5th March 1944 and on to Manipur in May. This unit received both of the 'Saddle Tank' Lancasters at one time during 1945.

No. 1384 Flight
No. 1689 Flight
No. 6 (C) OTU (later became No. 236 OTU)
No. 1 Ferry Unit
No. 16 Ferry Unit

Lancaster B Mk I of No. 1653 HCU being loaded with flares *(©RAFM P0019722)*

### G-H Training Flight
Formed at Feltwell in December 1944, this flight operated B Mk I & IIIs with F.N.121 turrets and G-H equipment. They continued in this role until the Spring of 1945, when the HCUs took over G-H training

### Photo-Reconnaissance Squadrons
No. 82 Squadron (PR Mk I)
Benson, Leuchars, Eastleigh (Kenya), Takoradi (Gold Coast) & Wyton - 10/46-12/53
No. 541 Squadron (PR Mk I)
Benson - 6/46-9/46
No. 683 Squadron (PR Mk I)
Fayid (Egypt), Kabrit (Egypt), Eastleigh (Kenya), Khormaksar (Aden) & Habbaniya (Iraq) - 11/50-11/53

### Air-Sea Rescue Units
No. 1348 (ASR) Flight, Pegu, Burma (from 1/46)
No. 179 Squadron (ASR Mk III) Code: OZ
St Eval - 2/46-9/46
No. 203 Squadron (ASR Mk III) Code: CJ
Leuchars, St. Eval, St. Mawgan & Topcliffe - 8/46-3/53
No. 210 Squadron (ASR Mk III) Code: OZ
St. Eval, St. Mawgan & Topcliffe - 6/46-10/52
No. 279 Squadron (ASR Mk III) Code: RL
Beccles - 9/45-3/46
No. 621 Squadron (ASR Mk III)
Aqir (Palestine) & Ein Shemer (Palestine) - 4/46-9/46

### Government & Research
Airborne Forces Experimental Establishment (AFEE)
Aircraft & Armament Experimental Establishment (A&AEE)
Air Photography Development Unit (AFDU)
Anti-Submarine Warfare Development Unit (ASWDU)
Blind Landing Experimental Unit (BLEU)
Bomber Command Instructors School (BCIS) - *This school was formed at Finningley in December 1944 by combining the Night Bombing Tactical School, the Bombing Analysis School and some other units. The school operated the Lancaster (B Mk I & III) up until 1946, when they were replaced with Lincolns.*

Bomber Command Film Unit (BCFU)
Bomber Development Unit (BDU) - *This unit operated both Manchesters and Lancasters from its Gransden Lodge base from July 1942. It moved to Feltwell in April 1943, Newmarket in September 1943 and Lindholme in October 1945. This unit became part of the Central Bomber Establishment at Marham in 1945.*
Central Bomber Establishment (CBE)
Central Gunnery School (CGS)
Central Navigation School (CNS)
Central Signals Establishment (CSE)
Central Photographic Establishment (CPE)
Empire Air Armament School (EAAS)
Empire Air Navigation School (EANS)
Empire Central Flying School (ECFS)
Empire Test Pilots School (ETPS)
Joint Anti-Submarine School (JASS)
National Gas Turbine Establishment (NGTE)
Pathfinder Force Navigation Training Unit (PFF NTU)
Radar Warfare Establishment (RWE)
Royal Aircraft Establishment (RAE)
RAF College
School of Maritime Reconnaissance
Transport Command Development Unit (TCDU)
Telecommunications Flying Unit (TFU) - *Several special installations were tested by this Special Installation Unit of the TFU. Post-war both Lancaster and Lincolns continued in this role.*
Torpedo Development Unit (TDU)- *Lancasters were attached to the special bomb and mine development side of this unit. The title changed to Aircraft Torpedo Development Unit in September 1943. Lincolns were allocated to this unit post-war.*

### Foreign Service
For details of all the foreign operators of the Manchester, Lancaster and Lincoln please refer to Appendix VIII.

Lancaster GR Mk III, RE206, A•F that was used during Glowworm trials. Note the rocket rails under the wing tip *(via R. Sturtivant)*

# Foreign Operators

One of the five ex-RAF Lancasters used by the Aéronavale in the Search and Rescue role

*What follows is a brief run-down of the countries that operated the Lancaster and Lincoln.*

## ARGENTINA

**Argentine Air Force (AAF)**
II Grupode Bombardeo, III Brigada Aerea

**Other AAF Squadrons & Units**
Paratroop Training School, Cordoba

## AUSTRALIA

**Royal Australian Air Force (RAAF)**
No. 460 (RAAF) Sqn - See Entry in RAF Section
No. 463 (RAAF) Sqn - See Entry in RAF Section
No. 467 (RAAF) Sqn - See Entry in RAF Section
No. 460 (RAAF) Sqn - See Entry in RAF Section

**RAAF Squadrons in Australia**
No. 10 Squadron (Lincoln MR.31)
No. 12 Squadron, Amberley (Lincoln B Mk 30) - Renumbered No. 1 Squadron 17/2/48
No. 21 Squadron, Amberley (Lincoln B Mk 30) - Renumbered No. 2 Squadron 17/2/48
No. 23 Squadron, Amberley (Lincoln B Mk 30) - Renumbered No. 6 Squadron 17/2/48
No. 82 (Bomber) Wing (Lincoln B Mk 30), Amberley

**Other RAAF Squadrons & Units - (All Lincoln)**
Air Armaments School, RAAF East Sale
Aircraft Research & Development Unit (ARDU), Laverton
Central Flying School, RAAF East Sale
Detachment B, ARDU

Lincoln Conversion Unit, RAAF East Sale
Lincoln Development Flight
School of Air Navigation, RAAF East Sale
School of Photography, RAAF East Sale
No. 1 Aircraft Performance Unit, Point Cook
No. 1 Air Trials Unit, Salisbury
No. 2 Air Trials Unit, Edinburgh

## CANADA

**Royal Canadian Air Force (RCAF)**
No. 405 (Vancouver) Sqn, RCAF - See Entry in RAF Section
No. 408 (Goose) Sqn, RCAF - See Entry in RAF Section
No. 419 (Moose) Sqn, RCAF - See Entry in RAF Section
No. 420 (Snowy Owl) Sqn, RCAF - See Entry in RAF Section
No. 424 (Tiger) Sqn, RCAF - See Entry in RAF Section
No. 425 (Alouette) Sqn, RCAF - See Entry in RAF Section
No. 426 (Thunderbird) Sqn, RCAF - See Entry in RAF Section
No. 427 (Lion) Sqn, RCAF - See Entry in RAF Section
No. 428 (Ghost) Sqn, RCAF - See Entry in RAF Section
No. 429 (Bison) Sqn, RCAF - See Entry in RAF Section
No. 431 (Iroquois) Sqn, RCAF - See Entry in RAF Section
No. 432 (Leaside) Sqn, RCAF - See Entry in RAF Section
No. 433 (Porcupine) Sqn, RCAF - See Entry in RAF Section
No. 434 (Bluenose) Sqn, RCAF - See Entry in RAF Section

**RCAF Squadrons (in Canada) - Maritime Patrol**
No. 404 Squadron - Mk 10MR
Greenwood, Nova Scotia (4/51-9/55) Code: AF & SP
No. 405 Squadron - Mk 10MR
Greenwood, Nova Scotia (4/50-11/55) Code: AG
No. 407 Squadron - Mk 10MR
Comox, British Columbia (6/52-5/59) Code: RX
No. 408 Squadron - Mk 10P

Rockcliffe, Ontario (1/49-3/64) Code: AK & MN
No. 413 Squadron - Mk 10P
Rockcliffe, Ontario (1/49-4/49) Code: AP

**Miscellaneous RCAF Units**
No. 2 (M) OTU, Greenwood, Novia Scotia - Operated Mk 10MRs in maritime training role. Code: XV
No. 103 Rescue Unit (RU) - Operated Mk 10S&R and one Mk 10S in transport and Air-Sea Rescue roles
No. 107 Rescue Unit (RU) - Operated Mk 10S&R and 10MR in transport and Air-Sea Rescue roles. Code: CX
No. 121 Composite Unit (KU) - Operated Mk 10S&R in transport and Air-Sea Rescue roles. Code: QT
No. 123 Rescue Flight - Operated Mk 10S&R in Air-Sea Rescue role. Code: CJ
No. 405 Squadron, Greenwood, Novia Scotia - Operated Mk 10MR in maritime reconnaissance role
No. 405 (BR) Squadron, Greenwood, Novia Scotia - Operated Mk 10BR in bomber-reconnaissance role & Mk 10MR in maritime reconnaissance role
No.664 Wing - Operated ex-RAF B Mk I/III/X in preparation for Tiger Force (never operational) 5/45-9/45
Air Navigational School, Summerside, Price Edward Island - Operated Mk 10Ns in navigational training role
Central Experimental & Proving Establishment (CEPE) - Operated Mk 10s for trails and evaluation. Code: PX
Central Flying School (CFS) - Operated Mk 10 in multi-engine training role. Code: GS
Winter Experimental Establishment (WEE) - Namao, Alberta - Operated two Mk 10S for climate evaluation trials

## FRANCE

**Aéronavale**
No. 2F, Port Lyautey (Morocco)
No. 5S, Lartique
No. 9S (No. 24 Flotille), Lahn-Bilhoué (later moved to Noumea and Tontouta, New Caledonia)
No. 10F (No. 24 Flotille), Lahn-Bilhoué
No. 10S, St. Raphael
No. 11F, Lartique
No.52S, Morocco
No.55S, Morocco
No.56S, Morocco
ASR Flights at Maison Blanche (Algeria) & Agadir (Morocco)

***Zenith*** **was one of five Mk 10N aircraft built for the Air Navigation School at Summerside, PEI. Four of the aircraft sported names which coincidentally started with the aircraft identifying letter, in this case 'Z'**
*(©Public Archives Canada via J.Lyzun/FlightDecs)*

# Manchester, Lancaster & Lincoln Production

## Manchester

### Prototype

**Air Ministry Specification P.13/36**
Ordered 8th September 1936. Contract No. 624973/37 dated 30th April 1937
• L7246 (First Flight 25/7/39) & L7247 (First Flight 26/5/40)

### Production

**200 Ordered (A.V. Roe, Woodford)**
August 1936. Air Ministry Specification Number 19/37 Contract No. 648770/37 dated 1st July 1937
• L7236-L7584 (L7236-L7526 built as Manchester Mk I/IA [L7483-L7526 = Mk IA], L7527-L7584 built as Lancaster B Mk Is)
L7295 - Rolls-Royce engine test bed
L7297 - Rolls-Royce (Derby) engine test bed
L7305 - Trials aircraft
L7517 - Damaged by fire prior to delivery, subsequently scrapped

**1 Ordered (A.V. Roe, Manchester)**
Contract No. 7625/39 dated 25th July 1937
• R2671
R2671 - Cannon turret trials aircraft

**150 Ordered (Fairey Aviation)**
September 1939 - Cancelled
• R4525-4554, R4572-4611, R4630-4649, R4670-4694 & R4710-4744

**150 Ordered (Armstrong-Whitworth Aircraft)**
September 1939. Contract No. 982865/39 - Cancelled
• R5273-5320, R5339-5380, R53997-5426 & R5448-5477

**200 Ordered (A.V. Roe, Manchester)**
September 1939
• R5482-R5763 (Ordered as Manchesters, but built as Lancaster B Mk Is)

**100 Ordered (Metropolitan-Vickers, Trefford Park)**
1939. Contract No. 982866/39
• R5768-5917 (R5768-R5797 & R5829-R5841 built as Manchester Mk I/IA, R5842-5917 built as Lancaster B Mk Is and delivered to A.V. Roe for assembly & testing)
NOTE: First 13 destroyed by enemy action at factory 23/12/40, serial numbers reallocated)
R5773 - RAE, then to TDU (Gosport), later became 3892M
R5774 - TDU (Gosport), then No. 11 SofTT becoming 3890M
R5830 - A&AEE 11/1/42

**150 Ordered (Armstrong-Whitworth Aircraft)**
Contract No. B.982865/39 dated 12th January 1940 - Cancelled
• W1280-1299, W1319-1350, W1374-1410, W1426-1475 & W1488-1498

## Lancaster

**1st Prototype (BT308)**
First Flight 9th January 1941.

**2nd Prototype (DG595)**
Ordered from A.V. Roe (Chadderton), 1940. First flight 13th May 1941.

Lancaster prototype BT308 (©RAFM P004010)

### B Mk I Production

**200 Ordered (A.V. Roe, Manchester)**
August 1936 Air Ministry Specification Number 19/37
• L7236-L7584 (L7236-L7526 Built as Manchester Mk I/IA, L7527-L7584 Built as Lancaster B Mk Is)
L7527 - A&AEE & Avro, test airframe
L7528 - TFU (Hurn), Avro (Woodford) & AFEE for trials
L7535 - A&AEE, becoming Inst Airframe No 3107M at No. 4 SofTT and No. 12 SofTT.

**200 Ordered (A.V. Roe, Manchester)**
September 1939
• R5482-R5763 (Ordered as Manchesters, but built as Lancaster B Mk Is)
R5489 - Named 'George' by King George VI
R5539 - A&AEE (dived into ground on test flight)
R5546 - Initially to Handling Squadron, A&AEE.
R5548 - Named 'Elizabeth'
R5606 - AFEE, later become Instructional Airframe No. 4130M at No. 4 SofTT
R5611 - Initially with RAE
R5660 - Initially with AFEE
R5694 - To Middle East July 1942. Later issued to No. 207 Squadron

**450 Ordered (A.V. Roe, Chadderton)**
January 1940
• RW4102-4700 (Ordered as Manchester Mk I/IA, but built as Lancaster B Mk Is. Only 207 delivered between July & November 1940.)
W4114 - Retained by Avro, becoming Mk III prototype
W4115 - RAE with F.N.79 turret
W4385-4400, W4414-4463, W4481-4524, W4537-4586, W4600-4641 & W4655-4700 cancelled

**200 Ordered (Metropolitan-Vickers)**
1940
• W4761-5012 (Built as 170 B Mk Is [W4761-4982] and 30 B Mk IIIs [W4983-5012] between September 1942 & May 1943. Delivered to A.V.Roe at Woodford for assembly & testing.)
W4777 - Only served with No 1656 OCU
W4779 - No 1565 OCU, No. 1 LFS and No. 4 SofTT. Became Instructional Airframe No. 49903M.
W5010 - Initially with BDU

**200 Ordered (Metropolitan-Vickers)**
1941
• DV155-DV407 (Built as 91 B Mk Is and 109 B Mk IIIs [W4983-5012] between May & November 1943.)
DV155-276, DV283-290, DV298, DV310, DV383 & 4 = B Mk III
DV277-282, DV291-297, DV299-309, DV311-382, DV385-407 = B Mk I
W4779 - No 1565 OCU, No. 1 LFS and No. 4 SofTT. Became Instructional Airframe No. 49903M.
W5010 - Initially with BDU

**640 Ordered (A.V. Roe, Chadderton)**
1941
• ED303-EE202 (Built as 129 B Mk Is and 491 B Mk IIIs [up to ED782], and all as B Mk IIIs after ED782 between November 1942 & June 1943.)
Note: B Mk Is = ED303-361, ED363-370, ED372-377, ED379-382, ED384-386, ED389, ED391-392, ED394-395, ED409, ED411-412, ED414, ED418, ED420, Ed422, ED425, ED430, ED436, ED439, ED443, ED446-7, ED451, ED498, ED521-522, ED525, ED528, ED533, ED537, ED548, ED550, ED552, ED554, ED567, ED569, ED586, ED588, ED591, ED594, ED600, ED601, ED604, ED610, ED615, ED622, ED631, ED650, ED661, ED692, ED703, ED715, ED732, ED735, ED749, ED751, ED754-755, ED757-758, ED761-763, ED766, ED773-774, ED777-778 & ED780-782
ED735 - Reserve aircraft 617 Squadron

**200 Ordered (Vickers-Armstrong, Castle Bromwich)**
September 1941
• HK535-806 (Originally ordered as B Mk IIs, order changed to B Mk IIIs in February 1943, but eventually all built as B Mk Is from October 1943 to February 1945)
HK543 - Initially with A&AEE
HK710 - Converted to B Mk III, to A&AEE, became Instructional Airframe No 6234M with No. 10 SofTT

**450 Ordered (Armstrong-Whitworth Aircraft)**
April 1942
• LL617-LM296 (Built as 100 B Mk IIs [Hercules XVI], delivered October 1943 to March 1944, and 350 B Mk Is [Merlin 24] delivered between November 1943 and August 1944.)
LL780/G - Initially used by RAE, later used by CFE for ventral and dorsal gun barbette trials as DF•N (1946-7)
LL809 - To Flight Refuelling Ltd as G-AHJT for in-flight refuelling trials
LL813 - Initially used by A&AEE, later operated by de Havilland Ltd
LL937 - RAE
LL948 - Converted to B Mk III

**350 Ordered (A.V. Roe, Yeadon)**
• LM301-LM756 (Built as 10 B Mk Is (LM301-LM310 and 340 B Mk IIIs, delivered between October 1942 and October 1944)
LM306 - Converted to B Mk III
LM307 - Only operated by Conversion unit (No. 1661)
LM308 - Converted to B Mk III

**200 Ordered (A.V. Roe, Yeadon)**
• ME295-ME551 (Built as 44 B Mk Is and 156 B Mk IIIs, delivered between October 1944 and March 1945)
Note: B Mk Is = ME328, Me330, Me350. ME352, ME371-375, ME383-4, ME419-421, ME431-440, ME445-451, ME455-8, ME470, ME475-477, ME479-480, ME482, ME490 & ME495
ME375/G - 433 Squadron ('Guarded' airframe)
ME420-1 - Only operated by Conversion Unit (No. 1654)
ME435 - Only operated by Conversion Unit (No. 1661 as KB•M)
ME436 - Only operated by Conversion Unit (No. 1654)
ME477 - Only operated by Conversion Unit (No. 1660)
ME479 - Only operated by Conversion Unit (No. 1660)
ME480 - Only operated by Conversion Unit (No. 1651)
ME482 - Only operated by Conversion Unit (No. 1651)
ME490 - Only operated by Conversion Unit (No. 1660)
ME495 - Only operated by Conversion Unit (No. 1661)

ADD43 Lancaster B Mk I, PD328, 'Aries' of the CNS at New Plymouth, New Zealand in 1944 (©RAFM P015671)

**Lancaster B Mk II, DG602** *(©Real Photos)*

**250 Ordered (Metropolitan-Vickers)**
May 1942
- ME554-868 (Built as B Mk Is between November 1943 and January 1944.)

ME554 & 555 - 617 Squadron
ME559-562 - 617 Squadron
ME567 - Converted to B Mk III
ME570 - Used by ATDU, Gosport
ME620-623 - Converted to B Mk III
ME625 - Converted to B Mk III
ME698 - Initially used by A&AEE
ME861 - Operated by RAE

**400 Ordered (Armstrong-Whitworth Aircraft)**
- NF906-NG503 (Built as B Mk Is between July 1944 and February 1945.)

NF920 - 617 Squadron, landed in Sweden after Tirpitz raid
NF923 - 617 Squadron
NF992 - 617 Squadron
NG180-181 - 617 Squadron
NG228 - 617 Squadron
NG234 - Converted to B Mk III
NG339 - 617 Squadron
NG340 - 617 Squadron. Later became Instructional Airframe No. 6421M (RAF Locking)
NG408 - Initially used by A&AEE
NG435 - Crashed in transit from Armstrong-Whitworth Aircraft Ltd
NG445 - 617 Squadron
NG465 - Latter fitted with Dart engine in nose by Rolls-Royce for trials (10/47)
NG489 - 617 Squadron. Later became Instructional Airframe No. 6501M (RAF Lindholme)
NG494 - 617 Squadron

**100 Ordered (Austin Motors, Longbridge)**
- NN694-NN816 (Built between March 1944 and February 1945.)

NN723 - Converted to B Mk III
NN786 - Initially used by RAE, subsequently used as target on Shoeburyness ranges
NN801 - B Mk III prototype, used for turret trials

**200 Ordered (Austin Motors, Longbridge)**
March 1943
- NX548-NX794 (Built as 50 B Mk Is and 150 B Mk VIIs between February and November 1945.)

NX558 - Never used operationally, operated by Avro and Austin before storage and scrapping
NX560 - Later became Instructional Airframe No. 5845M

**500 Ordered (Vickers-Armstrong, Chester)**
5th April 1943
- PA158-PA835 (Only 224 built as B Mk Is from June 1944 to September 1945)

PA227-8 - Operated by BCIS
PA315 - Became B.036 in Argentina
PA334 - Used by ATDU, Gosport
PA337-8 - Both passed to Royal Navy 12/46
PA339 - Sold back to Avro 2/48
PA343 - Operated by Miles Aircraft Ltd (3/48) and RAE
PA344 - Became B.037 in Argentina
PA346 - Became B.039 in Argentina
PA348 - Became B.035 in Argentina
PA349 - Became B.036 in Argentina
PA350 - Became B.034 in Argentina
PA365 - Became B.040 in Argentina
PA367 - Used by RAE for night photo trials
PA369 - Became B.038 in Argentina
PA375 - Became B.031 in Argentina
PA376 - Became B.032 in Argentina
PA377 - Became B.033 in Argentina
PA378 - Became B.045 in Argentina
PA379 - Modified to F.E. standard, later PR Mk I
PA380-1 - Modified to F.E. standard
PA382 - Modified to F.E. standard. Later became Instructional Airframe No. 6505M (RAF Yatebury)
PA383-6 - Modified to F.E. standard
PA387 - Modified to F.E. standard. Became WU-25 with the Aéronavale
PA388 - Modified to F.E. standard
PA389 - Modified to F.E. standard. Became WU-24 with the Aéronavale
PA390 - Modified to F.E. standard, later PR Mk I
PA391 - Modified to F.E. standard
PA392 - Modified to F.E. standard. Became WU-36 with the Aéronavale
PA393 - Modified to F.E. standard
PA394 - Modified to F.E. standard, later PR Mk I
PA395 - Modified to F.E. standard. Became WU-32 with the Aéronavale
PA396 - Modified to F.E. standard
PA410-411 - Modified to F.E. standard

PA412 - Modified to F.E. standard. Became WU-38 with the Aéronavale
PA414-5 - Modified to F.E. standard
PA416 - Modified to F.E. standard. Became WU-39 with the Aéronavale
PA417 - Sold to Avro 11/49
PA418 - Modified to F.E. standard
PA419 - Modified to PR Mk 1 by Armstrong-Whitworth Aircraft Ltd
PA420-21 - Modified to F.E. standard
PA424 - Modified to F.E. standard
PA425 - Modified to F.E. standard. Became WU-29 with the Aéronavale
PA426 - Modified to F.E. standard. Became WU-34 with the Aéronavale
PA427-8 - Modified to F.E. standard
PA429 - Modified to F.E. standard. Became WU-46 with the Aéronavale
PA430 - Modified to F.E. standard
PA431 - Modified to F.E. standard. Became WU-43 with the Aéronavale
PA432 - Modified to F.E. standard. Became WU-40 with the Aéronavale
PA433 - Modified to F.E. standard. Later used as gunnery target
PA430 - Modified to F.E. standard. Later became PR Mk 1 and Instructional Airframe No. 6493M
PA436-447 - Modified to F.E. standard
PA452 - Modified to F.E. standard. Became WU-35 with the Aéronavale
PA473 - Modified to F.E. standard
PA474 - Modified to F.E and PR.1 standards. Operated by Flight Refuelling and Cranfield Technical Instituite. Extant - Airworthy - BBMF, RAF Coningsby.
PA475 - Modified to F.E and PR.1 standards
PA476 - Modified to F.E. standard. To Egyptian Air Force, 1950
PA477 - Modified to F.E. standard. Became WU-33 with the Aéronavale
PA478 - Modified to F.E. standard
PA509 - Modified to F.E. standard
Cancelled - PA479-508, PA510-512, PA526-563, PA579-625, PA646-687, PA752-799 & PA816-835.

**800 Ordered (A.V. Roe, Yeadon)**
April 1943
- PA964-PD196 (756 built as 255 B Mk Is, 500 B Mk IIIs and one Lancastrian, delivered between May 1944 and March 1945)

B Mk I - PB592/G, PB643-7, PB671-674, PB686-692, PB695-6, PB703-705, PB708, PB721-727, PB730-732, PB734-757, PB759-768, PB780-PB823, PB836-PB881, PB893-PB936, PB949-PB961, PB981-990, PB995-PB998, PD112-PD139
PB592/G - B Mk I (Special) Grand Slam, A&AEE
PB822 - Ended up as gunnery target on Shoeburyness ranges, 3/49
PB873 - EAAS 'Thor'
PB926 - Became Instructional Airframe No. 5966M at Empire Radio School
PB986 - BCIS, later became Instructional Airframe No. 6304M at RAF Marham
PB995-998 - B Mk I (Special) Grand Slam
PD112-139 - B Mk I (Special) Grand Slam.
NOTE: PD140-146 and PD159-171 reserved for BOAC Lancastrians, later cancelled except PD163
PD174-196 allocated
PD167 and PD179 built and renumbered as VH737 and VH742 respectively

**200 Ordered (Metropolitan-Vickers)**
April 1943
- PD198-PD444 (Built as B Mk Is between June and December 1944)

PD328 - ECNS 'Aries'
PD337 - No. 5 Group Film Unit
PD371 - No. 617 Squadron
PD381 - Converted to B Mk I
PD418 - Became Instructional Airframe No. 5736M, RAF Locking
PD435 - A&AEE
PD438 - Blind Landing Experimental Unit

**200 Ordered (Vickers-Armstrong, Castle Bromw)**
- PP663-PP918 (Only 100 built as B Mk Is from 21st February to 22nd August 1945)

PP688 - Became G-AGUK 'Star Gold' with BSAAC
PP689 - Became G-AGUJ 'Star Pilot' with BSAAC
PP690 - Became G-AGUL 'Star Watch' with BSAAC
PP734 - Became G-AKAM with Flight Refuelling Ltd
PP739 - Became G-AKAB 'Sky Trainer' with Skyways
PP741 - Became G-AJMW and sold to Alitalia, 1948
PP742 - Became G-AKAL with Flight Refuelling Ltd
PP743 - Became G-AKAK with Flight Refuelling Ltd
PP744 - Became G-AGUN 'Star Belle' wiht BSAC/BOAC. Later became G-AHVN with Flight Refuelling Ltd
PP746 - Became G-AGUO 'Star Bright' with BSAAC
PP751 - Became G-AGUM 'Star Ward' with BSAAC
PP755 - Used by RAE to test Bristol Brabazon elevator controls
PP778 - ATDU, Gosport
PP786-7 - ATDU, Gosport
PP789 - EPTS, Cranfield
PP791 - Rolls-Royce
NOTE: PP793-806 and PP880-918 cancelled

**250 Ordered (Metropolitan-Vickers)**
August 1943
- RA500-RA806 (Built as 121 Lancaster B Mk Is, 28 Lincoln B Mk Is and 52 Lincoln B Mk IIs between December 1944 and April 1945)

B Mk Is - RA500-607, RA623-627, RA787-805
RA510 - 1,000th built by Metropolitan-Vickers
RA604-5 - Sent to Near East, 10/46
RA606-7 - Sent to Near East, 12/46
RA623 - Sent to Near East, 10/46
RA624 - Sent to Near East, 11/46
RA625 - Became B-041 with Argentinian Air Force
RA626 - Converted to F.E. standard, and later to PR Mk 1
RA627 - Became WU-49 with Aéronavale
RA787 - Converted to F.E. standard. Became WU-30 with Aéronavale
RA788 - Became B-043 with Argentinian Air Force
RA789 - Became B-044 with Argentinian Air Force
RA792 - Converted to F.E. standard
RA793 - Converted to F.E. standard. Became WU-44 with Aéronavale
RA795 - Converted to F.E. standard. Became WU-50 with Aéronavale
RA796 - Converted to F.E. standard. Became WU-51 with Aéronavale
RA797 - Converted to F.E. standard. Became WU-26 with Aéronavale
RA798 - Became B-042 with Argentinian Air Force
RA799 - Converted to F.E. standard. Became WU-31 with Aéronavale
RA800 - Converted to F.E. standard. Became WU-52 with Aéronavale
RA803 - Converted to F.E. standard. Became WU-52 with Aéronavale
RA805 - Became G-11-29, and later 80001, of the Royal Swedish Air Force (jet engine test-bed)
NOTE: Last seven Lancasters (RA800-806 were transferred, unassembled, for completion by Vickers-Armstrong, Chester)

**370 Ordered (Armstrong-Whitworth Aircraft)**
October 1943
- RF120-RF599 (Built as 65 Lancaster B Mk Is and 105 B Mk IIIs between February and May 1945. Also 2 Lincoln B Mk Is and 198 B Mk IIs were completed)

B Mk Is - RF120-161, RF175-197
RF142 - Operated by Air Survey Flight 1/46
RF144 - Ended up as gunnery target on Shoeburyness ranges, 4/49
RF187 - Became Instructional Airframe No. 6294M at RAF Wyton
RF189 - To Alvis Ltd, Coventry 5/47

**100 Ordered (Vickers-Armstrong, Castle Bromwich)**
December 1943
- RS102-225 (Ordered as Lancaster B Mk IV (Lincoln B Mk I) and B Mk V (Lincoln B Mk II) but changed to Lancaster B Mk Is)

B Mk Is - RS102-147, RS159-198 and RS203-225.
Cancelled before construction started

**250 Ordered (Metropolitan-Vickers)**
March 1944
- ST477-790 [See Below] (Mark not specified in contract, as cancelled before any construction commenced)

Serial Number Allocation- ST477-513, ST528-569, ST583-627, ST641-680, ST693-735 and ST748-790

**37 Ordered (Metropolitan-Vickers)**
- SW243-279 (Built by Metropolitan-Vickers but assembled by A.V. Roe between November and December 1944)

SW244 - A&AEE fitted with Saddle Tanks
SW259 - To Near East
SW279 - To Near East

**34 Ordered (Armstrong-Whitworth Aircraft)**
October 1943
- RF120-RF599 (Built as Lancaster 31 B Mk Is and 13 B Mk IIIs from May 1945)

B Mk Is - SW297-316 (all converted to F.E. standard)
SW296 - Modified to PR Mk 1
SW297 - Became WU-02 with Aéronavale
SW298-301 - To Near East
SW304 - Modified to PR Mk 1
SW308 - Became No. 1803 with the Egyptian Air Force 7/50
SW312 - To Near East
SW308 - Became No. 1808 with the Egyptian Air Force 11/50

**280 Ordered (Vickers-Armstrong, Chester)**
March 1944
- SX558-921 [See Below] (Mark not specified in contract, as cancelled before any construction commenced)

Serial Number Allocation- SX558-589, SX605-648, SX663-698, SX713-759, SX772-813, SX828-863 and SX879-921

**150 Ordered (Austin Motors)**
1944
- TG758-TG799 [See Below] (Mark not specified in contract, as cancelled before any construction commenced)

Serial Number Allocation- TG758-799, TG813-856, TG870-908 and TG921-945

**75 Ordered (Armstrong-Whitworth Aircraft)**
- TW647-TW911 [See Below] (Built as required and all (except TW647) converted to F.E. standard by AWA or Short & Harland in 1946/7)

Serial Number Allocation - TW647-671 & TW858-911
TW647 - Never converted, destroyed in crash 11/47
TW648 - Became WU-28 with Aéronavale
TW651 - Became WU-27 with Aéronavale
TW653 - Became Instructional Airframe No. 6506 at No. 2 Radio School
TW654 - Later modified to PR Mk 1
TW655 - Became WU-17 with Aéronavale
TW656 - Became No. 1809 with Egyptian Air Force, 11/50
TW658 - Later modified to PR Mk 1
TW661 - G-H Survey Mk II fitted (82 Squadron)
TW662 - Later modified to PR Mk 1

TW665 - Later modified to PR Mk 1
TW669 - To Near East 1953. Special photography aircraft
TW671 - Later modified to PR Mk 1
TW859 - Later modified to PR Mk 1
TW868 - Later modified to PR Mk 1
TW884 - Later modified to PR Mk 1
TW890 - Became No. 1807 with Egyptian Air Force, 11/50
TW893 - Became No. 1804 with Egyptian Air Force, 11/50
TW896 - Became Instructional Airframe No. 6638M
TW899 - Later modified to PR Mk 1
TW901 - Later modified to PR Mk 1. Became Instructional Airframe No.
6899M at RAF Spitalgate
TW904-5 - Later modified to PR Mk 1
TW911 - Used as Python test-bed

## 15 Ordered (Metropolitan-Vickers)
• TW915-929 (Built by Metropolitan-Vickers but transferred to
Vickers-Armstrong (Chester) for assembly)

TW915 - Converted to F.E. standard. Became WU-42 with Aéronavale
TW916-7 - Converted to F.E. standard
TW918 - Converted to F.E. standard. Became WU-45 with Aéronavale
TW919 - Converted to F.E. standard
TW920 - Converted to F.E. standard. Became WU-47 with Aéronavale
TW921 - Converted to F.E. standard. Became WU-48 with Aéronavale
TW922 - Converted to F.E. standard. Became WU-37 with Aéronavale
TW927 - Converted to F.E. standard. Became WU-53 with Aéronavale
TW928 - Converted to F.E. standard. Became WU-41 with Aéronavale
TW929 - Became Instructional Airframe No. 6425M

# B Mk II

### Prototypes (DT810 & DT812)
• Ordered from A.V. Roe (Chadderton). Only DT810 built, and
first flown on the 26th November 1941.

### B Mk II Production

#### 200 Ordered (Armstrong-Whitworth Aircraft)
1941
• DS601-852 (Built as B Mk IIs between September 1942 &
October 1943. Up to DS627 had Hercules VI engines, while all
subsequent had Hercules XVIs.)

DS601 - Initially at A&AEE
DS602 - Initially at A&AEE
DS606 - A&AEE, TDU, No. 4 SofTT. Became Instructional Airframe No.
3995M
DS611 - Used for ballistic trials. To No. 1 SofTT becoming 4947M.
DS628 - TFU
DS671 - BDU
DS672 - BDU, becoming 4958M at School of Aero Engineering.
DS687 - TDU (Gosport)
DS708 - RAE for test with servo spring tab controls.
DS819 - AFEE

#### 450 Ordered (Armstrong-Whitworth Aircraft)
April 1942
• LL617-LM296 (Built as 100 B Mk IIs [Hercules XVI], delivered
October 1943 to March 1944, and 350 B Mk Is [Merlin 24]
delivered between November 1943 and August 1944.)

LL619 - Operated by RAE & A&AEE
LL735 - Used as test-bed aicraft for Metrovick jet engines
LL736 - Used by TFU for AGLT trials
LL737 - Used by TFU and RAE for armament trials

### B Mk III Production

#### 640 Ordered (A.V. Roe, Chadderton)
1941
• ED303-EE202 (Built as 129 B Mk Is and 491 B Mk IIIs [up to
ED782], and all as B Mk IIIs after ED782 between November
1942 & June 1943.)
Note: See B Mk I entry for relevant serial numbers
ED371/G - RAE fitted with Lincoln nose
ED388 - Converted to B Mk I
ED474 - Converted to B Mk I
ED485 - Converted to B Mk I
ED565 - Never saw operational service, retained by A.V. Roe before storage
and scrapping (March 1949)
ED595 - Initially retained by A.V.Roe
ED765/G - RAE (4/43), 617 Squadron (6/43)
ED825/G - Dambuster (A&AEE)
ED817/G - Dambuster, 617 Sqn (AJ•C)
ED825/G - Dambuster, 617 Sqn
ED864/G - Dambuster, 617 Sqn (AJ•B) lost during Dams Raid
ED865/G - Dambuster, 617 Sqn (AJ•S) lost during Dams Raid

**Lancaster B Mk III** *(©Real Photos)*

ED866 - Post-war use by Flight Refuelling for in-flight refuelling trials
ED872 - RAE
ED886/G - Dambuster, 617 Squadron
ED887/G - Dambuster, 617 Sqn (AJ•A) lost during Dams Raid
ED906/G - Dambuster, 617 Sqn (AJ•J)
ED909/G - Dambuster, 617 Sqn (AJ•P)
ED910/G - Dambuster, 617 Sqn (AJ•C)
ED912/G - Dambuster, 617 Sqn
ED915/G - Dambuster, 617 Sqn
ED918/G - Dambuster, 617 Sqn (AJ•F)
ED921/G - Dambuster, 617 Sqn (AJ•W)
ED923/G - Dambuster, 617 Sqn (AJ•T)
ED924/G - Dambuster, 617 Sqn
ED925/G - Dambuster, 617 Sqn (AJ•M) lost during Dams Raid
ED927/G - Dambuster, 617 Sqn (AJ•E)
ED929/G - Dambuster, 617 Sqn (AJ•L)
ED932/G - Dambuster, 617 Sqn
ED933/G - Dambuster, 617 Sqn
ED934/G - Dambuster, 617 Sqn (AJ•H)
ED937/G - Dambuster, 617 Sqn (AJ•Z)
EE146 - Converted to B Mk I

#### 550 Ordered (A.V. Roe, Chadderton)
late 1941
• JA672-JB748
JA894 - 617 Squadron & A&AEE
JA903 - Flown by No 1577 Flight to India, 5th October 1943
JA904 - Flown by No 1577 Flight to India, October 1943
JA918 - Initially operated by A&AEE
JA981 - 617 Squadron
JB127 - Converted to B Mk I and oeprated by A&AEE and Rolls-Royce
JB240 - Never delivered, crashed in transit from No. 32MU, 15 September
1943
JB415 - Operated at RAE Farnborough 1943/4
JB456 - Used by A&AEE and Bristol (Filton) for various turret trials, later
became Instructional Airframe No. 5338M
JB457 - A&AEE, later became Instructional Airframe No. 5533M
JB558/G - Trials aircraft with H2S Mk IIIF (Lincoln) radome fitted
JB675 - Converted to B Mk VI, used by Rolls-Royce
JB683/G
JB705 - Used by TFU at Defford
JB713 - Converted to B Mk VI, used by Rolls-Royce

#### 350 Ordered (A.V. Roe, Yeadon)
• LM415—LM756 (Built as 10 B Mk Is (LM301-LM310) and
340 B Mk IIIs, delivered between October 1942 and October
1944)
LM395 - Initially used by RAE
LM448 - Converted to B Mk I
LM451 - Used by AFEE and EAAS only
LM492 - Converted to B Mk I
LM522 - First production aircraft to be fitted with H2S radar
LM681 - Converted to tanker (No. 18) for Flight Refuelling as G-AHJU
LM695 - Converted to B Mk I
LM730 - Used by A&AEE for mine laying trials

#### 200 Ordered (A.V. Roe, Yeadon)
• ME295-ME551 (Built as 44 B Mk Is and 156 B Mk IIIs,
delivered between October 1944 and March 1945)
See B Mk I entry for associated serial numbers
ME325/G
ME351/G
ME354/G
ME358/G
ME364/G
ME380 - Converted to ASR.III, March 1945

ME387/G
ME422/G
ME425/G
ME525 - Converted to ASR.III, March 1945
ME527 - Converted to ASR.III, March 1945
ME528 - Converted to ASR.III, March 1945
ME531 - Became Instructional Airframe No. 6334M (RAF Henlow)
ME540 - Used by Boulton Paul Ltd for trials
ME545 - Became Instructional Airframe No. 6295M (RAF Upwood)

#### 600 Ordered (A.V. Roe, Chadderton)
• ND324-NE181 (Built as B Mk IIIs between December 1943
and May 1944.)
ND348 - Became Instructional Airframe No. 5727M
ND418 - Converted to B Mk VI and initially operated by Rolls-Royce. Later
used by RAE
ND448/G
ND479 - Converted to B Mk VI, operated by Rolls-Royce, Avro and A&AEE
ND558 - Converted to B Mk VI, operated by Rolls-Royce and A&AEE
ND574 - Later operated by Flight Refuelling Ltd
ND575 - Not delivered to RAF
ND673 - Converted to B Mk VI, operated by Rolls-Royce and RAE
ND743 - Operated by RAE
ND784/G - Converted to B Mk VI, operated by Rolls-Royce and Power Jets
(Mamba engine fitted in nose)
ND794/G - Used by A&AEE for test of F.N.150 turret
ND843 - Flight Refuelling Ltd
ND991 - Flight Refuelling Ltd
NE147/G - Operated by BDU, modified by Flight Refuelling Ltd
NE165 - Converted by Rolls-Royce Sept-Dec 1944
NE181 - Earmarked to fly to New Zealand but subsequently scrapped (9/47)

#### 800 Ordered (A.V. Roe, Yeadon)
April 1943
• PA964-PD196 (756 built as 255 B Mk Is, 500 B Mk IIIs and one
Lancastrian, delivered between May 1944 and March 1945)
B Mk III - PA964-999, PB112-158, PB171-213, PB226-267. PB280-308,
PB341-438, PB450-490, PB504542, PB554-596, PB609-642, PB648-670,
PB675-685, PB689-90, PB693-4, PB697-702, PB706-7, PB728-9, PB733,
PB758, PB923, PB962-980 & PB991-994
PB151 - TFU Defford
PB179 - Converted to B Mk III
PB284 - S Mine experiments, RAE
PB414 - Not delivered to RAF, retained for exhibition purposes
PB415 - Converted to B Mk I
PB529 - Converted to ASR.III, then GR Mk III. To Flight Refuelling Ltd, 1951
PB579 - Crashed on initial test flight at Woodford, 11/9/44
PB619 - BBU Woodbridge
PB640 - A&AEE
PB641 - Initially with TFU. Later converted to ASR.III and GR Mk III and to
Flight Refuelling Ltd
PB972 - Flight Refuelling Ltd, Staverton. Later registered G-33-2

#### 700 Ordered (A.V. Roe, Yeadon)
• RE100-RF119 (Built as 87 Lancaster B Mk IIIs, 50 Lincoln
B Mk Is and 112 Lincoln B Mk IIs between March & June 1945)
B Mk IIIs - RE115-140. RE153-188, RE200-226
Note: RE100-114 cancelled
RE115/G - Later converted to GR Mk III
RE116/G - Converted to ASR.III, sent to Middle East and later converted to
GR Mk III
RE117- Converted to ASR.III
RE120- Converted to ASR.III
RE121 - Became Instructional Airframe No. 6586M ar RAF Watton
RE123 - Converted to ASR.III
RE129 - Converted to ASR.III
RE139 - Converted to ASR.III and later to GR Mk III
RE140 - Converted to ASR.III
RE158 - Converted to ASR.III and later to GR Mk III
RE159 - Converted to ASR.III and later to GR Mk III
RE164 - Converted to ASR.III and later to GR Mk III. To Flight Refuelling
RE165 - Converted to ASR.III and later to GR Mk III
RE166 - Converted to ASR.III
RE167-170 - Converted to ASR.III and later to GR Mk III
RE171 - Converted to ASR.III and later to GR Mk III. To ML Aviation and RAE
RE173 - Converted to ASR.III and later to GR Mk III
RE175 - Converted to ASR.III and later to GR Mk III
RE179 - Converted to ASR.III
RE181 - Converted to ASR.III and later to GR Mk III
RE184 - Converted to ASR.III
RE185-7 - Converted to ASR.III and later to GR Mk III
RE188 - Converted to ASR.III
RE189 - Converted to ASR.III and later to GR Mk III
RE205 - Converted to ASR.III and later to GR Mk III
RE206 - Converted to ASR.III and later to GR Mk III. Later to Flight
Refuelling, RAE and ASWDU. Fitted with RP rails
RE207 - Converted to ASR.III and later to GR Mk III
RE208 - Converted to ASR.III
RE211 - Converted to ASR.III and later to GR Mk III
RE216 - Converted to ASR.III

**Lancaster B Mk II, DG602, October 1942** *(©Real Photos)*

RE217 - Converted to ASR.III and later to GR Mk III
RE219 - Became Instructional Airframe No. 6599M at EFS
RE221-222 - Converted to ASR.III and later to GR Mk III

### 370 Ordered (Armstrong-Whitworth Aircraft)
October 1943
- RF120-RF599 (Built as 65 Lancaster B Mk Is and 105 B Mk IIIs between February and May 1945. Also 2 Lincoln B Mk Is and 198 B Mk IIs were completed)

B Mk IIIs - RF198-216, RF229-273 & RE286-326
RF201 - Became Instructional Airframe No. 5848M at No. 12 SofTT
RF210 - Converted to ASR.III and later to GR Mk III
RF2331 - Converted to ASR.III
RF244 - AFDU, Gosport
RF246 - BSAAC, 10/45
RF250 - BSAAC, 10/45
RF258 - Became Instructional Airframe No. 6313M at RAF Waddington
RF268 - RAE, fitted with auto-control guns. Later became Instructional Airframe No. 6206M at RAF St. Eval
RF269 - Converted to ASR.III and later to GR Mk III
RF271 - Converted to ASR.III. Later became Instructional Airframe No. 6673M
RF272-3 - Converted to ASR.III and later to GR Mk III
RF287 - Converted to ASR.III and later to GR Mk III
RF289-92 - Converted to ASR.III and later to GR Mk III
RF294 - Converted to ASR.III and later to GR Mk III
RF300 - Converted to ASR.III
RF301 - Converted to ASR.III. Later became Instructional Airframe No. 6679M at RAF North Coates
RF302 - Converted to ASR.III
RF303 - Converted to ASR.III and later to GR Mk III
RF305-8 - Converted to ASR.III and later to GR Mk III
RF309 - Converted to ASR.III and later to GR Mk III. To Flight Refuelling Ltd 4/51
RF310 - Converted to ASR.III
RF311-3 - Converted to ASR.III and later to GR Mk III
RF314-6 - Converted to ASR.III
RF318-20 - Converted to ASR.III and later to GR Mk III
RF321 - Used by Flight Refuelling Ltd and Dowty for equipment trials
RF322 - Converted to ASR.III and later to GR Mk III
RF323-4 - Converted to ASR.III
RF325 - Converted to ASR.III and later to GR Mk III. Later to ML Aviation and RAE. Last Lancaster in RAF service
RF326 - Converted to ASR.III. Never delivered, crashed on take-off after conversion

### 34 Ordered (Armstrong-Whitworth Aircraft)
October 1943
- RF120-RF599 (Built as Lancaster 31 B Mk Is and 13 B Mk IIIs from May 1945)

B Mk IIIs - SW283-295 (all converted to ASR.III)
SW283-289 - Later converted to GR Mk III
SW293-5 - Later converted to GR Mk III

### 47 Ordered (A.V. Roe, Yeadon)
- SW319-377 (Delivered between June and September 1945)

SW319-20 - Converted to ASR.III, and later to GR Mk III
SW323 - To Middle East, 12/45
SW324 - Converted to ASR.III, and later to GR Mk III
SW325 - Converted to ASR.III, and later to GR Mk III. To Middle East 11/52
SW326 - Converted to ASR.III
SW327 - Converted to ASR.III, and later to GR Mk III
SW328 - Became Instructional Airframe No. 6761M at 10 SofTT
SW329 - Converted to ASR.III
SW330 - Converted to ASR.III, and later to GR Mk III
SW334 - Converted to ASR.III, and later to GR Mk III. To Flight Refuelling Ltd
SW336 - Converted to ASR.III, and later to GR Mk III
SW337 - Converted to ASR.III
SW338 - Converted to ASR.III, and later to GR Mk III
SW339 - To Middle East, 12/45-5/46
SW341 - To Middle East, 12/45-6/46
SW342 - To Flight Refuelling Ltd 9/45, Air Service Training 3/47, and Armstrong Siddeley Motors 1/49
SW343 - To Middle East, 12/45-6/46
SW344 - Converted to ASR.III, and later to GR Mk III
SW345 - To Middle East, 12/45-6/46
SW359 - To Middle East, 12/45-6/46
SW361 - Converted to ASR.III
SW362-70 - Converted to ASR.III, and later to GR Mk III
SW371 - Converted to ASR.III
SW372-4 - Converted to ASR.III, and later to GR Mk III
SW377 - Converted to ASR.III, and later to GR Mk III

### 19 Ordered (A.V. Roe, Yeadon)
- TX263-290 [See Below] (Delivered as 11 B Mk IIIs and 8 Lancastrian C Mk IVs)

TX263 - Converted to ASR.III
TX264-5 - Converted to ASR.III, and later to GR Mk III
TX266 - Converted to ASR.III

**Lancaster B Mk VII** (©RAFM P005193)

TX267-8 - Converted to ASR.III, and later to GR Mk III
TX269 - Converted to ASR.III
TX270-3 - Converted to ASR.III, and later to GR Mk III

### B Mk VII Production

### 200 Ordered (Austin Motors, Longbridge)
March 1943
- NX548-NX794 (Built as 50 B Mk Is and 150 B Mk VIIs between February and November 1945. All B Mk VIIs were to F.E. standard)

NX611 - Became WU-15 with Aéronavale, later G-ASXX. Extant (East Kirkby)
NX612 - Never used operationally, stored and then to Austin Motors before scrapping
NX613 - Became WU-1 with Aéronavale
NX615 - Became WU-12 with Aéronavale
NX616 - Became WU-22 with Aéronavale
NX618 - Used for Dopler trials at TFU, 1949
NX619 - Became WU-11 with Aéronavale
NX620 - Became WU-20 with Aéronavale
NX621 - Became WU-19 with Aéronavale
NX622 - Became WU-16 with Aéronavale
NX623 - Became WU-14 with Aéronavale
NX627 - Became WU-09 with Aéronavale
NX679 - Became Instructional Airframe No. 6735M (RAF Cosford)
NX634 - Became Instructional Airframe No. 6216M (No 12 SofTT)
NX636 - RAE, used for aerial photography work
NX639 - Sold to France 10/53
NX663 - Became WU-10 with Aéronavale
NX664 - Became WU-21 with Aéronavale
NX665 - Became WU-13 with Aéronavale. Extant
NX666 - Became WU-05 with Aéronavale
NX667 - Became WU-23 with Aéronavale
NX668 - Became WU-24 with Aéronavale
NX669 - Became WU-18 with Aéronavale
NX679 - 617 Squadron
NX703 - Became WU-08 with Aéronavale
NX726 - Became G-ALVC of Eagle Aviation
NX735 - Became Instructional Airframe No. 6713M (No. 12 SofTT)
NX737 - Became Instructional Airframe No. 6736M
NX739 - Operated by English Electric and 617 Squadron. Later loaned to Silver City Airways
NX744 - 617 Squadron (KC•J)
NX745 - 617 Squadron
NX755 - 617 Squadron
NX757 - 617 Squadron
NX776 & 777 - 617 Squadron
NX780 - 617 Squadron
NX783 - 617 Squadron (KC•G)
NX785-7 - 617 Squadron (786-KC•H)
NX789-91 - 617 Squadron

### 240 Ordered (Vickers-Armstrong, Chester)
- RT140-456 (See Below)

Serial Number Allocation - RT140-183, RT197-228, RT245-290, RT315-350, RT362-403 and RT417-456
Cancelled before construction started

### 68 Ordered (Austin Motors, Longbridge)
- RT670-750 (30 built between November and December 1945.)

RT671 - To Middle East 2/46
RT673 - Sold to France 4/53, became FCL-04
RT674 - Sold to France 4/53
RT676 - To Far east 2/46
RT679 - Sold to France, became FCL-05
RT681 - Became Instructional Airframe No. 6748M at RAF Cosford
RT682 - Became WU-04 with Aéronavale
RT688 - Ended up as gunnery target on Shoeburyness ranges 1/51
RT689 - Sold to France, became FCL-03
RT693 - Sold to France, became FCL-01
RT697 - Became WU-03 with Aéronavale
RT698 - Became WU-06 with Aéronavale
RT699 - Became WU-07 with Aéronavale
NOTE: RT7001-1 and RT713-750 cancelled

## Lancaster Foreign Production

### B Mk X Production

### 300 Ordered (Victory Aircraft, Canada)
- KB700-999 (Up to KB774 had Merlin 38s installed, all subsequent aircraft had Merlin 224s. Delivered between September 1943 and March 1945)

KB702-3 - Retained in Canada
KB721 - Initially used by A&AEE
KB729 - Became G-AKDO, later modified as 10P for RCAF
KB730 - Retained in Canada
KB783 - Initially used by A&AEE for trials of Martin mid-upper turret
KB790 - Retained in store, never issued to unit (scrapped 5/47)
KB805 - Used by TFU for American remote control gun trials
KB825 - Crashed in transit, 25th September 1944
KB882 - Returned to Canada and converted to 10AR
KB883 - Modified to 10MP (RX883) 6/45
KB844 - Returned to Canada and became Instructional Airframe No. A526
KB885 - Became CF-IMF with Spartan Air Services
KB889 - Returned to Canada and converted to 10MP
KB890 - Returned to Canada and converted to 10MP
KB892 - Returned to Canada and converted to 10MP
KB893 - Returned to Canada and converted to 10MP
KB894 - Returned to Canada and converted to 10MR
KB901 - Returned to Canada and converted to 10MR
KB902 - Returned to Canada and became Instructional Airframe No. 606C
KB903 - Returned to Canada and converted to 10MR
KB904 - Returned to Canada and converted to 10MP
KB907 - Returned to Canada and converted to 10ASR, later sold to Spartan Air Services (4/56)
KB909 - Returned to Canada and sold to Spartan Air Services (4/46)
KB914 - Returned to Canada and converted to 10MP
KB919 - Returned to Canada and converted to 10MP
KB920 - Returned to Canada and converted to 10MP
KB932 - Returned to Canada and became Instructional Airframe No. 542C
KB925 - Returned to Canada and converted to 10MP
KB927 - Returned to Canada and converted to 10MR
KB929 - Returned to Canada and converted to 10MP
KB934 - Returned to Canada and converted to 10MR
KB937 - Returned to Canada and converted to 10MP
KB938 - Returned to Canada and converted to 10MP
KB940 - Returned to Canada and converted to 10MP
KB943 - Returned to Canada and converted to 10MP
KB944 - Returned to Canada and converted to 10S
KB945 - Returned to Canada and converted to 10MP
KB946 - Returned to Canada and converted to 10MP
KB948 - Returned to Canada and converted to 10MP
KB949 - Returned to Canada and converted to 10MP
KB950 - Returned to Canada and converted to 10MP
KB954 - Returned to Canada and converted to 10MR
KB955 & 956 - Returned to Canada and converted to 10MP
KB959 - Returned to Canada and converted to 10MP
KB961 - Returned to Canada and converted to 10MP
KB964 - Returned to Canada and converted to 10MP
KB965 - Returned to Canada and converted to 10BR
KB966 & 967 - Returned to Canada and converted to 10MR
KB971 - Not delivered to RAF, to RCAF, crashed during flight testing
KB972 - Returned to Canada and converted to 10MR
KB973 & 974 - Returned to Canada and converted to 10MP
KB976 - Returned to Canada and converted to 10AR
KB977 - Returned to Canada and converted to 10MP
KB986 - Returned to Canada and converted to 10N
KB991 - Returned to Canada and converted to 10BR
KB992 - Returned to Canada and converted to 10MR
KB995 - Returned to Canada and converted to 10MR
KB996 & 997 - Returned to Canada and converted to 10MP
KB999 - Presentation aircraft 'Malton Mike'. Returned to Canada and converted to 10MR

### 200 Ordered (Victory Aircraft, Canada)
- FM100-299 (Only 130 completed, FM229 being last B Mk X produced)

FM110 - Modified to 10MR 6/45
FM115 - Modified to 10MR 6/45
FM120 - Modified to 10P 6/45
FM122 - Modified to 10P 6/45
FM124 - Allocated (Canadian) Instructional Airframe No. A552
FM127 - Allocated (Canadian) Instructional Airframe No. B551
FM128 - Modified to 10MR 8/45
FM136 - Modified to 10MP 8/45
FM140 - Modified to 10MP 8/45
FM148 - Undertook winterisation Trials in Canada during 1946/7 (FC•D)
FM159 - Modified to 10MP 9/45
FM172 - Modified to 10MP 11/45
FM173 - Modified to 10MP 11/45
FM-184 - Became CF-CMX
FM-185 - Became (G-AKDP) CF-CMY used by Trans-Canada Air Lines
FM-186 - Became (G-AKDR) CF-CMZ used by Trans-Canada Air Lines
FM-187 - Became (G-AKDS) CF-CNA used by Trans-Canada Air Lines
FM199 - Modified to 10P 11/45
FM205 - Modified to 10O Orenda test-bed 1951
FM206 - Modified to 10N 'Northern Star' 8/45
FM207 - Last Canadian Lancaster accepted by RAF, all subsequent aircraft retained in Canada
FM208 - Modified to 10N 'Polaris', later became CF-KHH
FM209 - Retained by Avro (Canada) for Orenda trials work
FM210 - Modified to 10MR
FM211 - Modified to 10N, 6/49
FM212 - Modified to 10P
FM213 - Modified to 10MR
FM214 - Modified to 10P
FM215 - Modified to 10P
FM216 - Modified to 10P
FM217 - Modified to 10P
FM218 - Modified to 10P
FM219 - Modified to 10MR
FM220 - Modified to 10MP
FM221 - Prototype 10BR
FM221 - Modified to 10SR, later used by Spartan Air Services
FM223 - Modified to 10MR
FM224 - Modified to 10MR
FM225-8 - All modified to 10MP

# Lancastrian

## Prototype (C Mk I)
Air Ministry Specification
- 1 Ordered (A.V. Roe, Yeadon)

VB673 (Ordered for BOAC)
VB673 - Registered G-AGLF, certificate of airworthiness issued 7th February 1945

## Lancastrian (Special)
2 Ordered (A.V. Roe)
- VH737 & VH742

VH737 - Originally PD176, delivered 8th August 1945
VH742 - Delivered 31st October 1945

## C Mk I Production

### 16 Ordered (A.V. Roe)
- VD238-VD253 [See Below] (Lancaster airframes earmarked for conversion to Lancastrian, only three converted)

VD238 - Became G-AGLS
VD241 - Became G-AGLT
VD253 - Became G-AGLU

### 28 Ordered (A.V. Roe)
- VF137-VF167 [See Below] (Ordered for BOAC)

Serial Number Allocation - VF137-156 and VF160-167
VF137 - Became G-AGMR
VF138 - Became G-AGMS
VF139 - Became G-AGMT
VF140 - Became G-AGMU
VF141 - Became G-AGMV
VF142 - Became G-AGMW
VF143 - Became G-AGMX
VF144 - Became G-AGMY
VF145 - Became G-AGMJ
VF146 - Became G-AGMK
VF147 - Became G-AGML
VF148 - Became G-AGMM
VF149 - Became G-AGMN
VF150 - Became G-AGMO
VF151 - Became G-AGMP
VF152 - Became G-AGMA
VF153 - Became G-AGMB
VF154 - Became G-AGMC
VF155 - Became G-AGMD
VF156 - Became G-AGME
VF160 - Became G-AGMF
VF161 - Became G-AGMG
VF162 - Became G-AGMH
VF163 - Became G-AGLV
VF164 - Became G-AGLW
VF165 - Became G-AGLX
VF166 - Became G-AGLY
VF167 - Became G-AGLZ

## C Mk II Production

### 20 Ordered (A.V. Roe, Manchester)
February 1945
- VL967-986 [See Below] (This batch actually delivered after VM701-738 order)

NOTE: VL982-986 cancelled

### 18 Ordered (A.V. Roe, Manchester)
February 1945
- VM701-738 [See Below] (Delivered from October 1945 to January 1946)

Serial Number Allocation - VM701-704 and VM725-738

## C Mk IV Production

### 19 Ordered (A.V. Roe, Yeadon)
- TX263-290 [See Below] (Delivered as 11 Lancaster B Mk IIIs and 8 Lancastrian C Mk IVs)

Serial Number Allocation - TX283-290

# Lincoln

## Prototype

### Air Ministry Specification
- 3 Ordered (A.V. Roe, Yeadon)

PW925, 929 & 932 (Ordered as 'Lancaster Mk IV' and 'V')
PW925 - Delivered to RAF 22nd October 1945
PW929 - Delivered to RAF 13th November 1945
PW932 - Delivered to RAF 15th January 1946

## B Mk I Production

### 250 Ordered (Metropolitan-Vickers)
August 1943
- RA500-RA806 (Built as 121 Lancaster B Mk Is, 28 Lincoln B Mk Is and 52 Lincoln B Mk IIs between January and September 1945)

B Mk Is - RA628-655

---

**Lancaster B Mk I, R5868 of No 467 Squadron visiting a USAF base** (©RAFM P007009)

---

### 700 Ordered (A.V. Roe, Yeadon)
- RE100-RF119 (Built as 87 Lancaster B Mk IIIs, 50 Lincoln B Mk Is and 112 Lincoln B Mk IIs between March & July 1945)

B Mk Is - RE227-268 and RE281-288
Note: RE425-435, RE449-493, RE518-561, RE575-605, RE621-670, RE683-726, RE740-785, RE798-839, RE853-895, RE918-955, RE967-999 and RF111-119 cancelled

### 370 Ordered (Armstrong-Whitworth Aircraft)
October 1943
- RF120-RF599 (Built as 65 Lancaster B Mk Is and 105 B Mk IIIs between February and May 1945. Also 2 Lincoln B Mk Is and 198 B Mk IIs were completed)

B Mk Is - RF333-334
RF333 - Delivered 4th April 1945
RF334 - Delivered 7th May 1945

### 100 Ordered (Vickers-Armstrong, Castle Bromwich)
December 1943
- RS102-225 (Ordered as Lancaster B Mk IV (Lincoln B Mk I) and B Mk V (Lincoln B Mk II) but changed to Lancaster B Mk Is)

Cancelled before construction started

### 150 Ordered (Vickers-Armstrong, Castle Bromwich)
March 1944
- SR707-907 [See Below] (Ordered as Lancaster B Mk IV (Lincoln B Mk I) and B Mk V (Lincoln B Mk II))

Serial Number Allocation - SR707-749, SR766-790, SR814-851 and SR864-907
Cancelled before construction started

### 800 Ordered (A.V. Roe, Yeadon)
March 1944
- SS341-ST475 [See Below] (Ordered as Lancaster B Mk IV (Lincoln B Mk I) and B Mk V (Lincoln B Mk II), only six built)

Serial Number Allocation (B Mk I/II) - SS341-386, SS399-435, SS449-480, SS549-589, SS603-650, SS664-698, SS713-758, SS773-815, SS828-869, SS882-925, SS937-968, SS980-999, ST113-157, ST171-215, ST228-269, ST283-327, ST339-369, ST381-425 and ST438-475
SS713-4 - Only B Mk Is built

## B Mk II (later B.2) Production

### 250 Ordered (Metropolitan-Vickers)
August 1943
- RA500-RA806 (Built as 121 Lancaster B Mk Is, 28 Lincoln B Mk Is and 52 Lincoln B Mk IIs between September and December 1945)

B Mk IIs - RA656-658, RA661-693 and RA709-724.
Note: RA725-749 and RA763-786 cancelled

### 700 Ordered (A.V. Roe, Chadderton)
- RE100-RF119 (Built as 87 Lancaster B Mk IIIs, 50 Lincoln B Mk Is and 112 Lincoln B Mk IIs between July 1945 and April 1946)

B Mk IIs - RE289-325, RE338-380 and RE393-424
Note: RE425-435, RE449-493, RE518-561, RE575-605, RE621-670, RE683-726, RE740-785, RE798-839, RE853-895, RE918-955, RE967-999 and RF111-119 cancelled

### 370 Ordered (Armstrong-Whitworth Aircraft)
October 1943
- RF120-RF599 (Built as 65 Lancaster B Mk Is and 105 B Mk IIIs, 2 Lincoln B Mk Is and 198 B Mk IIs delivered between March 1945 and May 1947)

B Mk IIs - RF329-332, RF335-370, RF383-427, RF440-485, RF498-539 and RF553-577

### 100 Ordered (Vickers-Armstrong, Castle Bromwich)
December 1943
- RS102-225 (Ordered as Lancaster B Mk IV (Lincoln B Mk I) and B Mk V (Lincoln B Mk II) but changed to Lancaster B Mk Is)

Cancelled before construction started

### 150 Ordered (Vickers-Armstrong, Castle Bromwich)
March 1944
- SR707-907 [See Below] (Ordered as Lancaster B Mk IV (Lincoln B Mk I) and B Mk V (Lincoln B Mk II))

Serial Number Allocation - SR707-749, SR766-790, SR814-851 and SR864-907
Cancelled before construction started

### 800 Ordered (A.V. Roe, Yeadon)
March 1944
- SS341-ST475 [See Below] (Ordered as Lancaster B Mk IV (Lincoln B Mk I) and B Mk V (Lincoln B Mk II), only six built)

Serial Number Allocation (B Mk I/II) - SS341-386, SS399-435, SS449-480, SS549-589, SS603-650, SS664-698, SS713-758, SS773-815, SS828-869, SS882-925, SS937-968, SS980-999, ST113-157, ST171-215, ST228-269, ST283-327, ST339-369, ST381-425 and ST438-475
SS715-8 - Only B Mk IIs built

### 350 Ordered (Armstrong-Whitworth Aircraft)
- SX923-SZ493 [See Below] (Only 60 delivered between May 1947 and August 1949)

Serial Number Allocation - SX923-958, SX994-999, SZ113-158, SZ172-215, SZ228-259, SZ275-306, SZ319-363, SZ380-415, SZ429-471 and SZ488-493
SX923-958 and SX970-993 - Only examples delivered from this contract
NOTE: SX994-999, SZ113-158, SZ172-215, SZ228-259, SZ275-306, SZ319-363, SZ380-415, SZ429-471 and SZ488-493 all cancelled

### 21 Ordered (Armstrong-Whitworth Aircraft)
- WD122-149 [See Below] (Delivered between May 1950 and March 1951)

Serial Number Allocation - WD122-133 and WD141-149

### 18 Ordered (Armstrong-Whitworth Aircraft)
- B-013 to B-030 (For Argentina)

## Lincoln Foreign Production

### Canada B Mk XV Production

1 Aircraft Completed (Victory Aircraft, Canada)
- FM300

### Australia B Mk 30 Production

#### 54 Aircraft Completed
(Government Aircraft Factories, Fisherman's Bend, Melbourne, Australia)
- A73-1 - A73-54

### Australia Mk 31 (Later MR.31) Production

#### 19 Aircraft Completed
(Government Aircraft Factories, Fisherman's Bend, Melbourne, Australia)
- A73-55 - A73-73

# Manchester, Lancaster & Lincoln Bibliography

*Architect of Wings - A Biography of Roy Chadwick, Designer of the Lancaster Bomber.*
**Harald Penrose**
Airlife Publishing © 1985

*Avro Lancaster*
**Ken Delve**
The Crowood Press © 1999
ISBN: 1 86126 222 1

*The Avro Lancaster B.I/III*
**Francis K. Mason**
Aston Publications ©1989

*Avro Lancaster I - Profile No. 65*
**Michael Garbett & Brian Goulding**
Profile Publications Ltd ©

*Avro Lancaster II - Profile No. 235*
**Bruce Robertson**
Profile Publications Ltd ©

*Avro Manchester - Profile No. 260*
**Chaz Bowyer**
Profile Publications Ltd © 1974

*Avro Manchester - The Legend Behind the Lancaster*
**Robert Kirby**
Midland Counties Publications © 1995
ISBN: 1 85780 028 1

*Battle of Britain Memorial Flight*
BBMF © 1983

*The Design and Development of the Lancaster*
**D.C. Wood**
Royal Aeronautical Society (Manchester Branch) © 1991

*Flying Wartime Aircraft; ATA Ferry Pilot's Handling Notes for Seven WWII Aircraft*
**David & Charles © 1972**
ISBN 0 7153 53503

*The Lancaster Manual - RAF Museum Series No. 5*
Arms & Armour Press © 1977

*Lancaster - RAF Heavy Bomber*
**Dan Patterson & AVM Ron Dick**
Airlife Publishing Ltd © 1996
ISBN: 1 85310 775 1

*The Lancaster at War Vol 1*
**Michael Garbett & Brian Goulding**
Ian Allan

*The Lancaster at War Vol 2*
**Michael Garbett & Brian Goulding**
Ian Allan

*The Lancaster at War Vol 3*
**Michael Garbett & Brian Goulding**
Ian Allan © 1984

*Lancaster - The Story of a Famous Bomber*
**Bruce Robertson**
Harleyford Publications Ltd ©1964

*Lincoln at War 1944-1966*
**Mike Garbett & Brian Goulding**
Ian Allan © 1979 & 1999
ISBN: 0 7110 0847 7

*Manchester*
**Cliff Minney**
Air-Britain © 1990

---

**Official Publications**

*Air Publication (A.P.)*
Manchester Mk I/IA - A.P. 1600A
Lancaster B Mk I - A.P.2062A
Lancaster B Mk II - A.P. 2062B
Lancaster B Mk III - A.P. 2062C
Lancaster B Mk X - A.P. 2062F
Lancaster B Mk VII - A.P.2062H
Lancaster ASR Mk I/II - A.P. 2062J/K
Lancaster ASR Mk III - A.P. 2062K
Lancaster GR Mk III - A.P. 2062M
Lincoln B Mk I - A.P. 2847A
Lincoln B.2 - A.P. 2847B
B.P. Gun Turrets - A.P. 1659C
B.P. Type D (Lincoln) - A.P. 2796J
B.P. Type F Mk I (Lincoln) - A.P. 2796H
Bristol Gun Turrets - A.P. 1659B
Bristol Type 17 - A.P. 2768E
FN Gun Turrets - A.P. 1659A
F.N.121 - A.P. 2799A
F.N.121 Mk I - A.P. 2799F
F.N.150 Mk I & IV - A.P. 2799H
F.N.82 Mk I - A.P. 2799Q
War Equipment Schedule (Lancaster B Mk I/III) - A.P.3064

---

**General Titles**

*Aircraft of the Royal Air Force since 1918*
**Owen Thetford**
Putnam Publishing Ltd. © 1957, 58, 62, 68, 71, 76, 79 & 1988
ISBN 0 85177 810 0

*Aircraft of World War 2*
**B.Gunston**
Octopus Books Ltd. © 1980

*Armament of British Aircraft 1909-1939*
**H.F. King**
Putnam Publishing Ltd. © 1971

*Avro Aircraft since 1908*
**A.J. Jackson**
Putnam ©1990

*The Bomber Command War Diaries, An Operational Reference Book 1939-45*
**Martin Middlebrook & C. Eberitt**
Viking © 1985

*Bomber Group at War*
**Chaz Bowyer**
Ian Allan © 1981

*Bomber Squadrons of the RAF and Their Aircraft*
**Philip J.R. Moyes**
MacDonald & Co. © 1964

*Bombing Colours 1937-1973*
**Michael J.F. Bowyer**
Patrick Stephens Ltd ©1973

*British Civil Aircraft since 1919. Volume 2*
**A.J. Jackson**
Putnam Publishing Ltd. © 1973

*British Military Aircraft Serials 1878-1987*
**Bruce Robertson**
Midland Counties Publications © 1987

*Camouflage & Markings; RAF 1939-45*
**M.Reynolds**
Argus Books. ©1992

*Cologne - The First 1,000 Bomber Raid*
**C. Messenger**
Ian Allan © 1982

*Combat Aircraft of World War Two*
**E.C. Weal, J.A. Weal & R.F. Barker**
Arms & Armour Press © 1977
ISBN: 0 85368 191 0

*The Encyclopedia of the Worlds Combat Aircraft*
**B. Gunston**
Hamlyn © 1976

*Famous Aircraft Cockpits 2*
**H. Seo**
Asahi Shimbun © 1981

*The Hardest Victory, RAF Bomber Command in the Second World War*
**Denis Richards**
John Curtis & Hodder & Stoughton © 1994

*I Caccia Della Seconda Guerra Mondiale*
**C. Barbieri**
Ermauno Albertelli © 1971

*The Illustrated Encyclopedia of Combat Aircraft of World War II*
**by B. Gunston**
Salamander Books © 1978

*In the Cockpit. Flying the World's Great Aircraft*
**A. Robinson**
Orbis Publications © 1981

*The Jet Aircraft of the World*
**William Green & Roy Cross**
MacDonald © 1955

*Lincolnshire Air War 1939-1945*
**Sid Finn**
Aero Litho Co (Lincoln) Ltd © 1973

*Les Avions Britanniques aux Couleurs Françaises Pt.1*
**Jean Jacques Petit**
Airdoc ©

*Les Avions Britanniques Leurs Exploits dans la Guerre Aerienne*
Bureau d'Information Allie

*Maximum Efforts - The Story of the North Lincolnshire Bombers*
**Patrick Otter**
Archive Publications © 1990

*No. 83 Squadron 1917-1969*
**F.E. Harper & R.G. Low**
R.G. Low © 1992

*No. 207 Squadron 1942-1943*
**Barry Goodwin & Raymond Glynne-Owen**
Quarks Books © 1994

Operation Millennium - Bomber Harris's Raid on Cologne, May 1942
**E. Taylor**
Robert Hale © 1987

RCAF Squadrons & Aircraft
**Kostenuk & Griffith**
National Museum of Canada © 1977

The Right Line, The Royal Air Force in the European War 1939-1945
**John Terraine**
Hodder & Stoughtoon © 1985

Rolls-Royce Aero Engines
**Bill Gunston**
Patrick Stephens Ltd © 1989

Royal Air Force Bomber Command and Its Aircraft (Vol 1 & 2)
Ian Allan ©

Royal Air Force Bomber Command Losses of the Second War, 1941
**W.R. Chorley**
Midland Counties Publications © 1993

Royal Air Force Bomber Command Losses of the Second War, 1942
**W.R. Chorley**
Midland Counties Publications © 1994

RAF Bombers of WWII (Vol 1)
**Hylton Lacey**

Royal Air Force - The Aircraft in Service since 1918
**C. Bowyer & M. Turner**
Hamlyn © 1981

The Royal Air Force Yearbook 1976
**Ducimus © 1976**

The Royal Canadian Air Force at War 1939-1945
**L. Milberry & H. Halliday**
CANAV Books ©1990

The Story of a Lanc
**Goulding, Garbett & Partridge**
RAF Scampton © 1974

Squadron Codes 1937-56
**M.J.F. Bowyer and J.D.R. Rawlings**
Patrick Stephens Ltd © 1979

The Squadrons of the Royal Air Force and Commonwealth 1918-1988
**J.J. Halley**
Air-Britain © 1988

The Stategic Air Offensive Against Germany, Vols I-IV
**Sir Charles Webster and Noble Frankland**
HMSO © 1961

The Thousand Plan - The Story of the First 1,000 Bomber Raid on Cologne
**Ralph Parker**
Chatto & Windus © 1964

Very Special Lancaster
**F.E. Dymond**
RAF Museum

Warplanes of the Second World War
**William Green**
MacDonald & Jane's

War Planes of the Second World War - Volume 2
**W. Green**
MacDonald © 1961

Warplanes of the World 1918-39
**M.J.H. Taylor**
Ian Allan © 1981

What Were They Like to Fly?
**D.H. Clark**
Ian Allan © 1964

World Aircraft, WWII. Volume 1
**E. Angelucci & P. Matricardi**
Sampson Law Ltd © 1978

World War II Aircraft Fact Files, RAF Bombers Part 1
**William Green and Gordon Swanborough**
MacDonald & Janes © 1979

---

**Periodicals & Journals**

Aeromilitaria: 1993 No 1
Aeronautics: April 1965
(The) Aeroplane: 23/10/42, 25/5/45
Aeroplane Monthly: November 1979, February 1980, March 1980, May 1981, July 1981, June 1982, December 1982, November 1983, June 1986, June 1988, July 1988, August 1988, January 1989, February 1991, April 1991, May 1991, June 1992, May 1995, December 1998, January 1999, March 1999, June 1999, August 1999, February 2000
Aerospace: January 1991
Air-Britain Digest: Vol 34 No. 1, Spring 1994
Air Classics Quarterly Review: Vol.3 No.2
Air Clues: April 1995
Aircraft Illustrated: February 1996
Aircraft Modelworld: June 1987, April 1988, September 1989
Aircraft Production: Vol.5 No.51 [Jan 1943], Vol.5 No.54 [April 1943], February 1943
Air Enthusiast: No.25, Sept/Oct 1995, No. 38, March/April 2000
Airfix Magazine: August 1973, December 1979, June 1981, March 1982, May 1982, October 1983
Air International: December 1981
Air Pictorial: November 1988, May 1989, November 1989, May 1993, April 1995
Aviation Journal: 1976 No. 25
Aviation News: Vol.2 No.4, Vol.16 No.15, Vol.18 No.17, Vol.22 No.4
Bomber Command Association Newsletter: No.12 (October 1989)
Bomber Command News: 1991 (p25-6), 1993 (p28)
CAHS - Flying the Manchester by W.J. (Mike) Lewis (Journal of the Canadian Aviation Historical Society) Vol.32 No. 2 September 1994
Control Column; Vol.13 No.8
Flight: 13/8/42, 31/5/45, 26/10/56
Flightlines: Fall/Winter 1988
Flypast: January 1983, February 1983, May 1983, February 1985, February 1986, March 1986, October 1991, November 1991, December 1991, 'Bomber Special' 1991, February 1993, January 1995, May 1995, September 1995, August 1996, November 1998, February 1999, March 1999, October 1999
IPMS Quarterly: Vol 1 No. 1
Le Fana de l'Aviation: April 1984
Military Aviation Review: June/July 1981
Pilot: January 1973, August 1987, February 1991
RAE News: December 1979
RAF News: May/June 1986, Feb 21/Mar 6 1986
Roundel: October 1994
Scale Aircraft Modelling: Vol 6 No. 2 (November 1983), Vol 12 No 4 (Jan 1990), Vol 20 No. 12 (February 1999)
Scale Models & Scale Models International: March 1970, August 1975, January 1976
Tamiya Model Magazine International: Spring 1987
Vintage News Annual: 1998-1999
Warbirds Worldwide Journal: No.47
Wingspan: Nov/Dec 1986, June 1993

Note: The above periodical and journals listing is not, and cannot be, complete. The list above gives a broad overview of the subject and is offered as a reference guide for all those wishing to build the type. Further research into suitable source material is, however, still recommended.

# Index

Please note, this index does not reference the appendices.

No. 207 Squadron by Lancaster B Mk III, PB782, EM•Y at RAF Spilsby in 1945 (©RAFM P014999)

A group shot of No. 9 Squadron in front of Lancaster B Mk III, WJ•Z on the 7th September 1943 (©RAFM P007186)

Lancaster B Mk Is (Special), of No. 617 Squadron during an attack on Arnesberg Bridge on the 19th March 1945 (©RAFM P0022482)

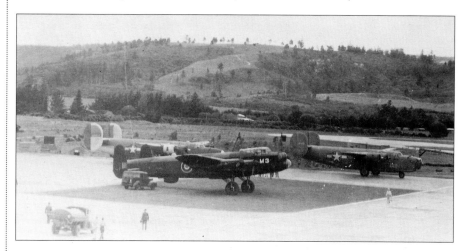

Lancaster B Mk I, PD328, 'Aries' of the CNS at RNZAF Whenuapai, New Zealand in 1944 (©RAFM P015679)

**Lancaster - loved by man and beast!**
**The NAM's resident cat takes a look at their newly arrived B Mk X**
*(©Bill Coffman)*

# Lincoln

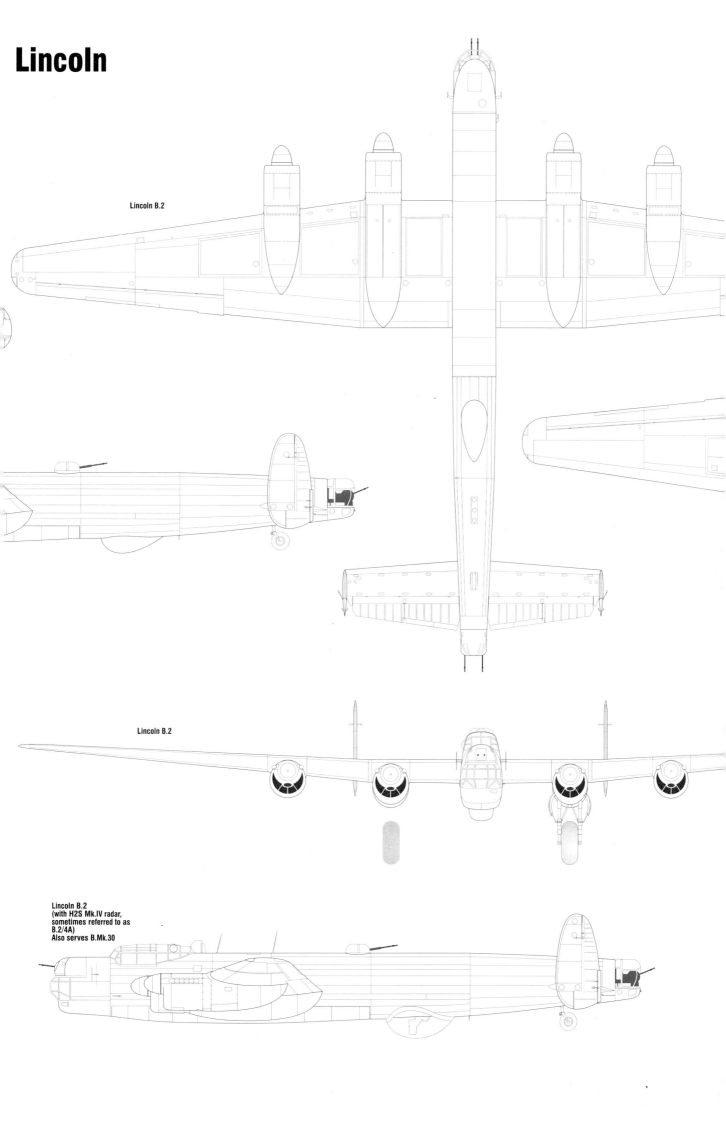

Lincoln B.2

Lincoln B.2

Lincoln B.2
(with H2S Mk.IV radar,
sometimes referred to as
B.2/4A)
Also serves B.Mk.30

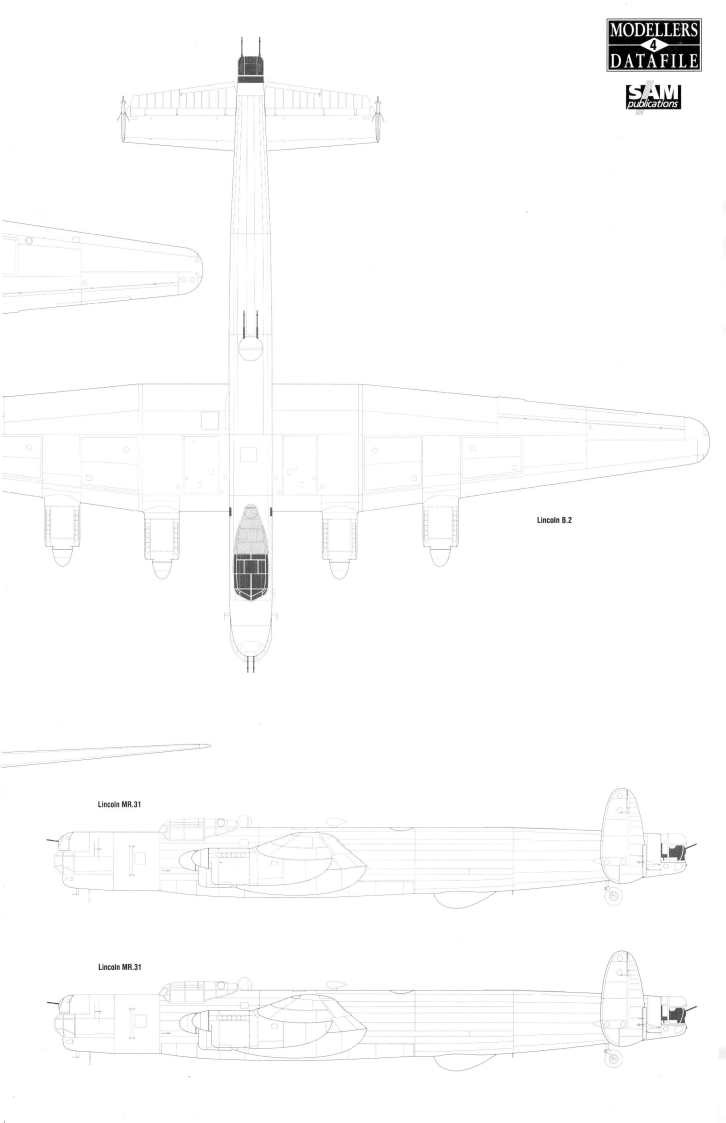

Lincoln B.2

Lincoln MR.31

Lincoln MR.31